PARADISE LABORERS

PARADISE LABORERS

HOTEL WORK IN THE GLOBAL ECONOMY

Patricia A. Adler and Peter Adler

ILR Press *an imprint of*
Cornell University Press
Ithaca and London

First published 2004 by Cornell University Press
First printing, Cornell paperbacks, 2004

Printed in the United States of America

Library of Congress Cataloging-in-Publication Data

Adler, Patricia A.
    Paradise laborers : hotel work in the global economy / Patricia A. Adler, Peter Adler.
        p. cm.
    Includes bibliographical references and index.
    ISBN 0-8014-4189-7 (cloth : alk. paper) ISBN 0-8014-8950-4 (pbk. : alk. paper)
    1. Hotels—Employees.   2. Hospitality industry—Employees.   I. Adler, Peter,
1951–   II. Title.
    HD8039.H8A35 2004
    331.7′6164794—dc22

                                                                    2004007178

Cornell University Press strives to use environmentally responsible suppliers and materials to the fullest extent possible in the publishing of its books. Such materials include vegetable-based, low-VOC inks and acid-free papers that are recycled, totally chlorine-free, or partly composed of nonwood fibers. For further information, visit our website at www.cornellpress.cornell.edu.

Cloth printing   10 9 8 7 6 5 4 3 2 1
Paperback printing   10 9 8 7 6 5 4 3 2 1

To Kevin and Regina
Who embody the *aloha* spirit of Hawai‘i,
The *chachma* of Judaism,
and the gentleness of humanity

C O N T E N T S

ACKNOWLEDGMENTS

Acknowledgments, as a writing convention, have never been analyzed. The latter part of the twentieth century witnessed a new turn in social scientific writing, as scholars such as Paul Atkinson, Howard Becker, James Clifford, Martyn Hammersley, George Marcus, and John Van Maanen, to name just a few, began to deconstruct our genres and tropes much as literary critics have been doing in the humanities for decades. Scanning the acknowledgments that serve as prolegomena to previous ethnographic works, it is apparent that this is the place where we are supposed to list all the people who have helped us during the course of our research, tip our hat in indebtedness for what they lent to us, but stereotypically, this is where we take the blame for whatever shortcomings might appear within the confines of the book you are about to read.

As many mystery and science fiction writers have learned, formulaic writing can sell, it fits into neat categories that people understand, and it serves as our "comfort food" during lonely times. We've seen it, we know it, and we can easily digest it. With this in mind, and with apologies, we will do the usual hurrahs, thank-yous, and expressions of appreciation, realizing, however, that doing justice to all the people who have helped along the way is a fruitless task. Please don't allow the conventionality of the convention to stand in the way of the sincerity of the remarks.

There have been several professional colleagues, some of whom we have never met, who through their editorial acumen and keen intellectual eyes have provided feedback that we have considered in crafting this volume. Peter S. Adler (no relation), Phil Brown, Norman Denzin, Jackie Eller, Calvin Endo, Cynthia Fuchs Epstein, William Finlay, Peter Heller, Kevin Henson, Charles Holm, Kiyoshi Ikeda, Arne Kalleberg, Vicki Smith, and Michael Weinstein all gave us ideas that were eventually used in this book. Special acknowledgments must go to the "MIT Mafia"—Stephen Barley, Wendy Guild, and John Van Maanen—who took an early interest in this work and advised us through some of the methodological nuances involved in negotiating access to organizations, particularly ones that are as surprisingly close-mouthed as hotel management. Peter Manicas, director of Liberal Studies at the University of Hawai'i, was perhaps more significant than any other single individual in assuring that this research was accomplished. Peter provided the "funding," in the form of summer teaching assignments from 1996 to the present that facilitated our forays into the field, and gave us key feedback on our developing work at conferences, in person, and via email.

We are fortunate to be blessed with friends in the sociological community who listened to our long hours of woes when gaining entrée seemed impossible and who had to bite their tongues when we complained about our "troubles in paradise," all the while cognizant that we were living where we wanted, waking up each morning to the sweet air of the tropics and to the dulcet tones of songbirds. Rather than expressing jealousy, they provided theoretical, methodological, and conceptual guidelines that helped us in the formulation of this book. Dan Cress, at the time our colleague at the University of Colorado, was particularly stalwart in pushing us back into the field and in buoying our sagging spirits during the long months between visits to our field sites. The intrepid Chuck Gallmeier, our dear friend and compadre in life, watched our children, made a site visit, and also spoke to us in detail about our burgeoning ideas. John Irwin's understanding of social scenes, especially the kinds reminiscent of the southern California where he grew up, provided insight into surfers and their culture, a key component of our study. His daughter, and a brilliant sociologist in her own right, Katy Irwin, helped more than she could ever know. She became a member of our family, intricately entwined in our everyday lives, giving us the freedom to take off for weeks at a time and not have to worry about our teenage children back home. It was only poetic justice that she ended up a professor at the University of Hawai'i, and then, in the latter stages of the research, discussed with us unique features of Hawaiian culture that she was learning during her own participant-observation of life.

Several friends, while not credentialed sociologists, added their own scholarly contributions: Diane Duffy, Sean Enright, Michael and Paige Geller, Jane Horowitz, Steven Kless, Dana Larsen, Angela and David Lee, the Miller clan, Marlin Vix, Adair Williamson, as well as our sister and niece, Kyra Sedgwick and Sosie Bacon, and cousins, Jamie and Laura Rosenwald. Most made the "arduous" trip to Hawai'i, not only to keep us company but to give us other perspectives to see the world in which we were becoming so intimately ensconced. In Colorado, friends and neighbors such as Linda, Bill, and Jennifer Jacobsen, Vince and Karen Porreca, and Susan and Sandy Schwartz supported us during the vicissitudes of our project, made sure that the mail arrived, and helped us through a particularly difficult period following open heart surgery.

We have been proud that many of our students have gone on to win major awards in the discipline and to land jobs or assistantships at good colleges and universities. During their time working with us, it was a symbiotic relationship, as not only were we able to lend our expertise to them, but they were our frequent sounding boards while the project was being conceptualized. Katie Coroso, Alice Fothergill, Rob Gardner, Molly George, Ross Haenfler, Joanna Gregson Higginson, Lisa Kraft, Katy Irwin, Jennifer Lois, Adina Nack, Lori Peek, Andrea Schmitt, Maren Scull, Elisabeth Sheff, and Kevin Vryan now know more about the inner workings of resort hotels than they ever expected, but without their help, this book would not have been completed. Our long interviews and copious field notes were transcribed through the years by a team of students. Rebecca Crane, Sarah DiBenedetto, Saira Hamidi, Christina Jason, Lori Lawson, Carolyn Matthews, Aurora Raiten, and Kevin Vryan all are owed thanks.

Departmental colleagues also gave us the freedom and sometimes the money to continue this research. All the departmental chairs who spanned the time period in which we conducted this study gave us support. Paul Colomy, the late Chuck Cortese, Dennis Mileti, and Nancy Reichman never questioned our sociological commitment to studying resort workers. Administrative assistants, such as Sam Abraham, Steve Graham, and Dorene Miller took care of our work "back home" so that we could traipse off to lands far away. Our schools, particularly the University of Colorado Dean's Fund for Excellence, provided mini-grants that paid our airfare or lodging during the days in the field.

Part of the convention of writing acknowledgments includes a section on the production team that puts a book together. We could not have been luckier than to have worked with one of the finest editors in the business, Fran Benson, who championed this research from the beginning, dogged us to move on with the project, and made the "pitch" to publish the book as simple as possible. Amazingly, when we were only a year or two into the research, Fran expressed interest in our work and got as excited about it as we were. She has been a joy throughout the process, and it was her work and vision at Cornell University Press that led us to them. Karen Laun, Carolyn Pouncy, and Lou Robinson were also helpful in moving the manuscript through production.

Words cannot express our gratitude to the people of Hawai'i who opened their doors, their arms, and their minds to us. Hundreds of people participated in this study, many of whom did not really understand what sociology is but trusted us enough to allow us into their lives. Special thanks go to the members of the management team at one of our hotels who let us behind the scenes, in the back of the house, and opened up the hotel to us in ways previously never allowed to researchers. We are also individually grateful to many people in the field, too numerous to mention, and whom we cannot explicitly acknowledge for reasons of confidentiality, who supported us during difficult phases of the research, helped us with key insights, assisted us in obtaining interviews, and generally took care of us when we were in the field, as friends do.

Children often pay the price for their parents' extreme work habits. In our case, this was no different, although as our son and daughter came into their adolescence we are not so certain that they minded mom and dad being away for months at a time, especially following on the heels of a ten-year research project focused on their worlds. Jori and Brye, our children and the loves of our lives, we thank for their patience and understanding and are grateful that they survived to tell the tales. That they both ended up majoring in sociology may perhaps be one of the best signs of the seriousness with which they took our work. We are proud to see them as young adults now plying the sociological trade in their own unique ways.

Last, we must thank our friends, Kevin and Regina, to whom this book is dedicated. They taught us the meaning of "aloha," housing us, feeding us, and sharing their family with us. Over long hours and countless discussions, Kevin, a true intellectual, helped us tease out the sociological implications of our observations, kept us up to date on happenings around the island, and paved the way for our future home there. Though he has many others, he has become like a brother to us. Regina, who knew us first as the Coloradans who descended on their home annually, took us in, learned to love us, and provided the humor and honesty we needed in a friendship. It is with heartfelt thanks that we dedicate the book to them.

Now is the time to take the blame, to recognize our shortcomings, and to ask you, our readers, to bear with us if any mistakes were made or toes stepped upon. We stand by our work and hope that we have offered a glimpse into a group of people that practically invisibly run the hotels and resorts at which you commonly stay. We invite all our friends, colleagues, and relatives to join us later in life when we move to Honua, the pseudonym for the island we studied. And, to you, our readers, if you see two tanned, smiling, and fit sociologists walking on the beach, come up, say aloha, and share with us the joys of sunshine, good spirits, and Polynesian hospitality. *Mahalo* for your interest in our work.

Portions of earlier versions of chapters 3, 4, 5, 6, and 7, appear as, respectively: Patricia A. Adler and Peter Adler, "Resort Workers: Adaptations in the Leisure-Work Nexus," *Sociological Perspectives* 32, 3 (1999), by permission of the University of California Press; Patricia A. Adler and Peter Adler, "Transience and the Postmodern Self: The Geographic Mobility of Resort Workers," *The Sociological Quarterly* 40, 1 (1999), by permission of the University of California Press; Patricia A. Adler and Peter Adler, "Seasonality and Flexible Labor in Resorts: Organizations, Employees, and Local Labor Markets," *Sociological Spectrum* 23, 1 (2003), by permission of Taylor and Francis Publishers; and Patricia A. Adler and Peter Adler, "'Off-Time Labor' in Resorts: The Social Construction of 'Commercial' Time," *American Behavioral Scientist* 44, 7 (2001), by permission of Sage Publications. We are grateful to the publishers and copyright holders for permission to reprint this material.

PARADISE LABORERS

1

ENTERING PARADISE

You land in paradise. Departing the airport in your canary-yellow rented convertible, you wend your way past mountains and beaches, past valleys and pastures, past cities and towns, past pristine golf courses and arid volcanic terrain, past sugarcane, pineapples, and coconuts. You head toward your vacation destination: an exclusive Hawaiian hotel. You see the tasteful and large sign at the resort's entrance. Turning off the main road onto the winding driveway, you see the rich, vibrant colors of the beautiful trees and flowers lining the peaceful path. As you drive up to the lobby, a potpourri of pleasurable sensations assaults you. You smell the fragrant plumeria and gardenia blossoms, indications that you are in a tropical Eden. You hear the rumble of the waterfall and then behold its magnificence, a torrent of rushing streams tumbling over rocks and crashing into a pool below. The cascading water and its splash fill the air with moisture and your nostrils with the hydrated aroma. You have entered paradise.

As you pull up to the *porte cochere,* a smartly dressed bell captain approaches and opens your door, welcoming you with a resounding "aloha." A bellman wheels up his cart and unloads your bags. You give your name and hand your keys to the valet and wander toward the lobby. You're a little disoriented from the long flight, so your car and bags are mindlessly forgotten behind you. Immediately, a beautiful Polynesian woman appears and, in soft tones, welcomes you, slipping a colorful and sweet-smelling lei over your head. Walking into the high-ceilinged, open-air lobby, you are escorted past grandiose floral arrangements, rock formations fashioned from native volcanic eruptions, marble-inlaid floors, a shock of delicate orchids in every direction, pools of azure water on both sides, and Hawaiian art and artifacts in all directions.

You are steered toward the front desk where another Polynesian employee greets you and begins your check-in process. Discreetly, your lei greeter re-

turns, carrying a silver tray from which she offers you glasses filled with tropical fruit punch and a sugarcane swizzle stick to chew on long after the last
sip of liquid ambrosia has gone down. As you navigate your room reservation,
your credit card imprint, and the details of your stay, you gaze around at the
impressive space, the many workers bustling around in diverse uniforms.
They range among the different Hawaiian hotels from the flowing raiment of
traditional Polynesian garb to the starched, dignified British uniforms summoning images of old-world butlers and high service.

After you complete your transaction, the front desk clerk summons a bellman who appears with your luggage and escorts you to your room, orienting
you to the mysterious and marvelous features of the property and the island.
Immaculately dressed in either a colorful aloha shirt or a white, starched uni-
form with gold buttons and rolling your suitcases on a gleaming bronzed cart,
he introduces himself and asks you about yourself, about your family, and if
this is your first visit to the Islands. He offers to assist you should you have
any questions or problems during your stay. You have made a new friend. As
you follow behind him, you feel the gentle trade winds moving through the
lobby and corridors, notice the perfect air temperature, and see the abundant
sunshine bringing diffused light all through the open-air hotel. Your bellman
takes you to your room via elevator, winding open-air hallways, or golf cart,
presents you with a view of the expansive ocean, brings in your bags, lays
them atop the unfolded luggage holders, and fills your ice bucket. You have
arrived in the lap of luxury.

This surreal guest experience is made possible by a set of carefully
planned structures surrounding and underlying what customers see. Most
guests do not notice the precise ethnic and racial stratification of those attending them. They do not recognize that the lei greeters and front desk clerks
are locals, selected for their Polynesian appearance;[1] that many valets and the
bell captain are "haoles" (Caucasians), selected to give an atmosphere of con-
tinental service; and that the bellmen are a combination of these two groups.
At the same time guests may completely overlook the new immigrants: outdoor housekeepers sweeping the lobby or gardeners raking the leaves. If they
notice a manager passing by in an elegant aloha shirt and slacks or pressed
skirt and heels, they take for granted that this person is a mainland haole or
a European.

The level of service accorded arriving guests differs markedly as well, with
one treatment offered new guests, another for returning guests, and yet another for celebrities and VIPs. First-time guests are greeted courteously with
the standard service. Returning guests are expected, and may be personally

welcomed by people they know. A card preprinted with their name may be placed on the dashboard of their car. Employee friends will pass them on their way to the front desk and chat or joke with them while they wait in line for check-in. Celebrities and VIPs get another class of service. Each day the roster of incoming VIP guests is distributed to all lobby personnel with the estimated time of their arrival. The VIP liaison personally waits at the entrance to greet them and to escort them to the front desk, chatting with them about their special needs and the custom accommodations that have been arranged. Bell and transportation clerks who normally stand behind desks at the front of the hotel emerge to personally greet these big spenders and important people by name, and to make them feel individually welcomed. Some have been picked up at the airport, in fact, by a resort driver in a limousine or special car. Managers from the front desk and guest services swing by during their stay to assure them of their personal interest in the comfort of their accommodations and service. For the biggest VIPs, the general manager may be present to greet them as well.

There will also be systems determining which faces returning guests are likely to see and recognize, as there is a hierarchy of seniority in each position, with some jobs incorporating a high turnover and others retaining the same people for years. Befriending people low on the seniority list or in a position with high turnover is less likely to give returning guests their desired sense of comfort, continuity, and community, as these people may not be there year after year like more entrenched employees.

Aside from individuals who arrive alone or with their families, there is also the hustle and bustle of groups entering the hotel, as tour buses, which some of the larger hotels accommodate, bring a different kind of rhythm. When large groups are expected, the group check-in desk is staffed, and bellmen stand at the curb awaiting their appearance. Suitcases are unloaded en masse, group handlers herd large numbers of people in the appropriate directions, and there is controlled chaos until everyone is processed.

Employees generally enter Hawaiian resorts through a different entrance from guests. They park separately, often in uncovered lots or on grass fields. To enter the property, they must pass through the cordoned-off security area, carefully observed by security personnel. They are required to swipe their employee ID cards through the time clock as they enter the back of the house, and to do so once again after they have changed clothes (and showered, if they so desire) and are ready to report for work. Penalties accrue for lateness. Employees then walk through the interior catacombs of the hotel to their work destinations, emerging into public sight only at their point of guest service.

Some resorts require six swipes daily, two for entering, two for leaving, and one each for going to lunch and reporting back to work.

Guests are also usually unaware of the complex systems that organize and track the services they receive. Valets and bellmen work on a rotation that calls them forth to fetch luggage or cars in a careful order. In tip jobs such as these, they wolf down their meals during their breaks so as not to miss more than one rotation. Unbeknownst to guests, the passage of every bag through the hotel is meticulously charted. Bellmen have cards on which they record the time and number of bags they take to and from each room, and whether these go to bell storage or are held on a rolling cart. When a bag is missing, this system marks the last time it was handled and by whom.

Guests often check out by calling both the bell desk to send someone up for their bags and the valet desk to get their car. When they arrive in the lobby, they may get the keys to the car from their valet, tip him, and leave, never seeing their bellman to give him a tip. Yet tips are vital to people in these occupations, and a careful system of "tip-tracking" operates. Bellmen record all their tips, and when they do not receive one from a guest they have serviced, they go to the valet desk to see who brought out that guest's car. They then claim two-thirds of the tip that the valet received, since they are entitled to a larger share for bringing down the bags. All this constitutes the complex underground functioning of a large resort that makes the guest experience invisibly smooth.

Resort hotels have become a ubiquitous part of middle-class life, as technology has made travel faster and easier and people have attained greater freedom to vacation. Resorts have become an important institution to society and its economy, as one in eight Americans is now employed by the tourism industry, tourists generate $900 per capita annually in tax revenue, and tourism as an American industry ranks first in terms of global international export earnings (Travel Industry Association of America 2002). In fact, although estimates vary widely depending on the source, global tourism is the largest industry on earth, employing somewhere between 100 and 230 million people, handling over 600 million arrivals a year, and having an estimated value between $476 billion and $3.4 trillion dollars (Apostolopoulos et al. 1996; "Beaches and Bucks" 2002). By 2020, the World Travel and Tourism Council predicts that 1.6 billion of the world's 7.8 billion people will make a trip abroad (Crosette 1998).[2]

In Hawai'i, tourism has been the state's leading industry since the mid-1970s (Stern 1989).[3] In 2002, the travel and tourism industry accounted for

$7.5 billion or 16.5 percent of the Gross State Product. It employed approx-imately 154,000 people, or 20.1 percent of the state's total employment. Taxes collected from tourism contributed $905 million to state and county revenues, or about 20.9 percent of their total income (Hawai'i Tourism Authority 2002).[4] Fueling these figures, the vacation has practically become a requisite of the American dream (Aron 1999). Yet despite the amount of time that peo-ple spend in hotels, little has been written about these institutions and those who labor there. This book offers a glimpse into what goes on behind the scenes in resort hotels from the employees' perspectives.

We focus on a group of luxury resorts situated, among others, along a sandy strip of Hawaiian beach, and examine the work and lifestyle experiences of its staff. To maintain the anonymity and confidentiality of our setting, we refer to our island as "Honua" (Hawaiian for place), and our beachfront strip as "Ali'i" (Hawaiian for royalty).[5] Clifford (1997) referred to resorts as post-modern organizations where people meet and pass each other, places of tran-sit, not of residence. Yet while guests may come and go, in a fashion the workers live there, and it is they who anchor these resorts.

Like nearly every resort—whether located near beaches, mountains, deserts, or on ships—the hotels we studied employed four distinct types of workers: new immigrants, locals, seekers, and managers (as we discuss more fully in chapters 3 and 4). These different groups ensure that hospitality work-ers constitute a broadly diverse population and therefore embody quite a few of the varied features distinguishing the essence of work and occupations in contemporary society. We examine the culture of this tropical island resort community and the workers' varied occupational subcultures. We delve into the kinds of work experiences and patterns evinced by resort employees as they service guests, follow management rules, and adapt to the personal dy-namics of their co-workers. Resort workers differ, however, among the four types, with two groups (seekers and managers) whose members are *transient* and two (new immigrants and locals) whose members are *trapped*,[6] com-pletely subject to the economic vicissitudes of the local labor market. Using this distinction, we examine differences between the alternative careers, life-styles, families, and relationships of those transient populations who have stepped off the normative track and their more conventional trapped coun-terparts. Another realm of contrast can be found in employees' differential "cultural capital" (Bourdieu 1984), stemming from distinctions based on race/ethnicity, gender, age, education, and class.[7] Workers' differences—whether they are transient or trapped, advantaged or disadvantaged—then lead them to react differently to their employment situations, with some more likely to stand up for their labor rights than others. Drawing on these distinctions, we examine the problematic nature of the politics of tourism labor relations and unionization. Finally, this is a study of the political economy of tourism, as we examine the role of resorts and their employees in economically adapting, each to its own benefit, over the short term, to local labor market conditions. We show that the result is that resorts and employees together unintentionally reconstruct the political economy of global labor market conditions, over the long term, to their mutual disadvantage.

Literature

A variety of sources have looked at resorts empirically and conceptually. Popular literature has focused on hotels—including works from highly acclaimed novelists such as Elinor Lipman (*The Inn at Lake Devine,* 1999), David Lodge (*Paradise News,* 1991), Alison Lurie (*The Last Resort,* 1998), Jeffrey Robinson (*The Hotel,* 1997), and Paul Theroux (*Hotel Honolulu,* 2001). While many of these offer insights, often satirical, of hotel life, none of them is based on rigorous social scientific research. *Thus, these works have used hotels as backdrops and settings, but they have not examined them systematically.*

Some academic attention has been paid to flophouses and other low-rent hotels,[8] cruise ships,[9] service at luxury hotels,[10] the location of hotel development,[11] the history of hotel and restaurant employees,[12] the social dimensions of hotel work,[13] the culture of a resort community,[14] new immigrant workers in a hotel restaurant,[15] and the labor (union) organization of hotel workers.[16] Related sociological research on the restaurant has examined its social structure,[17] the culture of kitchens,[18] waiters and waitresses,[19] the interaction between waitresses and their customers,[20] a licensed restaurant,[21] and fast food establishments.[22] *Nowhere, however, has there been empirical research on the culture and labor relations of exclusive resort hotels.*[23]

A third related area of literature involves workplace ethnographies, with studies conducted of hospitals,[24] schools,[25] factories,[26] domestic work,[27] high tech areas,[28] corporate and governmental organizations,[29] banks,[30] assembly line manufacturing,[31] and police, fire fighters, and rescue workers.[32] *Workplace ethnographies of hotels, however, are nonexistent.*[33] This book offers the first systematic, scholarly, ethnographic study of hotels and the people who work in them, examining worker cultures.

The composition of Hawaiian resorts' workforce is global, especially with regard to the new immigrants who moved to Hawai'i from all over Asia, the

Pacific, and Latin America. The social and cultural movements of these global workers cannot be understood without reference to international economic and demographic considerations.[34] Studies of global labor migrants have referred to these people as "transmigrants," or as "immigrants whose daily lives depend on multiple and constant interconnections across international borders and whose public identities are configured in relationships to more than one nation-state" (Glick-Schiller et al. 1995, 48). Most global labor migrants move back and forth between their host countries and countries of origin, retaining their core ties and plans for retirement in their ancestral homes.[35] In this book we show a different global relocation pattern and discuss how and why our resort workers established it for themselves.

Globalization scholars have also written about the feminization of the international labor force, with more immigrant women than men finding jobs in industrialized nations. This imbalance has fostered an upheaval and dislocation of gender relations in immigrant families. Many new immigrant women found employment in the often demeaning and repressive household labor force as domestics when higher-statused American women took work outside the home.[36] This removed immigrant women from their own households and families. We discuss two factors that set the circumstances of our new immigrants apart from this trend.

Organizations examined in the late twentieth century must be addressed from a postmodern perspective. As postmodern organizations, resorts operate incessantly (24/7), expecting workers to labor around the clock, through all the days of the week and seasons of the year. The culture of our society has been characterized as a rhythm of time, with interaction itself primarily a matter of cadence.[37] People may be tied together or isolated from one another by the invisible threads of pace and tempo and the hidden walls of time (Hall 1983), with consensus constituted by interpersonal coordination (Durkheim 1912). But Durkheim's (1893) mechanical conception of solidarity, lodged in people coordinating things together at the same time, is tied to a modern era of society. Postmodern society increasingly displaces this form of cohesion, replacing it with an organic temporal solidarity, where individuals do things at different times and are tied to one another by their interdependence. If modern society had a consonant rhythm based on coordinated movement, we are left to wonder what rhythm we find in postmodern organizations lodged in the postmodern world, with people working around the clock and calendar, in a blur of motion and sound. Brissett and Snow (1993, 245) have suggested that rather than having a simple organic rhythm, postmodern society is characterized by cultural arrhythmia: "the absence of entrainment associated with a decline in contrast in everyday routine and the destruction of rhythm through accelerated tempo." In this book we examine the temporal rhythms of resorts and their effects on both workers and guests.

But a postmodern community may have an impact on the people who work and live within it. Sociologists have long posited a relationship between society and self, so that change in the one fosters change in the other.[38] We analyze the selves of resort workers to see how they correspond to modern and postmodern images. The conventional, modernist model of the actor views the self as a genuine, real attribute—as reflexive, self-conscious, rational, and therefore autonomous. This self is seen as anchored in stable, mainstream social structures, in social values, in relationships to friends and communities— that is, in permanence (Mead 1934). The interactionist-derived model of the postmodern self posits that the self adapts to transformations in society. Dislocated from enduring social institutions, it has developed impulse (Turner 1976). Anchored increasingly in change rather than stability, it has become process- rather than product-oriented (Wood and Zurcher 1988). In a rapidly evolving, transformative society, it is mutable (Zurcher 1977).

Postmodernists reject this model as clinging to a modernist view of the real, or autonomous, self and failing to recognize its demise (Dowd 1991). They consider the self in the postmodern era as erased and dismantled by the bombardment of incoherent or "technologically saturated" (Gergen 1991) images coming from the media (Dowd 1991; Ewen 1988; Tseëlon 1992). These commercial images have replaced the constraints and framing supports of social structures like community and family, leaving individuals adrift in a world where the signifier has come uncoupled from the signified (Eco 1986; Manning 1991); the quest for self-presentation has replaced the quest for meaning. The self-concept has become an artifact of Baudrillard's (1983) hyperreality, replaced by the simulacrum, or the self-image. Postmodernists see the self, then, as an illusion, evoked situationally but adaptive and fragmented, emotionally flat and depthless (Goffman 1959, 1974; Jameson 1984). Fundamentally eroded, the postmodern self is like the layers of Goffman's metaphorical onion: devoid of a core, it is decentered and ultimately dissolved.[39] We show here how people exhibiting classical postmodern lives and inhabiting a highly postmodern community cling to a modernist model of the self.

Finally, the labor of resort workers falls into several areas of interest to scholars. In a review of the literature, McCammon and Griffin (2000) have suggested that service labor is a vastly understudied topic, especially given the huge percentage of the labor force that it encompasses. Little is known, in particular, about hotel work as service labor (although see Sherman 2003). The vast majority of service labor research focuses on the direct interactional experiences between workers and their customers or clients. Hodson (2001) has suggested that employees' dignity may be affronted by mismanagement and abuse, overwork, challenges to authority, and contradictions in directives. Leidner (1999) has traced the stages at which service workers may be forced into demeaning emotional labor from their selection to their training, the scripting and feeling rules they receive, and their monitoring, leading them eventually to break out in resistance. We examine here not only the way resort workers feel about the direct service labor they deliver but how they explore new territory by considering the indirect effects of a service labor economy on both the workers and their broader community.

Issues of ethnicity abound in the labor literature. In a multiethnic labor force, workers may be racially stratified. Lieberson (1980) has suggested that racial and ethnic groups have historically come to inhabit occupational niches for one of two reasons: they have some cultural characteristic (perceived physical, mental, or social ability) that is associated with a given job, or they find a ripe opportunity structure available for this job at the time they enter the employment market.[40] We examine the racial and ethnic stratification of jobs in the Ali'i resorts, from the way workers seek and are placed into various ghetto-ized departments to the stratification in pay scale between ethnically associated jobs and the way workers legitimize and feel about these inequalities.

A spate of literature has addressed labor studies in the new economy. During the twentieth century, the United States shifted from a manufacturing economy to one dominated by its service sector.[41] The growth in what the Bureau of the Census terms "service—producing" industries has been monumental, increasing from 30 percent in 1900 to 50 percent in 1950 and 80 percent by 2000, with 90 percent of all new jobs created by 2000 falling into the service sector.[42] In addition, companies outside the service sector also contain service occupations, including 13.2 percent of employees in manufacturing who work in clerical, customer service, telemarketing, and transportation jobs (Kutscher 1987).

Service industries foster the existence of a dual labor-market economy, with large numbers of jobs requiring little to no skill that pay poorly and a smaller number of high-skilled, high-income jobs (Macdonald and Sirianni 1996; Nelson 1994). Labor segmentation theory suggests that in this new economy, race/ethnicity, age, class, and gender differences have increasingly stratified the labor pool.[43] People with demographic advantages have a greater opportunity to capture primary market jobs, while their more disadvantaged counterparts generally land in the less skilled secondary labor-market economy.[44] This has been exacerbated by the greater migration of workers from one country to another in search of jobs, as we have witnessed the rise of the global economy.[45] The tourist industry, with its preponderance of unskilled and semiskilled jobs, draws heavily from the secondary labor market.[46] Moreover, the secondary market is increasingly composed of contingent jobs.[47]

The contingent labor force has its roots in what Morse (1969) first called "peripheral workers"—mostly blacks, women, and European and Asian immigrants, dating back to the turn of the nineteenth century, who were assigned to or accepted secondary, disposable, or "marginalized" employment roles (see also Harper and Simpson 1983). Contingency work became a meaningful lexicon in labor parlance when the term was coined in the mid-1980s by labor economist Audrey Freedman (Freedman 1985) in response to the corporate restructuring and downsizing that thrust, for the first time, many skilled, professional, white people into peripheral work roles.

The 1980s' economic boom saw a great rise in employment that created a large number of temporary, part-time, and other forms of unaffiliated positions that never converted to full-time jobs, burgeoning instead into their own segment of the economy (Golden and Appelbaum 1992). By the turn of the twenty-first century, the proportion of workers falling into the contingent labor force was estimated to have grown to between one-quarter and one-third of all those employed (Smith 1998). This situation has benefited management greatly, as prior to the 1980s only finance and marketing were considered flexible costs; employing people on a contingent basis added human resources to this list (Belous 1989; Osterman et al. 2001). Businesses have been able to expand without assuming the costs and obligations of affiliated workers, while increasing numbers of individuals have found themselves unable to find access to permanent, secure employment.

Like peripheral workers, certain populations are demographically more heavily represented in the contingent labor pool. Women hold approximately two-thirds to three-quarters of contingent jobs, although some indicators suggest that the United States may have more men in the contingent labor force than other countries.[48] By age, contingent workers are bi-modal, the majority being young people looking for their first or supplementary job (Tannock 2001), with another group falling into the bridge retirement category.[49] The service and retail sectors are those most commonly employing contingent workers, with 40–50 percent of their employees falling into this category (Rogers 2000; Tilly 1996).

All contingent work is not alike; it is patterned by several characteristics. Contingent work may be either voluntary—with individuals choosing to divide their time between several positions, employers, and pastimes—or involuntary—where people want full-time, permanent jobs but are unable to find them (Levenson 2000). Some contingent jobs are tightly controlled, having little freedom, and may involve assignment to more dangerous or unpleasant tasks (Bronstein 1991). Others have a great deal of flexibility or autonomy, liberating workers from the monotony of a daily grind and enabling them to plan work schedules around other commitments.[50]

While some workers prefer more flexible employment relationships,[51] contingency work almost always favors employers.[52] In assessing the pros and cons, Kalleberg et al. (2000, 274) have stated: "Nonstandard work arrangements represent a potential source of employment flexibility for both employers and workers, and they are doubly attractive to employers because they often reduce employment costs. For many nonstandard workers, however, any gains in flexibility come at a high price, and for the society they are likely to exacerbate socioeconomic inequality if qualified workers who seek regular full-time jobs must settle for less desirable alternatives." Individuals working on a contingent basis may be skilled and highly trained, but most of them are drawn from the secondary labor market with its lack of skills, low pay, high turnover, and diminished career ladders for advancement (Barker and Christensen 1998; Bridges 1994).

Contingent work may be short-term, done on an interim or entry basis, or it may be permanent, with individuals stuck in jobs where they have no opportunity to acquire the long-term and ancillary benefits of full-time labor. Some contingent jobs fall at the point of origination, serving as stepping-stones into organizations and industries (Houseman 2001), while others are retention-oriented—created to hold onto the skills, knowledge, and expertise of valued individuals (Tilly 1996). Contingent workers may be integrated into departments and offices with full-time workers; or they may be relatively segregated, located in all-temp environments (Rogers 2000).[53] Despite rhetoric suggesting that contingent workers embrace this occupational form, by far the majority of contingent jobs are involuntary, highly regulated, point-of-origination positions located in the secondary labor market.[54] Negrey (1990) has argued that contingency work is debilitating, exploitive, and fraught with instability.

Unionization is an important labor issue in Hawai'i, with its strong democratic tradition. The last three decades of the twentieth century witnessed a decline in union membership in the United States (Osterman 1999). Unionization was challenged during this period for a number of reasons (see Parker 2002). First, contingent workers are considered hard to unionize because their relationship to their employer is unstable and fragile (Carré et al. 1995). Second, certain categories of workers are less likely to unionize. Women may be inferior union prospects because of their family responsibilities, their marginal commitment to the labor market, and their submission to a patriarchal system. Workers of color and youth may also be difficult to organize because of their large participation in the secondary labor market.[55] Immigrant workers, too, may represent challenges to unionization because of their submissive attitudes, their strong work ethic, their satisfaction with low wages, their linguistic barriers, and their potentially problematic citizenship status.[56]

Labor segmentation theory suggests that in this new economy, race/ethnicity, class, and gender differences have increasingly divided the labor pool (Wells 2000). To the extent that employers are successful in exploiting this segmentation by creating a stratified labor force within their organizations, they can maintain divisions between their employees, hindering workers' recognition of shared labor interests (Gordon et al. 1982). This structural situation represents a challenge to the politics of labor organization.

The history of labor relations and unionization in the hospitality industry in Hawai'i is a successful one. Although it began with frustration immediately following World War II and moved into hard-fought and sometimes violent strikes, by the 1960s and 1970s resort employees were largely well represented (Stern 1989). Hawai'i has been a notably Democratic state with a strong orientation toward unions since the 1950s.[57] Union representation of hotel workers first established a strong foothold on O'ahu and then spread to the outer islands (Stern 1989).

These major changes in the relations between employers and their employees occurred as the institutional structure that shaped the postwar labor market progressively eroded. Economic times became tougher, technology was substituted for human labor, unionization declined, and existing norms of loyalty between workers and their firms weakened (Osterman 1999). We have witnessed the evolving pattern of labor organization in the postindustrial world (Piore and Sabel 1984). To best understand employer-employee relations in the current, evolving context, organization theorists have adapted their perspective from focusing primarily on organizations to including other relevant factors in the equation. The "new structuralist" paradigm[58] abandoned a "closed system" approach focusing solely on the internal structures of organizations in favor of an "open system" paradigm that investigated how organizations interact with their employees and with labor markets (Kalleberg et al. 1996).

Resort hotels, as part of the tourism industry, have seen no such change in their production methods, forms of work organization, or employment relationships, because they have always been organized on a seasonal and fluctuating basis, capitalizing on high employee turnover and contingent labor. Yet these issues, recently raised about broader segments of the economy, are germane to hospitality organizations. Some of the labor studies cited engage a few of the issues noted above, while others focus more exclusively on a single dimension of work in the new or global economy. *In this research, the diversity of worker types we studied allows us to engage nearly the full spectrum of issues raised by labor scholars.*

Some of these labor studies are single-case studies, focusing on particular organizations or workplaces (Devinatz 1999; Graham 1995), while others are multiple-case comparative studies (Rogers 2000; Smith 2001). In this book we use a single-type organization approach, focusing on five different resorts all within the same industry. *While most single-type organizational studies are based on survey or archival research (Kalleberg et al. 1996), we employ ethnographic methods to delve more deeply into workers' experiences across a range of similar organizations.*

The Setting

Resorts in the Hawaiian Islands are some of the most spectacular and famous in the world, regularly gracing the pages and top one hundred lists of such upscale magazines as *Condé Nast Traveler, Travel and Leisure,* and *Gourmet.* The Ali'i resorts were elegant, located on a beachfront strip in a community which we call "Lanikai." Their tropical waters featured lava rock and reefs, complete with fish, whales, dolphins, and sea turtles. Their regal palm trees towered over their manicured lawns. Their rushing pools and waterfalls filled the air with a soothing sense of serenity. Fragrant smells perfumed the air; gigantic floral arrangements dazzled the eye. Their guest rooms were spacious and well appointed.

Some but not all of the Ali'i resorts we studied received the prestigious AAA five-diamond rating, reserved for the most exclusive and expensive properties, while others routinely achieved four diamonds (hotel ratings also changed from year to year). These hotels were built over a two-decade span, with some of the earlier ones featuring an older style and simplicity.[59] Newer, more recent additions incorporated the latest in resort design, with open lobby ceilings, vaulted room entrances, bathrooms suitable for royalty, and dramatic waterfalls and fountains. These Ali'i resorts ranged from family- to honeymoon-oriented, from modest to outlandish, from simple to elaborate. They included independents, small chains, and large chain resorts (and shifted among these modes frequently); were Japanese- or American-owned; American or European managed; and catered to a different mix of predominantly American clientele supplemented by some local, Japanese, and other international guests. We call these five resorts the "Lukane Sands," the "Kahana Surf," the "Pono Beach Spa," the "Lei Gardens," and the "Hula Club Towers."

Visitors to this part of Hawai'i could walk up and down the beaches, venturing into the lobbies and pool areas of the various resorts, enjoying the quiet privacy of some, while gawking at the majesty of others. Shopping was situated conveniently nearby, so that guests who tired of eating or shopping at the resorts' restaurants and arcades could have a variety of alternative choices.

Simulacrum and Hawaiian Resorts

Key to contemporary Hawaiian resort architecture is the construction of simulations of the natural beauty of the Islands. In the more elaborate properties, these went beyond representation, which tries to recreate the real, to simulacrum, which enhances the real. Simulation progresses, according to Baudrillard (1983), from reflecting the basic reality to masking and perverting basic reality, then to masking the absence of a basic reality, finally abandoning relation to any reality whatsoever; it becomes its own pure simulacrum. Baudrillard noted the relation of simulacrum to truth and nature, suggesting that it was once the case that we sought to make models of the real, to make maps or mirror images. The real would remain, but these models would fade over time. Now that has become reversed. We see "the generation by models of a real without origin or reality: a hyperreal. The real territory no longer precedes the map, nor survives it. Henceforth, it is the map that precedes the territory" (Baudrillard 1983, 2).

Hawaiian hotels, as some of the most exotic in the world, seek to attract and to retain their guests. Many are destination resorts, where guests are encouraged never to leave the property.[60] If there are natural sights to be viewed, these lure away guests and their spending dollars. Resorts able to construct representations of natural sites that compete with the existing reality may entice guests into abandoning their thoughts of touring the island. Once developers began to construct these simulations, they became so grandiose that they shot to eclipse the real. Baudrillard (1983, 3) noted that "Simulacrum no longer has to be rational, since it is no longer measured against some ideal or negative instance . . . it is no longer real at all." Destination development is a science and an art that relies on the construction of fantasy. Chuck Law,[61] the deputy director of the Pono Beach Spa, commented on the simulated atmosphere created at his resort: "We're always creating this fantasy world—the Hawaiian experience. The Far East, Las Vegas, they're super plastic, but they have a certain glamour to them. This is another world, totally opposite from that. . . . I wanted to associate myself with this kind of fantasy of what luxury is."

Different resorts up and down the Ali'i strip constructed various kinds of simulacrum. Waterfalls were the most common effect, and most had more than one. More elaborate waterfalls incorporated natural flowers and plants growing out of the rocks behind and around the water, or had water tumbling into ponds filled with peaceful and stunning koi fish. Some waterfall simulacra sought to imitate the natural dripping walls of the Islands, where water leaked slowly along open-faced rock, rather than tumbling or rushing down, promoting a growth of exotic flowers.

The use of natural and artificial materials to create the rock walls around the resorts' waterfalls, pools, ponds, and restaurants ranged from simple to elaborate. Some properties used the natural indigenous rock from the area to build displays. Others gathered lava rock from the Islands and incorporated this rugged texture. Rock was also imported from off-island to create particular mountainous effects. Finally, some rock was artificially created from synthetic materials. Molds of Hawaiian mountains were taken and used to cast synthetic rock formations that were assembled in varied positions so that repetitions would not be noticed. Artificial volcanoes were built, lava flows simulated, natural cascading rivers and streams reproduced, and lava tubes and caves constructed. Flora and fauna from all over the islands and beyond were imported, from an array of plant life to birds and fish. These were often complemented with elaborate art collections.

A resort developer at one of the Ali'i properties explained to us his aim in designing his hotel, his conception of the image he wanted to portray:

> The philosophy behind today's hotel development is based heavily upon
> commercialism. Seldom considered is the idea of creating it [a hotel] to
> be a cultural asset and making it the center of culture for the region. . . .
> Many years ago, as far back as the early 1990s, there were some dedicated
> people who had dreams and created very special hotels of extremely high
> quality. . . . Recently a number of so-called high-class hotels have been
> built in Hawai'i, but they fall short of the needed, true, high quality standards. Most of such "luxury hotels" tend to charge high room rates, stand
> on false pretense, and ignore the importance of harmony with Hawai'i's
> nature. Some of these hotels are no different than ordinary city hotels,

and many are more like a Las Vegas establishment, while others seem more like something from the Arabian Nights. A visitor may wonder where he had drifted to. Seasoned travelers find such hotels less than satisfactory. Unless someone with accurate vision creates a true quality hotel with real cultural value and flavor, the future of resorts in Hawai'i may be in danger.

What this developer was proposing was that the simulated images of Hawai'i he created offered a more real cultural representation and center of culture for the region than the genuine sites. It is this image that the Ali'i resorts wanted to sell to their guests, the notion that they embodied the "real Hawai'i," one that could not be found as accurately outside the hotels (see Desmond 1999). Baudrillard (1983, 25) echoed this concept, noting that the simulacrum of nature is there to conceal the fact that "real" nature is no longer real; the hyperreal is the real. Real nature is of the order of the hyperreal and of simulacrum. "It is no longer a question of the false representation of reality (ideology), but of concealing the fact that the real is no longer real, and thus of saving the reality principle."

Functioning of a Resort

The Ali'i resorts were complex organizational and social systems. They operated continuously; they employed hundreds, sometimes more than a thousand workers; and they encompassed many different departments. These resorts slotted employees into a range of work areas. Back-of-the-house departments included laundry, housekeeping, tailoring, room reservations, hotel operator, human resources, comptroller and accounting, information systems, and security. Food and beverage departments included the restaurants, kitchens (prep workers and chefs), room service, banquet, stewarding, housemen (who set up and broke down the functions), weddings, and catering. Front-of-the-house departments included bell, valet, front desk, concierge, beach and pool (also commonly referred to as either recreation, or simply, rec), fitness and spa, retail shops, beauty salon, camp, outdoor housekeeping, water features, and engineering.

The chain of command through various positions and departments at the Ali'i resorts shifted constantly, resulting in a frequent redrawing of their organizational flow charts. Different positions appeared and disappeared with the recruitment and loss of upper-level management. Chains of command shifted similarly, with changes in personnel and new strategies for efficiency causing departments to move out of one unit's sphere of influence into another's. The

Executive Committee
Organizational Chart

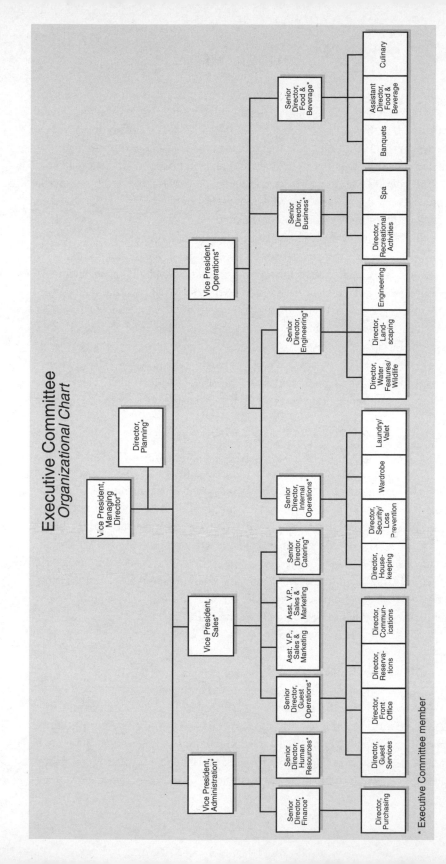

* Executive Committee member

Executive Committee Organizational Chart

composition of any Ali'i resort's executive committee was apt to change with shifts in ownership and management, and even while these two factors stayed constant. It is thus difficult to sketch out the key positions of authority in any of these resorts and to identify the departments that fell within the realm of various executives. We present one sample, composite organizational chart from the period during which we conducted our research, chosen because it represents the best example of what key departments and positions could be found in any of these resorts at a given time.

Hotels are notoriously ghettoized in their allocation of labor. Some of the Ali'i resorts' departments were marked by their gender assignment, others by age, and still others by ethnicity. While individuals might come in understanding this stratified placement system and request jobs in their demographically appropriate locations, those ignorant about it were quickly funneled into departments with others like themselves (see chapter 8). Women tended to work in laundry, housekeeping, hotel operator, human resources, weddings, beauty salon, and camp; male departments included MIS (management information systems), security, stewarding, housemen, bell, valet, water features, and engineering. The remaining departments were mixed-gender staffed.

Resorts tended to feature young workers; there were rather few departments where older employees could keep up with the work or feel comfortable. Attractive, slim, young workers populated the most visible areas. Older employees congregated in departments marked by little to no guest contact, mostly in the back of the house. Finally, a range of ethnic stereotypes existed, pushing workers into departments with others of their race and ethnic background (see chapter 8). Workers' pay scale was directly affected by the department in which they worked, and these ghettoized placements created a system of stratification that arose from the entrenched assumptions of what kinds of workers would be appropriate for each location. These employment trends are discussed more fully in later chapters.

Overview of the Book

Chapter 2 brings to life the resorts we studied and our role within them. We discuss the evolving nature of our research and the character of the resorts. In explaining our methods, we specifically examine our early research interests and our formal application for study, establishing our membership role, gathering data, expanding our focus, and reflecting on our methodology.

The major typology of workers is introduced in chapters 3 and 4. Here we begin introducing the many people we studied (for ease of reference, we include an appendix with a complete list of individuals, their hotels, and the departments in which they worked). We use these chapters to set the framework for all the work we subsequently develop analytically, as these groups have distinctly different work and living arrangements. Chapter 3 focuses on the trapped workers, the new immigrants and locals. Chapter 4 looks at the transient workers, the seekers and management. We discuss the background, composition, lifestyle, family arrangements, and customs of each group, using extensive quotes to give readers a flavor of the types of people who fall within each. These chapters articulate the various kinds of leisure pursued by each group and its relation to its work.

In contrast to the embedded nature of the new immigrants and locals, the trapped population, the seeker and management categories of workers are highly transient groups, as we will see in chapter 5. Occupational transience has been given scant attention sociologically, and it is tied in to the increasingly global flow of workers. In this chapter we look at these workers' lifestyles: their types of transience—transient careers, transient families, and transient friendships. These are postmodern workers with postmodern lifestyles.

Dealing with seasonality is one of the organizational challenges faced by resorts, as many of them are located in areas that are favored by weather and the seasonal fluctuations of families with children in school. Organizations that can streamline their staff during slow seasons and expand it during busy seasons can operate more profitably. Resorts thus have an economic incentive to maintain a flexible workforce. In chapter 6 we discuss the three seasons faced by Hawaiian resorts: group season (when corporations bring their workers for incentive reward and convention trips), "FIT" season (when families take their vacations), and slow season (when guests are scarcer). Departments in the resorts are affected differently in these periods, as groups use the convention, catering, and banquet services, while families throng to the restaurants, shops, beaches, and pools. During slow season employees are released, although cutting the workforce too sharply is damaging, as it shrinks the reliable, year-round steady core of employees who know how to operate the resorts. We discuss the seasonal adaptations made by these resorts as they expand and constrict their labor pool. We then discuss the lifestyle adaptations workers must make as they plan the yearly fluctuations in their patterns of work and anticipated income.

Time is a dimension that has become increasingly relevant to our "incessant" society in the postmodern age. We have increasingly conquered what was once referred to as a new frontier with a society that operates around the clock. In chapter 7 we contrast the rhythms of "natural time," so important to the beach- and sun-seeking guests in the Hawaiian Islands, with the "commercial time" artificially constructed by the resorts that keeps many departments operating around the clock. More time to sell makes resorts more profitable and increases the convenience for guests who can order food, make reservations, or speak to a concierge at any hour of the day or night. Experientially, however, breaking out of the rut and rhythm of the workday time clock offers freedom to guests, who take vacations to be freed from the constraints of temporal management. To provide this service to guests, however, resort employees must labor around the clock in daytime (first), evening (second), and graveyard (third) shifts. We discuss the experiential dislocation that occurs for employees who work in atemporal shifts and the adaptations they make.

Resorts are organizations where the ethnic ghettoization of their multicultural workforce is dramatic. Employees are steered into departments populated by members of their ethnic/racial groups by administrative stereotyping. In chapter 8 we go in-depth with several cases that dramatically illustrate this occupational stratification. Focusing specifically on the departments most affected by seasonal fluctuation, the catering and convention arena of food and beverage, we present the work and leisure lives of workers in three departments—new immigrant stewards, the most poorly paid of the three areas; local housemen, from the median-paid area; and haole banquet servers, who make the most money. This chapter delves more deeply into these workers' lives, discussing how these individuals came to Hawai'i and to work in the Ali'i resorts, how they came to their particular departments, what their work is like, and how their income is figured. They specifically discuss their placement in these highly stratified departments and the way they feel about their differential pay and work conditions.

Chapter 9 begins our examination of the occupational careers of resort employees. To understand the differential fluctuations of these workers' span of resort employment, we focus on each of our four worker groups and consider those who last for short-term (two to three years) or intermediate (up to eight or nine years) lengths of stay. In each category, we look at factors that led workers to remain in or depart from paradise, taking into consideration both their initial intentions and how these may have changed along the way. In so doing, we examine reasons why people leave resort employment, influenced by a variety of push-out and pull-out factors from becoming burned out to getting fired to seeking preferable jobs.

A variety of factors lead employees to stall in their jobs. Encountering adverse working conditions, they may become dissatisfied or uncomfortable. In chapter 10 we consider a variety of glass ceilings and other factors that shorten the careers of women, people of color, and older people. We then turn to those who make the hospitality industry their lifetime career, what the motivations and experiences are for each of our four worker groups, and why even those who decide to remain in resort work to the end usually leave at an earlier age than they might retire from other occupations.

Finally, in chapter 11, we examine the theoretical implications of the data presented in the previous chapters and the nature of resort work in paradise locations. We begin by analyzing resorts as postmodern, global communities, from their demographic composition to their temporality and to workers' social psychological self-portraits. We then look at work and labor issues, beginning with the nature of the service work involved in the hospitality industry, the demographics and characteristics of the Ali'i resorts' contingent laborers compared to the broader contingent workforce, examining why some contingent jobs were considered good and others bad. We consider the influence of ethnicity on the Ali'i diverse tourist labor force, examining how people of color are ghettoized, commodified, exploited, tokenized, socially closed, and ethnically stratified by job queues. We look at the difficulties cited in organizing hospitality labor in the tourism industry and discuss how the Ali'i resorts and their employees dealt with the issue of unionization, analyzing the particular impact of the two dimensions of transient/trapped as well as advantaged/disadvantaged on their labor organizing. Finally, we discuss the political economy of tourism, bringing issues of the relationship among resorts, employees, and the local labor market to the fore, as each factor plays a part in contributing to the structure of labor opportunities in paradise. We examine the short-term needs of each group and how these contribute to the long-term implications for the paradise workforce and the economy.

2

RESEARCHING RESORTS

Vacations are special times that we vividly remember from our youth.[1] Growing up affluent in urban New York, we were taken by both of our families to warm-weather enclaves during the winter in Florida and the Caribbean and to summer houses near the ocean in the "fashionable" Hamptons or to mountain resorts in the now-famed Catskills in upstate New York. Taking a "time out" became an annual event to which we looked forward, a time to renew family bonds and to recuperate from the labors of daily life.

However, as young, peripatetic, and relatively low-paid academics with a growing family, the only kinds of vacations we had known were spent visiting friends or relatives. Never could we afford to take an annual vacation on our own. We had once been to Hawai'i, in 1980 with Patti's family, a visit unfortunately cut short by the untimely death of Peter's father. Although our glimpse of the Islands was brief and encapsulated, it captured our imaginations, and we vowed that we would one day return. Garnering the airline mileage that we had so assiduously saved for years as well as hotel points, mostly accrued from attending professional meetings over a fifteen-year span, in March 1990 we packed our bags, excitedly prepped our children for our "dream vacation," and flew off to the Hawaiian Islands for a two-week spring break. This visit proved to be a major turning point in our lives.

We were delighted; we were enthralled. Hawai'i was fresh, magical. The air was softer there, the colors more vivid, the food fresher, the culture enchanting; romance was everywhere, even for us with our two preadolescents in tow. From that point on, we returned to our tropical paradise every year, increasing our trips from once to twice annually beginning in 1994. We experimented with different ways to vacation: at hotels or condominiums, staying at the houses of friends or living in ramshackle bungalows, searching the Web for special deals or finding charter flights to save costs. No matter what, we were bound and determined to find a way to get back to the spots we chronicled in our yearly photo albums.

Eventually we found a hotel that had everything that the kids and we wanted, the Lukane Sands, where we kept returning. As "inquiring" sociologists we naturally chatted with the management and staff about their lives and the way they ran the resort. Having spent the better part of our adult lives interviewing people, our questions ran deeper than most. To our initially unseasoned eyes, resort workers had it all. They lived where the weather was always temperate, they had enough discretionary income to pursue leisure activities, and even on the grimmest day at work, they could look at the scenery and find all tranquil with the world. Far removed from the rapid speed of American lives, they appeared to be in a laid-back groove. We wanted to know what it was like to live in paradise and what it took to make paradise for others.

Consistent with our investigative approach to ethnography (Douglas 1976), we wanted to penetrate "behind the scenes" and discover the mechanisms upholding the public presentations. We became intrigued by the concept of a resort as a social system, with its vast machinery of workers churning out food, towels, sheets, landscaping, and service. We also noticed that the Lukane Sands and the resorts around it were undergoing organizational transformations, as they shifted from chain to independent management and back, changing their names, owners, and management companies every few years. Our initial broad curiosity shortly gave way to sociologically fueled questions and ideas.

Beginning the Study

Approaching the final writing stage of our then-current research project (Adler and Adler 1998), we were casting around for our next topic of study. With a sabbatical on the horizon, we thought about transforming our role as tourists into that of ethnographers.[2] Aikau (2001) noted: "As ethnographers we walk the fine line between being tourists and researchers. Tourists leave home temporarily to escape into difference, while ethnographers dwell in a place to understand cultural difference. Tourists travel for pleasure, while ethnographers travel for work. Despite these tensions, both potentially share a colonial gaze."

Transforming membership roles (pre-established roles in a setting) into research roles has long been a hallmark of our work (Adler and Adler 1987), as we have turned neighbors (Adler 1985), students (Adler and Adler 1991a), and our children (Adler and Adler 1998) into research projects. Changing our role as regular guests at the resort into resort researchers seemed natural.[3] In 1994, with the hopes of doing an organizational study of this rapidly changing resort, we began negotiating with the management team at the Lukane Sands for permission to conduct a study.

The vast majority of our previous research had been conducted with unorganized groups (see Adler and Adler 1991b), and formally navigating the resort's organizational pathways proved difficult.[4] We had done well in the past negotiating entrée face-to-face, where we could explain our interests and convey our integrity and friendship personally. A letter of introduction—despite our titles, professional affiliations, previous publications, and any other sources of legitimation that we could muster—failed to capture our love for the resort, our interest in its organizational dilemmas, and our sociological expertise that might help the staff with personnel issues. But we tried. Little did we know how tenuous and difficult this negotiation would prove. Working our way, painstakingly, to the upper tiers of management, we finally were able to write and/or to speak to the general manager (GM). Explaining our research interests to him, we tried to differentiate ourselves from what he kept hearing: that we were muckraking journalists or, even worse, that we were freeloaders who just wanted free access to paradise. At long last we were successful in obtaining his official approval for our study, and we made our sabbatical plans for the following spring.

But before we could go, the resort's tempestuous owner fired the GM and his management company, hiring a new group of individuals whom he could personally control. Busy settling into their domain, changing the things most pressing to the owner, and hiring their own upper management people, these members of the new independent management company had little time for us. We were put on the back burner and pushed aside until they felt they had the resort under control. After several months of delay, we resumed our negotiations and were once again successful in obtaining the new management's permission to study the resort.[5]

In March 1995 we arrived in Hawai'i to begin our research, only to find that the new GM had been fired the day before and the deputy GM elevated to the top position. Management morale was seriously shaken by these changes at the top, and people were uneasy. We began interviewing members of the executive committee, with an eye toward speaking, once again, to the new GM. We finally were able to get an interview with him and went to his office at the end of a long day. Offering him a copy of our book on college ath-

letes (Adler and Adler 1991a)—a topic, fortunately, in which he had great interest—we explained the type of ethnographic research we did and the types
of access we would need to his property, and we had a stimulating and wide-
ranging discussion on a variety of issues. After over two hours in his office, he
assured us, as we shook his hand on the way out, that the way was clear for
us to talk to anyone at any time and to travel through any portion of the resort as we desired. In exchange, we would meet with him periodically to give
our assessment of the running of the resort, employee morale, guest experiences, and other organizational issues. His executive assistant would type up
a letter specifying this permission for us to pick up the next day. We were
elated. We went out to celebrate that night, thrilled with our success.

The next morning, on our way to the hotel's gym, we stopped by the office of the spa director, a good friend, to tell him of our fortune. We were in
the clear. But his words fell like a bucket of water on our high spirits. Within
an hour of our leaving the GM's office, he, too, had apparently been fired and
escorted off the premises. His executive assistant had emptied his desk that
morning and taken the contents to the security desk for him to collect. Independent manager no. 2 was gone and with him, our luck. We were deflated.
Our roller coaster had taken a downturn once again, and we were back at
square one. Nobody knew what to do with us, and we didn't know what to
do with ourselves. A new person was immediately brought in from the mainland to be the interim GM and was closeted with high executives and the
owner. Our friends in management assured us that we should continue our
interviews, since we had been given permission during each turnover, and the
control of the resort was ambiguous.

We went about our business, waiting for our turn to speak to the new
GM, cognizant of the fact that moving too quickly can be the ethnographer's
demise. Before we could get an interview with him, however, he was transferred back to the mainland and the third member of the independent management team installed in the top slot. We applied to see him but were unable
to get scheduled before our time evaporated and we had to return to the mainland. This kind of turnover continued to haunt our research for much of the
next year and a half. On many occasions, ruminating in our Colorado house
far away from our primary setting, we figured that the project had experienced
an untimely death.

Eventually the resort achieved greater stability and we reached some accord with the next GM. Over the course of our twice-yearly visits there in the
second half of the 1990s we were able to interview the entire management
team. We conducted these interviews on hotel property, usually in people's of-

fices. We never had the nerve to request permission to bring a tape recorder, as employment was unstable and people were on edge. Sometimes we both did the interviews, sometimes only one of us. We noticed that the management often compared notes among themselves about us, some bragging to others that they had gotten both of us while others got only one.

We continued conducting interviews with management even though we had covered all the positions, as the turnover at this level was so high we were guaranteed a continuing fresh selection of individuals each time we returned. This also allowed us to continue the relatively unfettered access we had to all the other employees. Top-level management and the long-time director of human resources, who had managed to survive the various internal coups, were aware of our existence and could vouch for our being on site, should security or other employees stop us. Eventually we reached data saturation, as we heard the same basic stories told and retold.

We supplemented these data with interviews at mainland and international sites we visited. Each time we traveled around or outside the country and stayed in a major hotel, whether it was urban or resort, independent or chain, we called and wrote ahead to arrange interviews. This was generally easier, we found, if we were staying there as hotel guests. Our trips, for instance, to the convention sites of the annual American Sociological Association meetings became times not only to catch up with colleagues and to exchange research ideas but to interview management and workers in the hotel chains we frequented. It was not unusual to see us engage a young waitress at a bar or a table-setter at a banquet in a conversation. Our colleagues began to marvel at our "hotel-speak." We interviewed resort executives on the East and West coasts, in Chicago, Anaheim, and Atlanta, and in the Colorado ski areas near our home. We also made several trips abroad, including one sweep throughout the South Seas intended specifically to gather data from this region and to present our developing ideas to colleagues at universities in Australia, New Zealand, Fiji, and Tahiti (home to major tourism research centers).

We affiliated with the Tourism Research Group at the University of Colorado and were asked to present our research to tourism executives. On several occasions we served as consultants for these executives, as they were particularly concerned about the personnel turnover and lack of continuity in their resorts from one year to the next. Although we weren't paid for the consultations, we sometimes received vouchers, amenities, and other perquisites that were not usually available to other guests. The stories of these executives proved remarkably similar to the ones we had been hearing, although hotels

in different locations varied in their seasonality, type of clientele, employee demographics, and expanse of operation.

Establishing a Membership Role

Simultaneous to these formal interviews we were also conducting casual
participant observation among the employees at the "Sands" and other hotels.
Walking around the resort, we engaged workers in friendly conversation, often going beyond casual chats about daily events to inquire into their lives.
We told them that we had official permission from management to talk to
them, but this often created suspicion, since, given the resort's history, people
imagined that we might be spies. We honestly answered no to this, but it
showed us the level of unease that existed.[6]

We found it too awkward to introduce our research project every time we
began a conversation with someone new, as we were generally talking with
people while they were working. They would gladly stop what they were doing to talk to us for five or ten minutes; we were aided by the hotel's edict to
its employees to maintain friendliness at all times with the guests. However,
these encounters were expected to be brief, and after a short time workers began looking around, fearing that a supervisor would accuse them of slacking.
We adapted ways to talk to people as functionally and efficiently as possible while still informing them of our research interests. Whenever possible,
we sought out supervisors and department heads and asked to attend their
pre-shift meeting. These fifteen-minute gatherings were occasions where information about occupancy, special groups or guests, and various new developments were announced. We were introduced to groups of employees, and
then later we would wander around their department to give people a chance
to see us or to ask questions.

We selected obvious places to park ourselves and to write up field notes,
so that employees could see us at work. This helped establish our working
role. Although we were staying at the resort off-and-on during this period, we
did not want people to think that we were simply interlopers, encroaching on
the property. Employees who didn't know us often inquired what we were doing, and this gave us the opportunity to explain our situation. As we wrote,
we asked ourselves questions, which we also recorded in our notebooks,
about trends and patterns that we were noticing. We were aided in our organizational analysis by the resort's color-coding of jobs by uniforms.[7] We could
easily distinguish people into their departments (i.e., landscaping, water fea-

tures, housekeeping, outdoor housekeeping, security, and engineering) because they all wore outfits that differentiated them.

Eventually we refined a methodology we termed the "chat swing," where
we would walk around, talk to a few people, and then retreat to a place in the
shade to write field notes in our notebook.[8] We regularly sat on a bench in
the shade, which we termed our "office," where employees knew we could be
found. A day filled with several chat swings yielded a good haul of information. We might begin a conversation by saying, "Boy, that's a big function
you're setting up for down here; let's hope it doesn't rain." The employee
would look up and we would talk about the weather. Then we might move
on with, "Say, your name tag says Ramon, do you come from South America?
How did you happen to end up working here? What do you do in the slow
season? Do you go home, stay here, or what?" In ten minutes of such conversation we could begin to put together little stories of people's lives.

Ordinarily, in our everyday existence, we have trouble remembering details about people—their names and their stories. But writing them down in
note form and reviewing them often helped us to remember things. The fact
that employees wore nametags was also a big boon (in fact, we often wished
we could too, so that they could remember our names). Then, when we ran
into people again, we could build on our previous conversations and extend
our knowledge. Employees appreciated our interest in them, as this was rare
among guests who were used to being pampered. Seeing us regularly, year after year, gave them a feeling of connection with us and a feeling that they had
friends among the often-arrogant tourists. We shared that feeling and enjoyed
walking around the property bumping into people we knew, where we could
catch up on their lives and the tales of their families.

Gossip in a resort is a daily pastime, as things change quickly. With over
1,000 people working at the Sands, there was a lot going on all around us. We
tried, as much as possible, whether we were staying in-house or not, to do as
much for ourselves as we could. Employees appreciated this and often commented on how easy we were to have around. In fact, we tried to pitch in at
times to make their jobs easier, keeping them company when they were doing mundane tasks, helping out bothersome guests, giving people directions
to the resort's myriad activities or through its circuitous corridors, and cover-
ing for them. After several years we knew better than most employees how
many departments operated. Many were impressed with the long-term institutional memory we had. In a place so transient, ironically, we became some
of the few fixtures that remained around year after year.[9]

There were special places where we felt most at home, where we formed the closest friendships. The resort's spa, gym, and exercise facilities were among the main factors that had drawn us to the Sands in the first place. We became known as gym rats, using the equipment, swimming laps in the pool, and taking a variety of exercise classes. When we were not staying as registered guests at the hotel, they sold us punch passes to use the facilities, a privilege accorded only to locals. They eventually created a more elite spa and gym membership for locals designed with us in mind. We were referred to as "regulars" by the spa staff and invited to their weddings, parties, master classes, and demonstrations of new equipment. Patti was invited to teach exercise classes when people couldn't come in at the last minute. In the gym, in fact, she helped out guests and trained new employees so often that the manager jokingly presented her with her own Lukane Sands "trainer" business card.

We emailed people during the off-season and exchanged videotapes, photos, and letters. On extended visits, we stayed at their houses, and they stayed at ours, sometimes rooming with us at condos we rented and sometimes visiting us in Colorado. When we were fortunate enough to be invited to stay at people's houses, our accommodations ranged from the dilapidated conditions of a two-room bungalow without air conditioning to the palatial opulence of a mansion with an ocean view. When one special friend left the hotel and moved to Europe, we visited him there and kept up with his travels through his parents. We extended our membership role by joining the resort's membership program, where for a down payment, we could reduce the price of our room nights or our friends', an investment that quickly paid for itself. When higher levels of membership were offered, we upgraded. This gave us a better status with employees and new management we met and befriended and allowed us legitimately to use the property when we weren't staying in the rooms. This was especially beneficial when we probed beyond the reach of most guests.

Talking with people in front of the house areas, such as beach and pool, bell, valet, fitness, and front desk was the easiest, as part of these people's job description involved talking to guests. Penetrating back-of-the-house areas was more difficult and required a different strategy. We formed close relationships with several housekeepers, many of whom were Filipino, during times when we stayed in the hotel. We tried to be in the room when they came by and talked to them about their lives and their families. With special friends, we requested lodging in their bank of rooms so that we could spend time with them. When we were not staying in the resort, we came by their floors and caught up with them, often exchanging small presents and photos.

All this proved fairly expensive, and we needed to minimize our costs.

We participated in every airline mileage game we could for the free travel. We found a regular condominium rental arrangement, with a long-term cheaper rate, and got our rental cars from locals offering banged-up vehicles. Using our exercise pass or membership to work out in the mornings, packing our own lunch and cocktails, hanging out when eating or taking notes on the (public access) beach, and sharing entrees for dinner, we reduced our costs.[10] To make our trips more affordable, we looked for work on Honua. In 1995, we went to the annual meeting of the Hawai'i Sociological Association to present our first paper from this research, and people there invited us to the Sociology Department at the University of Hawai'i to give a talk. They were gracious and warm to us, and we exchanged mutually interesting information. We were spending more time in Hawai'i during the summer, and they eventually invited us to teach summer school there. In 1996, we began teaching summer school every year, working for the University of Hawai'i. We developed a rotation of three or four courses that we each taught. This offered us a schedule that would have pleased Karl Marx (1845), as we exercised in the morning, did research in the afternoon, and taught classes at night.

The teaching experience far surpassed our meager expectations, as this opened up a whole new world for our research. Instead of just interacting with resort people, we made friends with students who were locals and local transplants. We went out with them and visited their houses and their places of work. Now, in addition to the resort workers we were meeting, we had another group to tap for data. As with the resort workers, we attended our students' baby showers, were invited to their weddings, made them dinners, became godparents (auntie and uncle)[11] to their children, and helped them find things back on the mainland they couldn't get in the Islands. They introduced us to local culture and to the delightful way that local people speak when they are not talking to resort guests.[12]

Our pronunciation and the cadence of our Hawaiian words and expressions began to change. We became more aware of the racial politics infusing the Islands and of the sensitivities local people had to different groups, both from the Islands and the mainland. To keep abreast of what was going on, we subscribed to the local newspaper when we were back in Colorado, bought subscriptions to numerous magazines that covered Hawai'i, and voraciously read any book we could get on the history of Polynesia. Our trip to the South Seas was especially helpful in giving us a comparative view of the relationship of indigenous peoples to their colonizers. We came gradually to understand the view of ourselves through the colonialist lens, although only one student ever specifically made us feel like encroachers or outsiders.

Mostly our students embraced us warmly, sharing their aloha spirit and culture with us. We learned that no one ever leaves a Hawaiian party hungry, and that a party with a few "pupus" (snacks) meant a feast. Like their ancient ancestors, people were generous to a fault. They appreciated the knowledge and education we brought to them, even dedicating a Hawaiian chant in our honor at the end of one semester. On Thursday nights we did late night happy hour with our students, and at the end of every summer we held a class party where we brought in dinner, then went out to drink and to shoot pool. Our students were a mix of traditional college people and nontraditional older people, working full-time. These latter were employed, trying to enhance their credentials to get a raise or to qualify for a better job. As a compassionate welfare state, Hawai'i had a call for people with social science training.

An unintended consequence of our teaching was the expansion of our membership research role. Now, not only were we regular hotel guests, island visitors, and resort researchers, but we were also gainfully employed as professors at the college. Although we were clearly mainland haoles (see Geschwender et al. 1988; Whittaker 1986),[13] we reached the exalted status of *kama'aina*[14] (local residents) who gave to, rather than just took from, the culture. Coming from a more privileged class background than many (although not all) resort workers, we had an expanded base of connections with employees outside the resort, particularly college-aged people. Our local knowledge, connections, and wardrobe increased to the point where we could comfortably converse with most resort workers, easily finding areas of commonality and mutual acquaintances. In fact, we were often mistaken for Island residents.

We thus settled into a regular lifestyle, traveling to Hawai'i twice a year for two weeks in March and six weeks in the summer, what Burawoy (2003) has called "punctuated revisits." Spending eight weeks a year there gave us a consistent presence, but it never felt like enough. We were able to use March as the launching period for catching up with people and arranging interviews for the summer, and returned soon enough so that we still felt connected. The long period in between August and March was more difficult, as things changed and we fell out of touch.

Expanding the Study

Back at the Sands, things were getting tense. Just as individuals can come to question the trust they may have initially granted a researcher, organizations may do the same. Several lawsuits by employees had left the managers feeling vulnerable to outsiders, and they began denying their people permission to conduct interviews with us. We then got into a conflict with the deputy director, and management blocked our research even further, eventually revoking our membership. The hotel fell on tough financial times, as was common in Hawai'i during this period due to the downfall of the Japanese economy, the aftershocks of the first Gulf War, and later, the deleterious effects of September 11 on leisure travel (Witeck 2001). The years of ownership stability came to a close and the resort was sold. From then on, a pattern of revolving ownership and management existed. New ownership and management was good for us, as new people had no worries about us and we could start afresh. A new membership program was launched, and we were invited to join. We were continually reminded, though, that our presence was tenuous, as was our research; and while we were careful to remain within prescribed grounds, the power of organizations, compared to unorganized individuals, in dealing with researchers is noteworthy (see Adler and Adler 1991b).

Our research mode at the other Ali'i resorts involved more in-depth interviewing than participant observation. We used our students and friends as contacts who helped us meet people working on these properties. From these, we got help snowballing to others through chain-referral sampling (Biernacki and Waldorf 1981). Many people held jobs at more than one of these resorts and sponsored (Burgess 1991) us to their co-workers along the strip. In this way we were finally able to get greater access to those people with whom we could not easily talk through our guest and chat swing approaches.

We delved deeper into local and new immigrant populations, groups that we had more difficulty interacting with casually, partly due to racial, cultural, and class barriers. Sponsorship proved the most effective way to bridge into these groups. In conducting these interviews, for the first time we were able to use a tape recorder, which greatly enhanced our data gathering. This was possible with mainland and local haoles and with locals, but less so with new immigrants, who generally felt embarrassed to be recorded because of their broken English. Several people, in fact, brought friends or family members to translate for them during the interviews, although they soon saw that this was not necessary. With these people we took written notes as closely as we could. We regretted losing the enriched culture and language associated with their exact spoken words. Our quotes from people in this book thus represent a combination of direct, taped interviews, interviews hurriedly taken as they were occurring, and notes of conversations reconstructed as soon as we left an interaction and retreated to a quiet location. As recommended by Emerson et al. (1995), in no instance did our note taking occur later than the morning after the interaction had occurred. In all, we observed and interacted with over 500 workers, conducting interviews with approximately 90 of them, some more than once.

We wrestled with being stood up for interviews, not being called back by people who appeared initially enthusiastic, and trying to find suitable places to conduct interviews.[15] Whenever possible, we went to people's houses for the privacy this offered. Some respondents preferred to conduct their interviews at work; this afforded us several opportunities to tour back-of-the-house areas in other resorts. We also conducted interviews on the beach, in churches, in public parks, and at our rental condo, at the convenience of our respondents.

Our new approach gave us the opportunity to search out more kitchen personnel, stewards, housemen, banquet servers, housekeepers, security guards, telephone operators, bookkeepers, and room reservations people. With the exception of one student, one secretary at the college (formerly employed in the resorts), and one director at the Sands we interviewed early in our research, we stayed clear of people working in human resources. We quickly learned that employees considered these "bureaucratic rangers," people who "wrote others up" (a formal complaint or a mark of violating company rules that was put into employees' permanent records), who looked for rule infractions and made trouble. Freed from the confines of a single resort and studying individual workers rather than the resorts themselves, we no longer needed organizational permission to talk to people.[16] We used Institutional Review Board (IRB) approved consent forms when interviewing and gave out more business cards.[17] When we took photos for the book we used model release forms supplied by the publisher.

In preparing to write each article, we transcribed our taped interviews and reexamined our handwritten field notes, coding and analyzing our data to discern patterns related to the topic at hand. These yielded preliminary concepts that we refined further as we proceeded with the gathering and analysis of our data through continuous, emergent inductive research (Becker and Geer 1960). Once we had formed an outline for each article or chapter, we conducted more interviews and casual conversations to fill in holes that we perceived in the data. As a result, we continued to engage in waves of data gathering over the course of years, never leaving the field, even throughout the writing process.

For each article, and for the ideas forming the main conclusions for the book, we typed up a one- to two-page sheet summarizing our general ideas in everyday parlance. We then took this overview around the resorts to engage in respondent validation (Burgess 1984), showing it to people to get their feedback. We let our key informants in each of the relevant departments and worker typologies read these to give us suggestions for modification or to affirm them. With each overview summary, the list of reviewers expanded, as people looked forward to seeing what we were writing about and increasingly appreciated their role as "experts" providing the final line of quality control. After each article was published we also offered these to people we thought might be interested in reading them, but with each article the list of people who had this kind of interest shrank (they found articles too dry). We used our South Seas lecture tour to get more academic feedback from scholars in the field. While we eventually brought some closure to this project by putting together this book, we maintain an ongoing interest in these organizations and occupations, with an eye toward future writing.

Reflections

Every research project yields some methodological insights previously unrecognized and offers its own particular set of challenges and rewards.

Distance

This was the first project we have conducted where we were not gathering data in our own "backyard." While we have done research in the past that was more dangerous (i.e., among drug dealers), more sensitive (college athletes), and more ethically controversial (our own children), the geographic distance involved in this research made it, in many ways, our most difficult challenge. It has always been our practice to immerse ourselves fully in our settings, to be there in the evenings and during the days, on the weekends and the weekdays, during times of crisis as well as calm; we have cherished the depth participant-observer role.[18] But we could not do this here because we lived more than 3,000 miles away. The demands of our work and lives precluded our being away from home for too long. With the cost of airfare to Hawai'i at times running at more than $1,000 a round-trip ticket per person, visits for less than two weeks never seemed worthwhile. We settled on traveling there twice a year and considered ourselves lucky to be spending two months out of twelve at our research site. However, we paid a price for not being "on island" more often.

As hard as we worked to forge a membership role, our continued absences undercut this. When we were there, we picked up our friendships, our relationships, and our role in the setting, but this role was limited by our transience. Like Simmel's (1950) strangers, we were neither fully part of nor outside the group; we were recurring, permanent fixtures but not people who were completely there. At times we toyed with the idea of applying for jobs as seasonal banquet servers at one of the resorts to get a better inside view of that scene (and to help defray expenses), but we thought our IRBs would not approve of our applying for jobs with the goal of gathering data without making a full research disclosure, and we thought that the resorts would not be interested in hiring us once we made such a disclosure.[19] Nor were we complete member-researchers, living there year-round and being in our subjects' worlds. We considered ourselves peripheral member-researchers, part of the social circle, friends whose involvement went beyond the role of customers.

We became meaningfully involved in people's lives and cared about them and their partners, their children, and their general overall well-being. Thus, we witnessed and counseled people through childbirth, childrearing, marriage, divorce, and the death of loved ones, since we were either seen as older (having lived through these phases of life) or wiser (a status conferred upon us due to our advanced degrees). Undertaking a research project where the field is far from where researchers live is nothing new to anthropologists; it is the hallmark of their discipline. These scholars, generally working in foreign countries, spend years learning the indigenous language. Their linguistic investment serves as a side bet (Becker 1960), binding them to that location for a lifetime of continued return. As sociologists, and as people working within our own linguistic domain, we have had no such commitment and have shifted our research focus nearly every decade. Our research patterns resemble anthropologists in some ways but differ in others. For some social scientists, the idea of a research location at a distance is appealing because it enhances individuals' outsider perspective and enables them to take a naïve role for data-gathering (Vail 2001). For us, it hurt our research relationships and role.

It also changed our lives because of the cost involved. Our sporadic forays into grantsmanship have never been fruitful. While many people in our setting suggested that we apply for private funds through tourist boards and other avenues of hotel management, we decided against that approach. We preferred to work without strings, at our own pace, and without the taint that our research was bought or influenced by a funding agency. We feared losing the anonymity of our setting to such agencies, and we had little desire to conduct applied sociology, wrapping our gaze around practical matters that would enhance the operation of such organizations. As in all of our previous research, we were self-funded, and we had to work out ways to creatively come up with the money we needed for our travels. We applied for small research stipends from our schools to cover airfare. During times we had previously reserved exclusively for writing, we signed up for teaching. We overloaded during the regular semesters with additional courses to teach. This hurt our writing productivity, but it kept us in the field.

After a while we felt that we had a life in Hawai'i that existed independently of our mainland lives. We became different people in our Hawaiian lives—more relaxed, loving, healthy, and social. Our perspective on being there and on the sacrifices it took to get and keep us there shifted once we arrived, justifying all the expenses. When we returned home to the bills and to the time cost of being away, we shifted again. We undertook a sort of schizophrenia, experiencing the "shock of unrecognition" (Wiley 1987) each time we moved from one location to another, one life to another, one outlook to another. We jealously guarded our time on Honua, meagerly parceling out permission to visit us to our closest friends and relatives, feeling that they consumed our attention and removed us from our local scene, local friends, and research immersion. Having an adolescent (high school) child at home severely limited our travel as well; and during the weeks we were away, when we left him with a housesitter, we were wracked with worries and guilt.

Studying the Other

Ethnographers have written much about the problems associated with studying people in different social and status positions. With many of the usual difficulties and solutions, we studied up to management personnel and studied down to workers who were younger, poorer, and equipped with less cultural capital than we.[20] We had the greatest problems, however, with studying those of different races/ethnicities. In the beginning we noticed that we more easily befriended people like ourselves: the managers and seekers who came from similar class and racial/ethnic backgrounds. We had more in common with them, we could talk to them more easily, and they trusted and interacted with us more readily. As college professors, we had the easiest times with the seekers, most of whom closely resembled our students back in Colorado. As middle-class, well-educated haoles, we had less in common with new immigrants and locals. We ultimately became close to some locals who were our students or who worked in departments where we had more contact: fitness, beach and pool, bell, and valet. Time spent together gave us more to talk about, more familiarity, a greater history, and more trust.

The longer we lived on Honua and the more we formed close bonds with residents, the more we came to understand the way we were viewed by new immigrants and locals. What we had taken for granted, we came to recognize as racial/ethnic, class, and educational privilege. The history of the Islands, like many other places, is a history of racial and ethnic subjugation and domination.[21] While we were not rich by mainland standards (nor compared to the elite groups of mainland haoles who bought extravagant vacation houses on Honua), we were considerably more affluent than many of these workers. While most resort workers could communicate readily with us, we could not speak the pidgin or foreign languages through which they talked to each other. Managers, though easier to converse with, were employees who still had to distance themselves from us since we were often seen as potential hotel guests. Not only were our biographies different from most of these people, but we were also connected to raced and classed educational institutions, both in Colorado and Hawai'i. We worked hard to overcome these barriers and to gather data. At times the obstacles seemed insurmountable.

As the research neared its close and we determined specific holes that needed to be filled, we particularly strove to schedule interviews with locals and new immigrants from the banquet departments: local housemen and new immigrant stewards. We conducted insightful interviews and even were invited into the homes of some people, such as housekeepers, whom we had befriended through participant observation over the years. Being sponsored to other people for "cold" interviews through mutual friends was much more challenging. After being frequently turned down, stood up, not called back, and subjected to a host of other refusals, we asked our local friends to explain people's reluctance to be interviewed.

It had been our experience in previous research that most people enjoyed talking about themselves. Lorraine, a secretary at the college who had worked at the Lukane Sands for eight years, said that local people don't want to be noticed. They are reticent to draw attention to themselves, to rock the boat. Fearful of what people might want of them, they would rather not do anything chancy or risky. Carol, a banquet server at the Hula Club Towers, tried to arrange an interview for Patti with one of her best friends there, a local houseman. When she was unsuccessful, she sent us an email explaining what happened: "I have mentioned it to him and he just smiles and says it will make him famous and then the guys razz him." She felt that the peer pressure from other local housemen deterred him from becoming the "subject of a book." Angie, a spa attendant at the Pono Beach Spa, said, "local women are very jealous and possessive of their husbands and that's one of the ways they show their love." She heard through the grapevine that one person who failed to show up for a scheduled interview balked "because of his girlfriend who's controlling and jealous. She wears the pants in that relationship." Angie was eventually successful in helping us to get another interview by first calling the worker's wife to explain the situation, setting up the introduction so she could "calm her down about it."

Beyond these difficulties of access, it is important to acknowledge that such "otherness" can never be fully overcome. Feminist standpoint epistemology suggests that the construction of research and its analysis is situated within the wider space of social relations (Hill Collins 1987; D. Smith 1990). Members of dominant groups conduct and represent social research from the perspective of their situated interests (hooks 1984). In so doing, they incorporate and recreate master narratives about other groups (Frankenberg 1993), such as views of Hawaiian locals as fun-loving but lazy and of new immigrants as hard-working and frugal. While we cannot claim to have avoided problems associated with privilege and difference, we have sought, like McCorkel and Myers (2003), to acknowledge them. Despite our best efforts, the colonial gaze noted earlier in this chapter, may, in part, shape our work.

Stigma

Turning a leisure setting into a research setting brought upon us a certain amount of stigma.[22] Like our work in the fields of drugs and sport, our resort research was regarded with a certain amount of frivolity by our acquaintances and colleagues.[23] This sense of triviality and superficiality contagiously spread to us. Returning from a trip to the field with a tan, or telling people where we had been, often meant that we had to endure snide comments from others, such as "Oh, that must really be hard," or "You must be researching something really important there." What made these remarks especially difficult to take was our feeling that it really was hard to do what we had done, to find a genuine research project in a place where we wanted to be, to struggle for years with research entrée, to work overtime to fund it ourselves, to construct a teaching opportunity where few had thought it possible, and to be far away from our home.

Life Changes

Any long-term and deep ethnographic research experience should change in some way both the researchers and those they study. This research was no exception, bringing serious life changes. Looking back over our research lives, we are proud that we have maintained meaningful, long-term friendships with people we met during each of our major research endeavors. Even though we have moved away from most of our research settings, we have kept significant ties to the key research friends we formed when we studied our "backyards."[24] Although we left behind the hedonistic and materialistic world of drugs and drug traffickers when we moved from graduate school,[25] we kept in touch with some of the dealers and continue to see and to talk to them. We left the world of college athletics behind when we changed jobs and moved to Colorado, but we call and visit our now-grown former student-athletes when we travel and when they come through town with their teams. We have probably seen more of the preadolescents we studied, although they grew up and many moved away, because they remained friends of our children and children of our friends and neighbors; some have pleasantly graced our college classrooms.

But with Hawai'i as a research setting, so far removed from our backyard, one might expect that this would be more likely to fade from our lives after the intense research period came to a close. A shift happened to us over the course of the research, however. Our short-term commitment to the Islands was reconstructed into a long-term commitment. Every time we went there, as corny as it may sound, it stirred something in our souls. We felt at peace there, at home. We craved an existential connection to the Islands, even though we are terminally fated to be mainland haoles, forever despised and resented by some politically conscious locals (see Trask 1993). We wanted a piece of the "rock." Buying property, we thought, was unaffordable and infeasible for us, but we became attached. Our perspective for the long haul changed, and we began to see ourselves as one day living there. Hawaiian art and cultural artifacts filled up our Colorado home, Hawaiian words permeated our mainland life (like our dog, named Lana'i, after the island in the Hawaiian chain), and Hawaiian culture and philosophy crept into our lifestyle. We began planning for our retirement with the idea of moving to Hawai'i and eventually bought a vacant lot upon which we someday intend to build. This affected our research and our roles and relationships in the field, as we knew that in addition to gathering data, we were also forming a community of people with whom we hoped to grow old, people whom we hoped to have as friends long after (or if) the research was completed. In effect, our peripheral membership role started changing toward an intended complete membership role.

Value Commitment

We believe that there is a value commitment in membership roles unlike that associated with other research strategies. Trained in the ideals of Weberian value neutrality, we have eschewed the feminist or critical epistemological stance that the personal is the professional or that praxis should guide our research actions. But making a long-term commitment to a setting and its people does not preclude, in our eyes, the possibility of taking a critical perspective toward our analysis. It has not kept us from seeing the sometimes-conflicting interests of workers and their employers, or of recognizing the inconsistencies between what people say and what they do. Yet we have a certain pride in feeling that when conflicts arose between what we might do to enhance our research careers and how this might affect resort workers, our enduring commitment to the participants was there to guide us into making a choice that respected the integrity and good of those others.

This is realist ethnography. As such, it meets many of the criteria Van Maanen (1988) first advocated as part of this long tradition. We offer thickly descriptive (Geertz 1973) portraits of the people we studied, based on firsthand observation (Adler and Adler 1994) and longitudinal, rigorous, cross-checked (Douglas 1976), depth ethnography in a way that we hope is fair, measured, and accurate. We have also been swayed by some of the advances made in ethnography following the postmodern turn of the late twentieth century.[26] As much as we were able, we have incorporated the voices of the people who extended us their friendship and cooperation. We have empowered them with the authority to make the ultimate assessments on our presentations by taking our findings back to the field and inviting participants' feedback. We have been self-reflexive about the way our privileged, colonialist gaze influenced our position in the setting, and how we strove to overcome this, all the while recognizing our limitations.

We believe that realist ethnography that is sensitive to contemporary epistemological concerns offers the best compromise between positivism's objectivist detachment and postmodernism's subjectivist self-absorption. It has the power to combine systematic understanding and theoretically informed analysis of social worlds, while representing them through the combined efforts of researchers and participants. For our final interpretations and extrapolations we take sole responsibility, a privilege that we allow ourselves based on the near decade of involvement we had as peripheral members (Adler and Adler 1987) in this complex, layered, multiethnic, and polyvocal scene.

3

TRAPPED LABORERS
New Immigrants and Locals

Workers in the hospitality industry comprise a variety of social and occupational types. Their backgrounds, lifestyles, and employee-management interactions vary with their subcultural values. In this chapter we look at the occupational cultures and work adaptations of the two groups of resort workers trapped in the local economy by their decision to live on Honua: new immigrants and locals. In describing each group we note members' structural situations, their cultural backgrounds, their type of work, their placement in the occupational hierarchy, their lifestyle and living situations, and their future work opportunities.

Estimating the breakdown of workers at each resort into these four groups is difficult. Over the course of any given year the number of people employed in each department fluctuated due to attrition, the economy and expected occupancy, the availability of replacement workers, and the time managers could make to interview and to fill vacant positions.[1] Beyond that, the banquet departments underwent huge seasonal fluctuation, swelling enormously during the busy group months and shrinking when these were over. Lorraine, our college secretary who had formerly worked in human resources (HR) at the Lukane Sands, offered us the best estimate we were able to obtain about the relative size of these four groups of employees. She did most of the HR reports when she was there, and she also helped construct the Equal Employment Opportunity Commission (EEOC) reports in the department. Based on these data, and using the number 1,300 as the best average figure she could come up with for the base employee size (including full-time, part-time, and casual workers), she estimated the following breakdown of people:

Table 1: Population of Worker Groups

325	Immigrants	[new immigrants]	25%
390	Mainlanders	[seekers]	30%
455	Locals	[locals]	35%
130	Management	[management]	10%
1,300	Total		100%

New Immigrants

Occupying the lowest rung of the occupational hierarchy was the new immigrant group.[2] These people accounted for a significant portion of the base-level line employees, those individuals who filled the lowest, most menial positions at the Ali'i resorts. New immigrants to the Hawaiian Islands began arriving in waves over periods of decades and centuries. Beginning around 1850, the Royal Hawaiian Agricultural Society imported laborers, mostly men, to work in the pineapple and sugarcane plantations. Over the next eighty to a hundred years, approximately 400,000 such immigrants were brought into the state (Lind 1996). The Chinese (particularly southern Chinese from Kwangtung and Fukien provinces) constituted the first wave of arrivals, followed by workers from Japan, whose emigration was eventually curtailed in 1908 (Espiritu 1995; 2003). Arriving the earliest, these two groups grew populous in Hawai'i and eventually gained a stakehold in local positions.

Immigrants from the Philippines arrived next, initially from the central Visayas but eventually more prominently from the more Northern Ilocano regions. Filipinos were a particularly favored source of labor because, due to their colonial legal status as U.S. nationals (the Philippines was a "ward" of the United States), they could migrate freely to the United States until the passage of the Tydings-McDuffie Act in 1934. Later waves brought masses of immigrants who were primarily Samoan, Filipino, Vietnamese, Korean, Portuguese, Micronesian, Thai, and Tongan.[3] Most recently, populations forming the major immigration streams in the late twentieth century have continued to bring workers to Hawai'i from the Philippines, Samoa, Tonga, the Marshall Islands, and many of the small Micronesian islands, such as Palau.[4] Members of these populations sought to build a better life in Hawai'i with its American-driven economy and infrastructure. They fled countries immersed in poverty and lacking avenues of economic opportunity (Espiritu 1995). Hired from the age of eighteen, men and women were equally represented during our period of research in the Ali'i resorts. As Santo Duque, a Filipino stewarding manager at the Pono Beach Spa noted, "There is always a fresh new supply of immigrants."

Many of these "labor migrants" (Portes and Rumbaut 1996) came in the first large wave of Filipinos in the 1920s and early 1930s or the second wave after 1965, arriving from the Ilocano linguistic group and bringing with them strong values of hard work, thriftiness, deferred gratification, future-orientation, and sacrifice for their family (Espiritu 1995; Junasa 1996; Woo 2000). A common theme found in the Filipino and other new immigrant cultures was, "Life is hard in America, you really have to work, no monkey business" (Robillard 1996). New immigrants' focus was on adaptation and survival in the new world. As Andaya (1996) has noted, new immigrants and their children believed in the American dream and sought to take advantage of the opportunities that beckoned. With the demise of Hawai'i's sugar and pineapple plantations in the late twentieth century and their replacement by the tourism industry as the largest employer, new immigrant workers moved into the hotel industry.[5] By far the largest group of new immigrant workers at the Ali'i and other local island resorts consisted of Filipinos,[6] followed distantly by Tongans, then further still by Samoans, Chinese, Vietnamese, and a smattering of others.

Job Characteristics

Entering the country with no local education, poor command of English, and few occupational opportunities, new immigrants assumed positions that many indigenous Americans rejected as undesirable.[7] Kam was a Chinese naval welder who migrated to the United States at the age of twenty-five as a "boat person" from Vietnam. He took an advanced welding class at the local community college and was offered work teaching the class but was unable to accept it because of his weak English. When he went to report for a welding job, he found that although the work paid well, it was unstable. He took the first available full-time job he could find instead, at the Lei Gardens. He explained:

> I finish my course at [the community college] as welder, and so I go down where my teacher tell me I find welding work. Guys all hang around every day, wait someone pick them up for job. Pay good, but work no steady. I no like that. I rather work full-time for less pay than work no steady. So I apply at hotel, look for busboy job with my friend. They had no opens, no more job opens. Only thing they had open was the steward graveyard from eleven nighttime to seven in the morning. So I took that. When I

come working my job is to wash pots and pans, and they so busy you can't stop. After a month they transfer me to make food. I work in the morning.

When we asked him how his language limitations affected his ability to find employment in the resorts, he replied, "I don't talk too much. My job, I don't have to, you know."

Similarly, Maximo, a doctor in the Philippines, could not get his medical license in the United States and ended up scrubbing pots and pans in the Hula Club Towers' kitchens. George Clark, the haole executive director of housekeeping and deputy director at the Lukane Sands in his early thirties, discussed the demographic composition of many of his staff members: "The stewards and housekeepers are the lowest end of the pay scale and they are at the bottom status level. They are the two lowest classes of employees in the hotel. They are untrained. No skills are necessary. They do completely manual work. For a lot of other jobs in the hotel where there is more guest contact, there are minimum standards of English-speaking. But these are departments where immigrants can work with few skills."

New immigrants dominated the entire housekeeping, landscaping, and stewarding departments.[8] They preferred being clumped together into these enclaves,[9] as one member of a group of stewards noted: "We have whole areas of hotel that are ours. We like it because we speak Filipino to each other."[10] Tongans, too, mentioned that they found comfort in being able to fall back on Tongan with other immigrants in the housekeeping, stewarding, and landscaping departments, although they claimed to converse primarily in [broken] English. While these people could not qualify for many different kinds of jobs, they approached their work with pride and diligence, had low absentee rates, and had the lowest turnover rate in the hotel (Stepick and Grenier 1994).

Favi, a thirty-six-year-old Tongan housekeeper at the Kahana Surf with four children, noted that upon first arriving in Hawai'i from Tonga at the age of twenty-one, she got a job in a retail store but quit because the work was "too easy." "Tongans," she noted, "just picking hard job. They always work hard in Tonga, so hard work is easy for them." Most Tongans on the island chose physically demanding labor, with "ladies working housekeeping, men working construction, the stone wall, stewarding like Moka [her husband], or landscaping, cut trees." Kam was an extremely hard worker as well. Having spent many years as a Lei Gardens cook, he noted: "I don't see anybody who work more hard then me. I am the main hard work person in my department. My chef, she know how hard I work, so she tell me ahead of time always that whenever you need overtime you go ahead. She approved. 'Cause you have to get approved to stay to work overtime. But she approve me because she know when I take overtime, I really need the hour. Other people, they look up every time they do the job, you cannot find them. They go smoke."

Employed as laborers, new immigrants were admired by management for their high job performance. Junasa (1996) has suggested that Filipinos' cultural lack of assertiveness, their aversion to direct personal confrontation, and their conflict avoidance led them rarely to complain or make trouble.[11] They executed tedious jobs—cleaning the guest rooms, maintaining the landscaping, buffing, polishing, and sweeping the lobby, gardens, and restaurant areas—keeping the Ali'i hotels in immaculate condition over long hours for very low pay.[12] New immigrant women worked in stewarding washing dishes, packing them onto rolling carts, bringing them down to the functions, and taking them back. These women also filled the ranks of the housekeeping, laundry, and wardrobe departments, as well as doing food preparation work in the kitchens.

In addition to working low-status, low-paying, difficult jobs, new immigrants often worked multiple jobs. It was not uncommon for individuals to work a forty-hour week at one job and then hold another job, either part-time or full-time, as well. Family members often held three jobs between two people, if not more. Santo Duque, the stewarding manager from the Pono Beach Club, noted the working patterns of Filipinos: "They may work the 11–7 [graveyard] shift here, and then in the morning they work some place else. On their day off they work again some place else. I have one friend, I asked him, how many hours do you sleep? At least three, he said."

Leonardo, a steward at the Hula Club Towers, spoke about the number of jobs he and his fellow stewards held:

LEONARDO: Antonio only has this one job; he's young. But most of us work more than that, like two or three jobs. Andres does stewarding at the Kahana Surf. He works the 8–3 shift there and then the 4–12 shift here. Most of us work sixteen-hour days. Some guys have one full-time job and two part-time jobs.

Q: Why do you work so hard?

LEONARDO: We are sending money back over to the Philippines to our relatives there. And then we can go visit over there. Most of the people here, they look down on us for the work we do, they wouldn't take our jobs. But when we go to the Philippines we have more money to spend. We are big shots there! (group laughter and poking each other)

Values and Goals

Their values and goals strongly motivated new immigrant workers. Instrumental in their orientation, they supported their extended family unit, working hard to advance themselves.[13] They wanted to buy land, to acquire the material possessions that were part of the American dream, and to make themselves a part of their new country (Espiritu 1995). Key to this goal was buying a house. With land and housing prices astronomically high, as in most resort areas, new immigrants slaved to accrue a down payment for a house and to make the monthly payments. Relatives pitched in to buy a house, often living in it together (Junasa [1996] has called this form of reciprocal dependency the "kinship alliance").[14] As Hope, a young local woman who worked in the human resources department at the Kahana Surf, remarked: "The Filipinos build big homes; five to six families live together. The elderly family members stay home and take care of the children. To care for their kids' kids. Because the parents are working at least one job each."

Santo Duque, the stewarding manager from the Pono Beach Club, explained one reason why Filipinos lived in multigenerational arrangements: "Among the Filipinos, many husbands and wives live like that: their parents still live there; the kids live there. In the Filipino culture people are very close with parents. You try not to get separated from them. You always see them. You can share things. You can take care of each other, even though married."

A second reason was that once these extended families were financially secure in their first house, they often began saving for a down payment for another. Then they rented their first house to others, accumulating capital to borrow against for a third. Santo explained this aspect of the Filipino lifestyle: "In the Filipino way, you keep the old house, pay it off, then you move on and buy a new house. My stepmother's friends work in a bank. She sees a lot of Filipino people borrowing money to buy houses. They are still living together. Even though they have a house already, they still have to buy another house."

New immigrants used their time to seek employment and to acquire resources. They knew that they could not carry out such intense physical labor as they got older. Enrique, when we chatted with him at age forty-four, was the oldest houseman at the Lei Gardens. He offered this perspective: "I work five sixteen-hour days a week, eight hours here, and eight hours at the Hula Club Towers. I'm the last diehard man. I will work both of these jobs until I feel I can only work at one. The way I figure it, I won't be strong enough to do this kind of heavy work forever. So I'll do it as long as I can, and then cut down to what I can do. When I'm older I won't be able to earn as much money, so I've got to earn what I can while I'm able." Six years later, Enrique was no longer working both jobs.

Although new immigrants worked to provide material comfort for themselves, they were also motivated to create opportunities for the next generation. To varying degrees, they hoped that their children, raised in America, would have better skills and earning power than they, and would climb the ladder of upward mobility (Espiritu 2003). They sacrificed considerably for their offspring, working multiple jobs and saving. Favi, the Tongan housekeeper, hoped that her children could have "a good education and a good life. . . . A job that they can do—that they can keep it. They can handle that job." Claro, a Marshall Islands groundskeeper at the Lei Gardens in his late twenties with a three-year-old child, voiced his concern, "I want make sure my daughter's life is better than mine. I won't have money, but I hope give her security." Wendy, the wife of Kam, the Lei Gardens cook, talked during his interview about the family's goals for their children: "Even if I cannot afford, I do my best. I want my kids go to the best school. I drive them always to the best school on Honua, even though far. I want them go college on the mainland. I know a lot of people say we're crazy. You know, we don't have money, but my kids they have nice stuff. I have them learn piano. We cut every corner, but I want them have opportunity."

Consonant with this family orientation, new immigrants expended considerable energy and resources in helping their extended kinship network. Before acquiring simple comforts for themselves, they often scrimped to help family members. Wendy described how she and Kam conserved their resources:

> We know a lot of people who don't know how we do it. We never go movies, we never go out. You know, we don't have anything. When we got married we never had reception. We eat rice, vegetables, and a little bit chicken. Our lifestyle is more simple; it the way we manage. We don't go out like people does. We never go to movie or going out like people's restaurant or anything. We survive okay. I have friends who even tell us you know you qualify for food stamp. And he won't take it. I don't want it. I never let you hungry so we make it pretty good independent.

New immigrants helped relatives not only in America, but also in the old country.[15] Kam and Wendy sent money back to support his mother in Vietnam. "Over there the problem is unemployment. It not like here where it easy to find jobs." Alva, twenty-seven years old, was born in the Philippines. Married with two children, he worked full-time at the Hula Club Towers as a houseman, and at the Lukane Sands for part-time work. He described his employment situation and his financial involvement with his family abroad:

> I am a houseman here [the Sands], but if they are short-handed I help out with turndown service. I haul dirty towels, fill carts with ice and stuff. Other male housekeepers on the day shift do butler-type jobs such as brass polishing, floor cleaning, and stuff like that. My wife also works full-time as a housekeeper at the Kahana Surf days, and used to work turndown service at the Lukane Sands. But she had to quit because she is pregnant with our third child. Life here is very hard, but it's harder, still, in the Philippines. I send money every month to my sisters and brothers in the Philippines.

More commonly, new immigrants saved their money to help relatives living abroad move to the United States. Reunification became a focus of their lives, as they navigated their way through financial straits and immigration bureaucracies (Espiritu 1995). It became a major project for an extended family to help members, one at a time or in groups, to immigrate.[16] Evelina, a clerk in the Lukane Sands' lobby's transportation department, was brought to Hawai'i from the Philippines as a child through the efforts of her older sister. Raised and schooled in the United States, she described her situation: "My oldest sister who's forty-four works in accounting. She moved here first. Then she applied for citizenship so she could petition to bring my parents over. That took two years. Once my parents got here it got harder to get citizenship and bring more people over. It took five years to bring my seven brothers and sisters over."

Tongan workers in the Ali'i resorts reported a similar bond with their extended families. Favi, the Kahana Surf housekeeper, confirmed that Tongans saved to send money to their siblings and parents back home, noting that life in Tonga was tough: "Sometimes it hurts that what I have over here they don't have over there. But I always keep on my mind that I'm going to help them out what I can do. But I think it was right for my sister to send for me to come here."

At the same time, she maintained that Tongans were more community-oriented than Filipinos.[17] Speaking to us in an interview conducted one Saturday afternoon at a picnic table on the front lawn of her church, Favi explained:

Tongans do not save and build up money or houses like the Filipinos. The Filipinos, they save for their own, but the Tongans really help out their community. Like we raise money here to build a school or church in Tonga. We give money even if we don't know them. . . . For us here, everything is the church. When we can, we go every Sunday and on Saturdays we have church picnic. I sing in the choir. Tongan youth too. We help them out to make them together and strong in church to have a good life. Every family go to church.

New immigrants represented a stable workforce in the Aliʻi resorts. With few marketable skills and strong language deficiencies, they had little possibility of occupational advancement. For the length of their working lives, they made their careers in these positions. While some new immigrants who initially arrived on Honua moved through to other places, people who stayed for longer than a couple of years tended to remain there. They made secure lives for themselves, found satisfying employment, surrounded themselves with family members, became American citizens, and put down roots. Their attachment to Honua was not particularly to the beauty or spirituality of the island, but to these critical pragmatic features it offered.

Locals

The second category of resort employees, distinctly different from the new immigrants, was the locals.[18] Although this term was more loosely defined and liberally applied before World War II, recent social movements (including Hawaiian sovereignty) have politicized it and made it more exclusive in its use (Trask 1993). Locals consisted of "brown"-skinned people (those having racial blends of Asian, Polynesian, Pacific Island, Hawaiian, and Portuguese descent) born and raised in Hawaiʻi, socialized through the primary school system there, who spoke "pidgin," also known as "creole," and who were mostly working class.[19] To get work in the resorts, however, local people had to be able to speak standard American with a minimum of competence. As Alika, a Japanese-Hawaiian-Chinese front desk clerk at the Hula Club Towers, explained:

Local is primarily a racial category. People who are brown can be considered or become local more easily. Haoles can never be considered locals,

even if they're born and raised here. They're called local haoles. But being a local can also be influenced by where you went to school. If you
move here after school age you can never be considered a local, but if you
move here and grow up here and go to school here with the locals you
can become a local, if you're brown. It's also affected by your speech, your
mannerisms, and how you act. If you talk like a local, have the local accent and way of talking, show the local ways of acting and being, you are
more likely to be perceived as a local.

Her Hawaiian-Chinese-Filipino-Swedish-English friend, Leilani, echoed her
assessment, noting: "I went to the mainland for two years to go to college at
Creighton. When I came back people criticized me for speaking too much like
a haole and having haole ways. I had to work hard to shed my haole accent
and ways in order to be re-accepted. And my mother, who moved here from
the mainland when she was twenty-three, still thinks of herself as a haole."
Locals, then, were generally American citizens. They were people with homes
and families to care for in the Islands.

Just as the new immigrants were affected by a new immigrant culture, locals were embedded in a polycultural, indigenous environment (Manicas 1998;
Yamamoto 1979). Local Hawaiian culture represented a conglomeration of native, assimilative, melting pot, and pluralist cultures. Local culture was distin-
guished from mainland American culture in several ways. Rooted in the ancient
"*aloha*" tradition of affection and embracing, it emphasized the leisure-time,
carefree, and simple lifestyle of the idealized former Hawai'i. Two other key values incorporated in the culture were "*kokua*," the extension of generosity or aid
toward others, and "*aloha 'āina*," preserving the balance among life, land, and
sea. Communally oriented, nurturing, and mutually supportive, local culture
embraced a web of reciprocity and a code of helpfulness toward the family
(*'ohana*) and community over personal recognition and social status. Finally,
local culture was oriented toward the values and behaviors of youth. It thus
represented a complete lifestyle, orientation, and value system.[20]

The category of locals is more diverse than that of new immigrants, comprising a variety of different styles. Some locals' (mixed) Hawaiian heritage extended far back, with their families having lived in the Islands for many
generations. These "family-entrenched" locals had a large network of extended kin living in close proximity and were usually strongly raised within
the Hawaiian culture. "Limited-family" locals were long-time natives as well,
but lacked an extended family in close proximity. This was often the case for
individuals who had moved to Honua from another island and left most of

their family behind. Without extended kin nearby, their knowledge and practice of local customs tended to erode. "New immigrant" locals were the children of new immigrants, born in Hawai'i and educated in the public school system. If their skin and physical appearance were consistent with the general local look and they spoke with the local cadence and expressions, they were accepted as locals. Some immigrants moved to Honua to join existing kinship networks, while others arrived with few friends or family members, giving their children widely different family situations. They held to some of their families' old world customs but augmented these with local and broadly Americanized ways of living, as is common among many second-generation immigrants (see Portes 1996).

Work

Although the hospitality industry was the biggest employer on Honua, not all locals sought employment there. Skimming themselves off the top, the more ambitious young people moved to the mainland. Chad Nakamura, the executive director of food and beverage at the Pono Beach Spa, a family-entrenched local with what he estimated to be six hundred relatives living on Honua, figured that 20–30 percent of his cousins had left for the mainland. The rest, he said, would be content to remain. Once people moved, he noted, it was unlikely that many would return. Of those who stayed, however, not all were even capable of working in the resorts. He explained one occupational barrier:

> You know, to be honest with you, the hotel industry is probably the easiest and the highest-paying industry for local people in Hawai'i. And not anybody can go into the hotel industry. Like, for instance, I have a younger brother. He wouldn't ever be able to go into the hotel industry because, number one, he speaks really broken English; he can't—I mean, I have like an accent, but his is really really, like, he's *real* bad, like, you can hardly understand him. He wouldn't get past the interview phases, he wouldn't. So, anyway, my point is like, growing up in Hawai'i, like, saying when I graduated, I'd say maybe 80 percent of the people I graduated with, maybe that's kind of over-exaggerated, maybe 70 percent was like my brother. And so, 30 percent of us could go in the hotel industry and deal with, y'know, high-end clients from Pono Beach Spa or Kahana Surf, or Lukane Sands.

Many locals, who disdained tourists, were not interested in working in the hospitality industry. Tourists had discovered their favorite places on the island, were buying choice real estate and developing it, and were swimming and surfing on local beaches. Some locals gave "stink-eyes" (dirty looks) to haoles and occasionally got into physical fights with them. Chad Nakamura, the Pono Beach Spa's executive director of food and beverage, spoke about locals' sentiment toward tourists: "Y'know, you've got people who's pro-tourist and like anti-tourist, and I'm pro-tourist of course, 'cause I'm in the industry. . . . And yah, I hear all of my cousins, and friends that's local, grumbling and y'know like they cannot handle tourists and all of this. But I think as far as looking at the big picture, without the tourists, y'know a lot of jobs would be cut, our economy would be shot."

Many locals had mixed feelings about tourists, but most regarded resort work as desirable. For children of new immigrants, resort jobs represented upward mobility, especially if their parents had worked in the plantations. Second-generation immigrants rarely performed the physically harrowing and dirty work of planting and picking, either staying with the industry as "lunas" (foremen), moving indoors into pineapple cannery work or the sugar mill, or getting out of the agricultural business altogether.[21] For them, any job in a hotel was an upward step. Children of immigrant resort workers usually fulfilled their parents' aspirations by moving into more prestigious departments than their parents' ghettoized hotel enclaves, landing jobs as housemen, bellmen, valets, at the front desk or as concierge, or in various supervisory positions. Felma Dela Cruz, the daughter of an immigrant hotel-working mother and a plantation-working father, completed her bachelor's degree and then obtained a managerial job in accounting at the Kahana Surf. She spoke about the values her parents taught her:

> FELMA: My parents imbued me with a strong sense of drive and upward mobility. I have to do better than they did, and I would like my children to do better than I have. To get this you have to have an education, that's what they taught me. That education is the most important thing.
>
> Q: More important than family?
>
> FELMA: Yes, that's what we believe. But if anything bad ever happened to the family, you'd better believe that everyone would come back home in a minute.

Felma's upward drive reflected her new immigrant parents' values. Long-term locals often lacked the focus on education more common to the children of new immigrants.[22] They sought work that would enable them to have a good life on the island. When locals' value on upward mobility conflicted with their emphasis on the importance of staying close and interconnected to kin, they came clearly down on the side of family as the most important factor.[23] They therefore envisioned their futures within the range of opportunities available locally. Some went into family-owned businesses; others aspired to establish their own, independent ventures; and many tried to get "hooked up" with politically connected county jobs. At the same time, they considered resort work one of the respectable options.

Locals who worked in resorts were scattered into different levels and departments. Edward Bacon, a thirty-five-year-old executive in the Lukane Sands' rooms division, made reference to the pervasiveness of locals, noting: "Line employees are mostly made up of local people. They were born and raised on Honua. The local lifers like working here because everyone they know works here. They get referrals for job openings from employees who work here."

While new immigrants filled the lowest categories of jobs, locals occupied the strata above them. With their language skills, locals qualified as workers for jobs that required guest contact, filling such areas as recreation (pool, beach, ocean), front office (front desk, room reservations, hotel operator), guest services (valet, bell, lei and aloha greeters, transportation), engineering (water features, wildlife, engineering), food service (restaurants, banquets, cafeteria), human resources, financial services (payroll, accounting), and clerical (secretarial, administrative). Locals worked in many of these departments with the haoles who had either temporarily or permanently moved to Honua.

Family
Local people had many different family and living arrangements, and these varied by the categories discussed above.

Family-Entrenched Locals. Individuals with large families living nearby were afloat in a sea of relatives. Chad Nakamura, the Pono Beach Spa's executive director of food and beverage, described his family:

I come from a big family, y'know here on Honua, my immediate family. I try to talk to them every other day. Like, my grandmother's eighty-six, I just called her today. I mean, I try to like call her, 'cause she's a real strong lady, and she still drives, and she still y'know does her hair, and I mean she's really hip. But my family is like real big, hundreds of them, and like my cousins are all like three hundred pounds, I mean, *big* Hawaiians.

Chad described family gatherings as mandatory events where he would spend
the entire time talking to first one relative and then another. These occurred
on an average of once monthly. He recalled the last gathering:

> We just had one last week Sunday, was my little niece's third birthday. We
> had like eighty to a hundred people at the beach in front of [another ho-
> tel]. They had like a big, Hawaiian-style gathering there. And when we have
> 'em, it's local food all the way. Good grinds! We barbecue a lot of steaks,
> lau lau, we eat a lot of pork, like kahlua pig, 'cause, y'know, a lot of my
> family's houses have emus [underground ovens]. They bring a lot of poke,
> sashimi, tako poke, squid luau, luau leaf [taro leaves], squid, and haupu
> fern salad, all kinds of different ways. Got to have macaroni salad, poi, al-
> ways gotta get rice. Real like local style of food. Which is good, but I mean
> you know like me, being over here, I don't get to eat those foods, 'cause
> I don't cook those kind of foods, so when I go there, I just indulge.[24]

Annie, a local girl from a more remote part of the island working as a
concierge at the Hula Club Towers, described her relations with her family:

> Q: And do you think that for locals, the sense of family is more nuclear,
>   or extended?
> ANNIE: Extended. It's not just our immediate; it's cousins, lots of cousins
>   and aunties and uncles. I mean, when we go to the beach, it's like, "Hey,
>   Auntie, we're going to the beach, we're gonna go be in Opeka." They're
>   like, "Okay!" The other auntie calls the cousin, calls the cousin, and
>   next thing you know everybody's there, and we've got y'know thirty,
>   forty people (laughs), and we all just hang out and barbecue, pulehou,
>   and just share within each others' company and just, sometimes we
>   don't even say anything to each other, we just kinda enjoy the scenery,
>   and just kinda be, be there. I dunno.
> Q: And family gatherings like that, would they take place, once a week?
>   Or how often?
> ANNIE: Mostly on the weekends, because within the week, you kinda stick
>   with just your immediate family, y'know, within your household, because
>   everybody works, everybody got things to do. But once there's the week-
>   end, it's like, "Ohh . . ." Y'know, we're kinda already planning by Wednes-
>   day, "yeah, we're gonna go to so and so place, this weekend. C'mon."

Many young family-entrenched locals had multigenerational living arrangements. Few moved on to college after high school, and many continued to live

with their parents for extended periods, especially while they remained single. Annie talked about her younger brothers who ended up still at home with her parents:

> ANNIE: Two of my brothers, they're still home. Yeah. One works for the county, but he doesn't do much. And my youngest brother, who is about ten years younger than me, he just works side jobs, y'know, working at the coffee bean plantation, or macadamia nut farm, or coffee bean farm, or just doing that kinda work.
>
> Q: Is that common on this island for kids to live like that?
>
> ANNIE: Live with their parents? Yeah.
>
> Q: And not work too much?
>
> ANNIE: Yeah. Because they got it made (*laughs*).

Not only did children live for extended periods with their parents, but Annie and her brothers had been raised by their grandparents for several years during a time when their parents were separated, another pattern not uncommon in cultures where people have children at a young age.

When young marrieds lived with their parents or other kin, they were usually just fit somewhere into the house. Local parents commonly built onto their housing capacity in some way, however, when their children were expecting. BJ and Delores renovated their house when their daughter married and became pregnant. They constructed a new "dream bedroom" and moved into it, giving the newlyweds their old room. Another common arrangement involved young families building additional structures onto family-owned land. These were ways locals coped with the high cost of housing in this increasingly populated and expensive resort destination.[25]

Limited-Family Locals. Not all locals lived such a family-entrenched lifestyle, however. Limited-family locals lived more separated lives, either because their family members lived on other islands or because their family members lived nearby but saw them rarely.

Locals often moved from one island to another. Some left their family's home island because jobs became scarce there and they moved to find better work. This particularly drew locals from the smaller islands to those that were more commercially viable. In so moving, they often followed other family members who had already migrated. For example, Jeffrey, a twenty-five-year-old hapa-haole (part Hawaiian, part Caucasian), moved to be near his cousin who had a job in water features at the Pono Beach Spa. He moved in with his cousin and was able to find employment as a houseman at the same hotel. For two years they lived together, until Jeffrey met a girl and moved out to live with her. Jeffrey and his cousin returned to their home island for family weddings or other special events, but they did not have other relations on Honua.

Kaniho, a twenty-four-year-old personal trainer at the Pono Beach Spa, was the son of a Hawaiian father from a small island and a Japanese mother from Honua. His father worked as a landscaper and his mother at a hotel. All his father's relatives still lived on the small island and his entire mother's family lived nearby. He went to high school locally and then moved to a different island to attend college. Returning after college with a fitness degree, his original intention had been to work in a hospital. But he decided that he would rather approach fitness from a health and wellness standpoint. His mother saw the job opening advertised at the Pono Beach Spa and suggested that he apply. For a year he worked as a fitness attendant, and he was promoted to trainer when someone left. Kaniho moved in with his brother, who worked at a golf course, while his younger sister still lived at home. He felt no pressure from his parents to move in with them. Kaniho described the size of his local family as moderate, maybe thirty to forty people, but he did not see them often. They had family reunions from time to time, but he described them as "not a part of his regular social calendar." Kaniho's family relations can best be considered more nuclear-focused than extended.

Palomi moved to Honua fourteen years before our interview when she was twenty-two years old, following her husband's job as a construction worker. With a food and beverage background as a hostess, a cashier, and then as a restaurant supervisor, she landed her first job on Honua at the Lei Gardens as a restaurant hostess. After three years, she moved up to a job at the Hula Club Towers as a concierge and remained there, although she worked part-time as a concierge for one year at the Pono Beach Spa. She explained her reasons for leaving the exclusive Pono Beach Spa and staying at the more low-key Hula Club Towers as related to the type of service work required: "The clientele was unbelievably demanding at the Pono Beach Spa. Very different. Two to three years is the maximum a lot of people I know can work there without burning out because the guests want so much service. You have to provide everything they want. People are demanding so much all the time. And the management wants you to just give it, give it. I just couldn't keep it up."[26]

Although she lived apart from her extended family, she considered the bond strong. "They come here or I go there every two months. We're very close. We just don't want to live with each other." Her mother once tried to move to Honua to be near her, but returned home after two weeks. "She couldn't take the pace." Divorced for five years, she was single-parenting a nine-year old son. Maintaining Hawaiian traditions was important to Palomi, who danced hula twice a week and sent her son to a special Hawaiian elementary school to make sure that he learned the local culture and practices.

New-Immigrant Locals. Although they inherited a mantle of extended family closeness, new-immigrant locals did not always maintain this. As they assimilated and moved comfortably into the established working class, these locals often lived in nuclear family situations. Pepito, a twenty-six-year-old fitness attendant at the Lukane Sands, grew up on another island, the child of Filipino immigrants who divorced. While there, he met his girlfriend. When she moved back to Honua to be closer to her family, Pepito moved with her. Reflecting on their housing decision, Pepito commented, "When we moved here we got our own place. Otherwise we would have had to live with her parents. They're Filipino." Pepito's mother, stepfather, and a variety of aunties, uncles, and cousins also moved to Honua, living on another part of the island. He ran into them when he shopped at the malls or at family parties, which he attended occasionally, but this was not a significant way he spent his time. Pepito spoke Ilocano before English, and so was able to converse with his girlfriend's parents in that language, which they appreciated. He discussed the importance he placed on holding onto his culture: "I think it's important to celebrate the traditional Philippine holidays, like fiesta in the summer. I've heard it's wonderful. There's lots of traditional food and dancing. I've been five times to the Philippines, the last time when I was nineteen. But I've never been for fiesta. When I go, I visit my grandparents, my aunties, my uncles."

Yet despite what he described as his closeness with his mother, Pepito admitted that he only spoke to her once a month, even though she lived on Honua. A year after we interviewed him, Pepito got fired for goofing off. He got a part-time job working retail at the mall, and another part-time job at a rental car agency.

In contrast, Eduardo, a bellman at the Lei Gardens, had never been to the Philippines, spoke no Filipino language, and practiced few of the traditional customs. He spoke of the pressure he got from his Filipino parents to live with them and to attend numerous family functions:

They [the extended family] tend to stick together and be a cliquish culture. If they were born in Hawai'i it would be different. But they'd rather be with each other, where they can speak the same language. They spend every minute in family gatherings. My wife and I have two children now, and we only see our parents on weekends every once in a while, the rest of them more rarely. My parents, they never go out. All they do is sit around every night and watch TV or be with the family. It's not something we want to do.

Some new-immigrant locals did live in familial arrangements that resembled their parents'. It was not uncommon for these children to remain with their parents well after they finished school and had worked for several years. Frank Thorpe, a food and beverage executive at the Kahana Surf, described the situation for many of these local employees:

The younger children of immigrants are usually living at their parents' house so they don't have to pay rent. Then they only have to work a full-time job. They may be saving, or they may be blowing it. A family with kids, and they tend to have children early, will have the mother and father working full-time. Then the father usually has a night job too, but the mother can't because she's watching the kids. The money from the father's night job goes to pay the babysitter so the parents can work during the day.

This partial multigenerational family living was more socially costly for adult new-immigrant locals than it had been for their parents. Socialized to the American dream and daily witnessing the affluence of the hotel guests, they aspired to the single-family dwelling and the other material accoutrements that made up that image. Kyle, a bell captain at the Lukane Sands, indicated how this often put a strain on family relations: "There is a high divorce rate among locals working multiple jobs to make ends meet. People live with their parents, work three jobs among two people. The cost of living is high. That is one of the pressures involved in being in an area with a high cost of living. The jobs in the tourist economy won't support your lifestyle."

This acculturated group reflected assimilationist values; they had lost the motivation of desperation survival, extreme future-orientation, and self-sacrifice.[27] With greater comfort and leisure, they began thinking about the frustrations of island living and their limited occupational options, many of them revolving around servitude to mainland tourists (Kent 1993). Some accepted their island life, work, and location as the best and only possibility, never considering the option of leaving. Others grew frustrated with the limited economic opportunities available on the Islands and thought about moving to the mainland. Those with greater aspiration and education became part of the

"brain drain" (Kent 1993; Stern 1989) and left;[28] those content to accept the
meager offerings available to them remained.

Leisure

Not as steeped in the hard-working ethos, all types of locals had a greater
emphasis on leisure pursuits than new immigrants. Alex, a twenty-four-year-
old recreation attendant at the Kahana Surf from a Hawaiian mixed-ethnic
white-collar family, explained locals' attitudes toward hard work:

> The Filipinos are thought to be hard working, but I think there are other
> reasons for that. People who have families they need to support are go-
> ing to work harder, as well as people who are sending back money to rel-
> atives in other places. When my siblings and I were growing up, my dad
> got maybe four hours of sleep a night because of all the overtime he was
> working. I'm not working that hard now because I'm young and not mar-
> ried, kick back. I like to go out to the clubs, party, meet women, travel
> around, have a good time. Young [local-assimilated] Filipino people are
> more like me.

Locals valued recreational experiences. As they aged and acquired greater responsibilities, they reluctantly assumed an increased focus on work for the
purpose of family support and survival. But in accord with their culture, they
cherished the carefree lifestyle of their youth. Not all locals had similar leisure
lifestyles, and these varied, once again, by the three family-related categories
noted earlier.

Family-Entrenched Locals. Family-entrenched locals tended to engage
in leisure that was cultural and spiritual. They spent time outdoors com-
muning with nature and pursuing traditional Hawaiian activities. Annie, the
concierge at the Hula Club Towers, described how she was raised in an extended family that spent many weekends hunting, fishing, and camping out.
Willy, an aerobics instructor at the Lukane Sands, spent time with his family
fishing, throwing net, boogie boarding, paddling outrigger canoes, and spear
fishing. Chad Nakamura, the executive director of food and beverage at the
Pono Beach Spa, described his attachment to the ocean, and how he could
never live anywhere far from it:

> In leisure, the ocean is very important, for me. I have to live near the
> ocean. There is something about the ocean that cleanses you, cleanses

your aura 'n' stuff, and when you're dealing with guests and management and all of their crazy personal problems, the only thing that refreshes me is the ocean. I used to do that more often, like make time out for me to jump in the ocean to *hiʻuvai,* and *hiʻuvai* means when you cleanse your aura, and I need to do that more often. And so one of the best leisures for me is like going to the beach with a big bottle of Evian, or bottled water, and just like, absorbing the scents, and the ocean breeze the salt breeze on your face, jumping in the water, swimming as deep as you can, until your ears pop, swimming as far out as you can, like, don't care about nothing even though you cannot see anything around you. Just like, you just feel the ocean and its energy. And you know, you say a prayer, and you just let everything go, all the aura around you, all the negative things that people around you like pulling from you from all directions, and when you come out it's finished. In Hawaiian we call it *pau,* y'know, it's done. You come out, you walk down, I went home, showered, got into my work clothes, came to work, and y'know, I feel great. . . . So even if I work for other companies, I would have to live somewhere that I could turn to the ocean. Like, even going to a picnic, or y'know barbecues or whatever, as long as I'm nearby the ocean, I just feel very, like tranquil.

Most family-entrenched locals had a deep appreciation for the beauty and spirituality of the Hawaiian Islands. Just living there gave them a sense of serenity and happiness. It was important to them to make time to get into nature and the Hawaiian ways. They did not want to live in paradise if the cost was that they could not enjoy it.

Limited-Family Locals. Limited-family locals pursued leisure that was active and outdoors. They bought motorbikes and rode them around the island, traveling to the remote parts of the island to camp out on weekends or holidays. BJ and Delores bought a camper so that they could spend nearly all of their "weekends" from June through November camping out at various beaches around Honua. They engaged in activities that were contemporary in nature, being less likely to go on wild boar hunts or fish the old-fashioned way, with nets and spears, than to swim or to picnic at the beach. They took their dogs to parks and exercised them with balls and sticks. They jogged, played in adult softball leagues, or golfed with friends. Palomi, the concierge at the Hula Club Towers, spoke about the lifestyle she shared with her nine-year-old son: "I go to dance class for three hours, two times a week. I work as a hula dancer for private functions. I hang out at the beach. I take my son to canoe paddling and swim classes and to football. We go out to eat two times a week. Saturday is family beach day and we do nothing."

Palomi could have moved up the ladder of resort management many times but turned down promotions because she so strongly valued her leisure and her time with her son. Working at her current job from 7 a.m.–to–3 p.m., Sundays through Thursdays, enabled her to drop off and to pick up her son at school, and to be with him on their Saturday beach day.

Seth was a twenty-seven-year-old fitness trainer at the Lukane Sands. A local haole, his haole father and Filipino mother moved from the mainland to Honua when he was five. After high school he went to college in Boston, as far as he could get away, just to try a different experience. But he eventually got homesick and returned, finding work first at a private gym and then at the Sands. He described the nature of his leisure activities and how they anchored him in living on Honua:

> For instance, on Monday, on my day off, I wake up and go shoot hoops at the courts eight to ten o'clock in the mornings. It's not snowing, it's not cold, there is no crime, we don't have to worry about people shooting at you or taking your shoes. You can get a tan. You are playing with guys that are very cool. Maybe go play some tennis outdoors. Can still go to the beach. It's very laid-back. I like the laid-back atmosphere. You've got the trade winds, the palm trees blowing; it's very relaxed. If you're stressed out, all you have to do is think about the fact that you're here at Honua and people would love to live and die here and you're given the opportunity to do just that. That's what I love. I'm not stuck in a place like LA or San Diego, where there's freeways and concrete gardens, a lack of trees, a lack of fresh air, a lack of everything that basically makes you happy. I'm not into running into the ground. I'm ambitious but I'm not crazy. I just like being relaxed.

New-Immigrant Locals. New-immigrant locals pursued leisure that was mundane. When they had time off they lounged at home, watched television, went shopping, and saw friends and family. Pepito, the fitness attendant, enjoyed taking his girlfriend to the mall. Although they were not as single-minded in their dedication to family as their parents' generation, they shared the new immigrants' lack of involvement in active leisure. Kaniho, the fitness trainer, spoke about what he did with his leisure time:

KANIHO: I don't know. Not much.
Q: Do you do outdoor stuff or go to the beach?

KANIHO: No, I don't usually go out or go to the beach. If I didn't live here
    I'd go a lot when I was here, but since I live here, I take it for granted.
Q: Do you fish?
KANIHO: No, I don't do that.
Q: What do you do?
KANIHO: I like to go to the movies. I always have done a lot of that.

Even though he didn't get out much, Kaniho vowed he would never think of
leaving Hawai'i. He proclaimed Honua the place to be because they had everything there, good stores, things to do, friendly people out there: "You can walk
down the street anytime you want, you don't have to worry about crime, you
can go out the park anytime you want, there are no permits required, and you
can watch the sunset if you want to."

    Joseph was a local Filipino, the thirty-six-year-old native-born son of new
immigrant parents. A houseman at the Hula Club Towers, he lived with his
wife and daughter in a house on the property of his in-laws. Living by her family, he saw a lot of the extended relations. But he considered it a good trade-
off for the house. He talked about his leisure time and his feelings about living
on Honua:

> The mainland's all fine and dandy but you can't even, in my whole life-
> time I couldn't see every place on this island and I don't have time to do
> anything. Today look at, the water was nice all day and I was working.
> You know I hate doing that. When I'm driving to work and I see that it's
> variable wind. You know what I mean, that's very rare to be able to have
> no wind. You know, I want to go fishing all day. I don't want to be going
> to work. I want to call in sick. But ah, family, family, my family is the best
> thing in the whole world. Ya, you know I talk about going fishing and
> stuff, but I got the best family and the best wife and little girl ever. You
> know, I'm stoked. You know, I got a killer place where to live. It's a beau-
> tiful house and it's almost free. I'm so so lucky. Ya, I'm the luckiest guy
> ever really.

Joseph rarely did anything more with his leisure than go fishing in his boat.
    Without their home culture and relations to support them, new-immi-
grant locals were the most likely to assimilate to dominant American cultural
ways.

The new immigrants and locals were trapped in paradise by choice. The former had already shown their mobility in making the jump from their coun-

tries of origin to Hawai'i. Although their disposable income was limited, once they had paid their mortgages, car payments, and other expenses, and after they had sent money to their relatives back home, they could have saved for and made another move if they so chose. But they were happy in this poly-ethnic melting pot that embraced them. Unlike in mainland America, people of color outnumbered haoles, and they were accepted. Although they tended to segregate themselves in ethnic enclaves, their children went to the public school and became locals, American citizens, and well-integrated members of the community. As global migrants, some new immigrants continued to fol-low their children or other family members (usually to other locations in the United States), but the majority lodged themselves firmly on Honua.

Locals who did not move to the mainland for college or shortly thereafter were also usually committed for the rest of their lives. Their experiences in visiting other states, and the stories they heard from locals who had moved away and returned home, convinced them that they were living in the best spot on Earth. Locals were committed to Honua because of the spirituality of the Hawaiian culture, the beauty of the Islands, the tropical weather, the com-fort of their families, and the safe, relaxed, outdoor lifestyle that enabled them to go to the beach, engage in outdoor leisure, and live in a manner and pace that continuously renewed them. They would not consider trading these as-sets for any other experiential or material attractions. Once these two groups found their niche on Honua, they became committed to it.

4

TRANSIENT LABORERS
Seekers and Management

Demographically, the transient laborers were primarily haoles. They also shared in common a more affluent background than the new immigrants and locals. Originally from a variety of locations all over North, Central, and South America (although concentrated primarily in the United States), their mobility began in making the long trip to Hawai'i. For many, it did not end there. In this chapter we examine the shared and divergent characteristics of the two groups of transient workers: seekers and managers.

Seekers

Seekers formed the third group of workers at the Ali'i resorts.[1] Like new immigrants, seekers were imports to the Hawaiian Islands; but unlike new immigrants, many did not remain there permanently. Exercising high mobility, seekers sought to maximize their immediate life satisfaction. Escapists, they desired to rid themselves of the routine, scripted monotony of the everyday world (see Cohen and Taylor 1976), even if only temporarily. They pursued alternative lifestyles and careers, shaped by their intense focus on recreation. They explored all corners of the world looking for paradise. Many of them found it in Hawai'i.

Seekers lodged their sense of identity in their leisure rather than work lives (see Mitchell 1983; Stebbins 1979). They traveled to pursue the ultimate leisure experiences—windsurfing the world's most famous beaches, diving the most exotic coral reefs, surfing the greatest breakers. Others sought spiritual connection to the mystical and metaphysical soul of the Hawaiian Islands located in its rugged and craggy terrain, its ancient and unspoiled nature.[2] Still others fled the cultural, climactic, and recreational constraints of the mainland. They came to Hawai'i for its beauty and warmth, its freedom and ease, its vestiges of the Polynesian culture.[3]

Characteristics

Seekers working in the Ali'i resorts came overwhelmingly from the North American mainland. Demographically, they were predominantly young, since many people lived as seekers only briefly, exploring the world in their youth and then returning afterward to mainstream lifestyles. They were also more male than female.[4] Women were less likely than men to embark on the transitory life of seekers because of its increased difficulty and danger, its highly physical nature, and its abandonment of security and home.[5] Finally, seekers were typically middle-class or more affluent haoles raised in financially secure environments, unplagued by fears of survival.

Seekers held several kinds of positions in the Ali'i resorts. Many of them worked in unskilled line positions where self-investment was not required. They valued the ability to follow the directions of others, to detach themselves, and to avoid thinking about their work. The most popular unskilled jobs among seekers were in the beach and pool (recreation) department where they could wear shorts, be outside, and bask in the beauty of the pools, the ocean, and the resorts' lush surroundings. Other seekers found semiskilled jobs in the restaurants working as waiters, bussers, and hostesses, in the banquet department as servers, or in guest services, being valets and bellmen. Another large group clustered in skilled areas such as the spa, where they worked as personal trainers, aerobics/fitness instructors, estheticians, or massage therapists; in the kitchens, where they got jobs as food preparers and chefs; in the water sports area, where they instructed guests in scuba diving, windsurfing, and kayaking; and in the more academically credentialed specialties such as aquaculture (care of fish), horticulture (chemical and organic fertilization), and waste management (recycling and water treatment).

For Ali'i resort management, it was considered advantageous to place as many workers whose demographic characteristics corresponded closely to the guests in the point-of-service positions as possible. Seekers, who were generally middle-class, well educated, and from mainland America, had the most in common with the customers they served. These features of their cultural capital enabled them to interact on a more equal footing with guests, to befriend them more easily (see McCormick and Kinloch 1986), and to give them the feeling that they were receiving a higher class of service (see Moss and Tilly 1996).[6]

Philosophy

Seekers thrived on the culture of hedonism. As Sosie, an exuberant massage therapist at the Pono Beach Spa in her twenties, put it, "As many days a year as you can be here or have a good time, you should do it." Much like the hippies of a previous era (Berger 1967), their focus on the present was paramount, with the future occupying less importance. Hank, a spa and fitness professional at the Lukane Sands in his forties, explained his philosophy of life:

> Life is this → fast [superquick one-hand crossover motion to a clap]. If it's
> so fast, why are you wasting your life working? Why kill yourself in a hotel? Travel around the world, enjoy yourself. I'm into making enough
> money to survive. To me, location is everything. That's why I'm here. I've
> been all around the world, and this place calls to me. It seems right.

People did not necessarily begin their working lives as seekers. Many started in mainstream careers and value systems but fell off that track after experiencing a taste of paradise. Larry Caplan, an up-and-coming middle-level manager at the Lukane Sands with a promising future, got waylaid by the lure of the Islands and made a dramatic life shift:

> When I first got here and I was the manager of the front desk and I worked
> nights, I was determined to learn to surf. I bought a board, had a couple
> of local buddies take me out and teach me. I surfed every day, rain or
> shine, hot or cold, sunny or cloudy, choppy or glassy, no matter what the
> climate or water conditions. Then I got shifted to days. Now I surf once
> a week in the winter and every day in the summer, when the big waves
> are on the south shore. I leave the house at six [a.m.], surf from 6:30 to
> 7:30, shower at the beach, carry my aloha clothes on a hanger in my jeep,
> fasten my surfboard onto the roof of my car, shave with an electric razor
> on my way to work, and start work at eight. You can't do that just anywhere. I knew when I first maneuvered that surfboard through the curl
> of a wave, and came out the other side, that I would never leave here. If
> I got fired from the hotel today I would walk down the street to another
> hotel and apply for a job. Not for nothing would I leave. It would take a
> crowbar to pry me out of here.

Goals

Different types of seekers pursued different goals. Connor, a seasonal banquet worker at the Lei Gardens in his late thirties from Alabama, was impelled to seasonal seeking by his athletic drive. He worked double shifts throughout the banquet season so that he could rock climb in Joshua Tree, California, during the off-season. Paul, a twenty-eight-year-old recreation employee at the Lei Gardens from Louisiana, noted his focus on working outdoors: "I got out of college with a business school degree and got a job as an accountant. It was what I had trained for, but I hated it. All day long I was looking out the window wishing I was out there. Finally I couldn't take it no more. I wrote to every dude ranch in Montana until someone hired me. I worked there two years. Then I moved to Honua and applied to all the hotels until I got a job here. I can never go back to working in an office. I need to live outdoors."

Gabriela, a fitness professional at the Kahana Surf in her late thirties, expressed her travel lust. Although she grew up in the Midwest, much like Simmel's (1950) adventurers, she had always wanted to move around and discover the world. She eagerly questioned new people she met about various international locations: what they were like to live in, to travel through, or to earn a living in. Her move from the mainland brought her to Hawai'i, but she expressed the desire for more travel and discovery: "I always wanted to be in a position to travel if I wanted to. It's taken me a while to figure out how to do it and get the confidence to know that I could do it. I have traveled to other places on vacation, but not lived there. I want to try living in Europe over the next couple of years. Then the Pacific area. I'm just taking it one step at a time. . . . I have no idea where I'm going to end up. Maybe an island. Maybe a cottage on the French Riviera." Three years after we interviewed her, Gabriela left Honua to pursue a singing career in Los Angeles. She was in the midst of trying to cut an album and put together a European tour.

Experience versus Materialism

A vital dimension characterizing seekers was their experiential rather than material orientation. Seekers sought and collected experiences, considering these the fundamental capital of life. This focus differs significantly from the values embedded in the dominant American culture, further marking seekers as deviants from normative career patterns. Lance, a twenty-five-year-old recreation attendant who had worked at the Hula Club Towers for one year, articulated his rejection of materialist pursuits:

> I'm not making the same kind of money as the doctors and lawyers, and I won't drive their cars, but I don't need it. I never need to own my own house. If someone gave me a pack of money I might, but I'm not going to work sixteen hours a day, two jobs, like the Filipinos do, so that I can

buy a shack. I've got the life now. My father's seventy-one and spent all his life acquiring material things, and now what does he have to show for it? I've made up my mind that in my life I will not spend my time chasing money. I'm pursuing the antimaterialist life. I'm living the life now, full-time, that all the people who slave year 'round only get to live on their two-week vacation a year.

Gabriela complemented Lance's remarks by explaining her feelings about the materialist lifestyle:

I moved over here from Ohio, and my friends back home can't understand it. They're so busy working to acquire material things, but I feel that they get trapped by those material things. I was trapped by my job in the bank, trapped by my lifestyle, trapped by my material possessions. When you have a lot of material possessions you have to worry about them: accumulating them, storing them, protecting them. They become a ball and chain around your life. When I moved here I cast that all off and escaped. Now I feel so free. I have freedom from those material cares. I want a lifestyle of experiences and not of material possessions.

As Feldman (1990) has suggested, seasonal and temporary employees experienced a "split loyalty" between commitment to the job and to other lifestyles or organizations. Freeing themselves from the imprisonment of their material and conventional lives, seekers embarked on journeys designed to rejuvenate their spiritual selves.[7] They traveled for adventure, to experience danger, to endure harsh conditions, and to overcome heroic obstacles. They were also driven by the sheer physicality of the experience, the need to use and to challenge their bodies. Many spoke about "testing," "strengthening," or "tuning" their physical selves, focusing their identities in their bodies.

Beyond physical exploration, seekers engaged in journeys of self-exploration and discovery.[8] Leaving the security of conventional life behind, they put themselves "out there" to discern their personal capabilities. Maia, a waitress at a mainland hotel restaurant, told us why she abandoned her earlier life of seeking: "I had been traveling around, living on my own, seeing the world, exploring and doing new things. I wanted to see what I was made of, what I could handle. On my last trip I found the edge. It was too much for me. I went through the Grand Canyon on my own and I sort of broke down emotionally. I didn't have the inner strength I thought I had. I found my limits, sad to say. So after that I came back and settled down. But I felt like I had tested myself, like I knew myself." Seekers thus took their journeys to the depth of their bodies and souls.[9]

Skill Accumulation

Consonant with their experientialist orientation and immediate focus, many seekers eschewed traditional career tracks and the commitment those required. Instead, they adapted to their financial needs by consciously acquiring a repertoire of occupational skills that would enable them to move anywhere and find a job. Paul, the Lei Gardens outdoorsman, noted how skill development enhanced his freedom and survival: "Learning to dive was one of the motivations for moving here. I got certified in the hotel and now I help out sometimes on dives. It helps me learn more, developing my expertise, and keeps the cost of my diving down. I want to become a dive-master. You can never learn too much, have too many skills. I can go anywhere and get a job, support myself. I can go camping, rock climbing in the mountains, and never take any food. I can always catch a trout to eat."

Gabriela cast her skill acquisition as credentialization. She felt comfortable moving around the world trying to obtain work if she brought with her a variety of certifications: "A hotel job is a good business to be in. It's stable. As a certified trainer you can go any place to train. I was lucky to get into a top resort. Being certified and having the credentials of having worked here and training people, I could take this job anywhere. I could train people in their homes. I could train people on the beach; on a cruise ship; any hotel all over the world. That's what's good about this job."

To further reduce their expenses, many seekers found creative ways to minimize their lodging expenses. Bob, a Kahana Surf massage therapist, exchanged landscaping work at a bed and breakfast for a long-term discounted room rental. Hank, the Lukane Sands fitness and leisure professional whose wife, Susie, worked as a pool waitress at the Hula Club Towers, found free rent as a landscaper for a ten-acre estate, necessitating ten hours of hard outdoor work a month for each of them. Connor, the Lei Gardens rock climber, became adept at stringing together a series of several-months long house-sitting gigs for dual home owners from the mainland who wanted someone to care for their homes, their plants, and their pets while they were gone. Bud, a fitness pro at the Pono Beach Spa, was able to land the ultimate lodging deal: after years of trying, he convinced a rich businessman building a large estate on the island to build a separate two-bedroom caretaker cottage for his massage therapist girlfriend and him, with its own pool, for them to live in year-round, in exchange for his caretaking and managing the property.

Leisure

Seekers pursued a different kind of leisure from new immigrants and locals, although some of their activities overlapped. Essentially defined by their
leisure interests and identities, many seekers were passionate about extreme
sports.[10] While new immigrants socialized with their families and locals followed historic cultural patterns of outdoor activities, seekers engaged in the
leisure activities that drew tourists to the Islands. One of the first of these was
scuba diving. Camille, a twenty-four-year-old recent college graduate from the
Pacific Northwest, moved to Honua with her best friend whose parents owned
a condominium for their future retirement. In the meantime, the girls, family
friends from childhood, were living in the apartment. Both got night jobs as
cocktail and restaurant waitresses along the Ali'i strip, but Camille's passion
was scuba diving. She got a job working at the Kahana Surf with the scuba
subcontractor. She gave instructions in the pool for novices and led groups
into the ocean for shallow dives. The subcontractor also owned a boat that he
took resort guests out on for deeper dives to more distant locations. Camille
dove every day and used her position with the company to make dives with
some of their other boats at a free or cost basis. She explained her passion:

> It wasn't intended, but I have developed a passion for diving. I try to go
> whenever I have the opportunity. I feel different, special, underwater. I'm
> exploring a world that is gripping and fascinating to me. . . . So right now
> I lead dives nearly every day. I sometimes do three group dives over an
> eighteen-hour period. I can't get enough. I prefer to take the "greenies"
> groups. No one else wants them and everyone is happy to be on the boat
> with me because I always take them. I figure I can guarantee them to have
> a good time because I have such a great time. I'm passionately enthusi-
> astic about what I do.

Kathy, an aerobics instructor, had a passion for windsurfing. She taught
a few step aerobics classes a week at the Pono Beach Spa and the Kahana Surf,
but she also gave instruction, in another part of the island, on windsurfing.
One of the few female windsurfing instructors, she was much in demand by
women students and those who admired her near-perfect form. Aerobics students similarly enjoyed her energy and creative choreography. Sinewy, lean,
and tanned, she spent nearly all her time outdoors. Kathy had a seasonal
lifestyle, spending half of the year on Honua instructing and the other half
teaching skiing at Lake Tahoe. She had skiing and windsurfing friends she
bunked with at each location, taking a minimum of possessions with her. At

forty-six, one of the older seekers in her mostly male group of friends, she dined out and partied most nights with her athletic buddies. Once married, but disillusioned by that experience, she had vowed not to be tied down again.

One of her best friends was Eric, who ran the kayak concession at the Lukane Sands. Lifeguard certified, Eric came to Hawai'i when he was twenty-four to lifeguard, surf, and windsurf. At thirty he decided to start his own sub-contracting business at the resorts, looking for more independence. His contracting business began with himself as the only employee, but within a year, he had three people working for him. Married to a local girl, with a four-year-old daughter and another child on the way, Eric had developed his business so that he could spend most of his time kiteboarding. One of the most daring windsurfers, Eric moved into the new sport of kiteboarding as soon as it appeared on the scene. Kiteboarding is more technical than windsurfing, so Eric had several rigs for all kinds of weather and wind conditions. Eric's little daughter could often be seen with her father at the kayak concession stand, charming the resort guests, who ended up entertaining her while her father arranged for rentals and lessons. Eric was an avid and expert surfer of all kinds and always wanted to try the most extreme activities.

Two of Eric's friends, Dick and Denise, lived a seasonal lifestyle similar to Kathy's. In their late fifties, they spent their winters in Aspen ski-instructing and their summers on Honua, teaching windsurfing. Among the oldest and most seasoned of the seeker crowd, Dick and Denise had organized many international windsurfing events. Although they began their seeker careers working in the resorts, they achieved a level of prominence in the windsurfing scene that allowed them to support themselves entirely through their sport. This was the ultimate dream of many seekers.

Less daring and technical were the numerous surfing seekers. Many came to Hawai'i either to learn how to surf or because they were already avid surfers, to exercise their passion. They caught waves before coming to work, no matter how early, or after getting off work. Shifts at any time of day could accommodate a surfing habit. And surfing was a relatively cheaper sport than diving or windsurfing. Other popular and less costly seeker activities were cycling, running, and swimming. Many marathoners and triathletes lived and trained in the Hawaiian Islands, competing in the Ironman, Xterra, and other popular events. The fitness areas of the Ali'i resorts offered employment to many of these serious athletes.

Coming to paradise to experience the indigenous forms of leisure, seekers also sought out some of the traditional forms of recreation practiced by locals. Palomi commented on the way seekers adapted to local forms of leisure,

"When the haole people come here they get involved in the Hawaiian lifestyle. They paddle canoe, they fish, and they surf. Haole people are catching on to Hawaiian ways. They're very different from the new immigrants."

Finally, some seekers were more sedate, being content to just enjoy the weather and beautiful surroundings. They came to Hawai'i to enjoy paradise, to swim in the ocean and to take long walks or hikes outside on a year-round basis, but they did not participate in the extreme sports. Danielle felt the pull to Hawai'i when she first went there on vacation. She had grown up in a small town in the upper Midwest and moved to Florida when she dropped out of college. There, she found a job at a clothing store. She immediately decided never to return to a cold climate. But she found Hawai'i greatly preferable to Florida on her first visit there at twenty-seven, and within six months of her visit moved out with no job. She had saved enough money to get an apartment, and she got a job at a clothing boutique at the Pono Beach Spa. There, she catered to the exclusive clientele with her exquisite fashion sense. She spent her free time at the beach, taking yoga lessons, and power walking along the island paths. Her boyfriend, Marc, another seeker, worked as a chef at the Kahana Surf, and spent most of his leisure time on his days off drinking and playing golf or tennis with his buddies.[11]

These goals, values, and lifestyles marked seekers as a unique category of workers not only in the Ali'i resorts, but within the parameters of conventional society.[12]

Managers

The last category of employees was the resort professionals, the management workers who made their careers in the hospitality industry. New immigrants hardly ever rose into management positions, and seekers did so extremely rarely. Locals were more regularly promoted into middle, and occasionally executive, management positions.[13] The bulk of the middle and upper management was composed entirely of resort professionals. These were people who had entered hospitality careers either by going to hotel and restaurant schools, by being accepted into management training or lower management jobs, or by working their way into the management ranks starting at the very bottom.[14]

Demographics

Resort professionals were young, male, and haole. As Hope, the human resources worker from the Kahana Surf, noted, they came overwhelmingly from the mainland and passed through Hawaiian hotels as part of their "career streams" (Gunz and Jalland 1996). Hotels, especially corporate chains, moved their management around frequently, evaluating them annually and moving them up the occupational ladder. Management working in independent hotels moved more slowly, as there were fewer internal opportunities for advancement. They were also mostly male. Women managers were ghettoed into areas such as human resources, payroll, and housekeeping. Finally, resort professionals tended to be young. People entered management careers in their twenties and toiled through their thirties and forties. Few remained into their fifties, even at the top management ranks. A young person's business, hotels promoted their managers on "fast tracks" (Gunz and Jalland 1996) and then burned them out early. Management thus had relatively few women, older people, or people of color.

Motivations

More than any other group, resort professionals were dedicated to their work. They toiled long hours like the new immigrants but enjoyed their work more.[15] Immersed in careers rather than jobs, they reaped the benefits of identity, occupational prestige, and engrossment in their work. Although their salaries suffered in comparison to those in many other white-collar, professional arenas, especially given the long hours, there were many aspects of resort management that people found quite compelling. First among these was the challenging nature of the work. Steve Levy, a rooms executive and deputy director of a downtown mainland, luxury hotel noted: "Every day's different. It's always a challenge. I don't sit behind a desk all the time. I'm out, I have freedom to go wherever I want to go. I meet a lot of interesting people."

Enhancing the challenging nature of the work was the typical management career stream that moved individuals among levels and departments every couple of years. The philosophy was to develop individuals professionally by moving them around, at the same time as new ideas and fresh blood were reinfused into each position. Managers faced a series of new challenges to master, with each new conquest bringing a sense of elation. Scott Peraud, a food and beverage executive at a mainland ski resort in his late thirties, noted, "There's nothing better than walking away from a function where you just served 5,000 people and everyone's ranting and raving that it's the most unbelievable thing."

Second, management professionals had a greater opportunity to integrate their work and leisure interests than other types of hotel employees. This attribute was more common for managers working in resort destinations, where the full range of leisure activities, luxuries, and extra amenities were available.[16] Vince McMurray, a thirty-five-year-old executive in the group sales division of the Pono Beach Spa, remarked, "I played golf five times last week, all with clients. That's a lot of what I do. It mixes the work with the leisure." So whether it was coming to work in an aloha shirt and slacks,[17] stopping at the beach to watch the waves and smell the salt air, or hanging around with other managers during slack periods, management found the work enjoyable.

Third, managers were motivated by their co-workers. Depending on whether their jobs were in the front- or back-of-the-house, they interacted mostly with guests or other employees. Managers mingling with guests enjoyed the opportunity to meet new, interesting, and often famous people, especially at luxury resorts. Star athletes, entertainers, and politicians came through the hotel and were attended to personally by management. Managers interacting with employees often found themselves in awe of the hard work and pride of new immigrant employees, fascinated by the assortment of people located in the various departments of the hotel ("every department has its own personality"), or drawn to the people working around them. As Bucky Gregson, an executive housekeeper at a Southern, luxury, urban hotel, noted:

> I don't know how everyone else is, but I look forward to coming to work every day. I would have a tough time working in a job if I didn't look forward to coming in every day. Some days a little less than others, but I do. I get a hoot out of it. My employees, and the respect I have for 'em. I mean, these people are one step away from laying on the streets, you know they really are. And there's very little difference between coming in here and cleaning a room and not coming in and cleaning a room, and they're prideful, and I have a lot of respect for them. . . . I'm sure as in any other profession, hotel people are cut from a different cloth. The hours that you put in are frightening at times. . . . I just think that hotel business is not a high-paying profession. It's just not. So there's got to be something that motivates you to come in and spend twelve hours a day. I think it's the friendships that you build.

They formed "occupational communities" (Salaman 1971) on the job, integrating personal and professional friendships (see also Shamir 1981).

Others found the hospitality industry motivating because of the travel and career opportunities it offered. Working in hotels gave them the chance to move around, to live in different parts of the world, to try new things. Dumar Kouchi, the Nepalese front desk night manager of a downtown hotel in

Sydney, Australia, described the progression of jobs through which he had moved in Asia and the South Seas over the past six years. When we asked him how he felt about future relocations he explained, "I'm in this business for the travel." The structured hierarchy of the career ladder, with its opportunity for advancement, gave a shape and direction through which managers could climb. Managers expressed the belief that this was an arena where opportunities were limitless, where energy and effort determined success.[18] They advised their junior managers that careers should be their motivating impetus, as Scott Peraud, the food and beverage executive, noted: "If you're in this for the money, walk out the door, don't come back, go somewhere else, because this is not the place to be. If you're in it for the future, if you're in it for the career, if you're in it for the travel, this is the place to be."

Finally, resort managers earned some level of material comfort. Although they worked long hours, they were able to move up the ladder to positions where they could support their families well. They deferred gratification during their early years, working their way into positions that were better paying. They sacrificed the leisure time and immediate fulfillments of their age contemporaries to build financial futures. Bill Stone, the executive director of food and beverage at a mountain resort, compared the experiential orientation of his high school friends with his own, more materialistic, orientation: "When I leave here, monetarily, yeah I can afford some nicer things than maybe my friends that took ten years and you know what, they went out and partied and they had great times, but what do they have, they have memories. Yeah, memories are great to have, but I also have a comfortable environment for my family." Here, we see a crisp difference between the experientalist values of the seekers and those of management professionals.

Time Demands

For management professionals, at all levels and in all locations, the hospitality industry was a greedy institution (Coser 1974). Unlike other industries that close at night or on weekends, hotels remain open seven days a week, twenty-four hours a day. Shifts for middle managers often stretched from eight- to eleven- or twelve-hour stints. The time demands of executive management were unbounded. Since little of the work could be done at home, time-on-property demands were high; it was not unusual for management to work a six-day, twelve-hour week, dependent on demand and seasonality.[19] Woody Michaels, a former recreation attendant, described the transition he experienced after he was promoted to guest services manager at the Hula Club Towers: "I can't complain because they don't like complainers, but they expect a lot of work. When I was a rec attendant I used to work my forty hours a week and 'pau' [the end, finished]. But now that I am a manager, I'm salaried and there's no counting the hours. I am scheduled for five ten-hour days, but that doesn't mean that's all I'll work. I have to get the job done, and if it's busy, I'm here more. But it's usually not too much more."

The most notoriously time-intensive department within the hotel was food and beverage. Warren Williamson, the mid-thirties director of catering and convention services at the Lukane Sands, remarked: "I think catering and convention services is the place that if you want a job you really have to work. During the season the hours are brutal. From January to June, I took off one weekend in April. Other than that I had no days off. I worked 6 a.m. to 2–3 a.m., slept on this couch in my office most nights. It's basically a twenty-four-hour-a-day operation."

The costs of such time demands were very high. While they found their jobs compelling and rewarding, managers put a huge percentage of their energy into their work, saving little for family and home.[20] Steve Levy, the rooms executive and deputy director, remarked:

> I would say it's very demanding, and there's probably a lot of things from a family standpoint that might be missed because of the demands. I mean, my father was in education, so he was home at four o'clock every day. Growing up, there were a lot of things that, like he and I would go out in the back yard and throw a baseball, and spend time together. If I have a son, I couldn't do that because I don't get home until 6 or 7[p.m.]. There's a lot of things that I miss. I'm married to my career, to the hotel.

Leisure

Because they worked the longest hours, Ali'i resort managers, especially at the upper levels, had the least amount of time left to them off the job. For some this meant working at a hectic pace, missing sleep, slaving on the property, and giving up time at home with family members. Managers compensated for this by taking leisure satisfactions on or related to the job. Some blended work and leisure, courting guests or potential corporate clients in the leisure pursuits they shared (golfing, tennis, diving). Some invested themselves in their career accomplishments, taking great satisfaction in what they created. Others used their vacations to travel to other resorts around the country, taking advantage of lodging discounts offered them at other locations by their employers. Bucky Gregson, the executive housekeeper at the Southern luxury hotel, noted that he spent his leisure in other hotels:

My wife is a travel agent and she likes to travel as much as I do, so it kind of works out good that way. I get a certain amount of comp days with [my company], and I take them all. To me that probably is the number one benefit of the hotel. I'm one that takes advantage of it. I'm an avid golfer. We have wonderful resorts to play golf at. We get to play golf free or relatively cheap as well as after you've been with the company for quite some time, you know someone on the property or know someone who knows someone there, so you're treated very well once you get there. So, there's probably no way to put a dollar sign on that benefit, but it's huge.

Compared to the other groups, management had less control over their destinies. They moved when and where their careers took them. While the attractions of Honua might have impelled them into their work, they could only enjoy them as long as it lasted. Then they were on the corporate merry-go-round to another hotel in another destination.

Seekers and managers moved to, and often through, Honua. Although some became paradise relocators and stayed, the majority moved back to where they came from or on to new pastures. Hawai'i became a place they enjoyed, but that did not hold them the same way it did the new immigrants and locals. Their time on Honua may have shaped or changed them, and they often incorporated elements of the Hawaiian language, culture, and lifestyle into their lives, but they moved on.

The differences that separate managers and seekers from new immigrants and locals extend beyond the two groups' relation to paradise to encompass the way they managed the dimensions of work and leisure in their lives. Resort hotels offer a valuable arena for the study of work and leisure because they stand at a pivotal point in the leisure-work nexus: they manufacture and service leisure for their clients. Resort workers are in constant contact with individuals at leisure, while they are "on the job." As such, they represent leisure-workers. These four groups of resort workers arrayed themselves differently with regard to two factors: materialism, a focus on future-oriented material acquisition; and experientialism—group members' interest in rich, immediate, experiential lives.

New immigrants ranked low in the experiential dimension but high in the material dimension. Their long hours and menial jobs, sacrifices to attain upward mobility, multigenerational living situations, diversion of finances to family members outside the country, and future-oriented reinvestment of all available resources gave them little immediate, experiential satisfaction. Focused on survival and adaptation, their central life interest (Dubin 1956) lay in the family. Having little to no concept of leisure, they separated work from leisure. Their rewards were more instrumental than expressive, with property acquired and security attained. They embodied a *subsistence-driven work culture.*

What seekers lacked in the material domain, they overcompensated for in the experiential arena. Supported by backgrounds of relative affluence and driven by a philosophy that grounded them in experientialism, they organized their lives around the intense pursuit of their leisure pastimes. They consciously abandoned traditional careers to attain their recreational goals but were unwilling to sacrifice their enjoyment of the present for material gains in the future. They pursued a leisure ethos that sublimated work to its service. Their lives, goals, and identities were shaped by their leisure, their clear central life interest, giving them a *leisure-driven work culture.* But since their work supported and was shaped by that leisure, it was not always totally disintegrated from it; their leisure interests sometimes spilled over (Wilensky 1960) into and other times stood in contrast (Parker 1971; Staines 1980) to their work.

Locals exalted neither the experiential nor the material dimension. Constrained by the economic, educational, and geographic opportunities on the island, they set few future-oriented goals, had limits to their work interest, and attained only moderate material satisfaction. Yet, although leisure represented their greater central life interest, they did not seek out the intense leisure experiences characterizing the seekers. Many locals surfed, fished, hunted, and went to the beach, but they were not usually involved in the seekers' extreme sports. Their recreation was characterized more by satisfaction than exhilaration. They had separateness and disintegration between their work and leisure, displaying many of the classic resultant symptoms of absenteeism and restrained responsibility. These fit the patterns most commonly associated with manual and salaried laborers (Parker 1983). The fundamental thrust of their leisure-work nexus lay in their *living-oriented local culture.* They held work-a-day jobs that supported their own leisure and the leisure of others.

Managers netted a high degree of experiential and material satisfaction. They found their work intrinsically satisfying and made it their central life interest. They displayed a *career-driven work culture,* engulfing them in an occupational trajectory that elevated the career path to paramount status. Although their transient lifestyles differed from those of most white-collar professionals, their orientation and value systems were grounded in a middle-class ideology. They displayed the classic spillover pattern associated with professionals, hotel work, and service industries, engaging in leisure activities that were intense, challenging, and engrossing. Yet leisure was integrated into their work as well, as they found excitement, autonomous expression, and creative fulfillment on the job. Integrating creative and personal fulfillment in their immediate careers with the attainment of future material comfort, their concept of leisure was something that accommodated their work schedules, that was evoked in their occupational performance, or that they professionally produced for others.

5

TRANSIENT LIFESTYLES

Transience is a concept that has not been systematically examined in the sociological literature.[1] Yet recent changes in postindustrial society have transformed the nature of transience. Advances in communication technology have enhanced the flow of information, fostering international information diffusal and trade (cf. the "digital nomads" discussed by Makimoto and Manners 1997). Technological innovations in transportation have also enabled greater mobility, freeing large populations from their former geographic bondage. Families and communities have adapted to this mobility through the use of myriad forms of non-face-to-face communication. With this, the concept of the available world has broadened, internationally and globally, so that people increasingly think beyond narrow, nationalistic confines. As a result, we have seen a boom in traveling, for both work and leisure, over ever-greater distances.

Occupational transience has especially grown, moving travelers around the world over the span of days, months, and years.[2] Transient relocation has been growing during the postindustrial era among diverse populations. One such group is resort workers who play host to the global tourist trade. Different types of hotel workers are impelled to undertake transient lifestyles through a combination of self-selection and inner drive factors as well as through the external demands of career streams in the hospitality industry. In this chapter we explore the manifestations of this new category of employed transients. We focus on workers' types of transience, their transient families, and transient friendships.

Types of Transience

Of the four types of·resort workers discussed in the two previous chapters, two of these groups, the new immigrants and the locals, were geographically stable, growing up and remaining in Hawai'i or relocating there from other (usually developing) countries and making a long-term commitment to the new location. The other two groups, the seekers and the managers, possibly fueled or aided by their more affluent backgrounds, were highly transient. They traveled and moved across the United States, often around the world. The mobility patterns and the motivations fueling the migratory patterns of these two transient groups were often rather different, but at the same time they jointly shared many features of the transient life, community, and self.

Seekers

Seekers, the first of these groups, were recreational transients, lodging their mobility and identity in their leisure. While they maintained employment and—unlike hobos, drifters, and bums—were essentially self-supporting, they did not move to accommodate their work. Rather, their leisure interests drove their transience.

Seekers' travels often took them through the major and developing resort locations of the world, where they lingered for varying lengths of time. Seekers were drawn to these areas for their beauty and for the specialties they offered to test themselves against the elements, to experience and learn about the world, and to assimilate different cultures. Milo, a thirty-year-old redhaired doorman at an elegant Auckland hotel, moved to New Zealand to experience the lifestyle, to see what it would be like to live in a different country. Although he tried out the various adventure activities when he first moved there, he eventually settled down and obtained a work permit. When we asked him if he intended to stay and if he planned on applying for citizenship, he said no. His response: "I'm a citizen of the world."

Often beginning as "time-outers," intending to take only a short break from their conventional lives, many seekers found themselves enamored with the experience.[3] Many then abandoned their initial plans to visit only one location and expanded their focus. They discovered the international "seeker circuit" through which "drifter-tourists" (Cohen 1972, 1973) and others like themselves, "drifter-workers," tended to migrate. Luke, a Texan and in his early twenties working in beach and pool at the Lei Gardens, alluded to these destinations:

I have a checklist of things I want to do or experience before I settle down. I wanted to experience the mountains, so I did Colorado. I think I'll go back there. I wanted to experience the ocean, so I moved here. I'm learn-

ing all the water sports now. I got a job here within a week. After six
months I decided I needed to accumulate more money, so I got two extra jobs. . . . I want to quit this summer and start my around-the-world
trip. Two other things on my list are to live and work in Europe and to
live and work on a ship.

Many other seekers included the experience of working on fishing ships
in Alaska, windsurfing in Costa Rica, and backpacking through Australia,
New Zealand, or Micronesia on their itinerary.

As these locations were popular with ordinary tourists as well, seekers
found themselves in destinations where the hospitality industry was the major employer. They had to support themselves during their stopovers, so they
turned to resorts for jobs. Once they had worked in resorts, they found it easier to get similar jobs at their new locations.

Seekers exhibited several different transient patterns, depending on their
length of stay in a given location. The "time-outers" remained on Honua for
the shortest time, detaching briefly from their conventional lifestyles and career tracks only to return quickly whence they came. Emily, a recreation attendant, was a typical example: "I moved here from Tennessee with my
boyfriend three months ago. I had just finished getting my master's degree in
psych and elementary education. I'm really just here as a 'cerebral break' because I'm planning on going back soon."

Short-term workers could be single-stop seekers or those on the circuit.
"Circuit-travelers" extended their windows of seeking and became more committed to this lifestyle with each new destination. Most stayed in Hawai'i for
a year or two and then moved on to other popular sites. They soaked up the
knowledge and experience that they desired, mostly in the water sports, extreme activities, and in nature. Beyond them, temporary relocators remained
on a longer-term, but still impermanent, basis. They moved to Honua with
the intention of living there for several years, or perhaps forever, but eventually chose to return home. Moves back were usually prompted by the desire
to live closer to family members, by dissatisfaction with the educational system on Honua, by island fever, or by the wish for more intellectual and/or
conventional surroundings. "Seasonal workers" exhibited a fourth transient
seeking pattern. These were people who joined the hotel's workforce during
the group season when banquets were plentiful and the demand for waiters,
bartenders, catering, and convention service workers were at their peak. Rick
Douglas, a Lukane Sands executive director of food and beverage, spoke about
the seasonal seekers:

The people who work the banquet season are really the transient people. They live a very interesting lifestyle. They can earn a lot of money in the heavy banquet season from December through April or May and then travel the other six months. A lot of people go to New Zealand or other exotic places. Many of them are into heavily rugged outdoor recreational activity. They windsurf, surf, ski, scuba, hike, and more. Once you have worked for a place and they know you it is very easy to get hired back. It can become a base for you where you return during the season.

Other seasonal workers migrated for jobs, moving to resort areas that flourished during the summer months (New England, the American Northwest Coast, southern Europe) where they could pick up other seasonal work. Larry Caplan, when he was a mid-level manager in the Lukane Sands' guest services department, described his seasonal working employees and friends:

Lot of your valet parkers, lot of your bellmen, lot of your restaurant server staff, a lot of your pool attendants and recreation areas. They are all very transient because they work six months, leave for three, come back for three, leave again. My roommate, for example, this guy is a surfer and he's worked at the Sands for three years and now he's gone for a month to Peru. He takes a leave of absence, and he wants to be a server because he wants mindless work. He works five hours a day and he gets cash and he can take it home with him and he doesn't have to manage anybody and he can take time off for the most part and leave and in the winter he will take off to go snowboarding. He will go do something fun and exciting and if he can't get the time off he will quit and he will go, and then he will come back and find another job. Every restaurant in Lanikai and every hotel will want somebody to serve. They don't want the turnover, so they will give him the leave of absence for a month or whatever. So that's the typical mentality.

Like the circuit-travelers, these people were permanent transients, never staying in any one place for too long.

Managers

The other group of transient employees was the resort professionals, management workers who made their careers in the hospitality industry. While seekers lodged their transience in their recreation, it sprang for managers from their occupation.

Resort professionals got on the transient treadmill when they entered their careers and did not get off until they retired. Individuals who entered management careers knew this was expected. George Clark, the twenty-nine-year-old executive director of housekeeping and deputy director of the Lukane Sands, noted, "The hotel business doesn't offer big salaries. What they have to offer is the carrot of advancement. That means moving. You'll give up everything for the next promotion."

Young professionals typically started at a local hotel and from there began their journey. Kahlid Achmed, a thirty-four-year-old Egyptian rooms executive at a Midwestern luxury hotel who had spent his youth working for Hyatt International in the Middle East, explained, "Movement is the norm. Two years is max. If you stay any longer than that in one job you're falling behind. If you can't move up a rung you make a lateral move to another property, one that is bigger and better."

Individuals entered young and were captured by the growth opportunities. The fast pace got into their blood and it became hard to shake. Chuck Law, the mid-forties Pono Beach Spa's deputy director who transferred into the hotel business after spending ten years in a rock band, described the progression of his hotel employment:

> I got into the business through a friend. I worked for Stouffers for six years, two in Atlanta, two in Philadelphia, two in Chicago, moving up rapidly all the way. I started at the front desk, then went to night manager, then to director of sales. After two years in Chicago, I moved to Nikko Hotels International, a Japanese-owned chain. I worked four years there, eventually moving up to senior director of rooms. I was in charge of engineering, housekeeping, front and back office, everything except food and beverage. A friend from Honua told me about the opening at this hotel and they flew me out to LA for the interview. Two weeks from the time I was offered the job I moved out. My wife had to pack up the family and household, sell the house. I came with no contract, no security. They gave me housing and offered to pay for half my kids' schooling. . . . Yesterday they told me they were transferring me to LA. I'm leaving tomorrow.

While people may have been reluctant to move so much, they knew it was necessary. Neil Rosen, a thirty-five-year-old manager of the grill restaurant by the Lei Gardens pool remarked, "I'm looking around at all the hungry twenty-eight- and twenty-nine-year-olds snapping at my heels, wanting my job, and I know I have to keep running."

Moving around served several functions for management. It gave them depth and breadth of experience in different types of departments and hotels, it helped them climb the ladder of career advancement, and it propelled their salaries upward. When they entered the career they accepted the transience that accompanied it, committing to its lifestyle. George Clark posed and answered the question: "Is transience only a voluntary concept? Mobility and flexibility are the rule throughout the hotel industry. If you're in the ranks you have to move to move up. In a big company you can move up faster if you're willing to move."

When offered the opportunity to move, managers knew they had to be ready to accept new jobs quickly. Any sign that they were hesitant to jump might mean the difference between an offer and being passed over in favor of someone else. They spoke about how they had to maintain a "lifestyle of transience." Bucky Gregson, the executive housekeeper at a Southern luxury chain hotel, discussed how he did this:

> I guess staying mobile is a big thing. I recently married but we don't purchase a lot of things that we probably would purchase if we had a home. Maybe a big screen TV, or home entertainment type of stuff that's going to take a lot to move. We've got some very nice artwork that we haven't unpacked because it's probably not worth it to unpack it. We've put off buying really nice bedroom sets and just home furnishings. We've stayed fairly mobile from that standpoint because when it comes to marketing yourself that's important: how much stuff do you have, how quick can you be there.

Art Boggs, at age forty-five the general manager of the Lukane Sands, described his situation: "I'm one of those guys, I can pick up and move in twenty minutes. I'm single, and even though they gave me a condo, I fundamentally live in a room in the hotel, so I'm here all the time. If I had a better offer than here, I could have my whole life packed up and be at the airport, ready to move, really, in two hours."

Managers moved through the ranks in several ways. At first they were transferred around their hotel learning about different departments or divisions, until they reached a higher position. From there, they moved to either a larger hotel in the same position or a smaller hotel in a higher position. People in the hospitality industry relocated through both the chains and the independent hotels. When they were offered advancement in their own company they took it, but when they were unsatisfied by their career progression, they looked outside. Ed Bacon, the Lukane Sands front office executive director, recalled: "I spent four years at an independent hotel in Boston, four years at the Hyatt, part of the time in Savannah, part of the time in Orlando, a year at the Phoenician in Scottsdale, a year and a half at the Ritz Carlton in Houston, and I've been here for a year. I'm twenty-eight years old and I'm on the fast track. All the department heads here are hotel professionals who move for the job, not the geographic location. . . . Fast trackers have to be willing to take risks."

As they gained more experience in their business, hotel professionals were increasingly called upon to open new locations. This was one of the most glamorous and desirable features of their work. When domestic resort development became more saturated during the years of our study, more senior managers were recruited to hotels in the world's developing hot spots: Thailand, Bali, Vietnam, Costa Rica, and parts of Micronesia. They looked on these, like all other postings, as temporary. International work, especially in Third World countries, was demanding. Unfamiliar with the language and with no other means of social recourse, people working in the global industry tended to stay on property "24 and 7" (all day, every day). Resort executives often sought to protect themselves from such intense work by contracting for limited terms at international postings, committing for no more than two years at a time. Others, drawn by the advancement opportunities, made open-ended moves.

The personal costs of such transience were extremely high. For single people, especially, it meant rarely meeting people outside the hotel. This fostered a social life centered on work relations with a high commitment to the organization. People were conflicted over this, however. Managers tried to balance concerns about professionalism (which precluded fraternization with line employees) with the "plantation mentality" on the island (which fostered an occupational caste system) and the perception of favoritism that arose when they socialized too exclusively within an "old boys' club." Further, the financial costs of transience were high. With every move personal goods were damaged or lost, and families had to put down deposits for registration, utilities, and first, last, and security rent deposits.

Transient Families

Seekers' and managers' family lives were also profoundly affected by their transience. Frequent relocation complicated the commitments and attachments customarily found in the conventional family life of relationships, jobs, schools, and friends. Moving meant uprooting children and spouses. Job accommodations for spouses were rare, so moving meant women had to give up their jobs to follow their husbands or vice versa. Families had to move their children between school systems, deterring children from developing core, long-term friendships. Adults had similar difficulties forming deep relationships.

Seekers

Seekers' values and ideology spilled over into their family patterns, driving them further away from conventional norms. In abandoning stability and embracing transience, they also abandoned the traditional family modes of organization, embracing more alternative ones. They carved out family lifestyles and relationships that fitted their identities.

Seekers valued fluidity and flexibility, the freedom to follow their own whims. Commitment to significant others tied them down and restricted their lifestyle. An attached life partner might not want to move when they did, might not want to travel when they did or how they did. Serious involvement with another person complicated their lives, put thought, planning, and compromise into decision making and mobility. For this reason, they often dispensed with such meaningful attachments. Al, a twenty-eight-year-old seasonal transient originally from Texas, came to Honua to work in the recreation department at the Hula Club Towers in the winters during the off-season from firefighting on the mainland. We spoke with him about loneliness and asked him if he had ever wanted to get involved in a relationship. He replied, "Well, I've been in some, but no matter how much I liked the girl, when the fire season was ready to start, I was there. It's like a sailor; they feel the call of the sea and have to go."

Seekers who did become involved in relationships were likely to keep these casual, avoiding formal commitments. Often much to the frustration of significant others, they preferred the alternative mode of living together, unmarried. Connor, the athletically driven seasonal Lei Gardens banquet worker, lived with his girlfriend but usually went off by himself or with his male friends on his climbing and biking expeditions. Although they were firmly a couple, he made it clear that he would never marry her, be obliged to her, or yield control over his freedom to her. Bud, the forty-seven-year-old fitness pro at the Pono Beach Spa, had recently celebrated twenty-five years of living with his girlfriend. When asked why they had never married, he replied, "I'm not the formalizing kind." We teased him as he walked off with "Grow up!" and

he responded by saying, "Not that, not ever! I'm still a rolling stone, still enjoying my freedom. I'm not settling." For seekers, making permanent commitments infringed upon their sense of youth, of freedom, of individuality.

Some people who came to seeking later in life abandoned existing commitments as they adopted this new value system and lifestyle. Gabriela, the
fitness professional, moved to Honua with her husband, a doctor, in a career
relocation they had carefully planned. Once they arrived, however, she decided she wanted more from life than what they had designed. She wanted to
travel, to meet new people, to pursue a singing career. Her openness to an un-
certain future did not mesh with her husband's careful preparations, and so
she left her marriage behind with her old lifestyle. As she noted, she didn't
want the "encumbrances of the traditional family life."

Among seekers who did get married, few had children. Hank, the Lukane
Sands fitness and leisure professional, married his long-time girlfriend, Susie,
when he was thirty-five and she was thirty-three. Two years later we asked
them if they saw children in their futures. Hank replied: "Oh no! We're never
planning on having kids. There was a time fifteen years ago when I might have
thought of it, but the circumstances weren't right. And now we're beyond that.
But to tell you the truth, I've never really wanted kids much."

Seekers pursued alternative, minimalist family forms, eschewing commitment and conventionality. Although many of them, like Bud, were devoted
to their parents and sent money home to them every month, they decided not
to have offspring of their own. Seekers were thus less likely to make relational
commitments, when they did they were less likely to marry, and if they did
marry, they were less likely to have children.

Managers

Like seekers, managers often departed from conventional family patterns,
but for different reasons. They found traditional family life hard to maintain
in light of their transience. Rather than embracing alternative family modes,
they struggled to maintain some vestiges of the conventional family structure
and lifestyle. What they ended up with were modifications to the traditional
family life occasioned by their transient career patterns.[4]

When they embarked on hotel careers, managers committed themselves
to the kinds of long hours that made meeting people difficult. This was com-
pounded by their frequent career moves. Newly arriving in each destination,
they did not have the social bonds to find potential singles to date. They were
stuck at work all the time. And when they did form relationships, they often
had to give these up when they moved. Janice Thomas, a thirty-eight-year-old

comptroller at a posh ski resort, reflected: "There's men that I have left in the cities that I have been in that I have really cared about a lot. A great deal. And in most of the cases I still talk to them. But in a lot of the cases my relationships have gone no further after tremendous heartbreak because you make the decision to go with the career. I could have been married three or four times already, probably. That's obviously the sacrifice you make. If you want to do something, then your career comes first."

Several people similarly noted that they were "married to their careers," or that their mobility made relationships and family difficult. Divorce rates were high among upper-level management. Art Boggs, the Lukane Sands' general manager, expressed this attitude: "I'm not married because of my work ethic. I'm married to my job. I've been in three or four serious relationships and each of them has lasted five years. One wanted me to become an accountant and settle down. Another one I asked to come to Honua, but she wouldn't come. . . . I feel like I stepped off an eighty-foot cliff one day and I've been stepping off for the last ten years." Mobility and marriage were particularly incompatible because in contemporary couples both partners were likely to want or to need to work. Marriage to a hospitality professional meant getting continuously dislodged from a career placement.

Yet amid these obstacles, managers sought to retain features of the conventional family. They had no identity barriers or moral strictures against having spouses or children; in fact, they eagerly strove for these traditional family elements. When transferred, some tried to land a position somewhere in the hotel for their wives.[5] Some rebelled against the norm of sacrificing family life for their careers and created alternative family forms.

The first, and most traditional, of these was the sacrifice of career for family.[6] Several people gave up their jobs when offered a transfer that would have wrecked their relationship, moving to another hospitality job locally or into another industry. When Kahlid Achmed, the Midwestern rooms executive, moved, his wife, Marion, gave up her job in human relations at a Midwestern chain hotel and took a job in the human relations department of a local bank near his relocation. Others found more creative solutions. Janice Thomas, the ski resort comptroller, became involved with Matt Marshall, another resort professional in her hotel, both of whom faced eventual promotions out of the area. After much discussion, Janice and Matt decided to keep their jobs but to decline any further job moves or promotions so that they could stay together. Their location in a remote mountain resort, where securing and retaining qualified management was difficult, convinced their regional office to acquiesce to this arrangement instead of possibly releasing them.

A second solution involved the mobile family, where spouses and children followed resort workers throughout their transience. Several managers indicated that this arrangement was specifically discussed or negotiated in advance with spouses. Scott Peraud, the food and beverage executive at a mountain resort, discussed this: "I understand it's not easy. We talked about this. This was something that's very important to me, and it was a big discussion prior to marriage. Do you understand what my job is, what my career is, where we're going, what's going on? We had to get it worked out."

Managers were happy to find accommodating and understanding spouses who would make their careers primary. This was easier for male managers than for their female counterparts. Once children were born, the mobile family became more complicated. Moving meant not only uprooting spouses from jobs but separating children from friends and schools. Finding acceptable schools in the new location was often difficult. Barb Law, a trailing spouse (Maines 1993) and the mother of two elementary school children, followed her husband Chuck throughout his job travels. When he got his job in Hawai'i, she had to finish out the school year in Chicago with the kids, pack up and sell the house, and re-establish a new home at the new destination. Once there, she had to find a secondary job for herself, a task that took more than a year.[7] After three years at the Pono Beach Spa, her husband accepted a promotion onto another Hawaiian island with a chain hotel for which he had previously worked. She explained their new dilemma: "This new job is great, but it's in an isolated resort area, not near any of the good public, or even private, schools, which we couldn't afford anyway, because they cost $5,000 to $8,000 a year per kid. Right now he comes home every Friday night and stays until the end of the weekend. We've been planning on moving over there, but if we can't find good schools we may stay here and he will continue to commute." They maintained this arrangement for two years, as he worked on one island and she lived on another with the kids. Eventually she started dating another man in his absence and divorced Chuck.

The third alternative career and family form, that Chuck and Barb attempted unsuccessfully, was the mobile worker/stable family.[8] Here, resort professionals moved with their jobs and became "absentee fathers" (Benokraitis 1996), leaving their families rooted in a stable base where they could return for visits.[9] Rob Kumeho, a fifty-eight-year-old (now retired) chef and food and beverage professional, left his wife to bolster the home and family while he moved around from location to location. When the kids were young, she stayed home. As they aged, she got a job as an elementary school teacher. He noted that these years were severely tough on her, as she had to "do it all" alone. He returned whenever he could. By anchoring home and children, she was able to give him a semblance of the traditional family life he wanted despite his transience. This kind of arrangement was made possible only by his limiting his occupational mobility. For most of his career he restricted his work to the Hawaiian Islands. When he accepted a job opportunity for two years in New Zealand, he relocated the entire family there with him. Mobile managers, like many middle-class, educated professionals, tended to have fewer children and to begin their families later in life (O'Connell and Bloom 1987).

Transient Friendships

The patterns of difference between the seekers and managers disappear when we consider the types of friendships characterizing these two groups. Here we see a convergence in the ways seekers and managers related to networks and communities of friends and its effects on their selves.

Forming Friendships

One of the strongest features linking seekers and managers was the ease with which they formed new friendships. People drifted into and out of their lives regularly, and they maintained an openness toward accepting them. This contrasts with individuals in more traditional lifestyles who go through periods of openness to forming friendships in their youth, then settle down during the career climb and young family years to a more limited accessibility. Traditional nontransients also form close friendships that they retain over the course of their lifespans, growing old and marking the significant passages of time with a regular group of friends. But the resort transients found themselves moving around, thrust into new situations, separated from former friends and in the company of new people. The departure of old friends gave them repeated openings in their social lives for new friends to fill the void. Jake, a twenty-four-year-old recreation department supervisor at the Kahana Surf, noted that this fostered an environment beneficial to the hotel: "I've been transient my whole life. I don't want to be stuck in one spot. I'm used to meeting new people. The local kids are used to the tourist industry, they're used to meeting new people. Between them and the transients like me there's a good balance and it creates an openness toward meeting the hotel guests and becoming friendly with them." Whether they had moved recently or not, managers and seekers knew that relocation was always potentially imminent, so they kept themselves open to considering each new person they met as a potential friend. Forming friendships with other transients was enhanced by the similarities they all shared and the differences that separated transients, with their distinct lifestyles and values, from more conventional others.

New people might be accepted not only as casual acquaintances but as close friends. In fact, transient friendships often moved to depth levels more rapidly than did those for more established people, who had the time to gradually assess new people, to work them into their lives slowly, and to add them to an already full repertoire. Thrust into the whirlwind of movement, transients assessed those around them quickly, sizing up people who might be suitable. They formed tight relationships with individuals and networks of people based on shared interests, outlooks, and experiences. They readily discussed their common situations, exchanged intimacies with, and felt empathy for one another. Connor argued that his relationships with people he seasonally encountered were meaningful: "Like this guy, Dave, who I see in Joshua Tree every year when I go there climbing. Even though he lives in LA and I live on Honua, and we see each other only once a year, I feel like our relationship is deep. When he sees me he knows me. We talk about our lives. We do things for each other." Connor eventually left his long-term girlfriend for a woman he met climbing in Joshua Tree.

Some transients described themselves as having been open like this throughout their lives. They reflected back on their younger years and rooted their nature not in any psychological affinity but in transient social circumstances. Several came from military families, where they were transferred around a lot and had to re-form friendships every time they moved.[10] Others had parents in mobile business ventures who moved frequently, or earlier careers characterized by high mobility. Chuck Law, the former Pono Beach Spa deputy director, discussed the effect his earlier transience had on his propensity toward friendships:

I grew up in a transient lifestyle. My father was a grain merchant, commodities broker. He was moved around a lot by his company. When I was twenty-three, I went into the music business and was on the road for ten years with my band. At age thirty-three I finally decided that the game had become a younger man's game, so I got a haircut and a suit and I applied for jobs. But I like this job because it's exciting and always different. Sometimes the tried and true becomes boring. A lot of time at the hotel it's like the road. Hanging with the boys. It's like a road trip. I probably meet new people easily.

Finally, some people had more stable early lives, but always saw them-selves as highly open to meeting people and making friends. They carried over this friendliness to each new lifestyle and career. Bud, the fitness pro, de-scribed his early recreational adventures: "I grew up on the South Side of Chicago. I always liked to play basketball. All day long I dribbled my basket-ball all over town. I could go into any ethnic neighborhood and play. I learned how to interact with people of all different backgrounds. . . . So now I walk with my basketball around the hotel grounds. I 'cruise and schmooze' the guests, the management, potential hotel developers."

For people who were not naturally open, moving into transience occa-sioned changes in their selves. They dropped their barriers and opened them-selves up. They learned to read others and, as Neumann (1992) noted about adventure tourists, to read themselves in the eyes of others. They saw this as a situational adaptation to their new circumstances. Managers moved into ho-tels with new communities of co-workers, and seekers encountered a contin-uous array of new individuals and groups. Members of both groups needed to acquire information from these new people, to socialize and to form bonds with them. If they weren't good at doing this before, they had to develop these skills quickly. Kim, a twenty-seven-year-old massage therapist at the Lukane Sands, talked about her learning curve: "When I was in high school I was more inward, not very charismatic. But I left home when I was eighteen to travel all around Europe and the world by myself. At first I stuck to myself and I was lonely, but I could see that that wouldn't work. So I got used to being by my-self and meeting people easily." Transient workers found these qualities highly valuable in the resort hotel environment, meeting others like themselves as well as guests, who came out of their normal closure and opened themselves up while on vacation.

Location of Friendships

Seekers and managers lodged their friendships in their transient commu-nities, the enclaves and subcultures they found of like-minded and -lifestyled people. They found these informal social networks in the core places they gath-ered. For managers this was the hotel, the place where they spent all their time. They forged friendships within their occupational strata, avoiding close per-sonal relationships with line employees because these might compromise working conditions.[11] They made individual friendships with people who shared common interests, common outlooks. Managers formed friendship groups and cliques among themselves. In many resorts the upper echelon of chefs (the chef, his sous-chefs, and the top tier of cooks) went out drinking together nightly after work. Others in these departments felt that nonclique members were promotionally disadvantaged. Denise Jacobs, a management wife, discussed the boys' club she observed at her husband's hotel:

It's very tight at the Kahana Surf. There's Wes, Brad, Rick, and five or six other guys, all from the executive committee [the highest management rung]. And these guys are close; they do a lot of stuff together. Like, they all just came back from a three-day hunting trip in [a rural part of Honua]. They camped out, told stories, hunted and killed a wild boar. Then Rick [the executive director of food and beverage] cut it open and gutted it right on the spot. They skinned it and brought it home, like it was the greatest thing you'd ever seen. They were all pumped up with testosterone, I'll tell you.

Seekers found friends within the hotel and elsewhere.[12] They bonded with other seekers at work who shared their interests and values. These friendships tended to lodge within departments, matching unskilled, semiskilled, and skilled seekers within their own groups. Jake, the recreation supervisor at the Kahana Surf, noted the instant sociability employees of his department forged: "As soon as you get here, if you come to work in the Rec department, you have thirty-five friends. We are all here to do the same thing, to hang out, enjoy Hawai'i, party. Last night we went out together to [a nightclub]. Everyone who worked here now or in the past was invited, plus anyone we like and we think that's cool. Some of the local guys like to do local stuff, like fishing and surfing. The haole guys like to windsurf and bike. But we all like to party." Seekers also found friends in seeker communities formed around their serious leisure interests such as windsurfing, mountain biking, scuba diving, and surfing. These integrated people from the various hotels with people who worked as professional leisurists.

Moving/Networking

Some seekers were on the move, passing by people, living as Bud noted, like "rolling stones." The relationships they formed were often "situational friendships." With these people they shared travel tips, working tips, living tips, resources, and each others' company. Al, the firefighter from Texas, noted how this happened:

AL: I have to go to places a lot by myself. It's hard to find people to go with me. Someone can't take the time, another can't afford the trip, a

third can't go because his wife won't let him. So I make friends and
pick up traveling companions when I get there—people who are already there doing what I have decided to do.
Q: Have you ever hooked up with people who turned out to be assholes?
AL: I'm a good judge of character, so that doesn't usually happen.

At new destinations, seekers often networked through friends and acquaintances for a place to crash or a contact for work. They maneuvered
around these individuals into seeker communities, talking with others about
places to go, things to experience when there, inexpensive ways of traveling,
serious recreational opportunities, and miscellaneous subcultural lore. Seasonal and circuit-travelers had the most global networks, cycling through
them habitually. Connor, the Lei Gardens banquet worker, described the cohesive character and consequences of these communities: "Small worlds—
each enterprise has its own small world. People's regular, repeating relationships are anchored in their small worlds, the world in which you circle. It's
your passion that drives you to seek, and then your identity becomes anchored in that small world."

Managers also networked furiously throughout their moves, relying on
their personal and professional connections to enhance their career progression. Every transfer introduced them to an array of new people. Chuck Law
discussed the way managers in independent hotels maintained their networks: "You stay in touch with people a lot by relationships and phone calls.
I call them from the job, they call me. Or you go to conferences. Professional
conferences by insurance planners, where everyone in the industry is there—
other people's conferences. These are the places where you can meet people
and expand your networks. Because we don't have any conferences of our
own."

Independent hotel managers' networks developed on an ad hoc basis,
with connections forged in a patchwork manner. Networking was easier for
chain hotel management because it was structured: they met people during
corporate training seminars, when they used the corporate perquisite of free
lodging to travel, and when other executives traveled and stayed in their hotel. As Bucky Gregson, the executive housekeeper, noted, "It doesn't take long,
a couple of years, let alone, not that I'm a huge long-term employee, but after
seven and a half years, the network grows very fast."

Friendship networks also enhanced promotion and mobility. This was especially vital to managers at independent hotels, who were not promoted as
quickly as those in the corporate world.[13] Many people at the Ali'i resorts had

been recruited by friends currently working there who mentioned them to higher-level management or ownership. Similarly, former employees of the Ali'i resorts recruited away their best managers when they arrived at new destinations, often at crucial times when replacement was difficult. As Rick Douglas, the executive director of food and beverage at the Lukane Sands, noted, "You always feed from the people that you've worked with in the past because you know what they're capable of."[14] Word of people's mobility and availability was anxiously discussed, as well as the changing state of each independent and chain hotel. As David Kimble, a sales executive at the Pono Beach Spa, noted, "You get a gut feeling about how you perceive their company— how it is, where it's going to go. It's a very small industry; good news and bad news travels fast."[15]

Expendable Friendships

Seekers and hotel managers did not even have to move frequently to continue expanding their networks of friends and professional contacts; if they stayed in one place for any length of time, they met the continuing array of more transient seekers and managers who passed through their location—arriving, working, and moving to other destinations. Their lives involved a regular upheaval as they befriended people, spent time with them, and bid them farewell. As a result, they learned to meet people easily, to make friends quickly, but not to make the kinds of bonds that were too painful to break. Friendships were made with the expectation that they might not be permanent. Individuals focused on attaching themselves to compatible others who most closely shared their most immediate situations, often going beyond the bounds of the age, race, religion, class, and gender parameters that usually demark attachments. These included hotel guests as well as employees, as Keiko, a long-time waitress at the Hula Club Tower's pool bar and restaurant, noted: "I have a lot of guest contact. I get a lot of repeat customers. There are people who run a tab with me all day, and I really get to know them. I have some people I visit every year in Arizona. I've made some real friends from the guests in the hotel."

Transient friendships thus had particular characteristics. On the one hand, they evolved to fit the fluid situations of high mobility that members of these groups experienced. Functionally, they were situational, enabling friendships to spring up in less fertile circumstances, fueled by practical and social needs. They were also flexible and adaptable, transformed from traditional conceptions of friendship rooted in a stable, long-term, nontransient world. Transient friendships were less demanding, more prone to easy sociability and the nurturance of basic human needs. But as a correlate, they sacrificed some of the depth dimension that grew out of people's long-term association and mutual dependence. Transient friendships were more temporary and expendable than many of their conventional counterparts, formed with an immediate present, but not necessarily a long-term future in mind. Transient friendships lacked the self-referential features of deeper, more traditional ones, where people lodged their identities in the relationship and gained a perspective on themselves through it. As a result, seekers and managers made and held fewer deep, lasting friendships than is the norm, with the exception of friends made during and held over from earlier life. Trevor, a twenty-one-year-old recreational attendant at the Lukane Sands from Phoenix, expressed his frustration with the friendships he had formed in Hawai'i by saying, "I don't have many friends here because every night is Friday night on Honua. Friends are just drinking buddies."

Transient hotel workers stepped off the mainstream path and left behind, to varying degrees, the world of their more normative counterparts. Seekers carved out a journey through life, looking for adventure, excitement, and a sharpened appreciation of their world. They pursued this route to deepen their intrinsic selves through a heightening of experience, skill development, and self-actualization. In so doing, they invested in their social and physical selves, enriching their cultural capital in the most portable space possible: their embodied, corporeal beings. Theirs was a conscious and intentional abandonment of the conventional values and goals of materialism, security, and family for a life of experientialism and freedom, a redirection of focus toward immediate happiness rather than the pursuit of deferred gratification. They recast their conception of community away from a stable, enduring set of close family and friends to a fluid, shifting, and partially recurrent global postmodern community of like-minded others. From their communities they received practical assistance, companionship in their quests, and a reified sense of core values and self. Seekers redefined their selves in terms of who they were, what they had done, and what they could do, instead of what they had accumulated. They cast themselves free to float less predictably through the sea of life, guided first by the quest for new and deeper experiences, then by the quest for renewed peak experiences.

Managers pursued a more modified journey. They chose their path for a combination of material and, to a lesser extent, experiential goals. In many ways their life choices exhibited a modulation of the radical alternative modes chosen by seekers. Their work followed more traditional career paths, bounded by structure and goals, but they were transient nonetheless, voluntarily relinquishing all the accoutrements of life accompanying the stability that they left behind. Rather than embracing seekers' alternative ideologies, their lifestyle was driven by more conventional motivations, leading them to suffer normative deprivation. Their family patterns, similarly, deviated from traditional norms due to their circumstances rather than voluntary choice. They developed innovative transient-adaptive modes but sought, as much as possible, to recreate in these some semblance of customary family structures. Their friendships and community networks were partially composed by their occupational structures, so that while they floated either loosely or tightly within these, they did not create them entirely out of free-floating recreational subcultures. They found a greater confluence of national and global friendship and professional community networks than did seekers. They adapted to their transience, redefining alternate forms of career, lifestyle, family, and relationships from conventional to modified models. In so doing, they set new norms, adjusted to less security and structure, and learned to live with the vicissitudes of regular uncertainty. Key to their acceptance of this lifestyle was their ability to root in their self; when things became challenging, they learned to develop resourcefulness and flexibility. They forged small, transportable family modes and they developed openness to the new.

We see, then, a changing conception of transience itself, as it is transformed from forced to voluntary, as it moves out of lower socioeconomic status positions to employed populations, and as the global, mobile workforce expands. It used to be that transients were seen as deviant, shiftless, rootless, unstable, or untrustworthy. Now they have experienced, in part, the benefits of a moral passage (Gusfield 1967), being reconceptualized as on-the-go, highly mobile, international business travelers or just everyday people. As a result, we have seen the stigma associated with nontraditional lifestyles diminish. People are becoming more aware of deviations from mainstream career tracks and accepting of these alternatives.

The rise of employed transients has also brought more affluent and voluntary transience; drifters have been supplanted by drifter-tourists who have, in turn, been supplanted by various forms of drifter-workers.

6

SEASONAL LABORERS

One of the most distinctive features of the resort industry is its seasonality, the fluctuation in the numbers of guests, types of guests, and guest expenditures that occurs annually. Seasonal occupancy and the use of resort facilities can vary according to two types of determinants. "Natural seasonality" attracts guests during favored climatic conditions (usually sun or snow), school and work vacations, and religious holidays. "Commercial or institutionalized seasonality" coincides with business conventions and conferences, performance-based incentive or reward trips, and times when destinations have organized socially constructed events to draw crowds, such as festivals, races, or other events.[1]

Seasonality has traditionally been viewed as a significant problem in the resort industry. It has been held responsible for difficulty in gaining access to capital, trouble obtaining and holding full-time staff, low returns on investment, and subsequent high risk.[2] Seasonality represents a noteworthy management issue because some destinations have widely fluctuating tourist periods in which profits must be realized in a compressed time span, capital investments lie dormant for long periods, and resources vary widely between low levels of use and operation at overcapacity (Cooper et al. 1993). When capital investments cannot be adjusted seasonally, it becomes imperative to the cost-effectiveness of resorts that they be flexible enough to shave labor expenditures during slow periods and to boost staff levels during busy ones.[3]

Resorts, as organizational entities, foster such employee fluctuation. They must augment a core staff of full-time employees willing to be adaptable in their working hours with contingent workers they can hire during peak periods and then release when occupancy declines. Contingent laborers include all those not working full-time, who do not have a secure, long-term, committed relationship with their employer (Polivka and Nardone 1989). Included among these are individuals employed part-time, as temps, from internal (in-house) on-call pools, of short-term or limited-duration as well as call-ins, subcontractors, day laborers, guest workers, international migrant workers, floaters, casuals, buffers, and independent contractors. Paid by the job or the hour, and receiving reduced benefits or none of the standard fringe benefits given full-time help,[4] contingent workers are generally not unionized and lack the labor benefits (overtime, minimum salary, representation, fair treatment) accorded better-organized workers.[5] The combination of contingent workers and seasonally adaptive full-time employees can be considered a temporally "flexible" labor force (Murphy 1996).[6]

It is clear that attaining a flexible workforce benefits organizations, enabling them to cut direct and fringe labor costs, to solve scheduling problems, to adapt to daily and yearly fluctuations in the demand for their products or services, to respond quickly to economic downturns, and to screen workers for future full-time employment.[7] What is less well understood is how and why the labor force can accommodate to these varying organizational demands.

In this chapter we seek to understand how, in dealing with the ebb and flow of both natural and commercially constructed seasonality, the Ali'i resorts significantly adjusted their workforce in nearly all departments annually. We begin by examining the resorts' three seasons and the types of employment they offered. We then outline the four major types of contractual relations the Ali'i resorts had with their employees. Finally, we describe the way these resorts dealt with their problems of seasonality by expanding and constricting their workforce over the course of the year and the effects that this had on workers.

Seasonality and Labor

Similar to all hotels, the Ali'i resorts had busier periods at certain times of the year than others. They shared this in common with a variety of different kinds of luxury accommodations. Upscale downtown hotels commanded business and convention travelers according to these groups' needs and individual guests' holiday or other travel times of the year, mountain resorts commanded winter skiers, beach resorts attracted cold weather escapists, and family resorts were busy during school vacations.[8] To maximize their profitability, however, resorts have sought to expand their selling periods beyond these "naturally occurring" seasons, attracting guests on a year-round basis.

The Hyatt Regency at Beaver Creek (Colorado), in a sales brochure, has advertised itself as "A Resort for All Seasons." This contrasts sharply with its early years, when, like most other Rocky Mountain resorts, it closed down entirely between ski seasons. But to sustain their capital investments, these operations have needed additional revenue. Mountain towns such as Telluride, Aspen, and Vail have successfully re-themed the meaning of summer to enhance their appeal as warm-weather resort destinations, sponsoring music festivals, hot air balloon races, food and wine tastings and competitions and attracting people for family vacations and reunions, weddings, and summer mountain activities (river rafting, cycling, hiking, and horseback riding).[9] The development of the summer season meant that these resorts now had three seasons: ski season, summer season, and shoulder (Butler 1994; also colloquially known as "mud") season. At the Ali'i resorts, there were also three seasons: FIT season, group season, and slow season. Some of these were more "naturally" occurring, with others more "commercially" constructed.

FIT Season

The busiest time of year occurred during what the resorts termed "FIT" (Free and Independent Traveler)[10] season. Most strongly grounded in a temporal foundation of "natural" time, the yearly vicissitudes of FIT season had a traditional base in the combined product of the agrarian- and school-based calendar, and the Judeo-Christian/pagan holiday seasons. This schedule has historically moved children and adults through a regular and repetitive flow of work and relaxation that is tied to climatic fluctuations and the secular and sacred symbols of the year. FIT season came episodically throughout the year, at Thanksgiving, Christmas, spring break/Easter/Passover, and the heart of summer. This was when families came to Honua, in correspondence with their children's school vacations. Young adults without children naturally gravitated to Honua during these periods as well, due to the confluence between school schedules, holiday times of year, and the American culture's rhythm of work and play. Summer also attracted a lot of wedding and honeymoon business. Ali'i resorts brought in an average of one-third of their total yearly earnings during these limited periods.

As tropical island resorts, the Ali'i hotels offered a warm refuge to people living in wintry locations. As a vacation destination, they attracted people during holiday periods. These features shaped FIT season. Families came with their children; cell phones were abundant; entertainers, athletes, and royal families could be seen at the hotel; roll-away beds and room refrigerators were on wait-list; every lounge (including those requiring rental) was taken; restaurant and spa reservations needed to be made three days in advance; the shops were crowded; and money flowed freely.

During these periods, the Aliʻi resorts moved into their most hectic mode. Even though the resorts were often sold out during spans of group season, more people were in evidence during FIT intervals because groups were more likely to book a single person into a room whereas families filled each room with couples and one or more children. In addition, families used the public facilities more heavily, frequenting the beach and pool, the exercise facilities and spa, the restaurants, and the shops. FITs were more likely to be regular, return guests, who knew the employees and were seasoned travelers accustomed to tipping norms.[11] During FIT seasons, the areas serving these kinds of guests were both strained with handling the overflow numbers and rewarded by the tips. Deedy, a Lukane Sands pool waitress in her late twenties who had toiled at her job for six years, went home each day sunburned and exhausted, with shins and back aching from carrying heavy trays of food and drink to poolside diners. While she might take home as little in tips as $20 to $40 a day during slow season and average around $75 a day during group season, she often earned $120 a day from FITs.[12]

During these periods employees had to work much harder, serving more meals in the restaurants, doing more massages, training more exercisers, and serving more chilled hand towels and water to outdoor guests. An average day in the beach and pool area—which might see two six-foot-tall rolling carts of cleaned, folded, and dried beach towels dispersed—usually went through six of these when it was busy. That meant employees not only had to retrieve carts constantly from the laundry but had to pick up wet towels discarded everywhere by guests, reset the lounges and to provide them with new towels all day, load the used, wet towels onto the carts, and roll them back to the laundry. Bikes in the group cycle classes were snapped up the minute reservations began, outdoor lounges were all taken by 9 a.m., customers fought over weights in the gym, and the pools were overcrowded. Employees and security guards patrolled the grounds with walkie-talkies regularly, looking for unregistered guests, summoning help for specific problems, and fielding complaints. This left employees feeling overwhelmed and exhausted. One day in August our field notes documented the following interaction:

[We] went back [to the pool] at 10:30 and there was a woman in a bathing suit and dry-off with three-inch heels demanding a lounge at the pool. Koʻono [a Lukane Sands beach and pool attendant] was trying to explain to her that the chairs were reserved and the cabanas were rented, and that people came down at 8:00 before breakfast and put their things on lounge chairs, then went to eat. She saw four lounges without anything on them but which had the little reserved tags, indicating that they had been rented. She wanted to take one of them. Ko'ono explained that if she did, when the people who paid for them came down, there would probably be a fight. . . . She proceeded to scream at him about how she wasn't getting her money's worth and she deserved a wooden lounge. Ko'ono said this was the fifth major chewing out from a guest he had taken that day. Occupancy is 100 percent.

FIT season reached its peak during the Christmas holiday, with tempers flaring and accommodations tight. However, any employee who had access to lounge or cabana rentals in the exclusive part of the resorts could make good money, as Nohi, a local girl working in beach and pool at the Pono Beach Spa, noted: "Tips are around this season. Anyone who has a connection to cabana rentals is sitting on a gold mine. You can work your butt off down by the beach and get nothing, but up at the [exclusive] pool there are tips to be made. I set up chairs and towels for a family of ten at the beach and got a $1 tip. But when I was working in cabana rentals, I raked it in! Less work for more money in the higher strata."

Guests frequently tipped in advance to ensure their access to these assets, and tipped for service at them. At 11:30 one morning over the Christmas season, a guest offered Ted, a pool attendant at the Lei Gardens, $50 if Ted could find his family four beach lounges, which took Ted a full half hour of scrounging all over the property to find. He then had to fight his way toward the beach to find a place to lay them down, as the crowd was three lounges deep in places. Sarah, a pool waitress at the Lei Gardens, added that the father of another family offered her $50 to serve them their food down by the beach, an area that was not customarily serviced. Everyone agreed that these were the real "banker days."

Long-term beach and pool attendants, who had good rapport with returning big tippers, serviced these "special customers" extensively, and could take home as much as $200 a day each above their salary during these weeks. Palo, a local beach and pool attendant at the Lukane Sands, described the "racket" he and the two other locals with high seniority who worked the towel and cabana rental desk at the resort's exclusive adult pool area had going:

I have it all down in my computer. Every one of the "special customers" and their families. I have their names and their wives and children's names and birthdays. We send them birthday cards. We take their kids surfing around the island on our days off. I know which cabana they like and what they want. We hear from the Lisa [the Sands' VIP liaison] in advance when these people are checking in. I make sure that their cabanas are [illegally] reserved. If they need food or drinks brought down to them where the pool waitresses don't serve, we take their order and bring it down personally. We are all over them like flies. And at Christmas the three of us—me, Ku, and Koʻono—we order gift baskets with special things from the Hawaiian Islands and have them delivered all over the country. No one else in the hotel puts in this kind of trouble, but it pays off for us big time. When the big FITs are here, we can make $2,000 each a week above our salaries. We split everything we get.

Koʻono sometimes grumbled about the tipping arrangement and the service that guests expected, but he took the money anyway: "We get extra money from guests, in the form of tips, to get them certain lounges at the pool, or cabanas. They may be giving us $100 a day above the regular hotel charge for a cabana. On a ten-day stay from a rich FIT, we can get more than $1,000, all in cash. To me it's more like a bribe than a tip, though. These guys, they throw the money at us in advance, and then expect us to take care of them." Palo disagreed with Koʻono, saying that the word "tip" derived from the phrase, "to insure promptness." He argued that the best way for a guest to ensure good service was to give the money in advance.[13]

Other beach and pool employees who experienced this treatment, especially the casuals who were there for the season but not there every day, just took the money. Tiare, a local high school senior in a two-day-a-week summer training program at the Kahana Surf,[14] explained her behavior: "Some guy came over and asked me to make sure they didn't give away his cabana tomorrow, even though he wouldn't be down until 11. He gave me a $20 tip. I pocketed the money, wrote down a reservation form not to give the cabana away, and I was finished."

FIT departments spent their entire year preparing for the two Christmas weeks. Their managers looked at the reports that were previously made during these periods to plan ahead, seeing what people complained about and what the resort could do to serve them better. They agonized over how to allocate their limited spending budgets between the deluxe and the ordinary beach lounges, maintaining old equipment versus buying new things, and estimating the number of full-time employees needed.

The demographics of the guest population also changed. During the sum-

mer most of the FITs hailed from California and western Canada. Fares to
Hawai'i were less costly. The culture of Californians was more relaxed. But
during Christmas people traveled to Hawai'i from the East Coast. Their transportation was more time-consuming and expensive. Employees regarded
these guests as "pushy New Yorkers, and from other Eastern places that are
not so laid-back. They want what they want and they want it now." These
guests assaulted employees by demanding, "Do you know who you're talking
to?" "Let me speak to your manager right away." Another reason the Christmas season was more hectic was that it comprised two weeks in the midst of
winter. The weather was cold back home, and guests were frantic to escape to
warmth. Unlike in the summer, they had only these two weeks of vacation in
the middle of a hard-working period and they were stressed out. At Christmas, everyone had the same two weeks off, and they were all looking for it to
be the apex of their year. These factors combined to create a lot of pressure.
Ku, the beach and pool attendant at the Lukane Sands, described the intensity of the Christmas season:

> At Christmas two people have to come in at 3–4 a.m. just to set the decks.
> Reset the lounges at the pool, set up the cabanas, lay out the reserved tow-
> els, open the [recreation] desk. By Christmas every lounge is gone by 6
> a.m. and latecomers don't get them. People fly all the way out here from
> the East Coast with their families, spend $500 a night on their hotel room,
> and then sleep outside on the lounges, and make their kids sleep outside
> on the lounges, just to reserve them for the next day. And then they go
> up to breakfast and leave their stuff on their lounges, and someone else
> comes along and steals them. So when they come back, a fight breaks out.
> People go to fisticuffs over lounges, but only at Christmas.

Employees were constantly called to mediate guests' conflicting demands.
One time Kiloa, a beach and pool attendant at the Kahana Surf, was asked to
carry lounges for a family to their favorite spot under a clump of trees by the
beach. When they all got there, however, another family had already claimed
the shade. "You're on our spot," the standing father said to the seated guests.
"No we're not, this is our spot," they responded. "No, this is our spot," the
first guest reasserted, angrily, "we've been putting our chairs on this spot for
years." Then they both turned to Kiloa and expected him to fix the situation,
neither of them satisfied with its outcome. Kiloa explained, "People are crazy
here at Christmas. If you can take somebody swearing and yelling in your face,
you're good. One time a father told me, 'you're the devil—you took away my

family's Christmas.'" Incidents like this made time crawl through the busiest periods for employees.

Group Season

Like many resorts, the Ali'i hotels sought to break through the boundaries of traditional vacation concepts, artificially extending the spaces of time designated for relaxation and play, to enhance their profitability. They needed an additional strong season to put "heads on the beds," to sell their goods and services. Group season, the second busiest period, was one the resorts had to struggle harder to create. Hawaiian resorts actively worked to forge a profitable base of convention, business, and incentive travelers, coming in clusters. From January to early May, mainland companies rewarded their outstanding employees by bringing them on all-expenses-paid vacations, and elite professions held their annual conferences in this tropical location so that members could mix work and play while enjoying a tax deduction.

Some of the Ali'i resorts were more successful than others in attracting group business, as the newer properties had been built with greater convention space, and were able to house, feed, and provide work and entertainment space for larger numbers of people. Yet even the smaller, older Ali'i hotels did business with established firms and organizations. Large pharmaceutical companies, automobile corporations, insurance conglomerates, and telecommunications firms thus shared space with smaller professional athletes' players unions, tire salesmen, and groups of medical specialists. The sales forces selling room nights usually had a division dedicated to "group sales" and offered special deals on rates and functions to attract their business. Because of their desirability, groups were allowed to book longer in advance than the one-year-out restrictions offered to individuals; and their representatives were wined and dined, taken to golfing and scuba diving, and offered free advance trips to tour the properties.

Groups brought in large numbers of people who knew one another, placed them in meeting rooms for several hours daily, and often fed them breakfast and dinner in large indoor or outdoor functions, complete with (sometimes lavish) entertainment. This put a great demand on the Ali'i resorts' institutionalized food and beverage departments (banquet, kitchen, stewarding, houseman, and catering services), which expanded and constricted their pool of workers in response. To service the demands of group season functions, employees had to be hired on a temporary basis to set up and break down the seating, serving, and entertaining facilities and to prepare, serve, and clean up the food and liquor consumed. Locals working other jobs took part-time work at the Ali'i resorts, those who lived from group season to group season without employment in between were recalled to full-time work, and seasonal migrant workers returned to the island for the banquet months.

The Ali'i resorts were often sold out during spans of group season, as organizations competed against each other for access to the most desirable properties during the peak winter weeks. Yet these periods were less hectic for the resorts because even though the rate of room reservations was highest, fewer people occupied the hotels than during FIT intervals. Employees, then, were less pressed.

The impact on employees of this seasonal fluctuation was mixed. While the catering, convention, and banquet areas enjoyed a boom, other resort employees earned less money during group season. People working FIT departments suffered during group season. Their services were not in as great demand from this clientele. Many in retail areas were negatively affected, as group guests were not as rich as FITs. Bernie, a salesman at one of the Kahana Surf arcade shops, noted: "Groups are bad business for the shop people. FITs are the big customers; groups don't buy much. Tip people who don't get porterage [precontracted group tips] also suffer, like the valets and the waitresses. They can't fill a big hotel like this with FITs except on Christmas week, Easter week, and the two summer months. The rest is heavily infused with groups. The shops make the bulk of their yearly sales during that [FIT] time."

Many in tip careers were negatively affected as well, since groups tipped differently from FITs. Freddy, a former Pono Beach Spa valet moved to bell, reflected on the variance between tips in those two departments during group season:

From January to May I made more money [in bell] than the whole year I worked in the valet department. The porterage I get from the group bags is more than the five dollars an hour salary I make. I have a tip job salary. Tip jobs are more affected by the ebb and flow of the seasons. If it's FITs or groups. Valets like the FITs because the groups don't include tips for the valets in their arrangements, and the group members don't tip individually because they think everything is being covered by the group. Groups do give porterage to bellmen, though. So the valets only do all right during FIT season. It's three times the amount of work and only an average amount of money in group season [for valets]. That's fairly consistent. But for us in bell, those five [group] months are the butter on the bread.

Other employees who earned an hourly wage that was not supposed to be dependent on tips worked with both groups and FITs. They noted the difference between the FIT and group guests, however, and the way the rhythm of the resort changed over the seasons. Ku, the beach and pool attendant at the Lukane Sands, reflected:

> In group season, over five hours you could see maybe two or three people at the pool. Then they let out of a meeting or something and you have 1,000 people at the pool for about an hour, and then they leave and the place is trashed. They go back to some other group function, or a dinner. They don't worry about renting anything. Anything that's not paid for by the group, they don't do. It's expensive. They just sit there. It's a different kind of people. Basically, they've never been to this kind of place. They expect everything is free because their room and plane are paid for. The royal families [who come in August] don't care about money. They're on one end. They buy anything and everything. But when the groups come, they ask how much is everything first.

Thus, even employees who were neither in banquet nor in explicit tip jobs could be seasonally affected. Group guests were not used to traveling to exclusive resorts and were not as educated in the nuances of deluxe accommodation. They therefore "stiffed" employees whose service might customarily generate tips, such as beach and pool attendants, water features instructors, massage therapists, and housekeepers. Group guests also eschewed parts of the resorts that cost money unless their companies precontracted for them. This could mean spotty use of the water equipment rentals, room service, restaurants, shops, and exercise classes.

Slow Season

The residual months formed slow season, falling in late May and June, September through mid-November, and the first two weeks of December. During these months occupancy was extremely low. Although the occasional small group, wedding, or couple passed through the Ali'i resorts during this time,[15] slow season was fairly quiet. Devoid of most FITs and groups, guests at the hotel had the facilities to themselves, and it was a pleasant time to be there. Fewer guests in the resort meant less income, though, and cuts had to be made in labor to keep the organization operating profitably. This meant that the number of employees fluctuated dramatically over the course of a year, swelling in some departments during group season, in other departments during FIT season, and shrinking in all during slow season. With no groups, the banquet, stewarding, catering, houseman, convention services, culinary departments, and spa were affected. With no FITs, beach and pool, laundry, camp, and restaurants maintained smaller staffs. With neither, bell, valet, housekeeping, and front desk departments shrank. The mechanisms by which the Ali'i resorts reduced their workforce during these months are discussed later in this chapter.

Employees with higher seniority were advantaged by being called in to work when others languished at home with no pay. We chatted with Ryan, a banquet bartender at the Lei Gardens, who was setting up for a small function one day in July. He explained to us: "Even though I'm full-time, I don't always get forty hours of work a week, especially when it's not busy. This little party, I'm the only bartender, but it's not uncommon at a large party to have four or five bartenders. Usually, even in slow season they have some parties or other that they put on, and I get work because I'm one of the full-time force and I have high seniority. When I don't work I don't get paid. I do get full-time benefits, though." This brought the inequality of the employees' stratification hierarchy to the fore.

In departments where people generally came in every day—such as bell, valet, beach and pool, hotel operator, room reservations, fitness, and the restaurants—many sat or stood around doing little. They chatted and had fun for a while but often ran out of things to do other than to complain. Their reactions to lack of work differed, with some departments witnessing competition and others cooperation. For instance, in valet, when automobile traffic was meager, people discussed among themselves who wanted to be sent home early. Since the tips were poor when there was little work, people usually volunteered to leave. They amicably negotiated who could get to leave and who would agree to stay. In the spa, however, massage therapists fought over the few customers who remained. Don, a long-term massage therapist at the Lukane Sands, noted: "The politics of the massage department are a pain. There are lots of big egos, and when the hotel gets less busy they quarrel. People catfight over customers. If the full-timers are filled up with appointments they will call in part-timers. But if cancellations occur, they [the full-timers] will grab the appointments from the others. It's cutthroat."

Some people whose work evaporated during slow season left Honua. They traveled, vacationed, or visited friends and family. Others pursued supplemental work, augmenting their diminished hours with casual employment at other resorts or in other lines of business. People laid-off applied for and collected unemployment insurance.

Organizational Adaptation Strategies

In adapting to their seasonal fluctuation in employee need, the Ali'i resorts tried to strike a balance between the cost savings that they would generate by holding only a minimum of full-time employees, supplemented with expendable casuals, and the smooth functioning of the hotels, which was enhanced by a larger, more permanent, dedicated, and knowledgeable full-time staff. This required a careful balance of workers in all categories of employment.

Contractual Relations

Within each department, the Ali'i resorts employed a variety of different categories of workers, ranging from management to independents. Every area had its own particular composition of types, depending on the services offered, skills required, financial structure, and time demands. Management was a salaried class with a fixed income,[16] responsible for the resorts' daily operation. These individuals worked the longest hours, varying between seasons from five to seven twelve- to fourteen-hour workdays a week. Committed to careers in hotel management, they followed the profession's career ladder.

The largest group of employees worked on a full-time basis, (sometimes) putting in a forty-hour workweek and earning vacations and benefits. Full-time employees formed the backbone of the hotel, offering a base of stability. They were chiefly located in housekeeping, laundry, wardrobe, kitchens, stewarding, landscaping, water features, beach and pool, spa, fitness, front desk, room reservations, hotel operator, bell, valet, and clerical work. When their hours slipped, they lost their seniority. Another group of hotel employees worked part-time, fewer than thirty hours weekly. Richard Keen, the thirty-five-year-old executive director of food and beverage at the Hula Club Towers, noted that more than half the employees at his resort were working more than one job. The income they earned from one job, either full- or part-time, was not enough to sustain them, and they supplemented this with additional work. Part-time employees were paid according to the number of hours they worked and earned benefits only when they worked more than twenty hours a week. When their hours slipped, they lost their benefits. This was the smallest group of employees, consisting primarily of permanent part-time workers who voluntarily sought jobs to supplement other full- or part-time work.[17]

Casual employees were not defined by the number of hours they worked, but by their level of commitment from the organization. They were promised no minimum or regular number of hours, and they received no benefits. Casual workers were a boon to resort management, as they were the easiest category of employees to manipulate seasonally. They could be laid on and off with few negative repercussions. Enormous variations existed within the casual staff. Some were transitional employees, taking whatever hours they could get in the hope of moving into full-time employment. Some worked during the group season only, coming in to serve, to set up, and to break down banquet functions. Seasonal-only employees usually committed themselves to the resorts, working full-time hours (and more, taking jobs in multiple resorts) during the high season so they could earn nearly all their money for the year during this period. During the off-season these people either migrated to other states or countries or stayed on the Island. Seasonal-only employees could also augment their regular (part- or full-time) jobs every year by taking on extra work at the resorts, using this income to make up the difference between the cost of living and what they were earning elsewhere. Casual workers were also integrated into nonbanquet departments throughout the year, during FIT and group seasons, to help when things got busy.

Finally, some people were hired contractually, such as aerobics instructors, racquetball, basketball, and tennis pros, and personal trainers, who were paid to teach specific classes, to give lessons, and to offer training. These people were classified as independent operators who sold their time to the hotel and received no benefits or social security payments. These entrepreneurs worked out their own arrangements with each resort's management and ownership, often supplementing this work with other part-time jobs.

Workforce Expansion
During the resorts' busy seasons management scrambled to fill each department with enough people.[18] Although it was a challenge that had to be met anew each year, the Ali'i hotels nearly always succeeded in recruiting adequate personnel for their crowded periods.[19] They met their labor needs in a variety of ways.

Workforce Shifts. When the workload escalated in some parts of the hotels, management shifted personnel from one department to another.[20] On high turnover days, valets might be transferred into the bell department. When the hotel was filled with FITs driving rental cars, employees would shift from room reservations or hotel operator to valet. During weeks where a big group was in-house and eating breakfasts, lunches, and dinners, people might be moved out of landscaping or room service into convention services, and anyone with serving experience might be called to help in the banquet department. In particular, casuals were likely to request these transfers. Such temporary shifts, called "tt's" (temporary transfers), might be for the day, the week, or longer.

Expansion of Hours. Another easy solution to the problem of expansion involved increasing existing employees' hours. Part-timers were asked to stay overtime or to come in for additional days, often moving to full-time hours. This was especially common in housekeeping, which employed many part-timers for evening turndown service. Full-timers were asked to work additional days, beyond their forty hours, and to help out with turndowns as well. Krakover (1998) noted this as a way full-time employees looked forward to earning overtime pay during peak seasons. Nilda, a Kahana Surf Filipina housekeeper in her forties, told us: "Full-time housekeepers are supposed to work five days a week. Sometimes we work six, when the hotel fills up. When it's really busy they ask us to work straight through, seven days a week with no days off."

By far the greatest increase, however, went to casuals' hours, as they moved from two or three days a week to a regular full-time schedule. One day in March when group season was in full swing and FITs were also filtering in for spring break, Ray, a Pono Beach scuba subcontractor in his late twenties, commented on the work pace: "I haven't had a single day off in three weeks and don't have one planned until April, but I don't mind. [My boss] is around less and we're making more money, so it's okay. With the money I'm making now I'm going to buy a motorbike [a key lifestyle accouterment]."

Local Seasonal Workforce. The Ali'i resorts benefited from having a considerable pool of island residents to work as casuals in stewarding, houseman, and banquet. One group of seasonal workers, people who held full- or part-time jobs elsewhere, relied on the extra money they earned from these seasonal second (or third) jobs. They held flexible core work in fields such as massage therapy, consulting, or athletic training, which enabled them to pick up shifts, especially in the evening, for group functions. Many could not survive over the year financially on their regular income, and the labor demands of the banquet season offered them a way to pursue their regular low-paying careers, yet earn enough money over a twelve-month period to cover their expenses. Kim, a woman in her fifties, was a full-time elementary school teacher with tenure. She described her banquet work at the Kahana Surf:

I've been here twenty years. I got my Masters at UH [University of Hawai'i]. I've got no children, no husband. Just to support myself I work twelve hours a day, seven days a week. I hold three part-time jobs beyond my teaching job. I work through the Nanny Connection as a babysitter, I tutor kids after school, and I work as a waiter in banquets here. I work seasonally, regularly, and with good seniority. I come back every year, so I get my pick of the days and shifts I want. My teaching salary pays my mortgage and utilities. For the rest, I need my part-time jobs . . . I make 50 percent of my full-time teaching salary at my other part-time work.

Teachers were, in fact, a large pool from which the seasonal labor force drew, especially since the local public high schools paid them only $26,000 in starting salary. Others might be school administrators who also kept school hours and vacations; self-employed people such as tutors, artists, and music instructors; trainers; and independent contractors. Katie noted that seasonal banquet employment, since it was receptive to women, represented one of the only ways that they, especially single mothers like her, could earn this type of money on a part-time basis. For her it represented a sizable financial opportunity.

Cory, a local student who attended Honua Community College and worked part-time during group season as a casual in the Hula Club Tower's houseman department, described his work pattern: "Usually I can only work nights. I get the 6 p.m. to 2 a.m. shift. I break down from the functions. I get home late and don't get a lot of sleep. But the minimum for casual is two shifts a week, so I do that. But right now it's spring break, so I'm giving them a lot of days I can work."

Even people working in the Ali'i resorts in the nonseasonal departments availed themselves of this opportunity to earn extra money on the side. Many people in the spa, fitness, valet, room reservations, and other departments applied for and held seasonal work setting up for and serving the group banquets. They could take these jobs either at their own hotel or at one of the others on the island. A second group of casuals made themselves available for forty-hour or longer workweeks when the seasonal demand presented itself. The resorts relied heavily on this population, since nearly 80 percent of banquet, 60 percent of houseman, and a much smaller number of stewarding employees were made up, during the busy season, of casuals. Mostly seekers, these people either could not find other sources of regular employment or voluntarily chose not to take them. Tori, a seasonal banquet worker at the Lukane Sands, noted the composition of the banquet and houseman employees: "We call a large chunk of them the 'surfers.' These are people who surfing is their primary interest and whose work comes secondary. Banquet work is good for them because they can surf during the day and serve banquets at night. They will call in sick in a heartbeat if the surf is good today."

Not all casuals who worked major hours were leisure-oriented; another group was steadier, being available for work any hour, day, or evening. They worked as much as they could during the six months of banquet season, taking double shifts and "tt'ing" into other departments for extra work, often logging seventy to eighty hours a week. They could earn $40,000 to $50,000 serving banquets during the season, which they supplemented with unemployment during off-season. By cramming as much work as possible into their busiest quarter of employment, upon which their unemployment was calculated, they could then earn nearly half of their banquet salary during the off-season.

While many from this group maintained a seasonal working pattern, others were hired on during group season and hoped to translate this into more permanent employment. Jeffrey, the hapa-haole who moved to Honua from a neighboring island on the spur of the moment, described his working situation at the Pono Beach Spa during the early period of his employment: "Right now I'm a casual in houseman. They hired me for the season for two to three days a week, but I put down that I'm free all the time, so I'm getting forty hours. More of the local types go into this department, young strong guys. There are no skills required. They see I'm a hard worker, so I'm hoping that when the season is over I'll be able to 'tt' into a full-time job. This is the best job I've ever had."

Seasonal Migrant Laborers. A final group of workers, also casuals, left the island during the off-season. Like migrant farm workers who come for the harvest season, they left when the work evaporated.[21] These people could be divided into three subtypes according to where they maintained their primary residence. The first type vacationed off-island during the slow months. Their homes were local, but they regularly left when groups were not filling the hotel. Marcos, a twenty-five-year-old Lukane Sands banquet worker from Brazil, talked about his yearly migration patterns: "I like being a casual. When you work for the hotel they own you. They treat you shitty. When you're a casual you're your own boss. When I work is my prerogative. I can take off and leave whenever I want. I travel. I usually go back to Brazil in the off-season, because that's where I'm from, but this year I'm going to Europe. I backpack, stay in youth hostels. I try to save $5,000, $6,000 each year for my off-season and then live on that."

Many seekers visited friends and family during the off-season. Others left to pursue their leisure avocations, such as global travelers seeking waves for surfing and windsurfing. Some went to places such as Fiji, New Zealand, and Australia, where they benefited from the favorable exchange rate, or to Third World countries, such as Thailand and Costa Rica, where costs were low.

A second type left during the off-season to live somewhere else. They traveled to specific destinations, often maintaining a second residence near friends and family. For example, several young locals working as full-time Lei Gardens houseman casuals went to California colleges when their hours got cut in May. They timed their travel so that they could attend summer session and fall semester on the mainland, working in the resorts during spring semester. Others moved where they could earn additional money during the slow season. They went to summer resorts areas such as New England, the Pacific Northwest, and abroad. People from middle-class backgrounds were more likely to know such places to go and to have contacts there.

Finally, others migrated continuously. They stopped in one location to experience it, staying long enough to participate in the local sports, to soak up the lifestyle and culture of the area, and to expand their adventure repertoire. They might even stay a season, perhaps two, but then they roamed to other pastures (see Cohen 1972, 1973). One such nomad was Trevor, a late twenty-year-old Southerner who had spent time in Alaska and Costa Rica before coming to Honua. He described his travels: "I got a job at the Lei Gardens through a connection I made with a Canadian on an Alaskan fishing boat where we both used to work. Bell and banquet bartending are the best jobs you can get here. You can make $50,000–60,000 in nine months doing banquet bar. A lot of people who work the banquet season are really the transient people like me. We live a very interesting 'lifestyle.' You can earn a lot of money in six months and then travel the other six months."

Continuous travelers often found places to live and work through others on the "seeker circuit." Ranging from the relatively cyclical seasonal traveler to more continuous nomads, these types represented transient global workers who took advantage of the liberties in contingency work. Notably, they were mostly white, middle-class, and male. We asked Kamala, a forty-five-year-old long-term haole banquet worker at the Lukane Sands, how these migrating workers felt about the seasonal fluctuations in their employment, whether this kind of hotel employment represented exploitation or an opportunity:

Oh definitely, an opportunity. People who are into the serious leisure lifestyle, they look for this kind of hotel work from all the kinds of work you can do, 'cause then they can pursue their lifestyle. They can surf during the banquet season because they are living on a tropical island paradise, and they can make enough money during half the year so that they don't have to feel tied down to a job or a place and can take off and have their freedom during the other months. These kinds of people feel trapped if they can't travel, if they can't surf, or windsurf, or dive, or whatever it is that grabs them. They're gonna feel trapped by a job that makes them work too many months of the year.

Workforce Constriction

After the conventioneers had finished their pilgrimages and FITs were still hard at work, the demand for seasonal laborers in the banquet areas dried up and the traffic to stores, restaurants, and the recreation areas had yet to bloom. Late spring and early summer brought the first slow time of the year, to be followed with periodic lulls recurring throughout the fall. The Aliʻi resorts desperately needed to cast off workers during these times. Hotels that employed fewer full-time employees who had to be retained, and a greater number of part-timers and casuals whose hours could be adjusted downward, constricted their workforce more easily. The Aliʻi resorts, like others, used a variety of strategies to shrink their workforce during low occupancy times.

Vacations. The first, and easiest, strategy was to encourage, and then force, employees to take their vacations during slow periods. Few workers in seasonal resorts had much autonomy over the timing of their holidays. Employees took these when the guests were not pursuing theirs, in June, September, and October. Management scheduled their time off during the slow months, and employees had to do the same. Few workers were allowed to take vacations during the busy months, no matter what the reason. One time the general manager of the Lei Gardens went to a retreat during Thanksgiving, only to find himself fired upon his return. Yet, even during the slow months, many employees had little control over their own time. Tamora, a veteran of the Hula Club Towers' security department's graveyard shift, complained: "Last year they wouldn't let me take off the time I wanted, and my family and I had planned a vacation with our kids and everything. But even though I put in for it in advance, and it was in slow season, when the time came around this year they wouldn't give me the week off I asked for. They told me it's not convenient for us for you to take off now. You have to take your vacation then. You can only take your vacation when we want you to."

A frequent conversation among resort employees, then, involved their frustration over having put in for vacation time, even during the slow season, and waiting for it to be approved. This involved their managers coordinating the vacations of all employees in a given department, often a low priority. Employees had to put off purchasing airline tickets until their vacations were approved, and they frequently lost the best prices.

Worker Attrition. With a transient workforce, the Ali'i resorts shrank their payroll during the slow months by failing to replace workers who had quit. One byproduct of the hospitality industry attracting young people was burnout, as many workers eventually aged and could no longer take the hours, the hard work, and the mobility. When Tiffany, the Surf's long-term poolside waitress quit due to burnout, the resort cut down to a staff of two waitresses on the deck throughout the entire spring and summer, only returning (temporarily) to three for the heavy FIT August weeks and when the winter holidays began. When the executive chef at the Hula Club Towers and his wife, the assistant director of catering, transferred to another hotel right after the banquet season, the Towers went through the whole off-season without them. By not filling these positions, the Ali'i resorts used these turnovers not only to ease their payrolls during slow seasons but to tighten their rolls permanently where possible so that they could operate on a leaner budget.

Release of Expanded Workforce. When they had to take more active steps, the Ali'i resorts made the necessary cutbacks. Depending on the department and season, casual and part-time employees' hours were cut or completely eliminated.[22] As Krakover (1998) noted, employees were released from the periphery inward. Banquet employees expected to be laid off and figured this into their earnings cycle. Casuals and part-timers from other areas were often full-time island residents, however, who were hoping for longer-term employment. When their paychecks could not be justified by hotel occupancy, their employment suffered. Enrique, a nearly fifty-year-old local man of Filipino descent, was a full-time houseman with high seniority at the Lei Gardens. Having watched the ebb and flow of workers for many years, he described what his winter colleagues were doing in the summer months: "The casuals be happy during group season but now, summer, it different. We had seventy-five people working full-time hour, but now only ten. When the hotel is busy they get full-time work, but when it slack off, nothing. There's a lot of people out there crying right now."

Local residents with spouses, children, and mortgages had regular expenses that had to be met. Many did not earn enough during the busy season to tide them over for the year. Miguela, a forty-five-year-old Filipina house-keeper at the Hula Club Towers, talked about how people in her department managed financially when the resort released them: "They try to stretch their money. They try to cut back on things they're doing. Make do on less. These people all have large extended family networks. Nobody's going anywhere. That's why they put so much support into sending money back home and ringing their family members over here for reunification. If things got tough, I bet they could count on support from extended kin." Not only did em-ployees lose their hours, but cutbacks also forced some to lose their benefits. During the course of our research, one resort undertook a major employee restructuring through union busting, where many workers were dropped from full-time status and rehired as casuals.

Under the terms of nearly every union contract, when a resort was sold to new owners, a "successors and assigns" clause required the purchaser to be bound by the terms of the existing union contract. Many Ali'i resorts were sold and the employees maintained not only their union representation, but their years invested in their retirement plans, their days and weeks of vacations ac-crued, and their seniority. The loophole to this clause was that purchasers who hired back fewer than 50 percent of the existing employees could void the union contract (Stern 1989).

During one sale, the new owners decided to cut their labor costs by us-ing this means to drive out the union. Despite the fact that the sale became official at the end of the year, right during the busiest part of the Christmas holiday, the resort fired all of its employees and proceeded to reinterview them all. The newspapers were filled with advertisements calling for people to come in and apply for jobs. Some employees were rehired, while others were not. Everyone was urine-tested for drugs. Chaos broke out and morale plum-meted. Guests were severely affected, and shared in the employees' suffering. When the dust settled, some good people were rehired, while others failed in their efforts, the number of full-time employees shrank and casuals skyrock-eted, and there was no union. It took the employees the better part of three years to bring the union partially back into the hotel. It took the management little more than a year to winnow down the number of casual employees and to elevate the better ones to full-time status. In the interim, they "flexed" the labor of people employed as casuals, working them for full-time hours dur-ing high season but dropping their hours when the guest count diminished. Vida, a Filipina housekeeper in her forties at the Pono Beach Spa, remarked: "I was full-time, but when the hotel changed ownership, they cut me to ca-sual. I was working full-time hours, but I wasn't getting health benefits and I did get sick. The first time I went to the doctor he had pity on me and didn't charge me. The second time I went to the doctor he had pity on me and didn't charge me. But the third time I had to pay. I paid $30 out of my pocket, and then I had to pay $60 for the medicine. That was a lot of money."

Workers released during slow season had a variety of ways to spend the summer months. Those who did not leave the island picked up extra work, either legitimate or illegitimate, on a piecemeal basis. Romeo, a houseman at the Lei Gardens, augmented his income by selling cars. Hona, a houseman at the Hula Club Towers, grew marijuana, which he said brought in three times his houseman salary. Others did nothing, applying for unemployment insurance. Kiawe, a local boy who had worked for three years as a casual in the Sands' houseman department, was unsuccessful each summer in "tt'ing" into other departments. During these months he hung out on the beach, fishing, and collecting his meager unemployment insurance. His wife used to work, he noted, but at age twenty-five they had recently had their third baby, and so she quit to be with the children. These people tried to keep their expenses to a minimum, not fixing their cars when they broke down, and delaying making full payments on bills that came due until more money became available. Miguela, the Hula Club Towers housekeeper, discussed the adaptation patterns of new immigrant workers:

MIGUELA: Some casuals lose they hours in slow time. Kind of depend where you work, if you in the part of the hotel that don't sell as well, your rooms be more empty and they cut you back.
Q: What do these people do when less money is coming in?
MIGUELA: They try stretch they money. They try cut back on things they doing. Make do on less. These people have lots of family, cousins and uncles and aunties. Nobody going anywhere. That why they put so much into sending money back home, bringing they family members over here. If things tough, they can count on support from they family.

Diversion of Full-Time Workers. Slow season saw people moving around between departments and jobs in the resorts. Some individuals hired as casuals into banquet or houseman departments tried to keep working by transferring either temporarily ("tt'ing") or permanently into other locations, such as landscaping, beach and pool, engineering, or internal operations. There, they could fill in for the normal attrition of the transient work force. The core full-time workers in areas heavily affected by seasonal fluctuation, who could not be laid off, were temporarily transferred into other locations where they could be used for special projects. This group—drawn mostly from banquet serving, houseman, (male) housekeeping, and stewarding—did odd jobs such as spring-cleaning, maintenance, and repairs. At various times they ironed banquet table skirts, repaired the plumbing and tiles, varnished wooden lounges, mended banquet furniture (tables, stages, props), cleaned the spa, stripped and refinished floors, sanded and repainted walls, shampooed carpets, regrouted tile, and generally kept the resorts in pristine condition. They also assisted with major renovation projects usually scheduled for slow season, such as recarpeting the resorts; tearing down and reconstructing water features; repairing the pools' plumbing systems; resurfacing the racquetball, basketball, and/or tennis courts; installing new equipment in the gyms; and reflooring the aerobics rooms.

Shrinking Full-Time Hours. During slow season, even full-time workers' hours were shortened. Seniority determined who stayed and who got cut back. Some were only hired on a temporary basis, with the understanding that they would be released when the busy season ended. For example, one summer Susie, Hank's (the fitness professional's) wife, got a temporary full-time job as a cashier working in one of the Hula Club Towers' restaurants. It was specified in her hiring that she would be released at the end of FIT season. But full-time workers in permanent slots could also be curtailed. Scott, a thirty-eight-year-old valet at the Hula Club Towers from a neighboring island, noted: "They can take a full-time person and put them on call if the department is not union. Tell them not to come in that day because they're not needed. The less senior people get put on call. Everybody knows when they get hired that this can happen. You can go apply for unemployment insurance when you get your hours cut like that."

When the weekly schedules were posted, some workers found their days cut. Put on call, they could be summoned at any time if people failed to show up or were fired. Lauren Hali, the beach and pool manager at the Lukane Sands, noted: "I had two full-timers who got one day a week cut from them. But due to someone getting suspended for disciplinary reasons I got to call them back in." Full-time workers might also have their hours shortened. Many departments sent people home early on slow days, scheduling them for the full eight-hour shift, but dismissing them if it rained or business was poor. Managing schedules to keep labor costs as trimmed as possible, trying to anticipate the weekly, daily, and hourly demands of the resort during slow periods, was a complex undertaking. Ty, the bell captain at the Lukane Sands, explained how cuts to full-time employees were made in his department: "When it's a 50-percent week, the guys with the least seniority get only two days of work. The newer guys can go to the more senior guys and ask them if they want extra days off. The guys with the top seniority get the work opportunity."

David, a full-time banquet server at the Pono Beach Spa, who had moved to Honua with his wife and two children from Los Angeles over ten years before, talked about how he managed when his hours were curtailed:

> DAVID: I'm number seven on the seniority list. Jack, here [gestures to a local guy helping him set up for a banquet], he's number five. We're both full time banquet, but in the slow season we don't get full-time. I got four shifts this week, but only two last week.
>
> Q: How do you survive on the reduced hours?
>
> DAVID: I have to budget myself for the lean times. When it's busy I take some money out of my checking account every month and put it in savings. Then when it's slow, I don't take the car in to get fixed. We cut back on drinking and eating out, on movies. I collect unemployment insurance. And I pick up casual work at the [hotel on another part of Honua]. But I tell anyone who comes to work here, you'd better plan to budget your money between the fat years and the lean years.

When full-time workers' hours were cut during slow seasons they lost their hourly wages but still retained their benefits.

Termination of Regular Employees. Slow season also meant layoffs and "housecleaning" in some departments. At these times, management could examine the performance of their employees more scrupulously. Alex, the hapa-haole beach and pool attendant at the Kahana Surf from a neighboring island, complained:

> Slow season is "clean house" season. When it's busy, they need everyone they can get; and while they don't change the rules, they don't enforce them as much. They let the little things slide. Then, when it gets slow, they start to nit pick at the little things. People have been getting written up lately for wearing sneakers that were not all white, for wearing sunglasses that had gold or silver on them, for not swiping in when they get on property and again when they start working, and then out when they quit working and again when they leave property. That's another way they shrink the workforce during the slow season.

Management confirmed that slow season offered them the opportunity to plan ahead by weeding out employees with bad attitudes and replacing them with new trainees. As Lauren Hali, the beach and pool manager at the Lukane Sands, said, employees could be told, "they just have to get their act together. Otherwise it's just a matter of time before they slip up and get fired. Or, they can resign right now. I've seen people do it."

This workforce constriction yielded a hierarchical arrangement. When employment shrank, higher-statused people were mobile, leaving the area to vacation, to travel, or to find other work. Locals could sometimes move into their jobs, but management positions were usually filled by mainland haoles. Some locals left the island to find better work, although most who left began preparing for that while they were still young and moved out shortly after high school. New immigrants were the most often exploited; they were trapped.

Employees at the Ali'i resorts adapted to these seasonal fluctuations in occupancy and employment in a variety of ways. For some living on Honua and making meager amounts at their regular jobs (whether these were in resorts or elsewhere), they represented an opportunity to augment their income. Workers depended on their supplemental seasonal earnings to get them through the year. Although they labored hard during high season, they do not represent the overworked Americans depicted in so many studies of contemporary occupational life (Epstein et al. 1999; Hochschild 1997; Schor 1992). Whether they stayed where they found themselves or traveled to get there, their location on Honua represented their choice to live in paradise.

For others, it was a hardship, as their primary source of income was curtailed. They had to cut back their spending, to search for other ways to make money, and to apply for government or family support to make it through the year. Burman (1988) has noted a high level of dissatisfaction with leisure when it is forced upon employees through layoffs, cutbacks, and the reduction of hours. Even though they were financially disadvantaged, most of these Ali'i resort workers adapted their lifestyles to enjoy slow season.

Finally, there were those who welcomed the seasonal flow of work as a source of liberation, a way to more intensely experience the leisure activities that were their highest priority. Whether they were locals or seekers, they went to the beach, fished, swam, surfed, windsurfed, and more fully utilized the leisure opportunities available in this resort area. For all groups, seasonal variations in work availability meant that they had to plan their balance of work, leisure, and spending over the course of one full year at a time.

Local girl welcomes arriving guests with a lei

Bellman carts luggage to room

Front desk worker checks guests into resort

Concierge plans activities for guests

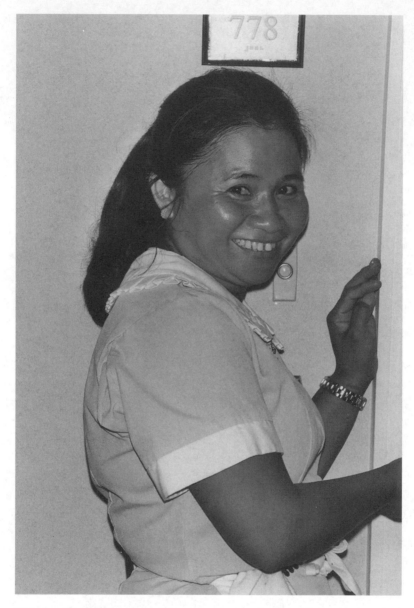

Filipina housekeeper welcomes guests to the room

Beach and pool attendant stacks lounges at the end of the day

Local takes break during slow period to relax with co-workers

Manager takes a break from his duties

Towel collections at the end of a long day

Scuba subcontractor prepares guests for ocean dive

Filipino immigrant keeps the grounds green and trim

Rolling out tables for a banquet function

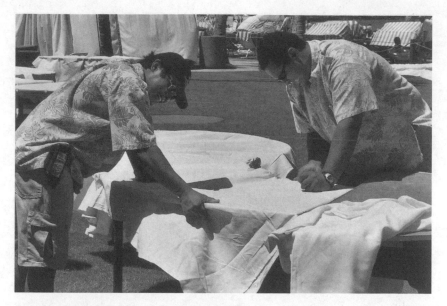

Housemen enjoying camaraderie while dressing banquet tables

Banquet server clears tables of used dishes

Dirty dishes and food go back to staging area for clearing by stewards

Some food prep is done early to enable faster meal service

Cook puts finishing touches on food

Worker transfers into window washing during slow season

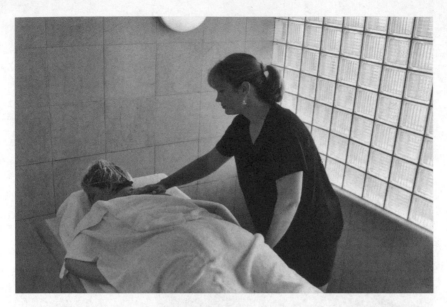

Spa worker offers nurturing treatment to relaxing guest

Local landscaper gives traditional
"shaka" sign of greeting

7

TEMPORAL LABORERS

During the twentieth century, our relationship with time was radically altered. Whereas we once lived in a world temporally dominated by the "natural" cyclings of the day, week, month, and year, technological advances have transformed these dimensions. We remain tied to these conceptions of time not as much because we have to, but because they are culturally ingrained. Increasingly, however, our ability to push the boundaries of time offers us, as a society, new opportunities that may or may not be attractive.

It was once considered a maxim that as societies advanced technologically, the amount of time necessary to the sustenance of life would decline, leaving people freer to pursue leisure.[1] De Grazia (1962), Schor (1992), and others exploded this myth, showing that machines have, instead, led to a decrease in freedom, a decrease in free time, and a decline in leisure.[2] Rather than offering a shorter workweek and greater relaxation, people have had to spend their extra time working additional hours and jobs, commuting, and doing errands and household chores. Later, Melbin (1978) proposed the concept of the "incessant" society. He suggested that our advance into the nocturnal hours was the result of a gradual, but inevitable, expansionist pressure. As consumers become dependent on the enhanced speed and broadened quantity of the goods and services that can be produced, ordered, shipped, and delivered around the clock, he predicted that we would learn to accept the inconveniences of working the twenty-four-hour day as routine.

Melbin's notion of the incessant society has since become relevant to weekly and seasonal applications, as many professional, corporate, and industrial work organizations have expanded their reach, remaining open continuously. Radio, television, and other news or entertainment networks; embassies; brokerage houses; airports; police and security firms; Internet products and providers; telephone and transportation companies; manufacturers; gyms and health clubs; shippers and delivery services; telephone and catalogue sales; hotels, restaurants, and gambling establishments; gasoline stations; and emergency, medical, and hotline services are but a few of the many organizations that have converted to the incessant schedule. While we have seen some investigation into the temporal dimensions of hospitals,[3] restaurants,[4] factories,[5] security guards,[6] and custodial workers,[7] there have been no investigations into how hotels manage this challenge. Yet they are classic "24/7" organizations, as they feed, house, and service guests daily, at all hours, throughout the year.

In resorts, two dimensions of time are relevant: quantitative and qualitative. Resorts produce a perishable product that goes to waste if it does not sell by the time it is "ripe." With capital invested in the basic facility and infrastructure, it becomes financially advantageous to use these resources to their maximum capacity. Resorts therefore seek to amplify the quantity of goods and services they can sell by augmenting the amount of their socially constructed "commercial time"—the hours of the day, days of the week, and seasons of the year when they can attract guests.

At the same time, especially in a resort hotel, attention to the qualitative dimensions of the guest experience is vital. Resorts market a particular kind of pause in the normal flow of everyday life where guests can relax from their usual rat-race pace. Pausing enables people to slow down their tempo, highly accelerated by the intensity of contemporary society, to de-stress their bodies and spirits, and rhythmically to get in touch with their selves (Snow and Brissett 1986). Periodic temporal breaks have a healing effect on individuals, refreshing them and permitting them to return to their everyday lives at peak levels, enjoying rather than being overcome by their challenges (Brissett and Snow 1993).[8] Temporal breaks represent an important and necessary component of the living cycle of time, rest, and play (Zerubavel 1985). Resorts recognize this and specifically market this feature to guests. For example, the La Samanna Resort invites guests to "Imagine a sanctuary outside the boundaries of time and responsibility" (Condé Nast Traveler). Princess Cruises offers guests "The freedom to do what you want, when you want" (Condé Nast Traveler), thereby associating time with freedom. The Utah Tourist Bureau suggests to visitors that "Life never seems to slow down. So one day I decided to stop trying to catch it" (Condé Nast Traveler). Their visitors have the opportunity to slow time down by getting off the time treadmill. These marketing campaigns reveal an intuitive insight into the subjective and objective dimensions of time, wherein time can be perceived to pass slowly or quickly, depending on people's surroundings and circumstances.[9]

In this chapter we look at how resorts market and manage these qualitative and quantitative temporal features, and where the resources come from to support these manipulations.

Goffman (1974) has suggested that we use frames to bracket and imbue meaning in assorted dimensions of the world. These frames can define and delineate temporal boundaries, ordering society and the people within it (Zerubavel 1991). Resorts manage the variable of time via several different frames. They bracket time in daily, weekly, and seasonal containers. In playing with time, resorts attempt to transform the character of guests' temporal experiences while simultaneously increasing their own profitability. Guests' emancipation from temporal routines is supported by the invisible and largely taken-for-granted mechanism of employee labor. Time is thus a palpable element for resort workers, one with which they grapple through each of these three frames.

Daily Flow of Time

Depending on their clientele and location, resorts have different goals for handling daily time. Some strive to expand the quantity of their serviceable hours by keeping their guests detached from the hours of the day, such as the Las Vegas gambling establishments where the activity is nocturnal, by designing their casinos without windows or clocks. This extends their commercially profitable time by enabling guests to remain ignorant of temporal cues that would remind them when they encroach too far into "natural" sleeping hours and suggest that they stop drinking and gambling. The Ali'i resorts, located in a tropical paradise, had fewer ventures into the late-night hours, although they operated certain departments around the clock. They took room reservations, sold and delivered room service meals, registered guests, did laundry, maintained security, and conducted other business during all hours of the day and night. This enabled guests to spend their money over a greater span than the traditional hours of the day. It also created opportunities to enhance the resort's earning capacity by augmenting the daily hours during which the same space could be commercially viable. This highlights the connection between space and time, as given locations can engage in additional or even distinctive enterprises during different periods, extending their capacity for "space-time units" (Melbin 1987).

It also created the sensation that guests could escape the restraints of the traditional daily clock, ordering meals or calling for service whenever they wanted. It was this qualitative manipulation of the time dimension that the Ali'i resorts more earnestly sought to attain. Detachment from the shackles of the daily rat race was a critical experience the resorts wanted to offer their guests. Freedom from time meant freedom from the pressure to accomplish things, to rush, to have obligations. People could read recreational books, could drink alcohol even at lunch, could sleep late, have sex in the daytime, could relax and unwind. This temporal escape from the everyday world is exemplified in the advertising campaign of Shutters, L.A.'s luxury hotel on the beach, where they entice guests by offering them "Lots of sand. No hourglass. There is a place where time is measured by the sun and the surf. Where your day planner is as bare as you are. Where you can check out as soon as you check in" (*Gourmet*).

Employee Shift Work: The Time Clock

The temporal flow of departments differed according to their hours of operation in the hotel. As Freddy, the former valet in the Pono Beach Spa's bell department, noted: "There's actually rather few departments here that stay open all night. Bell closes by 12–1[a.m.] and a "swing-valet" covers bell demands. The first bellman comes in at 4:30[a.m.]. Valets have staggered shifts. Workout room closes at 8[p.m.]. Pool closes. Camp and spa close. Restaurants and kitchens have certain hours. The main departments that stay open are laundry, room reservations, front desk, hotel operator, security, room service, and some kitchen to support that."

Departments that closed down ran two-shift operations, while those operating around-the-clock needed to bring in people over three shifts.[10] The length and timing of shifts varied within the resorts. Two-shift departments such as landscaping and water features regularly brought employees in from 6 a.m.–2 p.m. and 2–10 p.m. Others offered shorter hours, such as spa, camp, fitness center, and beach and pool, giving their employees more collapsed shifts. Housekeeping had full-time people working the day shift from 9 a.m.– 5 p.m., with part-timers doing turndown service from 5–9 p.m. Some departments staggered their shifts, such as bell and valet, bringing in one person very early to set up, increasing the load gradually as the anticipated need grew (varying by daily check-in and check-out expectations), and tapering into the late night hours. Each type of job involved varying shift schedules.

Three-shift departments tended to offer regular, unstaggered, eight-hour work stints. These have been referred to in other incessant organizations such as factories (Robboy 1983) and restaurants (Paules 1991) as day, evening or swing, and graveyard shifts. Banquet and front desk scheduled their workers from 2–10 p.m., 10 p.m.–6 a.m., and 6 a.m.–2 p.m., while security and laundry brought people in from 7 a.m.–3 p.m., 3–11 p.m., and 11 p.m.–7 a.m. These different turnover hours offered the advantage of moderating the flow of employees entering or leaving the property at any given time.

A second shift-work variation among departments concerned employees' schedules as either permanent or changing, what Melbin (1987) has called "flexible or fixed." Some areas—like housekeeping, water features, and internal operations—kept a stable workforce on regular hours. People there had the advantage of being able to take second jobs to earn additional money. This predictable structure was highly preferred. A security guard commented, "People like the shifts they're on and stay there."

The alternative was new work schedules constructed weekly. Supervisors made these plans, taking employees' seniority into account, so that those with the longest standing received the choicest hours. Reconfiguring work schedules weekly allowed management to work part-time and casual employees into the rotation as occupancy expanded or declined and to fill the busiest hours of the day as needed. Employees regularly grumbled about this, as they were unable to make plans with friends and family in advance, needing to wait until the weekly schedule was posted.[11] For people working the two-shift departments their options involved working mornings versus evenings, and having different days off or at work. Those in the three-shift departments' entire sleep and waking schedule could be affected. Wally, a married man with children working at the Lei Gardens, who had moved to Honua from another island, explained his shift rotation: "Being a fireman is my full-time job. That keeps me four days a week, a full twenty-four hours a day, at the fire station. So I'm a casual over here for the other three days in the security department. Security has three shifts: daytime, evening, and graveyard. Most of the full-time people work regularly on the same shift. I fill in for various people on their days off. That means I take different shifts all the time on different days. I have no hour of the day stability at all."

Preferences

Although their ability to influence their daily scheduling was usually minimal, employees had clear preferences about the hours they would rather work.[12] The strongest pull to the daytime shift was rooted in individuals' desire to participate in specific activities or to be integrated into the social life of their friends or community. Temporal synchrony of this sort (being "in synch") is a foundational component of societal cohesion (Hall 1983; Zerubavel 1981). Most parties and special events, workers noted, took place in the evenings.

People who worked evenings and graveyard shift tended to miss these. Kaipo, a local girl in room reservations at the Lukane Sands, indicated her aversion to the evening shift, although that was her regular stint. She would rather work days so that she could have her evenings free to go to martial arts classes, or work graveyard so she could have her days free to hike outdoors. Many others mentioned the desire to engage in water sports such as snorkeling and surfing, which were compelling avocations.

A second factor people cited as affecting their shift preferences involved their families' and children's schedules. Individuals with spouses tried to arrange their working hours to match their partners', and those with children needed to be home during after-school hours to provide childcare. This led some to seek the day shift, like Teresita, a new-immigrant local aerobics instructor at the Lukane Sands, who moved to Honua from the Philippines when she was five: "I've got to work school hours now. Dean has a job that keeps him away during the evening and nighttime hours. Alberto gets out of school at three, and I need to be finished with work so that I can look after him. We've made a deal that for awhile I will scale back my work while he's young and Dean will support us, so that one of us can always be with Alberto. That frees him up to work those crazy F&B hours."

Others, like Januaria, a local-born front desk worker at the Hula Club Towers of Filipino descent, took the graveyard shift because she was a single mother living with her own mother, a day worker. Januaria's mother told her that she could assist her with childcare only if Januaria took the graveyard shift to serve as a counter to her own evening hours at home. Without these kinds of flexible arrangements, parents had to rely heavily on the assistance of their friends and extended family members for babysitting, or pay exorbitant childcare costs. Workers' ability to adapt flexibly to different hours of the day were thus heavily influenced by their marital and parental status, making nontraditional hourly work, with a few exceptions, mostly a young person's game.

Third, people preferred certain hourly shifts to others so they could take care of necessary commercial or mercantile errands. Stores, the post office, banks, and other organizations were more uniformly open during traditional daytime hours, and being at work or asleep during these hours restricted employees' access to necessary tasks. As Melbin (1987) has noted, however, the increase in businesses operations over extended hours has eased this pressure on individuals to remain tied to the traditional temporal schedule.

A fourth consideration involved people's circadian body rhythms, the energy and vitality they naturally experienced at different times of the day. Most people were more energetic after awakening, losing stamina over the course of the day. Some preferred to spend their lively hours at work, so that they could effectively carry heavy serving trays, set up difficult banquet arrangements, run back and forth to the garage to fetch automobiles, and haul tree prunings around the property. Deedy, the pool waitress at the Lukane Sands, remarked: "I notice that when people come in to work later in the day, they are already tired from their day away from work. Maybe a little cranky too. I have energy in the morning. When the sun goes down, so do I."[13] Others preferred to have their energetic period for themselves and to come to work during physical lulls. They found that if they worked all day, they were too tired at night to accomplish other life goals. Gabriela, the fitness trainer working on her musical career, noted: "I can't stay up late regularly. I was sick for four months and couldn't shake it because I wasn't getting enough sleep. I would rather work at the Surf earlier or later and have the middle of my days free when I have my energy to do things, like writing and arranging my songs, working with my producer, marketing myself."

A significant number of Ali'i resort employees worried about shift scheduling because of its effect on other jobs. Frank Thorpe, the senior director of the food and beverage division at the Kahana Surf noted, "The majority of people who work in this hotel have two jobs. You've got to do what you've got to do." Younger employees who still lived with their parents rarely needed this extra money, but married people with children usually needed extra money to pay for housing, childcare, and education. New immigrants, among whom both husband and wife often worked in housekeeping, tended to work both daytime and turndown shifts, usually at two different hotels. They might have to drive around the island, commuting to different jobs. Enrique, who had worked two full-time houseman jobs at different hotels, had to give up one of these when his primary resort changed from a fixed to a flexible working schedule, where his days and times varied every week. A local man in landscaping who took an additional full-time job working for an outside pool maintenance company told us that he had almost fallen asleep in the car driving to work that day. The stewards discussed in chapter 3 noted that they often worked multiple shifts at different Ali'i hotels.

Unquestionably, night work was the most disruptive to people's lives.[14] Some occupations demanded night hours, especially food and beverage enterprises. People working nights accepted this as a lifestyle accommodation, centering their lives on it. Many came to like the style, flavor, and meanings associated with night work, with its elements of deviance, danger, adventure, alcohol consumption, flirtation with fellow employees, socializing on the job, less visibility and pressure, and freedom from the close supervision and scru-

tiny of day work. Night work also paid better for some, as waiters earned bigger tips, and some departments offered (meager) greater hourly wages.[15]

Others found themselves working at night against their wishes. Hermio,
Karl, and Esmeralda, three local Filipino front desk employees at the Lukane
Sands, discussed the rotation in their department, where new workers with
the lowest seniority rank had to begin their careers in the graveyard shift (10
p.m.–6 a.m.). Everyone with whom they worked had done their time working nights, waiting for people ahead of them to move on so that they could
work their way back to days, a period that usually lasted for around a year.
Hermio described how he handled the hours: "I would come home after work
and take a nap, two hours or less, then try to get up and spend some time with
my kids, play with them. My wife was not working, so she took care of the
childcare. Then I'd be up during the day and take a bigger sleep before going
in to work."

Esmeralda also slept in split shifts, napping right away and taking her
greater sleep later, freeing herself to do outdoors and commercial things during the daylight hours. She'd have a late lunch/early supper around 4 p.m.,
get to sleep by 5 p.m., and leave the house by 9:30 p.m. to get to work. Most
people in their area followed this pattern.[16] Only one person they knew didn't
"split-sleep," supplementing their main sleeping hours with a nap. Alan, a
haole seeker, who liked and remained on the graveyard shift, would strap his
kayak onto the roof of his car in the employees' parking lot so he could take
off right after work for the beach. He'd stay up most of the day, doing all of
his sleeping before work.

When they got their two days off, these transitional graveyard workers
most often reshifted their sleeping schedules to return to conventional time.
This involved two major adjustments per week of temporal dislocation, but
Melbin (1987) also found this to be the most common pattern among night
workers. Hermio described his hourly regime during his "weekend": "When
I got off for my 'weekend' I would always try to cycle back to regular time. Being on a graveyard sleep schedule cut me off from a social life, from seeing
friends, a lot of which is done in the evening hours. I would spend my first
day off staying up all day, 'recovering' back to normal time, and then effectively have only one day off. It's a drag, but if you want to feed your family,
you have to do it." While Hermio hated the graveyard shift, with two small
children, he needed the job.

Being assigned to rotating work was more difficult than steady night
work. Karl, another front desk employee, noted that there were times when
he had to work split shifts. After being on duty from 10 p.m.–6 a.m., he then

had to come in at 2 p.m. for the afternoon shift. He explained: "It was hard to stay awake for that. I couldn't get enough sleep during my time off to last me, and I'd start crashing in the late afternoon and have to fight my way through it. It stressed me out and made me really cranky. That was worse than a consistent graveyard shift." Regular graveyard shifts usually paid around one dollar more per hour. People who opted for these hours were often either single or holding down other taxing jobs.

Weekly Flow of Time

Perhaps even more than the daily flow of time, the traditional rhythm of the days of the week was intentionally disrupted at the Ali'i resorts. Resorts never close, so they had to be open when other organizations might be quiescent. This enabled the resorts to increase their quantity of commercial operating time. Jeff Carlson, the owner of a shop at the Pono Beach Spa, explained the economics of this:

> To operate a shop in a hotel is very different from running a normal shop. It's in the contract with the hotel that we can never close. We must be open every day. Since the hotel opened, there has never been a day Carlson's has not been open. I myself work the major holidays: Christmas, Easter, New Year's, Thanksgiving, because I don't want to ask my employees to. There are a couple of days that I have closed early, but the shop generally opens at 10 a.m. and stays open twelve hours a day. . . . Because we are open so much I get a lot more exposure of my merchandise for the money. Most stores would be closed Saturdays, Sundays, and holidays, which I figure is about 20 percent of the days of the year, maybe more. All it costs me to be open this additional time is labor, since I'm already paying for the rent, the inventory, the insurance, the utilities, and everything. So I have a lot more commercially usable selling time than a regular store.

At the same time, the Ali'i resorts manipulated guests' sensation of the temporal quality of their week. Obliterating the difference between weekdays and weekends was critical to the resort experience they sought to offer. The days of the week had to be socially constructed to make guests forget what "day" it was.[17] For example, a print advertisement for the Aruba Visitors Bureau reads, "There are no Mondays in Aruba" (*Condé Nast Traveler*). At the Ali'i resorts, the characteristics of the days were intentionally undifferentiated, annihilated. Guests were removed from their orthodox sense of the week and moved into the realm of the surreal (time out of time). This detachment from the weekly rhythm helped free guests from the feelings of routine, drudgery, and captivity associated with home and work. Each day at the Ali'i resorts was contoured to make guests feel as if they were free from the weekly time treadmill, especially from the morose Mondays and the sad Sundays that preceded them, signifying the end of their weekend and the return to labor. Ali'i guests were liberated from the fetters of the week by being encapsulated in a world of service and luxury, where everything they wanted was available any day they wanted. They could create their days as they desired, without the rhythm of the week impinging on them. David Horowitz, a jewelry shop owner in the Lukane Sands, offered his perception of the essence of guests' weekly temporal experience: "It's not like there are no weekends in a hotel. My concept is the reverse. Because people [the guests] are all not working, are relaxed, are together, and are in a romantic mood, every day in a hotel is a weekend—or more precisely, a holiday. I capture my customers for a better quality of their time. It's a hotel; every day is *yontif* [Yiddish for holiday]!"

But every day was not a holiday for resort workers. What was, for guests, a surreal temporal arena, was a world of work, of everyday life, for employees. They had to integrate being at work with running their routine lives. They were rooted in the world where weekdays and weekends mattered. To create this sublime temporal experience for guests, Ali'i resort workers had to adapt to losing their concept of the traditional weekend. While the guests were emancipated from weekly temporality, employees had to adapt to working around the week to keep the resort operational. As a result, they lost their weekly rhythm. When Enrique shifted to a flexible time schedule, he complained: "I liked the regular days off because then I had a certain rhythm to my week. I always knew when my weekend was and I could plan my energy around it. There was the building up to it, needing it, having it off. Now it moves around and I've lost my weekly rhythm."

Losing standardized weekends prevented employees from being home on traditional family or religious days, when their spouses or children might be home from school or work and social occasions were planned. By becoming dislocated from the weekly cycle of socializing, employees were cast out of the interactional patterns of "social traffic" (Zerubavel 1985). They lost their "entrainment," or synchrony with others' rhythms (Hall 1983). As Zerubavel (1985, 112) has noted, "The price one pays for being out of phase with the conventional weekly work/rest cycle is essentially a social one, namely depriving oneself of the opportunity to interact intensively with those whom one can see mainly during the weekend." It was for this reason that employees—despite the benefits they might accrue, such as less supervision and a more relaxing work atmosphere (sometimes employees goofed around on weekends when their managers were off-duty, jumping or pushing each other into the pools)—resented having to work on weekends.

Stratification and Scheduling

Working in a continuous flow of time, disconnected from the weekly rhythm, affected employees differently, partly according to their job classification. As people moved up the resort's occupational hierarchy, they could regain the temporal distinction of their days. The top management, although they worked long daily hours and were ultimately on call when crises struck, could command Sundays and often half of Saturdays off. Chuck Law, after leaving the Pono Beach Spa to become the general manager at a major resort on a neighboring island, arranged his schedule so that he could return home to spend every weekend with his wife and children, still on Honua.

After senior management, senior line employees had the most control over their weekly schedules. Regardless of competence or level of effort, employees who had the greatest length of service were given first preference in choosing hours and days to work.[18] The most senior massage therapists, for example, preferred the work shifts in midday and arranged their weekly schedules to facilitate outside employment. Rick, a Hispanic beach and pool attendant from Phoenix who worked at the Kahana Surf, arranged his weekly schedule so that he had Saturday mornings off to comb the flea markets for equipment necessary to his moonlight career.

The bulk of the employees had to accept the work schedules offered them. They picked up the days that others had passed over, regularly working weekends and holidays. Fortunately for many, the highly transient character of resort workers, especially in certain departments, kept the seniority list pretty fluid. As Nick, a beach and pool attendant, noted, "I've been here seven to eight months, and I'm more than halfway up the seniority chain in that amount of time." The most junior workers got the residual shifts, filling in for regular employees on their days off, like Wally the fireman, picking up days and hours that varied around the clock. Wally, whose wife had moved temporarily to the mainland with their children so she could live near her parents while she went back to school, described his indifference to weekly work scheduling: "What about days of the week? That doesn't matter to me. Weekends, weekdays, are all the same. This is a party island and people are partying any night of the week. It doesn't matter if it's Monday or Tuesday, they will go out. There's a lot of young people and this is paradise." This attitude varied greatly from when his family was there and he had been forced to rely on friends, siblings, and babysitters for childcare on evenings and weekends. Workweek flexibility was thus another young person's game, with single workers who were taking time-outs from their more settled career tracks able to adapt more readily. Many people preferred to have at least one weekend day off, even if they were single, as Matt, a gay valet at the Lei Gardens, noted: "If I had my choice I would rather have off one weekend and one weekday. The weekend to party and have fun at nightclub events, which are more likely to be hot and organized for gays on weekends, and the weekday so I can get all my errands around town done."

The Social Construction of Weekends

Although Ali'i resort workers labored on weekends, the cyclical rhythm of temporally moving through weekdays and weekends was so deeply ingrained in cultural conceptions of time that management socially constructed it artificially.[19] In particular, they strove to give employees their two days off contiguously. This recreated the cultural construct of the "pulsating week" (Zerubavel 1985), in which the forty hours of work were concentrated into five days of work and two days of rest, thereby giving relief to the continuous flow of working. Dennis, a haole bellman from the mainland at the Lukane Sands, who had lived in the Islands for seven years, discussed a situation that threatened this occupational norm:

> They have some big checking-in and -out coming up. Friday and Saturday of this week are huge. Sunday, Monday, and Tuesday are easier. They're trying to give everybody in the department off on those days because they can't spare them the rest of the week. Everybody is working. But they try to preserve the concept of the weekend when they schedule us for our days off. The supervisors came and apologized to us. "We've got to try to give everyone their days off on Sunday, Monday, and Tuesday this week. We're going to try to make most people either Sunday–Monday or Monday–Tuesday, but there will have to be some people who will have to get Sunday–Tuesday. We're sorry about that." So even though there's only one day breaking it up, they felt like they had to apologize for this violation.

The temporal importance of the two-day weekend suggests that it takes people more than a single day to relax, unwind, and renew their energy for another stint of work.[20]

Some employees responded to this situation creatively, rearranging their "weekends" to land in the middle of the week. Iris, a saleswoman at the Lukane Sands' art gallery, was informed that she could not have weekend days off work. Tuesday and Wednesday became her regular nonworking days. When her husband Bob finished school and got a job with a rental car company he was told that he had to work at least one weekend day. He accepted that gladly, agreeing to work for the full weekend. He requested Tuesdays and Wednesdays off and they were glad to give it to him. So now Iris and Bob had their "weekends" together again. It benefits an organization to stagger employees' "weekends" due to the characteristics that have become socially infused into different days. Mondays, the first day of the working week, is traditionally a slow starting day, where people need to recover from the weekend and to warm back up to their working rhythm. People call in sick disproportionately on Mondays.[21] Tuesday through Thursday they are in the groove, with people at maximum productivity. But productivity again begins to lag on Friday, as people anticipate the weekend and let down their effort (Zerubavel 1985).[22] At the Ali'i resorts, by spreading constructed "weekends" throughout the real week, management was able to diffuse the effects of these peaks and valleys.

The concept of the socially constructed weekend was so embedded in the resorts that it often superseded the traditional, outside concept of the weekend. We spoke with Lance, the recreational attendant at the Hula Club Towers, who was in a rush and getting ready to leave. He couldn't talk to us then, but wanted to tell us when he could. "I'll be back Monday," he said. "It's my Friday." By this he meant that he had the next two days off. This was a phrase commonly used at the Ali'i resorts. The ironic thing about Lance's remark was that it actually was a Friday. The real days of the week had become secondary in importance to the socially constructed days.

We see that in a tourist-oriented economy, where many businesses were open and running seven days a week, it was not uncommon for young people or people of lower seniority to work weekends. The days of the week were detached from their traditional meaning and the weekend became a more flexible concept. People who could afford to be especially flexible were single people such as Rick, or married people such as Iris and Bob, who had no children (otherwise they would be worrying about weekend childcare). People with built-in childcare, such as extended kinship networks, could also be more flexible about their weekly schedules.

Seasonal Flow of Time

Ali'i resort workers experienced holidays differently from most people whose work schedules were more traditional. First, the atemporal hours and the weekends were not the only nontraditional times they worked; they worked through holidays as well. We called the room reservations department at the Lukane Sands one Easter Sunday to make a reservation and talked to Kaipo, a local girl whose sister worked at one of the resort's restaurants. We asked her how her Easter was going. "Easter?" she asked. "It's Easter?" "You didn't know that?" we asked. "I knew it when I left home this morning." "But you've forgotten it?" "Yeah. I guess being here is like being out of time. There are no holidays here." By this she signified her sense that every day at the Sands was the same. In the outside world there were weekdays, weekends, and holidays, but at the Sands these were all blurred, stripped of their distinction and transformed into unidimensional workdays.

Resort workers thus had no holidays, as they sacrificed these to enhance them for guests. People most likely to be working holidays were those at the lowest end of the seniority hierarchy. The higher-ups got their pick of hours and days and jockeyed to avoid holiday work. But more people on a resort payroll had to be working on any given day than could be off, so most Ali'i employees worked through all the major holidays. Some tried to compensate for what they were missing by making private celebrations before or after work, or on other days. But, as usual, many missed the traditional parties with friends and relatives.

The necessity of working on holidays was something people entering into resort work needed to take into consideration more consciously, as Scott Peraud, the mainland food and beverage executive, noted. He reflected on his philosophy about this occupational demand: "You've got to know you're going to work every Christmas, New Year's, Thanksgiving. Every holiday, you're working. While your family is at home. And that's very tough sometimes. It's very tough. And you have a little three-year-old boy at home and he's wondering where's Daddy today? Daddy's at work. Well, when am I going to see Daddy? Well Daddy left at 6 a.m. and he's going to get back at 12 midnight, it's the busiest day of the year for Daddy. There's a lot of that aspect. People don't realize that coming into the business."

Being able to celebrate holidays with their families was a goal some resort employees held for their future, as they ascended the corporate ladder. Scott offered his thoughts on what he was missing, and tied it to his outlook of deferred gratification:

I know a lot of people who believe that there was a lot of time there, when I was an assistant restaurant manager, while a lot of my friends were in college and going out Friday and Saturday nights, going to dance clubs and things of that nature. And Friday and Saturday were my busiest nights and I'd work until 3 o'clock in the morning. And all my friends said I was crazy at the time. . . . But when I get to GM or whatever position it may be, I'll be able to take the weekends off. I'll be able to take the holidays off. Truly, if my son is six years old and I'm GM and I'm able to take the holidays off, that's when he's going to remember it, that I was at home, not when he was three.

Second, due to the seasonal nature of this resort work, many Ali'i employees sacrificed their choice to work or not during holiday seasons. People employed in the heavily seasonal banquet server and houseman departments, whose occupational fluctuations were either boom or bust, had little choice about which holiday seasons they would work. Those holidays coinciding with group season offered employment, while those outside it did not. Few groups booked into resorts during Thanksgiving or Christmas, for example, as their employees were unlikely to welcome conventions or incentive travel then. But spring break fell right into the middle of group season, and seasonal employees were on the job. Employees in heavily FIT departments, in contrast, were always in demand on holidays, as these were times when families took vacations. Depending on their department, then, employees worked the yearly seasonality of their jobs. They were in mandated work or mandated leisure to make the guests' experience optimal.

Third, Ali'i employees' experience of holidays was different from that of people in other occupations. Time passed differently in the Ali'i resorts during holiday seasons.[23] Their work was seasonally characterized by times of protracted inactivity during slow season, times of moderate activity scattered around the year, and times of hectic hyperactivity over the holidays. Csikszentmihalyi (1975) has noted that the most enjoyable state of existence, the "flow state," is characterized by a balance between boredom and anxiety. Although holidays spent at home with the family usually offered some peace and serenity, at work they rarely had this quality. One long-time beach and pool employee at the Lei Gardens highlighted the subjective character of time perception, noting, "The two weeks at Christmas feel like they take three months to get through." When things were deadly slow, though, workers liked it no better.

As a society, our temporal cyclings have traditionally rested on a foundation of "natural" time. Our conceptions of the hours of the day, days of the week, and seasons of the year are rooted in the circadian rhythms of the sun, the lunar movements of the moon, and the well-defined holiday seasons of the year. Like many hotels, the Ali'i resorts sought to break through the limiting boundaries of these traditional concepts, artificially extending the spaces of time designated for relaxation and play to enhance their profitability. These resorts made the time they sold to guests freer and more relaxing by staffing it with employee labor around the clock. To maintain their jobs, workers had to labor incessantly. They gave up their hours of natural sleep, natural weekends, and natural holidays in order to qualitatively enhance and quantitatively lengthen the holidays of guests.

The extension of work to fill the day, week, and year is not a new trend. We have branched beyond the daylight hours from our earliest days of fire and electricity (Melbin 1987) and altered societal conceptions of weekly cycles of work and rest over the course of history (Zerubavel 1985). Throughout, our pattern of expansion has been to pack ourselves as densely as we can into the time and space available (Melbin 1987). This expansion represents the technological conquest of society over nature.

At the same time, a dimension of stratification emerges within the foundation fueling this trend toward incessance. Time, as the maxim suggests, is money, and people with money can purchase the benefits that the incessant society offers: they can pay to have their goods manufactured and work orders processed more quickly, to have their packages delivered around the world overnight, to purchase goods and services whenever they want. Those with fewer socioeconomic resources are the ones toiling to support this temporal infrastructure.[24] In a classic Marxist fashion, they are producing the temporal freedom and leisure of others. Although the managers and more senior resort employees make less of this sacrifice than new immigrants and locals, the whole resort work population, as a tourism service industry, is obliged to engage in this labor.

8

STRATIFIED LABORERS

Despite over a half-century of legislation against discrimination in the workplace, racial and ethnic minorities as well as women continue to suffer from practices that limit their success in rising through the socioeconomic system in the United States. In the early twenty-first century, the labor market remains segmented and ghettoized, with specific groups over-represented in some areas and under-represented in others.[1] In this chapter, we explore the racial and ethnic stratification in the Ali'i resorts, the impact of these practices on various groups, and the ways in which these groups have adapted to the hiring practices of the resorts' management.

Ethnic Stratification

In the Ali'i resorts, one particular area displayed the most marked ethnic ghettoization and stratification. Group functions, popular when companies or conventions came and booked meals, primarily involved the work of three departments: stewarding, housemen, and banquets. Kamala, a haole banquet server at the Lukane Sands, explained this stratification system:

The whites grab up all the good jobs in the hotels and control the hiring and distribution of jobs. Most of the new immigrants and locals in the seasonal workforce do not get the higher-paying banquet jobs as waiters and servers. They work as housemen or stewards. These jobs require much heavier and difficult physical labor. They get paid maybe more per hour, but no tip pool. Those people do not travel anywhere during the off-season, and most of them wish they were working full-time, year-round. Departments in the hotel tend to be heavily stratified by ethnicity. The difference in salary between what the white people make as waiters and what the housemen make is great. The whites are making about double what the housemen are making. Waiters get around $2/hour salary and $20–25/hour from the tip pool. Housemen are making around $11/hour with $5/hour from the tip pool. And the Filipinos in stewarding get $12 an hour, but don't make anything from the tip pool at all.

Stewarding

The stewarding department was composed of new immigrants. Stewards, mostly men but some women as well, assembled all the dishes, serving ware, grills, glasses and silverware for the group functions, making sure they had the proper amount. They then stacked these onto carts and wrapped them with industrial plastic wrap to make sure that nothing fell off, then hauled the serving ware, along with the food from the kitchen, down to the function locations. They used small Cushman trucks to drag some of these, but many were hand-rolled, along winding and uneven paths, to the functions on carts with wheels. During the events, stewards waited behind the curtains at the staging area. As banquet servers brought back dirty dishes and platters from the event, put them down on the counters, and walked away, stewards took the food off the trays, separated the garbage from the dirty dishes, cleaned and stacked them, assembled the big high rolling carts, and wrapped them with plastic wrap so they could be safely rolled back inside.

At the end of the events, stewards brought back the dirty dishes, grills, and garbage. They then washed the dishes and silverware and scrubbed the pots, pans, and heavy, greasy grills. As each shift neared its finish, they cleaned the entire kitchen, from the cooking and preparation areas to the cabinets and floors. Frank Thorpe, the thirty-eight-year-old executive director of food and beverage at the Hula Club Towers, noted, "They do the dirtiest work in the hotel." Stewards also emptied giant garbage cans around the resorts and replaced filled liner bags with clean ones. They could frequently be seen wearing heavy-duty rubber gloves and smocks. A group of new immigrant employees from the stewarding department chatted with us as they moved around the Lukane Sands together, joking with one another and conducting their business:

We are the hardest-working guys in the hotel. We do the heavy work, "man's work." There is a lot of lifting involved. We wear the weight belts. Us guys, we work the late shift here: four p.m. 'till midnight. Sometimes when there is a big party, we don't get off work until two or three [a.m.]. We bring down and set up for the functions. Then we pick up the stuff after the functions and clean it up. Like the big, heavy, outdoor grills. We have to scrub them all down when the party is over.

Although standard American was mandated in most of the Ali'i resorts, when they were among themselves, the stewards generally spoke to each other in the various Filipino dialects. Jeffrey, the local houseman at the Pono Beach Spa, discussed the ethnic cliquishness of resort workers:

JEFFREY: Tell you the truth, Filipinos stick with the Filipinos, Tongans stick with the Tongans. I mean, if you walk in the cafeteria, all you hear is Filipino language. I don't think that's proper in a cafeteria—you should speak English.

Q: Is there a pecking order to these groups?

JEFFREY: In my opinion the Filipinos think they're better than everyone else, because they can do stuff that they can get away with, you know, things that we can't do.

Q: We being locals?

JEFFREY: Yeah. Yeah. But I just think that they have, like, they're invincible sometimes. They think they're invincible, because there's so much of them here, they think that they can overpower everybody else. And I'm part Filipino myself, but I still don't like it.

Stewarding was thus a department where new immigrants who were willing to do hard and dirty labor could work in an arena that was mostly insulated from guests and resort management, where they could interact with their own kind, and speak their native language.[2]

Housemen

Housemen were mostly locals and generally all men. The Pono Beach Spa tried a brief experiment one year hiring women into this department, but it did not last. Housemen set up the tables, chairs, buffets, bars, and stages for the functions, then broke them down and hauled them back into storage. Known within the resorts as "table rollers," they assembled tables and chairs, stages for entertainers, sound systems, and setups for competitions and games. Kevin, a thirty-one-year-old local haole working at the Hula Club Towers, noted:

KEVIN: Oh ya. Houseman is, I can easily say this, the hardest job in the hotel.

Q: Why?

KEVIN: Oh, physical. Physically setting up tables and chairs. You have, you know, five guys setting up for fifteen hundred or a thousand. A lot. Ya bust your ass at tables and chairs and linen it and break it down. You know, you might have four dinners a night and meetings. And it's a lotta work. From the time you walk in the door you're usually hustling the whole time, 'till you leave.

In fact, Kevin explained that housemen's work was so physically demanding, that once he began doing it, he had to give up his outside form of exercise. "It's like, I boxed for about ten years. I've boxed amateur, but once I started working at the Towers I can't do that any more. The kind of work you do just does not coincide with having a extracurricular sport like that." This was particularly true during the busy season, when the demand for his work was at peak.

Housemen were nearly exclusively locals; some originated in Hawai'i, while the rest, born in foreign countries or on the mainland, had moved to Honua early enough to complete most of their primary schooling there. They cultivated a local culture where they spoke to each other mostly in pidgin English and felt at ease among their own kind. Jeffrey described his clique of local housemen at the Pono Beach Spa: "There is, there's a good local clique. When the locals get together, they work hard. Good attitude. It's just about having fun all day—joking around, laughing, you know. The locals have a good clique here. And a lot of the younger kids are starting to work more. They're starting to get jobs earlier. But the locals, the locals are good, here. Work together. Camaraderie."

Housemen had more contact with guests than stewards, as they were sometimes stopped and questioned by individuals asking for directions or asking about what they were doing, as they brought stacks of chairs and tables down in the Cushman trucks, unloaded them, and set them up, but this was still occasional. They spent a fair amount of time by the function areas waiting for their co-workers to deliver tables, chairs, stage, lighting, and other equipment so they could assemble it. This gave them the opportunity to talk and have a good time and occasionally to meet guests. But their jobs did not involve direct guest contact except for the head housemen, who had to interact with the group handlers.

Banquet Servers

At most of the Ali'i resorts, banquet servers prepared the tables, served the food, and removed it to the staging area after it was eaten. Sam, a thirty-five-year-old haole banquet server at the Pono Beach Spa described his job: "They [housemen] set it all up, and then the servers come in and dress it up, make it look nice, and then serve it all, clean it up, but they move all the heavy stuff." This was the case for all the Ali'i resorts except the Lei Gardens, which employed no housemen, and so the banquet servers there had to do their own setups and breakdowns. Primarily mainland haoles, they spoke standard American. Most had moved to Hawai'i in their early twenties, either following friends or on a whim, after taking a vacation there. Most banquet servers held more than one job, working as banquet servers at other resorts on the strip in addition to their main job. Gary, a fifty-two-year-old mainland haole banquet server at the Lei Gardens, talked about holding more than one job:

> Some of us have like, myself, I'm not that fortunate yet to have one, but you know, a $2,000 mortgage when you're a waiter is a lot of money. You know, and the wife's doing a little bit here, and you're living in Hawai'i, and the cost of living and the gas, the gasoline is going up, and it's a lot of money. So you work your butt off when it's busy season, and then the rest of the year you work your one more stable job, that. So yeah, is it hard? It *is* hard. But it's something you have to do. 'Cause you can't work, and live a good lifestyle, take a good vacation, for $10 an hour. You can't do that. You can do it if you're living under Mom and Dad's house, or if you're living, like when I moved here, you know, we had a bunch of guys in one apartment for a while, and all we did was really drink and smoke (*laughs*), you know, all day long. Play on the beach, and work one job. But if you're gonna be here for a period of time, and wanna make your life on Honua, and you're gonna be in the service industry, you have to work two jobs.

When they worked at two or three different resorts, they constantly crossed paths with each other. People who worked part-time at one resort might have a full-time job elsewhere, or work two to three part-time jobs. Sam described it as a "strange way of life." He noted:

> You see so many crossover faces between hotels, and when you cross paths, and you pass people, you ask them "You work a double today?" So you're going like, "What's goin' on?" Y'know? "Is there a group coming in next week?" "Are we gonna get a good tip pool?" That's a conversation too, it's like, "How much was the tip pool over there?" Some guy worked that day, and he worked on that last tip pool, you go, "Well, how much was the tip pool?" And that's an actual thing, y'know, "Geez, the Lukane

Sands had $30 tip pools for two, two weeks in a row!" Y'know; it's like *high school*!

This crossover of working and living in the same local area meant that most banquet servers knew each other, forming a cohesive social community.

The broad pattern of this ethnic stratification and ghettoization, with some regional variation, was repeated in every hotel throughout the mainland that we visited. In the South, banquet servers were white, housemen were black, and stewards were new immigrants from Asia (Lao, Lu, and Hmong). In the Midwest, banquet servers were white, housemen were Mexican-American, and stewards were new immigrants from Africa and Asia. In the Rocky Mountain West, banquet servers were white, housemen were Mexican-American, and stewards were new immigrants from Asia. Similarly, in Australia and New Zealand, banquet servers were white, housemen were Maori or Aboriginal, and stewards were Tongan, Samoan, Fijian, or from other Asian locations.[3]

Occupational Funneling

Workers were funneled into various departments through a dual process of self-selection and organizational typification.[4] Under the former, prospective employees often chose to apply for work in specific departments because they had family members or friends who worked there. George Clark, the thirty-year-old director of internal operations at the Lukane Sands, discussed the "grapevine recruitment" (Grint 1998) people often used to get into the departments he supervised—laundry, wardrobe, and housekeeping: "When something opens up here, we hardly even have to post the job. Everyone knows when someone is leaving. They take care of filling the positions with their friends and relatives. Even before the person leaves, they have their relative come in on their day off to train under them. Then, when the job is officially open, the new person just steps into it. They like it, because they can take care of their own. We like it because if new people give us any problems, we just talk to our long-time employees and they handle it."

Others followed their friends into jobs. Kevin, a thirty-one-year-old houseman born in Cleveland of German and American Indian descent, moved with his recently remarried father and stepmother to Honua when he was in the third grade. He began his schooling at the local elementary school and continued in the public school system all the way through high school. After he graduated from high school he worked for five years as an agent and then a mechanic at a rental car company, a job he got through a friend from high school. Next he found a job through another friend as a restaurant cook and bouncer at a bar. When he got tired of doing that, he turned to still another high school friend:

Q: How did you get into hotels?

KEVIN: Shoot, I think a friend of mine, another friend, everything, wow. I think another friend of mine, I heard of it. How the heck did I hear of houseman? Why did I apply for houseman? I think my friend Chris, I known him since fifth grade. And so I think, you know, he was in houseman, so I think I asked him, and I told him I needed a job and was looking for something in the hotel and, um, I think he kinda got me in.

Q: So you just went into houseman because Chris was in that department?

KEVIN: Well, I heard, I didn't want to work in the front of the house with the guests.

Q: Why?

KEVIN: I mean that's what I had to do at the jeep rental company. There was only a few people working, so I would do contracts and, you know, sign out the jeeps, you know, do all the paperwork and, uh, just always having to deal with people, and then I kinda just didn't want to anymore. Didn't want to deal with the tourists so intensely. A lot of people that I see, a lot of the tourists are, you know, you know what I mean. Snobby, nasty, freaks. I don't like to deal with that kind of people, you know, at all. It's not good to say really rich people are all like that, because there are some nice ones. But, you know, it's good to be working around nice people.

Other employees chose jobs on the basis of their surroundings, the physical aspects of the job, and the potential for interaction with others. Jeffrey noted what was important to him in choosing his job at the Pono Beach Spa:

Q: So what made you go into the houseman department?

JEFFREY: It, you could be outside more. Being outside, meeting new people, getting to talk to people. I didn't want to be stuck indoors, you know.

Q: What were some of the other options?

JEFFREY: I could have been a chef, stuck in a kitchen. I don't want to work in a kitchen all day, it's too hot. There was a waiter opening, but I did that before. I've done fast food, I'm not really into that anymore, and, it's just, the work I've experienced is in and out. I don't really like being inside. I like coming to work early, starting early in the morning, and then being out by 2:30 or 3:00. I don't really see myself as a behind-the-desk kind of person, I don't think. I like being outside and doing work outside, I think. Physically. Physical labor. I guess I've always been doing that.

At the same time, human relations departments, the hiring arm of hotels, funneled prospective employees into areas that they deemed appropriate according to their ethnic typifications.[5] Andy, a twenty-five-year-old college dropout from Maine who had moved to Honua three years before and worked in various restaurant and sales jobs, described his initial experience applying for work at the Lukane Sands:

> ANDY: First thing I went in for the interview. I didn't know what hotels were like at all. I knew nothing. I just. . . . When they said, "What are you applying for?" for some reason a hotel like that, I figured, "Oh it's so exclusive," I was like, (*dumb, self-mocking sounding voice*) "housekeeping," 'cause I had no concept. I mean, there's no anything like that in Maine. So I'm like, "Housekeeping, landscaping, work, I'll work my way up, whatever." And then they're like, (*lisping*) "Well there's a beach and pool open, it might fit you better." I was like, "Cool."
> Q: What do you think they meant, "It might fit you better?"
> ANDY: Yeah, exactly. But that's what they said to me. Just now, thinking back, it makes totally sense, like I woulda stood out. I'm not in the racial category for those other two jobs (*laughs*).

Getting the Job

Workers in each of the three departments had different patterns of finding their jobs.

Stewarding

Nearly all the stewards were born outside the United States. Santo Duque was seventeen when his parents, who had immigrated several years earlier, brought him to Hawai'i from the Philippines. Happy at home, he had dropped out of high school because he was unmotivated and mostly hung out at the beach, partying with his friends. His parents sent home a monthly allowance from the United States, so he lived the good life and had no interest in moving. Dollars were valued there, and he imagined that America was a place of easy money where people did not have to work very hard. All of that changed when he arrived in the United States. He talked to us about how he came to work in stewarding:

> When I first came here I had to go to work right away. I worked my first job in a store selling shoes. I did that for three month, and then I got a job as a busboy at the Royal Hawaiian Hotel. I did that for six months, then they moved me up to the room service department, where I worked for three months. Then there was an opening for a waiter in their fancy restaurant, the Royal Hawaiian. I did that for nine years, and I was making good money. During that time I got married and had children. But then the [large chain hotel] opened, and they had a dishwasher job open. So I applied for that and I got it. It paid a lot less money, but I didn't have to talk to the guests anymore . . . In the long run I didn't like working with the guests.

Santo spoke about the Filipinos' work preferences:

> Many Filipinos are ashamed to move up, they don't want to move up. It's the language, they're afraid they don't speak English very well. They're afraid they won't understand the high-position people, like the head chef, if he wanted to talk to them. . . . We have people working as dishwashers here who used to be high school teachers in the Philippines. We even hired an administrator, a high school district supervisor. And when we interviewed him, two of my people came to me and said, he's an important man—he used to be our district supervisor back in the Philippines. So I asked him, "Are you sure this is what you want to do?" Because he was not a young man. And he said, "Yes, dishwashing is what I want to do."

Agrifina was a fifty-three-year-old steward at the Lukane Sands. Born in the Philippines, it had been her dream as a young woman to come to America: "I think I was eighteen years old when my cousin married the Hawaiiano. We called them Hawaiiano. They're Filipino, but they live in Hawai'i. So in that time I was dreaming, I wanted to know what it was like to get with a Hawaiian also. So I begin to be dreaming, you know. So I said I think, hopefully, I can meet a man like my cousin, you know a Hawaiiano from America."

Her cousin's mother arranged a match. She fixed Agrifina up with a Filipino man who had moved to America in his youth. Richard was twenty-two years her senior and divorced. For two years they corresponded, writing in English. Then they arranged a meeting. Richard came to Manila. Agrifina had been dating a young man in the Philippines who was distraught at the prospect of this new suitor, but she pushed her feelings aside to pursue her instrumental goals:

> But I can tell you, very hard. My pen-pal husband is all ready to come to meet me tomorrow, and then the one who like to marry me, one o'clock in the night is still there to ask me that. Very hard, I'm telling you. To asking me that okay, that he bring me somewhere so we can hide me, but I said no, I cannot. I really, really like that man; the only thing is my family, not only myself. So what can I say, I tell the truth. I cannot go with you because I get friend to come from Hawai'i, even though I like you very much. To marry you I cannot, because what I dream is, I can, if I can marry a Hawaiiano, I can brought my family here, I can brought my mother and my six sisters and brothers to America.

After forty-five days of courtship, Agrifina agreed to marry Richard and to move to the United States. In 1973 she moved with him to his home on Punalua [a small, remote Hawaiian island]. There, he worked in the maintenance department of a pineapple plant. Agrifina found work with the pineapple company as well, first growing and harvesting an experimental strand of corn, and later picking pineapples, one of the most difficult and arduous agricultural tasks. Eduardo, the bellman at the Lei Gardens of Filipino descent, whose parents used to work in the fields, talked about pineapple picking, "Pineapple fields are the prickliest and most dense crop. No animal will venture in there, not even a dog. The rows are planted close together, and you get cut and torn up if you go in there even five feet. Only the most desperate of people will ever work there, the newest of new immigrants." Agrifina worked in the pineapple fields as a picker for ten years, from 1973 to 1983. Some days she and her crew engaged in competition against male crews to see how many crates each could pick. Those who picked the most earned not only their $2.40 hourly wage but a bonus, depending on the number of crates they filled. She became pregnant with her first child and worked in the fields throughout her pregnancy, having to turn sideways to spare her belly from the sharp cuts.

During this time the pineapple company offered their long-term workers, like Richard, company housing. He used this opportunity to make some extra money: "So my husband house, is he living in his own house. He play smart. He would rent [his] house, and then he live in the company house. Because we only had to pay seven dollars a month [for the company house], so it's a good chance to make money little bit, so he rent them out, his house, for seven hundred a month. So that's still a nice start."

In 1983 Agrifina had her second child, just about the time that the pineapple plantation closed. Richard was laid off. As part of his severance package, he was offered the opportunity to purchase the house in which they were living, which they did. He also got a lump sum of money that they used to buy another rental house. They now had two children and three houses. During this time, Agrifina applied for and was granted citizenship, and brought her mother to the United States. Over the next six years, together they were successful in bringing her six siblings to the United States. None of the siblings wanted to work in the pineapple fields, so some moved to the mainland, some to Honua, and some to other islands. With new family living on Honua, Agrifina and Richard went shopping for another house. They bought one there and installed their family in it. They made the down payment and owned the house; the family made the monthly payments.

Agrifina stayed home for a couple of years with two young children, and Richard found another job. When he retired in 1987, she went to look for work. The only other industry on the island was hotels,[6] so she got a job as a housekeeper at a large chain hotel. She worked full-time there and part-time at another property, the Punalua Breeze Resort. Richard started his own business at home, "my husband he get farm, he get chicken, his pig, his cow. So really, really working hard." Richard raised livestock and grew Filipino vegetables; Agrifina helped him at night after she came home, "So me and my husband, even at ten o'clock at night, we still outside to work on our farm." They took the produce they grew to the local market, and they shipped some to their relatives living on Honua to sell at the market there.

Agrifina worked as a housekeeper at the two Punalua hotels but received no medical benefits. With two children, she had to pay $335 a month for health insurance. Her relatives on Honua urged her to move: "So my sister, my brother said, why don't you come here? You get plenty job here." She and her family moved in with them and added two more rooms onto the back of the house. She then looked for work. A job came open at the Lukane Sands in 1993 as a steward. Although she had previously worked in housekeeping, the only full-time job available was in stewarding, so she took it. With all these people in the house it felt crowded; she and Richard moved out and bought a five-bedroom house for their family: "We heard a new housing going up so we go and look at the model. It look good, so we apply to see if we qualify for a loan. We do, so we get a new house." Now Agrifina had a full-time job, health insurance, and her fifth house. Yet despite these assets (or maybe because of them), she always complained that she was broke.

Housemen

As noted, nearly all housemen were locals or assimilated locals. Nestor Kaono, a thirty-year-old houseman supervisor at the Kahana Surf, was left behind in Tonga at the age of three by his parents when they migrated to Hawai'i, placing him in the care of "aunties." They brought him over seven years later, and he started in the Honua public school system in sixth grade. Large, like many Tongans, Nestor Kaono spoke the local dialect. In his second year of high school he started working after school and during the summers for a landscaping company. Good fortune and coincidence landed him a more prestigious hotel job at one of the Ali'i resorts: "After my landscaping job was finished one day, I was walking through the resorts, and I saw someone unloading tables and chairs and offered to help. It turned out he was the food and beverage director for the Kahana Surf, and he offered me a job. That's how I got in. So I went back to school and finished up high school. I started working at KS the Monday after my Friday graduation."

Nestor Kaono had dreams of going to college on the mainland, and he had a football scholarship to Colorado State all set up, but when his father died the August after his graduation from high school, he put aside his college plans to stay with and to support his mother and siblings. He married when he was twenty-eight and was still living with his wife, mother, and child, aged one, at the time of our interview. He has been with the Kahana Surf ever since he graduated high school, for the last twelve years. Nestor Kaono described his job:

> The first department I worked in was houseman. We set up for weddings and the group functions. We bring down the tables and chairs from storage and set them up, set up the serving areas. If there's entertainment, we set up the stage and the sound system. There's no stewarding department here, so we've got to do the stewarding as well. That means that we also bring down the plates, silverware, and serving ware. We bring down the food from the kitchens and set up the staging area. They have dishwashers to do the heavy cleaning work, so we don't have to do the dishes, the bad grease work, clean the heavy grills and stuff. We set up the buffet, the chafing platters, the plates and silverware, the decoration and accessories. Then we pick up the food, drive it down in trucks, and set it on the buffet tables. When it's over, we take it away to the kitchen and they take care of it.

Nestor Kaono described his job as hard work, "It's a physical job. You're out there every day lifting heavy weights." But he preferred to stay in his department because, as a local, it suited him. "No, I just don't like the demanding of the guests. I wouldn't want to work in a department where I had more guest contact all the time. Then you're really serving them. You have to find a department that fits." Nestor Kaono described his department as very social. "We have fun hanging around with each other. Guys, they joke around, they laugh a lot." On their days off, co-workers socialized with each other and organized department barbecues, fishing trips, bowling, and golf tournaments.

Kevin, as noted earlier, wandered through a variety of local jobs he obtained through friendship connections, until he found employment at the Hula Club Towers. He was happy with his placement as a houseman. "Houseman is good 'cause you get to work hard, you makin' good money. For sure, it's one of the best paying jobs in the hotel." During the slow season, he either took off from work or tt'ed into other departments in the hotel. Kevin described his alternate labor: "Well, houseman is slow right now so what you call, I'm temporary transferred to engineering. . . . So me and my friend Herb is, you know, putting a new surface on a wall where there's usually a waterfall, up by the restaurant. So they closed the water off, and we're making it look a lot better. Sanding off all the old paint, working in salt water. You know wrist deep the whole day eight hours. You get kinda burnt out. And it's so dusty and salt water, it's just, whew, what a nightmare! It ain't really that bad, you know, [they] give you extra hours."

Like Nestor, Kevin felt some sense of camaraderie with his co-workers. But this was not universal to the whole department, nor did it extend beyond their working hours. He had heard about the extracurricular events at the Kahana Surf, but his department was not that social. He noticed a division between the born and the assimilated locals. Those who were born either on the mainland or the Hawaiian Islands socialized independently from those who were born abroad, despite their local acculturation (so he hung with the local clique, despite his early mainland years). Nevertheless, he found, like Jeffrey at the Pono Beach Spa, that there was a good bunch of local guys and a strong local culture in his department.

Jeffrey, as we noted earlier, got a job as a houseman at the Pono Beach Spa. He had moved to Honua with his girlfriend from another island to look for a job, after working at a honey factory back home for five years after high school graduation. His cousin Felix was living on Honua and working at the Pono Beach Spa, and they moved in with him at first. Felix helped Jeffrey get access to the Pono Beach Spa's job postings, and after working at a few unsatisfactory outside jobs in car rentals and fast food, he moved into the housemen department, doing setups for the banquets. A hard worker, he never slacked, and soon proved himself to his co-workers: "When I first started, all Tongans; I was working with all local Tongans [born locally of Tongan extraction]. And they kind of test you to see how strong you are. And they had me pushing stages up this hill just to see, it was a rainy day, and I was pushing these stages up. So I passed that test, but they're really nice, friendly people. They're strong, hardworking. I like working with them. A lot more hardworking than the local [born] Filipinos. Those guys been there the longest and they're the laziest guys I know." Within a year Jeffrey had moved halfway up the seniority list. Eager to work, he picked up a second job on his days off doing landscaping.

Banquet Servers

Sam, the Pono Beach Spa banquet server mentioned earlier, moved to Hawai'i following his Canadian high school friends. He described his career path:

> I started windsurfing in Canada. Just kind of as a summer activity, in high school. Then I got really interested in the sport, and I started going south to Oregon in the winter to surf there. After high school during summers I started going down to the Columbia river in Oregon, and I would spend my summers there windsurfing and teaching windsurfing, and then all my friends would end up going over to Hawai'i when I went back to school in Canada in the winter. And I always envied them and wanted to come to Hawai'i and live here and experience the lifestyle. And I never did. . . . I went to college. . . . I finished college and I worked for a company in marketing and sales and ended up moving to California. San Francisco, lived there for a couple of years. At some point in time I decided I didn't want to be doing what I was doing, and at that point I didn't really have anything to go to, I didn't have any money, I was around twenty-four, so I decided I would go to Hawai'i, just kind of on a whim. . . . One of the motivating factors for coming here originally was the windsurfing, and I was here for a couple of years and I worked in the hotel business.

Sam's path into banquets was typical. A seeker, he was drawn to Hawai'i by his interest in an extreme sport. His work became a means to further that end. Sam continued:

I ended up getting a job in a hotel and working the banquets, and I found that that was just a lot more pleasant of an atmosphere than a restaurant. You know, you didn't have to deal with the clientele in the same way and the stress level wasn't as good, but you could work in a seasonal manner in a sense that you could put in a really hard three or four or five months and save a lot of money and then be able to take off and do whatever you want. So I like the entrepreneurial feel to it and that I could make my money and then go do something else that I would enjoy.

Sam described his resort work aspiration:

At the time, when I first got in, I wanted to get into banquets, I knew that, but there was no position available, so I took whatever position that I could that was full-time. Because I knew that I wanted to get benefits and all of that. I knew that if I was full-time in one position in the hotel I could more easily get into a full-time position in another area, and a full-time position in banquets is pretty difficult to get, because they pay your benefits and you get a retirement plan, a 401(k), all those things. Whereas casual workforces don't get any of that. It's a certain stability too.

Carol, a forty-nine-year-old mainland haole, visited Honua for the first time when she was nineteen. "I was on my way to Fiji, and it was a stopover. It was only eighty bucks round trip, student standby." But instead of making it to Fiji, she got sidetracked and remained on Honua. "So I got off the plane and said 'This is great,' and hung out for the summer, went back, finished school, and then moved back here. I was in college. So, I just came here 'cause I always wanted to move to a tropical place, where the weather was good."

But she did not work in the resorts right away. She married, had two children, and became an elementary school teacher. Her husband left her when the second child was five months, and although he stayed on the island, she had to raise their children alone. To supplement her teaching salary, she started babysitting for guests' children in the resorts, where she could bring her own children along and not have to worry about childcare. From there she started working summers at the Ali'i beaches, teaching windsurfing and sailing to the guests. Eventually she found that she was making more money at the resorts than in the schools and cast around for day work in the resorts. She taught dance classes and took Pilates training, learned yoga and kickboxing. She wanted to do banquets right away, but she could not manage the regular evening hours when the children were young, and so she waited until her ex-husband took over a greater portion of the childcare when the youngsters were thirteen and fifteen. Carol never obtained full-time work at any resort but juggled casual banquet work at three different resorts: the Lei Gardens, the Hula Club Towers, and the Lukane Sands. "There's a whole troupe of people who work casual at all these resorts. They go up and down the strip, swinging to wherever has a function and needs them." There were a few times where Carol was offered the opportunity to upgrade her employment to part-time, but she turned it down, preferring to remain a casual: "I could work there as much as I want. I turned down part-time work. I'm top casual, but I, I don't want to *have* to work. Once you go part-time or you go full-time, you *have* to make those hours. You ha-, if the shifts are there, you *have* to work those shifts, in order to maintain your status. So I would rather be on casual on-call than have to commit." After thirteen years as a devoted casual, Carol had worked her way to the top of two resorts' seniority lists.

Ron grew up in Akron, Ohio, the son of two factory workers. He got his first part-time job at age fourteen, as a barback (bar busser) for the local chapter of the American Legion, and held it throughout high school. After graduation, he worked in a factory for five years, making good money, but decided that it did not seem "natural," and he did not want to follow his parents' career. Then he moved to Cleveland and went to bartending school, thinking that this would give him an opportunity to do something until he figured out what he wanted to do with himself. Ron got a job in a nightclub as soon as his schooling was completed, where he worked for six months, until he got the opportunity to lease and open his own bar. This lasted for a year and a half until he left his club and joined the Air Force. While in the service for five years, he tended bar at an Elks Club part-time. Ron then decided that the Air Force probably would not be his preferred career, so once again, he looked around for other alternatives. The next move was to Honua, and Ron explained his reasons for this move: "Probably the reason I came to Honua, more than, it wasn't just looking for a destination to work, it was more looking for a destination that I would like to be at. The ocean, the sun, the recreation. I play golf occasionally, I play tennis occasionally, I snorkel along, I dive occasionally, I might learn how to surf yet. And therefore, I had to work to stay here."

Ron thus represents another kind of seeker, one not so frenetically into extreme sports, one who moved to Hawai'i for the warm weather and lifestyle. Within the first week after his arrival, at age thirty-one, Ron got a job at the Hula Club Towers. Although he wanted work as a bartender, he recognized how difficult those jobs were to get, so he took work as a houseman, and ended up being the bar porter, doing the setups for the banquet bars. After a year, he had the opportunity to work as a bartender and worked in all the restaurants and bars in the Towers, from their fine dining establishment, to their pool bar, to their lobby bar overlooking the evening sunset. Ron described his progression into the banquet department:

> Basically I started at the bottom and I worked wherever anybody else didn't wanna work. I liked bartending all over the hotel better than being a banquet porter; I didn't like that at all. I mean it was a job, but it was not something I would've stayed at, for sure. But bartending was more what I had looked for and what I was accustomed to. I liked it. It was all part of, uh, progression to where I am now, as far as they call it, "paying your dues." I worked all the bars in the hotel, for quite a period of time before I worked, moved my way into banquet bartending, which is mainly all I do now.

Ron's job, which became full-time after the first five years, was supplemented by regular part-time work for fourteen years with the Air National Guard as a communications specialist, working on electronic communication equipment.

In the banquet department, Ron worked in a supervisory position, giving him the opportunity to earn more money than those who had been there longer. He explained the factors that led to this:

> Basically, I suppose maybe at thirty-three I was older than some of the other guys, I was used to having had my own bar and doing things that I'd done, assuming a lot of responsibility. So basically while I worked in the [lobby bar], the beverage manager at that time, who used to be the head bartender, knew that I could handle scheduling and responsibilities that other people might not necessarily wanna take care of, so I became his kinda unofficial assistant, and whenever he went on vacation or on his days off, I would take care of all the banquets, and there's a lot of paperwork involved and scheduling and things like that. And where the other guys wanted to come in and just work their shift, I was more probably able and willing to do the additional paperwork and spend a couple hours in non-bartending activities. So I took on supervisor responsibilities, and that was like, kind of more work, but along with it you got to tend the bar at the banquets.

At fifty-two years old, as the banquet bar supervisor, Ron claimed that he earned one of the highest salaries at the Hula Club Towers.

We see that for banquet servers, instrumental goals dominated their career placement, whereas the new immigrants made their decision to locate in stewarding for cultural and linguistic reasons, and the locals wound up as housemen due to their interpersonal connections.

The Work Experience

People's feelings about their resort work varied. Those who did not enjoy it moved on, while others who found it more suitable stayed. The highest turnover could be found in the banquet department, with moderate turnover at housemen, and a high degree of stability in stewarding.

Banquet Servers

Sam spoke highly about his work, claiming to be working where he most wanted. He discussed his initial feeling about his work:

> [Things] kind of clicked for me here. This was the first place I felt like I could really take care of myself. And I was able to get ahead. I felt like I could control my own destiny to a certain extent. When I was working for this company [back in California] I was in sales, I was 100-percent commission based, and there was a lot of pressure to perform. I was barely making ends meet. . . . Whereas when I was here, it was like I could put in eight hours and I knew I had $150 or $200, whatever. I could do that again and again. Or sixteen hours. And I could do it for three–four months. It was a lot of work, but then I could say I have $20,000 saved and I can do whatever the hell I want. I felt like I was in charge of my life. And I didn't ever feel that way before. That was a real attraction for me.

After a couple of years Sam married, and his wife wanted to move back to the mainland. They relocated to California, but things never quite worked out well for them there. He discussed their decision to return to Hawai'i and to resume their earlier lifestyle:

> We moved back with the intention of coming back here and getting ourselves set financially for a short period of time, like for six months. And we had two goals: one was to pay off my car, and Barbara's goal was to make enough money to go to New York for six months and study dance. Within three months we had that money made. It was easy. So it was,

okay, what can we do next? She was doing banquets full time then too. What's our next goal? Why don't we save for maybe an investment property on the mainland and we'll do this for another year or nine months. Within about a year, not even, like eight months, we had put that together. And so we bought an investment property here instead. And then it was kind of like, okay we did that, that was going pretty well. And we thought okay, we should buy a house. We can't afford to live up here, so let's buy an investment property that will generate some income and that will be our foray into real estate and that will be a good start. And so we did that, and after about nine months or a year, less than a year, we had the money to buy a house, so it was like, okay, well, so we did that. So now we've got the house and the condo and now we're cruising along, trying to figure out what we're going to do with our lives next.

Ron, the banquet bartender, also enjoyed his job. He compared it favorably to working in a nightclub, restaurant, or bar: "I've been at the Hula Club Towers twenty-one years. My daughters almost used to be embarrassed to tell all their friends that their dad was a bartender (*laughs*), but it's a very, it's a very good job for Hawai'i. They pay well. I'm working with people that are unusually happy, because they're all on vacation; this is a once-in-a-lifetime trip for almost everybody that I meet. For a bartender, I have a dream job. I don't have drunks; I have happy people on their best vacation of their life. And that's hard to beat."

But not everyone who worked as a banquet server found it as enjoyable as Ron, who readily admitted that the burnout rate for servers was greater than for banquet bartenders. One fifty-year-old female banquet server told us, "Tell people this is not a job for them; it's hot, it's sweaty, it's hard. They shouldn't do it. Tell them to do their art instead; they shouldn't work banquets."

Carol survived over the long haul by mixing her banquet serving with several different ways of earning money. In the beginning she moved into banquets occasionally, using them during the busy season to supplement her income. Then, after she quit her teaching job, she loaded on as many banquets during the season as she could and worked lightly during the off-season. Eventually she started trying to build up other businesses. She did dancing and dinner theater. She got into aerobics and sports rehabilitation. She became certified as a personal fitness trainer and built up a small clientele with whom she worked at local gyms. She taught aerobics and fitness classes at several Ali'i resorts. With all these other things going, Carol found the repetitive nature of banquet serving comforting. She explained:

Heh heh. Well, by the time I get to the hotel, I've already done two or three different jobs, and within those jobs, two or three different classes. I mean, I'm ready for (*laughs*) pretty mindless stuff. I think my co-workers though—I work with some *very* intelligent people, very talented people, and I do see a façade of them not really realizing their potential. And I think later on down in their life, they will say, y'know, "I went for that paycheck, that banquet paycheck, and I wish I'd, y'know, become a clothes designer," y'know, or built model cars, or, y'know what I mean? They don't, because a hotel does get demanding of your time, y'know. A lot of those functions are long hours and they're scattered, so a lot of times their sleep is scattered and everything else, that they don't have time to concentrate and really find their potential in where their real talents lie. But that's, I think, a cultural thing of the U.S. That a lot of people give up that inner inspiration, for a paycheck. For the money. And living here, it's important to people to live here. But the cost of living is expensive, so it's even more emphasized.

Stewards

While banquet workers appreciated their work for the way it enabled their lives, stewards talked about their feeling of accomplishment in the job and the sense of Filipino pride they felt for their whole departments. Santo stated:

There are mostly Filipinos working in this area. They can work longer than the local people here. If you hire the local people here, they are young guys, and when they get their paycheck they go out and party and then they get hung over and they don't show up the next day. The Filipinos, they are always thinking about their family, the future, sending money back to relatives in the Philippines, buying a house. They are willing to work longer hours. Young and strong is not better than old and reliable. . . . Asian people are hardworking and they always do the job. . . . Stewarding is the backbone of F&B [Food and Beverage]. We work with the cooks, we work with the chefs, we take care of everything. The employees are really happy here.

Agrifina had mixed feelings about working in stewarding. She preferred her days as a housekeeper because of the guest contact:

If you go out you meet all the people from other states, you visit them. I love that time to meet people. That's number one my hobby. I love to talk to people. I think that is the most I love about housekeeping. Because you know why? I can tell you, back in Punalua I get, two months our guests come, I try to remember that. I fall in love with them, all the family and the kids. They stay two months in our hotel. I just enjoy talking to them and then they enjoy talking to me too. So that's the most I always felt myself at work you know. I try my best to bring cleanliness for them to every day.

In stewarding, Agrifina spent most of her time in the back of the house, interacting with other women in stewarding, which she enjoyed. She had a large network of friends at the hotel. Yet she wouldn't think of transferring out of her department now. Once she had a job, she kept it. She, like Santo, prided herself and her people on their hard work.

You know what, Filipino people work so hard because they ambitious. I can say that because of my experience; for my property I work very hard. I so thankful because I can see how the working hard we do with my husband. Because I start, my husband been working very, very hard. We get full-time job and at the same time, we do the farm. But if you very, very you know work hard, and then you know how to do monies, you can be okay. . . . You know, my children used to be ashamed of me, work so hard in hotel and work in farm all night. They no understand. But now, they grow up, they go school in Las Vegas, we buy them model house [Agrifina's sixth house]. They proud of me now.

For Santo and Agrifina, as for others in their area, stewarding became a career job. The majority of the people with whom they worked would stay in their jobs until they retired.

Housemen

After two years as a houseman, Nestor was promoted to supervisor of his department. This meant that he was given full-time status, becoming the only full-time employee in a department of six. The rest were either part-time or casual, although everyone's hours increased to full-time during the busy seasons, January to June and August.

As the head, he was responsible for several extra duties. He made the schedules, ensuring that everyone got at least two to three days a week. "If you don't give them the two days they're going to find another job, that's the trick of making the schedules, you've got to take care of them, not just yourself . . .

they've got to take care of their family." He was also in charge of hiring and firing people. In choosing new people to hire, Nestor claimed that he noted no significant difference in the work ethic of different groups. His department had three [local] Tongans, a European, and a [local] haole. When he arrived at work, he checked his box to see what applications he received. "I pick up the applications I get. I don't know how they handle them in HR [Human Resources]. I don't get the applications from bell, valet, accounting. I don't get the immigrants wanting here. I get the people who have applied for houseman jobs." He then interviewed them, looking for their backgrounds ("what did they do before?") and their appearance ("do they have the right dress code for the interview?"). He found firing people an easy task. "People leave because they do something stupid. I don't think people will quit from working there. But they don't show up enough, and then you can't keep them."

Unlike the others in his department, Nestor interacted directly with supervisors from other departments and with outsiders. When groups booked their visits, their organizers, the "group handlers," came in a year in advance to meet with the people who would coordinate their visit. He regularly went to meetings where the head chef presented his ideas for the various banquet menus, and Nestor presented his diagrams and ideas for how he would set up and service the group. Nestor was very proud of his evaluations. "They have these rating sheets with evaluations going from one to five. So far I've been getting fives."

Nestor enjoyed his work and planned to stay. He made more money because he was a supervisor and had a good medical and pension plan: "A hotel job is a good job because of the benefits. I enjoy this work, and I've never thought of working in any other department." Nestor planned to remain in this job until he retired: "I know when I retire I'll be on the golf course and I'll be fishing. I think I'm going to make it to my retirement working here. That should be in my sixties."

Kevin originally chose the housemen department because of its seasonality. He could earn a good living and still find time for recreation:

KEVIN: Ya, when it's busy we're making like a thousand bucks a week. Who makes that kind of money? Like nobody does. You know, you can't work construction and make as much money as I make.

Q: But then it's not busy like that all year 'round.

KEVIN: Ah, but it's busy enough so you can put money aside. You can have nice things. And when it gets slow, hey you get to do all the things you like. You just watch your spending. You know, nobody wants to work hard, you know, that's why I got into houseman so I don't have to work year 'round. In my department the summer's slow and fishing is good in the summer time. So ya, I'll take three months off. . . . For the past four years I just collected unemployment and got to go fishing everyday.

In the beginning Kevin was very content with his work. One of the local girls working in the Pono Beach Spa commented on the way people in each of the three convention services departments seemed to prefer their own job over that of others: "It's the local way, I know 'cause I grew up here. Local guys, they find a place for themselves and they are satisfied to stay there. They have no ambition, they don't think about trying to make something of themselves, of trying to better their lot in life. That's not the local way. They are complacent."

After his first four years of work, however, the Hula Club Towers was sold, and the new owners started cracking down on the medical and retirement benefits they paid. They started strictly enforcing the hourly definitions of part- and full-time work. Even if people were hired at a full-time classification, if they failed to work a minimum of 1,560 hours a year, they would be demoted to part-time status. Individuals falling below 1,040 hours a year were bumped down to casual. Moving from full-time to part-time meant losing retirement benefits, but moving to casual meant losing health benefits.

In addition, moving down a classification meant losing seniority, which restricted both the choice of better shifts and the opportunity to work. For Kevin, with a wife and new child, this meant he could no longer afford to enjoy a summer vacation; he needed the hours. But when he tried to get them, he found this was difficult: "It's always, you know, you bust your ass when it's real busy. As soon as it gets slow they don't, you know. Oh nothing, we don't have nothing for ya. You know, it's either feast or famine." Kevin found this situation unfair and it angered him. "It's like when you hired me on you said I'm a full-time employee with full-time benefits. You don't have the work, now you know that's not my fault." He found himself competing with others, based on seniority, for seasonal work around the hotel.

Like Kevin, Jeffrey faced the seasonal lull in housemen employment at the Pono Beach Spa. During his early years in the resort, he eagerly sought all the work he could find, even taking additional jobs on his days off. During the summers he always tt'ed into other departments. But after a few years he began to feel resentful about the work he was asked to do there. Coming from the housemen department, he brought a strong work ethic, but he noticed that this was not pervasive. When he transferred into other departments, he noticed loafing. Managers of other departments asked for supplemental labor when they had the heaviest tasks to perform and stood by watching as he and his fellow housemen grunted over strenuous physical exertions. When tools or equipment ran out, the people in those departments sat around and did nothing; Jeffrey and his friends ran to local hardware stores to buy what they needed. On top of having to do the hardest work, Jeffrey began to feel resentful that he was doing work for which others were getting paid more, yet still making houseman scale:

> I don't mind doing tt into landscaping, but when you've got mason work, construction work, and then someone volunteers you for it, you should get more paid. You know? That's a project, that's a crew project. When you sign an application, it doesn't say for mason or build rock wall here. We're doing other jobs that isn't even on our contract to do. And that, that kind of aggravates me, you know? It kind of aggravates me a lot, because physically, it takes a lot out of you at the end of the day. . . . I've been getting back pain, major back pain, from doing a lot of carrying heavy trees, cuttings, just bending over a lot, carrying a lot of heavy things, and I'm only twenty-seven years old. That project stuff's been chasing me away from the landscaping. I enjoy landscaping, but when you have to do, when you feel like you're doing somebody else's job, you just don't feel right. You know? Because those guys are making $28 an hour, and we're making $12.75 an hour, you'd want that extra pay to do his job, you know?

As a result of his dissatisfaction with this exploitation, Jeffrey transferred permanently out of the houseman department into landscaping, which was not as seasonal.

Legitimating the Pay Scale

Stewards, housemen, and banquet servers all worked long hours, but this varied seasonally. Most held two full-time jobs, or a full-time job and other part-time jobs. Talking about stewards, Santo noted, "They work two to three jobs. They may work 11 to 7 here, say the graveyard shift, and work the morning shift somewhere else. On their day off they work someplace else." Jeffrey similarly described housemen's occupational patterns: "They work two jobs.

Housemen tend to have forty-hour weeks. They work more hours than servers, and they're usually scheduled like that. And most of them have two full-time jobs; a lot of them do, anyway. So a lot of these people are working eighty hours a week. And they don't get two months off a year. So they work a lot more, and as a result they're able to afford a home or do the things that they can do here, but I don't think it's quite as easy of a lifestyle."

When we asked Santo how many hours he slept, he replied: "More than some. At least four." Banquet servers logged long hours as well, but not for the entire year. Their busy times ebbed and flowed, giving them respites throughout the year. Function scheduling did not follow regular shifts but varied according to the specific event. They might find themselves working at odd hours that disturbed a regular sleep schedule. Sam noted: "My job is different because I work day and night. I work the 3:30 in the morning shift, at times during the winter. It messes up my body. And then the next day I'll work until 11 or 12 midnight, and then I'll get up and at 5 in the morning the next morning, and so my sleep patterns are all screwed up." We asked him how he adjusted to that and he replied, "You just deal with it. You take naps when you can. I definitely feel like I've been deprived this year of a certain amount of sleep."

Banquet servers seasonally worked overloads to get ahead. Sam held one full-time job and two casual jobs, more than he really wanted. He kept three jobs on the off chance that he might want to play golf, one of the benefits offered at the third resort that employed him. These three jobs kept the money coming in faster than he could plan for it. Santo, in contrast, just broke even working full-time. His salary structure was so poor that he earned considerably less. Santo talked about his stewarding pay scale compared to other possibilities: "These are the lowest-paid, hardest-working jobs in the hotel. But they pay well compared to country work. And office work gets the lowest pay. Outside by the sun gets more pay. But we get enough. Dishwashers get $12 an hour. Houseman work is more seasonal. With the tips they get paid more. It's a dollar an hour and some tip point more, but they don't work as steady. Not as many hours. Filipinos always like to work. It's not as good money, but at least we have jobs. Filipinos would rather work longer hours for less pay if it is steady than be paid more for seasonal work."

Agrifina said that she knew other Filipinos who had started their own businesses. At times during her life she had dreamed about opening her own restaurant ("If you get your own business maybe you're going to be rich"). But she backed away from that because she didn't want to come home after a full day of work and then have to worry. Working in a hotel enabled her to leave her job behind when she was finished. She reflected on why so many Filipino people stayed working for so long in the hotels at low pay: "Because that's the job, that's the job we can. I don't know if you aren't working for that same job what else we can do. We not, if you like to go work at another job, it's not that much. So the stewarding, or the hotel business, that's the open job you get. You know? I never graduate you know, in high school. But even in our department they have people they already teaching how many years, and they working for stewarding. So I guess you like the pay."

Agrifina accepted her salary and avoided dissatisfaction with its pay scale by avoiding comparisons to other departments: "I don't know how the people over here maybe different where I come from. I'm not the compare person. Their job is different from my job. And with my job I don't compare with them. But I think I compare with the one that has the same as my job. If he or she get more than me, then I would complain. So I don't compare with the waiter, the houseman; their money, they make more money, they're different."

Sam offered these reflections on his salary structure:

Generally a lot of back-of-the-house stuff is paid an hourly wage, and they don't have a part of the gratuities. They don't take part in the tip pool. Some of them do. Like houseman gets a percentage, but it's a very small percentage, much smaller proportion of the tips than the servers get. Because they do a smaller part of the job, even though they lift tables and chairs, it's fairly straightforward. They're not dealings with the guests, doing that kind of thing. So they do get a percentage, but it's not as big. And the stewards get an hourly wage, they don't get tipped at all.

At the Kahana Surf, Nestor discussed the salary structure:

Banquets get paid the highest of all the departments. We get tips, at least. Dishwashing [comparable to stewarding]—they get no tip. Dishwashing is a totally different department from banquets. Their base salary is a good $15. The housemen get a base salary of $11.50. The servers make a $6.00 base. But the servers get a large portion of the tip and we get some of the tip. In the end, it works out pretty even. The servers work less hours than we do, less than the dishwashers. But us houseman, we're happy with what we've got. We get higher hourly than they do, and more tip than the dishwashers. With our tip, that almost gives us $25 an hour.

When comparing the three jobs, Sam felt sanguine about the differential pay scale. His wife, Barbara, who also worked as a casual server, pointed out the heavy and physical nature of the housemen's work and the difficult and dirty nature of the stewards' work. She asserted that the unequal pay scale represented "racial factoring." Yet Sam brushed this aside, arguing: "Generally the job, the steward jobs, are usually foreigners that don't speak very good English, that wouldn't necessarily have opportunities other than that, because they either can't read or write properly, or they can't speak English to communicate very well. They would have trouble in that guest situation, one-on-one with the guest. So that's generally why the racial thing happens, it's based on education level and based on communication skills."

Sam expressed his belief that the high level of skills involved in speaking standard American justified banquet servers earning twice the salary of stewards. "I'm on the front lines with people. I'm constantly dealing with people and people's needs. You have tables that are assigned to you, and you have a buffet that you need to describe food to people and you need to describe where the restroom is, what they're eating, you need communication skills. And because they're affluent people, they expect a certain level of respect and courtesy and not some pidgin English." He felt comfortable with his position and his salary. At the same time, Santo legitimated the salary structure associated with his job by comparing it to other, less advantageous work. Office work was not as good because it paid worse, but work in the sun was harder. Stewarding represented the best work for the money, one that would hold him and his co-workers for the rest of their working lives.

Kevin was the only person with whom we spoke who expressed dissatisfaction with the salary structure and its inequality. He compared his houseman salary to the banquet servers:

KEVIN: I think it works out, um, you know. If they work as much hours they make more. Their tip pool, their tip rate is always just a few bucks more than ours. Sometimes five dollars more, you know. It's always a little higher. But we work more hours. So we get paid about the same.

Q: So they work less hours for the same money.

KEVIN: Right. Ya, and they don't work nearly as hard, too.

Q: How do you feel about the differences in the pay scales between departments?

KEVIN: Nobody likes that. You know, I don't like to see these banquet servers sitting down folding napkins. We have to set how many meetings and breakfast, you know. Lot of times I'll work, uh, like the morning crew shift. Well, I've worked everything. I've done everything from graveyard to morning shift. And uh, we'll be coming in working, you know, just like we don't know what Banquets has going on, so they'll just be kicking back. But we have a whole bunch of things going on. But they'll be there for their eight hours just folding napkins doing this and that. Yeah, we'll have a thousand things to do. And you know they're getting paid more than us. So like were kinda building the tip for them on those days. You know?

Q: So how come every time I ask people how they feel about that, everybody always says they feel great about it?

KEVIN: The pay differences? Like . . .

Q: [interrupt] Yeah, that's what I can never understand.

KEVIN I know. That's stupid to say that you feel great about it.

Q: Well, the wait staff people tell me, ah well, we deserve more money. 'Cause we have to do guest contact and, you know, we have superior language skills, and then the stewards all tell me,

KEVIN [interrupt] Ah, come on. Superior language? That's bullshit.

Q: Yeah. The stewards all tell me we don't mind, you know, working hard or doing less because we would rather have a job that's not seasonal and that's steady than make, than work less and make more money. So I kind of want to know how the housemen feel about it since they're kind of sandwiched in the middle?

KEVIN: Well, I'm just, I think we get by because, you know, we don't complain much, because we are getting a lot of money. You know, your back hurts all week, you get pain and you know. Nobody makes that kinda money, not policemen, not construction.

Kevin, notably one of the few housemen of mainland haole descent, expressed dissatisfaction with the stratification hierarchy of the pay scale. He pointed out that housemen, like servers, worked rotating shifts and had their sleep hours disrupted during the throes of group season. The work they did was as much or more physically demanding than the servers, and enabled the servers' work substantially. Unlike Santo, he did not prefer to work more hours just to have a steady paycheck coming in. He would rather not work, would rather go fishing. And unlike Agrifina, he did compare the work and the compensation among departments. But like the others, he did not challenge the inequality. He took his paycheck, was glad that he was making more money than people in other jobs, and went home.

These economic structures and their segregated racial base represent a strong bastion of institutionalized racism and explicitly stratified inequality. New immigrant workers were slotted into (and gladly accepted) the lowest strata of work. Their status as the relatively newest arrivals put them at the bottom of the hospitality pecking order, and the resorts gladly exploited their labor and dedicated service at low wages and poor conditions. Even so, the situation of these workers compared favorably to that of even newer immigrant groups from Micronesia and other places, whose only choices involved toiling outdoors in the agricultural industry. Newer immigrants could not manage even the clean, presentable appearance that the Filipino, Tongan, Chinese, and other resort employees had attained. Locals gladly ceded the jobs occupied by new immigrants to these groups, seeking employment in departments where their language skills and acculturation enabled them to work with haole co-workers (bell, valet, front desk, spa, beach and pool) and in better-paying houseman work that was still heavy but not as dirty. Here, they interacted with guests occasionally, were in view of guests frequently, but dealt mainly with one another. Haoles, at the top of the pyramid, still performed temporally shifting and somewhat physically demanding labor, but their efforts were more highly remunerated.[7]

Scholars have suggested that the stratification of workers in the service industry stems from employers' reliance on workers' demographic characteristics (race/ethnicity included) to assess their suitability for various service occupations, often using stereotypes as their best way of potentially anticipating workers' personality and behavior (Van Maanen and Kunda 1989; Woody 1989). Macdonald and Sirianni (1996, 14–15) have noted: "Even though discrimination in hiring, differential treatment, differential pay, and other forms of stratification exist in all labor markets, service occupations are the only ones in which the producer in some sense equals the product. In no other area of wage labor are the personal characteristics of the workers so strongly associated with the nature of work." Worker characteristics shape what is expected, not only by employers but by customers as well (Kirschenman and Neckerman 1991; Trentham and Larwood 1998). Research has shown that when there is a confluence of race and ethnicity in the "worker-customer dyad," interactions are friendlier, marked by more frequent verbal exchange and more smiling eye contact (McCormick and Kinloch 1986). Not only do salaries tend to rise and fall, then, depending on the demographic characteristics of workers filling the positions, but research has shown that customers are more likely to consider service more valuable if it is performed by demographically advantaged workers (Moss and Tilly 1996). Thus, white, middle-class banquet servers may indeed have more of value to offer resort employers than their language skills, making the service work they perform to guests worth the additional salary they earn.

Not only did these workers fit themselves within the system, but they also internalized a set of verbal rationalizations legitimating it. They legitimated the cultural differences in job preferences, they legitimated the class-based differences in aspiration, they legitimated the false consciousness associated with getting less pay for doing the hardest, dirtiest jobs, and they legitimated the importance of customer service as a means of stratifying income. As they offered these up, both to each other and to outsiders like us, they artfully constructed and perpetuated this system of differential economic opportunity structure and their places within it.

9

CAREERS IN PARADISE
Short-Term and Intermediate

We have already considered various factors that led the diverse types of workers to seek employment in the Ali'i resorts. In this chapter and the next, we explore why these workers remained in their jobs as well as what factors influenced them to terminate their resort employment. The analysis of resort careers is complex and requires the interweaving of several factors.[1] The first is demographic, as the length of time people are likely to remain working is influenced by the group into which they fall; seekers had different work and leisure patterns from managers, from locals, and from new immigrants. In these chapters we distinguish different types of workers' careers by their temporal length, ranging from short- to intermediate- to long-term. How each type of career is experienced over the course of its span varies, then, by the workers' demographic group and by the length of its duration. In this chapter we consider the short- and intermediate-term careers of Ali'i resort workers.

Short-Term (Youth) Experiences

Many of the Ali'i employees had a relatively short tenure in their jobs, lasting no more than two to three years.[2] Rarely did new immigrants stay for so few years, and management generally lasted longer as well, at least in the industry as a whole. We found the highest turnover among seekers and locals.

Seekers
Seekers varied in their commitment to the resorts, the Hawaiian Islands, and seeking as a value system and lifestyle. Some were passing through it as

a phase, while others made a longer-term investment. The least committed seekers were the short-timers, people who lived on Honua for relatively brief periods. *Time-outers* took breaks in their lives after high school, after college, or somewhere in between, to rediscover or refresh themselves, with the intention of shortly returning to the normative path (Hall and Lieber 1996).[3] People commonly took such breaks when they envisioned a traditional life in their future that would tie them to family and work, and they wanted to try something adventurous while they were young. Time-outs lasting a year or two were normatively accepted; pushing these temporal boundaries any longer could prove problematic, making it difficult to get back on track (Mannon 1997). Family members often alerted (or, more precisely, nagged) seekers that their "time was up," and that they should come home for more conventional jobs or schooling. Others sensed these boundaries themselves. For example, Emily, the recreation attendant from Tennessee whom we met in chapter 5, was just planning on a three-month time-out to Honua as a "cerebral break."

Transients were short-timers who strung together one time-out after another. Although their length of stay on Honua was similar to the time-outers, their experiential goals were grander in scope, putting them on the alternative track for longer. Many transients had a list of destinations that they desired to visit, experiences that they craved to reap. Recall Texan Luke, in the Lei Gardens beach and pool department, who had a checklist of places he wanted to go around the world.

Other transients visited various locations on the seeker circuit. Moving freely around the world, sometimes with buddies or more commonly alone, they were used to meeting new people, to making friends quickly. Paul, the Southerner in chapter 6, came to Honua on the advice of Mark, a Canadian he had met on an Alaskan fishing trawler. He contacted Mark's friends and arranged to crash with them when he arrived. Through them he found work as a bellman at the Pono Beach Spa. His group of friends consisted nearly entirely of this Canadian enclave.

Transients might or might not eventually return to the traditional track. Dana stepped off and never went back. From Nantucket, she graduated from college in 1982. She worked as a "ski bum" in Vail for ten years, pursuing outdoor sports: downhill and cross-country skiing, snowboarding, and snowshoeing. She earned around $100 a day, working nearly a hundred days a year, and cleaned houses during the summer, back home in Nantucket, where she was able to amass a nest egg. Finally tired of the ski scene, she received her fitness certification and moved to Honua. Although she had never been there, she remotely knew some friends of friends. Renting a room for $49 a night, she worked for a cleaning agency and as a casual in the banquet department at the Lukane Sands. She tt'ed into one of the restaurants, and from there found her way to a full-time job in recreation. Dana rode her mountain bike everywhere she went and was passionately interested in learning all the tropical sports. Vowing never to return to conventional life, a career seeker, she was the tannest individual we ever saw.

Seekers, especially the short-term employees, often made impulsive, unplanned decisions to move to Honua. Some were so impressed with the island during a two-week vacation that they went home, packed up and sold their things, and moved over, often with little money and no place to stay. Andrea came with her bicycle, $700, and no friends or employment prospects. Her sister, Ginny, joined a year later, bringing a bicycle and some cash, but at least she had a place to stay. Much to their chagrin, Ginny's former boyfriend, Burt, joined them the following year with $100 and no bicycle. He ended up sleeping in a tent in their backyard and hitchhiking to work, and he dejectedly left the island after four months.

Another common path to Honua involved following romance. Originally from Ohio, Joy met her boyfriend on the Internet. She came to Honua to meet him for a two-week vacation and they clicked. They became engaged. When we talked with her six months later, however, she was trying to get him to move back with her to the mainland. Janet took a Hawaiian vacation with her mother before a business-related move to Chicago and ran into a guy she used to date while taking a windsurfing lesson. When she returned to the mainland, he called her and asked if she'd like to give Honua a try. She moved out, lived with him a month, then married him. A year later they both run water activities subcontracts at two of the Ali'i resorts. But she was also reexamining her job prospects in Chicago. Seekers who moved to Honua without much thought often retreated back to the mainland after a moderately short interval.

Locals

As noted in chapter 3, locals held differing views of resort work, depending on their feelings toward tourists. One thing they all agreed on, however, was that the industry was lucrative, especially at the bottom-line positions. There were few other jobs that young locals could get with such little education and so few skills.[4] When locals began working at the Ali'i resorts, they were usually in awe of the grandeur of these properties. Seth, a fitness trainer at the Lukane Sands, described his initial feelings:

This was a job that I felt happy to get. I mean here is the Lukane Sands. I wouldn't have even dreamed of being able to step foot on the grounds much less work on it, you know. So I was all in awe with the immensity, the proportions of the resort. Of course, you know that fades over time, but I thought the first few weeks, gosh, I don't know if I'll ever be able to get over how impressive this place is, but I have. 'Cause you do, it's your workplace. It ceases to become the palace and the all-inspiring whatever it used to be. But I was just, you know, happy to get the job in the first place.

The fact that novice employees immediately earned the same amount of money as people who had been working there for years made it especially appealing to newcomers.

Victor, twenty-four, moved to Honua from the Philippines when he was fourteen and went through the public middle and high school system in the United States. Speaking broken English, he barely passed the language test at the Lei Gardens. His first job out of high school was doing landscaping for a small outfit, but he explained, "Everybody here know that the hotels is where the money is." He preferred to work for one of the large chains because then he could "go to other branches and get benefits."

Locals got their jobs through newspaper advertisements, through watching people they knew working in resorts and deciding to try it themselves, or through the assistance of resort-working friends. Once people had jobs in a resort they were privy to all the openings in other departments, and they could share this information. Many job openings thus never made it to the paper. This is how Felix from chapter 8 got his cousin Jeffrey a job at the Pono Beach Spa. Similarly, Grego, a twenty-one-year-old local who was born in the Marshall Islands but raised by his adopted father on Honua, was working in the meat department of a grocery store when he became friendly with one of his customers. A manager at the Hula Club Towers who always wore his slacks and aloha shirt when he went shopping, he asked one day if Grego wanted to work in the hotel. Grego explained: "I said yes, because I knew it was more money. The guy asked me what I wanted to do. I didn't know. I asked about meat jobs, but the guy said there were no openings there, so he gave me a list of all the different kinds of jobs and gave me fifteen minutes to decide. I picked recreation. And here I am now."

The paucity of other industries on the island let young locals with no clear aspirations slip easily into tourism work. Resort jobs were filled with other young people like themselves, and the atmosphere was highly social. They could meet people, make friends, and party.[5]

Locals who did not last long usually began with a *temporary orientation* toward their hotel employment.[6] They looked at their jobs as transitory, something to do while they were young, but which would not constitute their career. They "goofed off" while at work, frequently called in sick, and took a half-hearted attitude toward their performance. Alex, the hapa-haole at the Kahana Surf in his twenties who had been working there for a year and a half, described his thoughts about his future: "I plan to work here long enough to buy my own boat. I'm not looking to move up the ladder. I'm staying here to get a paycheck. I like interacting with tourists, with the guests. I like working in the hotel. It's beautiful. We have a good union. It's a good working environment with good pay. I am using it to build up money for my future career."

Temporarily oriented employees rejected management opportunities when these were offered, usually because they considered the additional hours and serious orientation required not worth the limited additional pay. Ken, a recreation attendant at the Lukane Sands, noted that supervisor jobs, the next level up, only paid one dollar an hour more and entailed a lot more responsibility. "It's like the first level of management, you know? For one dollar an hour is it worth having to write up all your friends and get everyone pissed at you? Not to mention having to stay late to fill out all the paperwork. No thanks, it isn't worth busting my balls getting nowhere."

Career Progression: Exiting

While low-level, relatively mindless jobs seemed enjoyable at first, people tended to lose enthusiasm for them. Ernie, a two-year recreation attendant at the Kahana Surf, talked about *burnout:*[7] "I like my job now in rec, but I couldn't endure past the burnout phase. I see the other people who have gotten burned out. They start to complain. They act rude to the guests. I don't want to get like that."

Exemplifying the epitome of burnout syndrome, Arika, a Norwegian-American activities desk employee at the Lukane Sands, sat at her station one day, a scowl completely framing her face, picking up and immediately hanging up the telephone every time it rang. She was fed up with talking to the guests. Roy, a local rec attendant, complained about the degrading nature of tourist service work. Seth, the fitness trainer at the Lukane Sands, talked about the exhaustion of doing emotional service labor for guests who were rude:

Q: So what do people get like when they start to get burned out here?
SETH: I think people are generally nice here. But I notice walking around in the hall that somebody is not as happy or expressive as you are, and

I'll say hello because I still remember Aloha service orientation. Say hello to your fellow co-workers, tell them hi. So I still remember that. But yeah, some days you just don't feel like being the hello, happy-go-lucky guy all of the time. It's hard to do that. I never really mentioned aloha, even though I grew up here, as often as I did the first day that I worked here. It's a local word that you use, but it wasn't used as often as I use it here. And mainly we are using it for the guests.

Q: You feel that the aloha is put on? Is that what you're saying?

SETH: In a sense, you are putting on your Lukane Sands face. You have to because it's not natural to be that happy all of the time; it just can't be. For some people it might be, but then you realize because some people treat you differently that might strike you if you're a happy person and you have a very expectant affluent FIT coming in and just giving you crap because that's just how their life is, you know they are wealthy but everything's just going wrong for them, that will probably stick in your head, embellish itself as a memory, and then you think some people just aren't happy, but look at what they have.

Burnouts soon left.

Locals and seekers who passed relatively quickly through the Ali'i resorts left in a variety of ways. Some who came from other places *moved back* home again. They returned to neighboring islands or to the mainland, often to jobs and lives they would have pursued had they not taken their Honua time-out. Tony, a kayak instructor from Tennessee, returned there to enter his father's tax preparation business. Ralph, a personal trainer, bought the thirty-six acres next to his father's two-hundred-acre ranch and began raising cattle. Nancy, a waitress, who had been an executive secretary in St. Louis, returned to that line of work. Ohua, who worked in room service, returned to her family's house on another island to work in her old preschool.

Others used the skills and connections they acquired in resort work to *move on* rather than moving back. Gabriela, the fitness professional, cut an album in Los Angeles and completed a successful European tour. She tapped into a network of people, many of whom were guests at the hotel, who worked in the entertainment industry to help her. Willy, a local aerobics instructor, got a referral from his spa director to a job in an exclusive Italian spa. After a year there, he moved to an Italian city and became a well-known aerobics instructor, dance choreographer, and drag personality, his dream of escaping the confines of Honua realized.

A certain number of short-term employees ended their jobs by being *fired*. Locals and seekers were often not heavily invested in their hotel careers and were fairly casual about following the rules. For example, Alex, the Kahana Surf rec employee, had a problem with time and had been suspended twice over time issues. Once he came in late, and another time he swiped the at-work time clock too soon after swiping onto the property (not allowing himself the time he legitimately needed to change into his work clothes). For each of these offenses he received a three-day suspension. One night when he stayed over at his girlfriend's house, he slept through the alarm and woke up at 7:30 a.m., the time he was supposed to be at work. "There's no getting around it," he said glumly. "I knew it was over after that."

Other offenses for which employees were fired included dress code violations (wearing sneakers with black Nike swooshes on them instead of all white as they had been repeatedly instructed, wearing sunglasses with gold trim instead of all plastic) and behavioral violations (drinking water in sight of the guests instead of retreating to a private location to do so, jumping into the pool when they thought no managers were around, trying to drop women's bathing suit tops with the water squirts, getting into fights with other employees, goofing off and fraternizing, taking showers in the employee locker rooms while on the clock). These ranged from minor offenses that employees considered "ticky-tack" to more serious infractions such as dating the teenage daughters of guests and giving away or selling pool passes to friends. Some employees, who had been "written up" more than once, took the proactive move of quitting before they were fired. Brad, a rec attendant at the Pono Beach Spa, explained his reasoning: "I need to get out of here anyway. That way I can go with a clean record, and if I want to come back all my violations are erased."

People with such short employment histories usually went on to other unskilled or semiskilled local jobs such as retail sales, restaurant service (hostessing and bussing), driving and delivery services, store stocking, clerical work, home and industrial cleaning, or employment in other aspects of the tourist industry, bouncing around from one job to the next.

Intermediate Resort Jobs

Another group of the Ali'i resort employees stayed working there for a span of longer than two to three years, remaining up to perhaps seven or eight years. These were people who survived getting cut for stupidity or careless behavior, and who did not just roll through on their way to somewhere else. They were people who began to take their jobs seriously, at least after a while.

Locals

Some locals looked immediately to the resorts as a *career* opportunity, since the hospitality industry was one of the few viable sources of large-scale employment on Honua, and it was cleaner and more pleasant than the plantation-style agricultural production, harvesting, processing, and canning that employed another large group of low-skilled and under-educated people. People who had gone to college, either on Honua or on another island, to get their degrees in fields that would be relevant to resort work such as information systems, recreational administration, or hotel and restaurant management were usually looking for careers as opposed to simple jobs. College degrees were relatively rare for locals, however, as the educational norm was to quit after high school. Koa got a bachelor's degree from the University of Hawai'i in the food and beverage unit of their hotel and restaurant management school but decided that he hated working in kitchens and got a job at the Pono Beach Spa in their beach and pool department. He worked there for a few years, and it was where we met him. When an opening came up in water features, he applied for and transferred into that department, where he had worked for three years when we ran into him again.

Hope, one of our students, worked in human relations at the Kahana Surf, then went back to school, part-time, at night, to complete her bachelor's degree in social and cultural studies, because she could see that her advancement opportunities in management would be restricted without this credential. After several years of working at the resort, the owner lured her away, with a raise and a promotion, to work for his wife and him in their private, family-owned hotel management corporation.

Other locals were *converted careerists*, who entered the Ali'i resorts without long-term career plans but after working there for a few years started thinking about what they wanted to do with their futures. Quite a few of these decided to turn their years of resort employment to best advantage by making a career out of a casual job. They shifted their attitudes and started trying to work their way up the occupational ladder into positions with greater pay and responsibility. Robby, a supervisor in the recreation department, talked about his future hopes: "I'm looking for a job where I can advance to the managerial level so that I can some day afford to buy a house and send my kids to school. There's a big gap between me and my employees in mindset, and between me and my managers in pay. . . . Some employees work hard, are responsible, and want to move up in the organization. Some just want a job at a pool so they can party and have fun." As these employees became immersed in hotel careers they shifted their focus from having fun to getting ahead. They advanced slowly, striving to show dedication and hard work.

Lauren Hali, the local girl from chapter 6 who started at the Lukane Sands as a recreation attendant and eventually worked her way up to manager of the beach and pool department, explained the progression of her attitude toward the resorts:

> I was born and raised here, but because I was smart I skipped ahead and graduated high school at sixteen. My first job was at the Sands in beach and pool. I was a rec attendant for a year and a third, but then I got promoted to supervisor. I did that for two years, applying all the time for assistant manager jobs. I got close to a lot that I didn't get, but I knew they were looking at me, because I kept going up in front of the interview panel. With the turnover here, I finally got an assistant manager position down here, in beach and pool. I have been thinking of going back to school, but with the baby it's hard. But I don't think that a degree in hotel and restaurant management is such an asset in a job like this. I have a girlfriend who's going for that, but I think my seniority will end up being more valuable. I think that by the time she gets out of school, I may already have a management position.

She categorized herself as someone who had moved into a careerist relationship with the hotel after starting out with a more temporary orientation. Leroy, a local boy who started working in the beach and pool department at the Hula Club Towers, began to think about his future after three years there. He had nowhere else to go, so he started applying for middle management positions. Like Lauren, he did not get the first several ones, but finally landed an assistant manager position in housekeeping. Other young people we knew who started in the beach and pool area, the gateway department for resort entry, ended up moving into more career-oriented positions at the front desk, laundry, guest services, the spa, and room service. They advanced slowly, striving to show dedication and hard work.

A third group of locals entered the Ali'i resorts with some kind of *specialized skill* that was suitable to resort work, and while they did not attempt to climb into the ranks of management, they stayed to further their careers in their chosen field. This was especially true for people in the spa department who had training and credentials in fitness, aerobics, massage, and facial or hair esthetics. Kaniho, the college-educated fitness trainer we met in chapter 3, is a good example of this, as his degree could have taken him into only a finite number of different types of organizations, from those geared toward working out to those in the broader health field. His interest in the resorts lay exclusively in the health and fitness area. Many of the exercise instructors and trainers also stayed for intermediate tenures, as these were the jobs for which their backgrounds and credentials qualified them. Locals also brought native expertise to resort entertainment, especially those who were brown-skinned (read: authentic looking) and could dance, sing, or play traditional Hawaiian songs. They got jobs in the cocktail lounges performing in the evenings or at the sunset hour.

　　Another group of locals, many of whom began their resort work in the beach and pool area, remained in these organizations and sought transfers after a few years into departments where they could *develop skills* that would foster future blue-collar work. Water features and engineering were popular with these individuals because they learned about operating and servicing heavy equipment such as pools, pool heating and filtration systems, air conditioning, plumbing, and a variety of assorted other machinery. These departments also offered the advantage of better pay and insulation from providing service to guests. These individuals focused on acquiring experience that would enhance their ability to promote themselves in the job market at a later time. Felix and Koa, two locals in their late twenties who worked in the Pono Beach Spa's water features department, discussed the mobility many locals envisioned in the hotel's blue-collar areas:

> KOA: Water features is a good department to be working in, better than rec, because we are learning a lot. We've learned about mechanical things from this job. Things like water stuff, pool maintenance, filtering systems, motors and engines, aquaculture. Some mechanics, some engineering. We could transfer these skills off-hotel to a lot of other blue collar, mechanical, masculine occupations. We could work for someone in air conditioning, pool maintenance, equipment or appliance repair, a lot of stuff. Or we could start our own small business. So this is a real stepping-stone job.
>
> Q: To what?
>
> FELIX: Engineering. Those guys make $16 and up an hour. That's a career job for many of those guys. They grow old in it, raise families in it, buy homes with it. Or if they get those skills from engineering, they can spin off into private work too.

Not all locals remained contented to continue working in the Ali'i resorts, even with a shift into greater career orientation. Mike Pinedo, the local manager of the Lukane Sands fitness department, a well-developed bodybuilder near thirty with several competitive titles to his credit, offered his analysis of three reasons local people left resort work. First, he explained, they got fed up with the bureaucratic politics and they could not take that anymore. "They look at the management above them and so many of them are young, under thirty, but they've got the educational credential, and that's necessary to the job. They have no experience and they don't know anything, but they're lording it over you."

Second, he continued, people left because they thought they could make more money elsewhere. "But they can't. You can work in a store and make $8 or $9 an hour, but you could be working the front desk here and making $14 an hour. The pay is better at the resorts than anywhere else on the island. But like Seth—he's getting burned out. He expects that with his education and his knowledge the trainings should just come rolling in to him without his going to have to go out and prospect for them. So then he will leave to go elsewhere and will have thrown two years of good experience here down the toilet."

Seth, the most evenly proportioned trainer in the Lukane Sands gym, also grew up on Honua. He echoed Mike Pinedo's point that with his credentials, he aspired toward a salaried career where he could both make a better income and earn greater respect from his employer. While he felt he was learning things at the Sands, he felt stalled professionally. Looking around, he saw few opportunities on the Islands to attain these goals. He wrestled with the idea of leaving Hawai'i to find the right career opportunity, and staying on Hawai'i where he loved the lifestyle and wanted to raise his family, ensconced in the Hawaiian cultural traditions. Seth articulated his conflict, "I understand that if I need to make money in this type of world that we live in, I might have to leave this relaxed-type atmosphere just like I did for school and make the money that I need to and eventually move back here." Seth eventually left to become a firefighter.

Ironically, Mike Pinedo himself echoed Seth's sentiment a little over six months later, emailing us to say: "I have been doing a lotta thinking. I think I may want to change my job, you know, for something a little more higher paying. I'm very tired of having a higher education and not getting compensated for it. So we will see, but I will keep in touch, one way or another. Things are going good in general, but I would rather have more gratification for my output." Mike's and Seth's situations both illustrated a critical difficulty faced by Hawaiian locals who wanted to stay on-island: the limited scope of career opportunities for educated and credentialed people.

Mike continued with his third reason he believed people left resort work:

to do nothing. He explained: "I spoke to Sally [a former trainer] today. When she left here she was going to start her own private training business with her own clients, working out of [a local gym]. But now she's quit that and is a full-time mom and sits on the couch all day long eating Oreo Lights."

A fourth reason we might add to Mike's three is that people leave resort work after an intermediate span of time because of the physical demands of their jobs. Both Jeffrey from the Pono Beach Spa and Kevin from the Hula Club Towers discussed how their work as housemen was causing them to develop serious back ailments. Neither of them expected to stay in these jobs for much longer. Bruce, the local bellman at the Lei Gardens, talked about the life expectancy in his department: "This job takes a toll on me and my knees. Lifting heavy bags as you get older is hard. Having to walk six miles every day, all over the hotel, is hard. I know of one sixty-year-old bellman in [another Hawaiian resort area], but most of the people here, they can't last that long. The oldest guys in this department are in their forties."

When locals left resort employment after an intermediate time span, they were usually ready to leave adolescent "social" jobs behind and look for adult work. A variety of occupations constituted what locals considered "real" jobs. Primary on this list was entrepreneurial work, where former employees set up their own independent businesses. Teresita, the aerobics instructor at the Lukane Sands, gave up her full-time job as the supervisor of the fitness classes to start her own gym. With a backer, she rented space, bought exercise equipment, and catered to a clientele of locals and second-home haoles. For two years she continued to teach some classes at the Lukane Sands, needing a source of income and a fallback job in case her gym flopped. But she grew weary of the politics in the fitness area, and eventually she felt her gym was doing well enough to quit entirely.

Pua, the local-born wife of Kevin, the houseman at the Hula Club Towers, worked in the hair salon at the Hula Club Towers, where he had met her ("I just walked by and saw her and I knew that was going to be my girl"). She was in the process of establishing her own hair business on the side (focusing particularly on weddings), while still working some days at the resort. Kevin talked about her independent business:

Q: Do you think she'll be in this [resort] job for a long time?
KEVIN: Oh, she'll probably leave for her own business. She awesome, she can do hair and makeup and she makes, she makes, you wouldn't believe what kind of money she makes. She makes more than me, and she only works two days a week.

Q: Really?

KEVIN: Yeah, really. Yeah, crazy. When she busy she brings home a thousand dollars a day.

Q: Really?

KEVIN: Ya, doing brides, braiding hair. Oh yeah, insane. Ya, she worked for four days last week, she brought home 2,900. And what kind of work did she do? Put on some makeup and braided some hairdos and you know. She gets a wedding and then she does the hair of the entire bridal party. It's a special occasion and everybody is in a good mood, so it's a lot of fun to do. She had to cut back on the number of days she worked in the Towers to do her independent side business.

Mike, the manager of the Lukane Sands fitness department, also started a side business that he hoped to move into one day. With a partner who minded the store during his hours working at the Sands, he opened a supplement (vitamins and other health products) outlet that he hoped to one day grow into a chain of stores with franchises, a Web site, promotional materials, and events. He placed a high importance on the value of entrepreneurial work in the Hawaiian Islands. "I'm teaching my kids to be entrepreneurs. It's the most important thing here—more important than college." He talked about his future in the resort:

> I like working at the Sands because of the interesting guests I meet and the people I work with. I talk to guests a lot in the gym and give people nutritional and supplement advice. I met the guy who manufactures the Champion line of supplements at the Sands. People come in there, say they like me, they like the energy that I put out, and they want to help me be successful. So I think I will stay there to meet more people until I find enough of the right people to help me achieve my dreams . . . I see myself in an intermediate resort career. I won't stay longer; I'm not like those Filipino housekeepers who are so happy and grateful to have the job and a free lunch every day that they will work here until the day they die.

Like these others, Felix was in the process of establishing a pool cleaning business on the side, Brian was starting a commercial cleaning business, and Matt was dabbling in a travel business booking package tours for locals to Las Vegas.[8]

A second "real" job option was to get work with the county. These coveted jobs often required local connections. Work as firefighters, police officers, lifeguards, road repair crews, and clerical staff, for instance, were highly prized for the good medical and retirement benefits and because of the relaxed work ethic.

Finally, many women left resort work to marry and have children. Deedy, the pool waitress at the Lukane Sands, started cutting her shifts back after her first child and quit entirely after the second. Married to a local, she kept the books for his thriving, independent pool maintenance business. Tammy, a concierge at the Hula Club Towers, left to go back to college to get her Montessori credential and to work in a school so she could be closer to her daughter.

Seekers

Intermediate seekers committed for mid-length time frames. Settling in Honua for a while, they eventually returned to the mainland. Some came over as *mid-termers,* with the express intention of only staying for a mid-length period. Brianna, an esthetician at the Pono Beach Spa, came to Honua with her husband Steve after they graduated from college.[9] He operated a mail-order business over the Internet, so he had mobility about where he could locate. They had saved for over a year to make the trip and planned on enjoying themselves while they were young on this warm, tropical island. While there, they tried not to work too hard and to enjoy hiking, biking, and entertaining their family and friends who came to visit. At the end of three years, their intended stay, they returned to the mainland to settle down and to have a family closer to home.

Some intermediate temps were just *extended time-outers* who had lengthened their stay, leaving them drifting "temporarily permanently" until something better came along. Hank and Susie had planned on staying for a short-term period but kept extending their visit. They planned on only being in Hawai'i for two years, but they ended up living there for four. Periodically, during this time, they gave notice at their jobs that they planned to return to the mainland. But each time something intervened to change their minds. Once, the people for whom they were caretaking begged them to stay long enough for them to find replacement tenants. Another time, things were tight in one of their departments and their manager asked them to stay. They even got as far as quitting both of their jobs and had to find new ones when they changed their minds again.

Some intermediates were *failed permanents,* who had planned to relocate to Honua forever but became disabused of this notion after living there. One group grew dissatisfied with the Islands because of the relaxed, hedonistic, atmosphere. They found the local culture too devoid of goals and drive. Others, like Trevor in chapter 5, complained that "every night was Friday night," and that the leisure and recreation lifestyle precluded intellectual engagement.

Come-and-goers, another group of intermediate seekers, stayed longer than mid-length temps, establishing themselves for five to ten years as residents. Many of these individuals were pushed out by factors they did not like such as the high cost of living, the weak educational systems, or by "island fever," a sense of being confined by the limited options on the island. Others were pulled back home by factors calling them from the mainland, such as crises or needs in their families. Colin, a bellman at the Lei Gardens in his early thirties from Montana, had been living on Honua for five years. He considered his future prospects: "My wife and my original plan was to stay for two years, but we liked it so much we stayed. We just had a baby girl. She works as a waitress in the [pool] bar. We don't know if we'll stay or go back. We miss our families. We go back once a year and the families come out once a year, but that may not be enough. We are also concerned about the school system. Once our kid gets to be school age, I think we might go back."

Some seekers who had planned on staying on Honua and working in the resorts were unable to do so. Barry, the bell captain at the Lukane Sands, had been planning on living on Honua and working at the Sands, but he got fired. One day he took home a glass ashtray, a knick-knack brought by a group to be given as an amenity to their members, that he thought was an extra. When management asked about it he said, "Oh yes, I have it, do you want it back?" They said yes, so he brought it in the next day. They never said anything to him about it, but a week later they fired him for stealing. Dennis, one of his closest friends in bell, said that if the department had a union contract, Barry would have gotten only a write-up, but with no contract, they could fire people "on a dime for no cause." Dennis subsequently became motivated to mobilize people for the union.

Barry then got a job at the Akaha Golf Course as an attendant. Larry Caplan, his former department manager, said of him, "He's working over at the course doing tee times and cleaning clubs. He makes good money. He makes a ton of cash in gratuity, he plays golf for free, he lives the lifestyle he wants, he pays his mortgage, and he's happy." Other intermediate-length seekers who would have preferred to stay but who got fired included RJ, who failed a drug test, and David, the Pono Beach Spa banquet server, who got fired in a banquet department drug-dealing scandal.

Like locals, some intermediate-length seekers *burned out* on their jobs. Camille, the Kahana Surf dive instructor, got tired of diving. "I'm doing the scuba, but I'm so over it. I wanted to work on a boat, but now I realize that I don't have to do that either. I can get out of the water." Deedy, the Lukane Sands pool waitress, explained:

I've been doing this job for seven and a half years now. I'm nearly thirty; it doesn't have the excitement and fun that it did. You see those new kids, they're bopping all over the deck, full of enthusiasm, but after all these years of bending down, carrying the heavy trays, I'm burnt out. And people can be so mean. Sometimes by the end of the day I'm so overloaded that I forget their drink orders and they have no sympathy or understanding for what I'm going through. And people are so dirty. They throw their trash down on the ground right in front of me, and I'm thinking, who do you think is going to have to pick that up? I'd be happy to put it on my tray, sure, but they throw it on the ground right in front of me and step on it. So I'm burned out on the guests too.

Deedy quit before the year was out.

Paul, a seeker working landscaping at the Kahana Surf, was also getting tired of his job. When he first started, he had been highly enthusiastic about his work. He loved the beautiful surroundings and working outdoors in the sun. But after five years his attitude shifted: "I'm thirty-four now, and my priorities are different. I'm trying to save money. In the past I was always saving up for some snowboard vacation. Now I want to move back to the mainland. I'm bored with this work. I want to do something more interesting, maybe use my artistic talent. I think five years is about as much as you can work a mindless job like this without burning out."

The *paradise relocators,* those seekers who moved to Hawai'i and settled there, took a final intermediate path out of resort work. Many of these people drifted into local patterns. So, like the locals, they looked to get out of resort work after an intermediate period by establishing their own businesses. Ann left the Lukane Sands spa for her own independent massage therapist practice. Jennifer left the Pono Beach Spa hair salon for her own weddings hair business. Kristy left a career where she originally worked at the Lukane Sands in beach and pool, and then did several more years at the Pono Beach Spa in their poolside restaurant, first as a hostess and then as a waitress, to start a restaurant with her husband. Six days a week you could find him cooking and her hostessing there.

New Immigrants

Few new immigrants abandoned the hospitality industry once they had entered it. In fact, new immigrants rarely left any job they obtained. As a group they were ideal workers who could be counted on for the duration of their working lives. But occasionally life changes led new immigrants to change jobs. When they did, they usually stayed within the same general industry. Agrifina, for instance, left the pineapple business only when the company closed down, and left her first jobs in the resort industry only when she decided to move to another island.

Santo Duque moved, over the course of his career, from the Royal Hawaiian to the [large chain hotel], to the Pono Beach Spa, but he did not make these moves lightly. His last job change, from the chain to the Pono Beach Spa, was occasioned by his family's need for a larger house. Only by quitting his job could he access the funds in his profit-sharing plan that he needed to build an extension onto his father's house for his wife and himself. He could have bought a new house without liquidating these funds, but he deferred to his parents' wishes that he remain living with them: "My dad said, 'don't build new house; stay with your family to save.' I was going to buy a new house. But the Filipino way is to stay together. So my wife and I ended up living with my Dad and Mom." When the GM of the chain found out that Santo had quit only to access his profit-sharing funds, he twice called him personally to beg him to stay, assuring him that he could have figured out a way to get him this money. But by that time Santo had accepted the new job at the Pono Beach Spa and he felt obliged to take it.

Favi, the housekeeper at the Kahana Surf, worked first as a housekeeper for a condominium complex for thirteen years. But when they had a management change, she felt that the new manager treated her poorly. She saw a job open at the Kahana Surf and moved over there. She expected to remain at this job for the foreseeable future.[10]

Management

As we saw in chapter 5, mainland haoles working management careers moved around considerably. Yet despite their frequent relocations, they tended to remain within the hospitality industry for many years. While some who tried out this line of work left it right away, once they recognized the hours expected and the pay scale, most who lasted past the six-month mark stayed for at least an intermediate period of time.

Some who spiraled out after an intermediate stay were those working their way up the ladder but who *burned out early*. Ben Masters, a middle-level manager in catering and banquet services at the Lei Gardens, had wanted to get out for a long time, but could not bring himself to do it. He could not stand the long hours and grueling day-after-day resort routine. But the money was good, and what he called the "accoutrements" or "trappings" were excellent. He loved the location and the environment in the Ali'i resorts and on Honua. By the end of his career he was making about $55,000 annually and had years invested in the occupation. Eventually, he went to a support group for help to get out of the industry. He described it as some kind of "realize your dreams" group. When that did not work, he got into nontraditional therapy and decided that was what he wanted to do with his future. But he did not go cold turkey. He started taking intensive weekend seminars in Santa Barbara every other weekend to get certification while he was still working. Only when he was far enough into it that he could see his new career did he quit.

Others who lasted no longer than intermediate length exited for *family-related* reasons. Elizabeth Direnzo, the manager of the Sunset dining room at the Kahana Surf, confirmed how difficult she found it to leave resort management. She had begun her career working for a prestigious chain and moved through their executive food and beverage training program. There, she met her husband, who worked as the executive chef at the Kahana Surf. Together, they successfully struggled to manage a food and beverage resort dual career. But after the birth of their first child, she extricated herself from the business, noting: "Without him [her child] I flat out wouldn't have been able to get out. It would have been too hard. And when I go back to work, I'm not getting back into this." She alluded to a friend of hers, Sandra, who had worked for many years as an executive secretary for various upper-level managers at the Kahana Surf. "She quit to get into selling cars. She needs to make more money to support her child."

While many people in management talked about getting off the corporate merry-go-round and *going local* (following the local pattern), few did so. Larry Caplan, who fell in love with Honua after taking up surfing and told us once that he was getting off the management track, saying that "it would take a crowbar to pry me out of here," could not quit. When he was fired from the Lukane Sands, in a post–September 11 flurry of cost cutting, he tried to find transient work that would anchor him to his home base.

Many people pointed to Terry Holland as the successful example of prioritizing life and family over career.[11] Terry rose through the ranks at the Hula Club Towers in the food and beverage department from being the DJ at the nightclub, to managing the nightclub, to moving into middle management in the catering and convention services area, to becoming the assistant director of food and beverage. When the Hula Club Towers underwent a change of ownership the new company tried to streamline management positions and bring in some of their own people from the mainland. To move Terry out of his management position, they offered him the job of banquet captain with the highest seniority. Although this offered a better salary, it represented a move off the management track. At that time Terry weighed his options. He could have turned it down and looked for a management job elsewhere, which he was confident he could have found. But he had an ex-wife living nearby with whom he shared a nine-year-old son, and the three of them were very close. He explained the basis of his decision:

> I came home one evening and Bobby [his son] said, "Dad, how come I don't see you anymore? How come you're always working?" This woke me up and gave me the realization that I was letting the important things in life pass me by. Since things didn't work out with Teresita, I want to make sure that they work out with Bobby. I guess we may have let things slide a little too much with Bobby's schoolwork last year, and I want to make sure that we stay on top of it this year. We want to make sure he gets a good education, and we want him to go to college.

Terry therefore accepted the banquet position and supplemented this with independent work as a DJ and emcee at corporate functions around the Islands. Six months of the year he was booked solid at the Towers, and the other six months he spent quality time with Bobby, who often traveled with him on weekends to his functions. He reflected on his decision: "I know that if the hotel hadn't sold I would have made it to the head of F&B by now, but it did, and that's the breaks. So this time I made my break. When the hotel isn't busy, I don't go to work, and I spend it with my kid. And I'll never have to move away from him now."

Finally, some resort managers got *fired* and had to leave during the intermediate time span. Melody, the assistant manager of beach and pool at the Pono Beach Spa, was terminated when she was caught getting a manicure and massage in the spa for free on company time. People speculated that if the upper management had liked her better, she might have survived this incident. Shortly after that, her boss, Daniel McLeod, the beach and pool manager, was dismissed as well. The word was that he was too "old-school," that he could not say the hard "no" to guests who complained, and was perennially "comping" people and costing the company too much. We later heard that he surfaced in Las Vegas as part-owner of a sunglasses concern, actually selling sunglasses himself (a step down). Few people wept at his loss either. But other, more pop-ular people hit the chopping block as well. Managers who refused transfers into different departments in the resorts were often released. The merry-go-round in the top positions was legendary. Fired General Managers often found it hard to get jobs they really liked, and sat at home in between jobs for months. Thus, although GM jobs were coveted, they came with a high degree of risk.

Short- and intermediate-term resort careers represent particular types of le-gitimate, organizational careers, since they are so heavily governed by several structural factors. Pay scales were fixed in each department, so that new em-ployees immediately earned the same salary as individuals there for years. This attracted and benefited young people, short-term workers who could move right into a job and earn the top wage. At the same time it disadvantaged in-termediate-term employees, whose cost of living rose while their paycheck did not. Resort employment therefore became less rewarding financially, the longer people stayed on the job.

Compensating for this was the presence of seniority hierarchies that re-warded longevity. Once people were hired, they were placed on the seniority list and began to work their way up the ladder. Separate seniority lists existed within each employment category for full-time, part-time, and casual work-ers. Shifting job status meant moving to the bottom rung of the list all over again. Degrees of seniority gave employees greater choice about the hours and days they worked, offering stability over the capricious whims of flexible scheduling. At the same time, seniority hierarchies accorded no significance to merit. Employees' competence, work ethic, job performance, and overall talent had little to no effect on their choice of shifts or pay. This discouraged responsiveness to the needs of both guests and management. Line employees who considered turning to management as a career were often discouraged by their initial experiences, as supervisor positions, the lowest managerial rank, offered little more and demanded significantly longer hours, bringing with it alienation from the camaraderie of their former work cohort. What this cre-ated in the Ali'i resorts was a group of companies that encouraged a high rate of turnover, a low level of organizational loyalty, employee disinterest in ca-reer advancement, and, aside from the tipping jobs, a moderately rote attitude toward guest service.

10

CAREERS IN PARADISE
Long-Term

Long-term Ali'i employees, who made their careers working in resorts, formed the backbone of these organizations. Many began as youthful workers and managed to last beyond the early, partying years to forge serious, adult jobs. As these employees aged, the change in their lifestyles resulted in a shift in their orientations and values. In this chapter, we examine the long-term employment patterns of locals, seekers, new immigrants, and management who made a commitment to resort work as a way of life. At the same time, we note that the Ali'i resorts, like many others, had employment patterns that affected people's likelihood of advancing, and hence remaining at work there. We therefore take into consideration the demographic factors of age, race, and gender as they influence workers' careers. We look at the possible glass ceilings characterizing resort careers as well as the working patterns of long-term resort careerists.

Age, Race, and Gender

Many current and former Ali'i employees alleged that these resorts, and possibly hotels more broadly, were marked by workplace environments and institutional barriers to advancement that favored youths, whites, and men. Studies of organizations have suggested that informal glass ceilings for women and people of color accrue under certain conditions. Factors that may specifically inhibit the advancement of these two groups include short job ladders (with nowhere to advance);[1] informal, ascriptive promotion criteria (rather than well-specified, achievable standards);[2] ghettoization and segregation;[3] and previous instances of lagging promotion.[4] Uncomfortable workplace cultures and glass ceilings encouraged women, people of color, and older people, particularly in the management ranks, to leave their jobs over the course of intermediate and longer-term stays.

Race

Since people of color in the Hawaiian Islands constituted a much larger percentage of the population than in the rest of the United States, they might be expected to hold more management positions than at mainland hotels, where their numbers were notoriously low.[5] While we did find more racial and ethnic diversity among the Ali'i resort management than on the mainland, it was not nearly commensurate with the percentage of people of color living in the Islands or employed in these resorts. People of color in the Ali'i resorts tended to be largely found at the line employee bottom level and in the middle management ranks. The number who made it to the executive level was very small.[6] Chad Nakamura, the executive director of food and beverage at the Pono Beach Spa, a large national chain hotel, noted that he was the only local on the executive council at his hotel.

In contrast, some of the other Ali'i resorts that were independents, small-to-mid-sized national chains, or Hawaiian-based chains (they all shifted ownership and management frequently) had a greater representation of people of color in their upper echelons. During the years the Lei Gardens was a Hawaiian chain hotel, it had many locals on its executive council; the others had somewhat fewer local executives. Over the near decade of our research, with each resort averaging a new general manager every year and a half to two years, only one of the five Ali'i resorts ever employed a local general manager. This individual had left the Islands to get his education and advance through his resort career and returned with solid credentials. People of diverse race and ethnicity worked, as noted in chapter 3, in an abundance of different departments around the resorts, however, and were not ghettoized into a few, limited departments.

Many locals were held back in their career advancement by their lack of education. Going directly from high school into the hotels, they could move up only so far before they found that their lack of a college degree stopped them. While resort management held that this was a main reason people of color were passed over in their advancement, locals regarded this as a convenient rationalization for discrimination. Hope, the local girl who worked at the human relations department of the Kahana Surf, offered her view on the matter: "*Prejudice* is the main reason so few local people are in management. Haoles think they are not smart enough, can't handle the job. They think it looks aesthetically better to have a white person in that job than a non-haole. More Caucasian people have *degrees,* so they use that as their *excuse.*"

Another reason cited by management to explain why people of color were often passed over for promotion was their unwillingness to relocate, a core feature of the management career.[7] Edward Bacon, the Lukane Sands senior director of the front office area, in talking about his reservations manager, noted the frustration of many local hotel careerists: "Take Tia [Ke'ahi], for example. She's a local girl who's climbed through the ranks. She had no hotel training or interest in the beginning. But she's done every job, knows how everything works, and was promoted to manager because of her performance. She was a local lifer who got into a hotel career. One day she wants to take over the whole reservations department. But it's not going to happen. Her career climb is slow. It bugs her a bit, as far as career growth, but not enough to leave. Most locals are not interested in leaving Hawai'i."

Tia's stalled career may have been influenced by her race/ethnicity, her gender, and/or the slow pace of her advancement. Staying in one job for a long time, without a continuing upward trajectory, signified to management that she was not a fast tracker for promotions, was not willing to do what it took to move up in the company. While people of color knew management most often blamed their lack of geographic mobility and lack of education for dampening their career potential, many recognized other structural racial barriers to their upward advancement. George Clark, the Lukane Sands deputy director, attributed managers' inexperience and lack of comfort in dealing with racial issues as the cause of some inequities in upward mobility for people of color:

> It can be very unfair. You can see a lot of really good local people who work really hard who should be placed in higher capacities, that have been passed by because their department head or their division head didn't have the spine that it took to step up to the plate and say this is the right individual for this position. Because they're too afraid of offending someone, or they're afraid someone is going to play the race card on them, or it's a union department and they're going to pay hell with the union trying to alter this, and it's not worth the battle. They don't want to deal with the problem and they don't want to inherit it or alter it or look as if they are racist about it.

Local people who felt that they had been discriminated against occasionally grumbled about it and had resentment but rarely did anything openly combative. Some who did were quietly terminated.

Yet, as we note in chapter 2, during the period of our research the Lukane Sands was sued for race discrimination by one of their employees. Although he was unsuccessful in winning his case, James, a cook in the employees' cafeteria, alleged that he had been repeatedly passed over for promotion. An African-American reared in the South, James finished high school and put himself through electronics trade school by cooking in various downtown and hotel restaurants. Hoping to escape the sweaty, greasy atmosphere of the kitchen, he moved to waiting tables in a hotel restaurant, which he enjoyed. From there he was recruited to work for the [medium-sized chain] hotel as a waiter in their fine dining establishment.

After several years, one of the guests at the restaurant offered him a job as his personal chef in Los Angeles, and James immediately took advantage of this opportunity ("So this is more enhancing to me, because now, instead of a hotel or a restaurant kind of a setting, it's all mine. I'm kind of like the chef of the house, more close up personal responsibility.") But his patron had a downturn after a few years, and James took a job at [a boutique hotel] in Los Angeles as a room service waiter. While there, James met a girl from Honua, got married, had kids, and moved to Hawai'i. For his first ten years on Honua, James worked as a cook for [a large chain] and was then hired by the Lukane Sands when it opened. He cooked for a number of the Sands' restaurants, by the pool, in the main kitchen, and finally wound up in the employees' cafeteria as the head cook. While trying to avoid specifically discussing his case since it was under litigation, he mentioned:

A lot of times, where you think that you are qualified, most qualified, or should get that job, it's who you are or who's next in line. I've seen 'em go and get cousins from, you know, out of town. On a race subject, I've seen a particular hotel get, uh, young white males from the mainland, and use the hotels here as a per se training camp to get 'em trained in different steps of management from, you know, first management to middle management, to senior manager, getting toward director. And then they can send 'em back to some of the other, you know, places or hotels or whatever, as a set manager that already know how. So they can use this area, which is really nice, as a training ground for their preferred people.

James noted, then, the informal, often ascriptive criteria his resort used for promotion: a panel of executive committee members, who could easily be swayed by personalistic factors or connections, made raises, hiring, and promotion decisions. James felt he was more qualified than many of the candidates who moved into sous-chef and other positions ahead of him, especially since he had moved extensively around the country and had a trade school diploma, in his view the equivalent of a college degree. Hope, from human relations at the Kahana Surf, was one of James' roommates, and she offered her view of his situation:

> He's felt like he's been discriminated against by the management at the hotel and he's taken some action. The majority of the kitchen management is haole, even some of them European, and snotty. From the local point of view, with haoles, the prejudice comes in. Local people are here to make a living, to survive. Haoles are here to get their money, to make their stepping stone, to move on. So there's resentment. The local people get hired. Then they have to train these people, who are making more money, who have a degree, and boom, they leave, and a new one comes and the same thing. So James had to train so many people, teach them what to do, and then they kept getting promoted over him.

This type of situation is exactly what Mike, the Lukane Sands fitness manager, alluded to when he noted that people left resort employment because of bureaucratic politics.

Gender

Women who wanted to forge resort careers also encountered frustrations. Many women we talked to up and down the strip assured us earnestly that men in the hotels were treated a lot better than women. They were promoted faster and further, people said, and tested less severely. Women worked in more segregated, ghettoized departments than men and had shorter job ladders for promotion. Judged most qualified to supervise other women only, women in departments where they were in the majority—room reservations, hotel operator, communications, front office, human relations, weddings, housekeeping, wardrobe, laundry, spa, and camp (where hotels had one)—were the most likely to rise to management levels.[8] Not all these departments had women managers, as men working in female departments often experienced glass elevators and rose to managerial positions (Maume 1999; Williams 1989). Moreover, these female managerial slots were often dead ends, rarely leading into the reaches of upper management. As a result, there were fewer women than people of color on the Ali'i resorts' executive councils, and not one general manager.

Second, the mobility associated with hotel management careers was more difficult for women, as they did not have the same familial support to move for their jobs as men (Gutek 1992; Reskin and Phipps 1988). Mainland haole women were more reluctant to relocate to exotic locations than men; and local culture, with its slightly machismo overtones, was less supportive of women's career advancement than haole culture.

Some managers attributed women's stalled careers to their lack of interest in promotion and their unwillingness to work the long hours required.[9] Matt Garvey, the senior director of guest operations at the Kahana Surf, referring to the stalled career of his front office director: "Rose was really gung-ho for a lot of years and had a rising career, but I guess that old biological clock started ticking and she decided to have a baby. Now she doesn't want to work the six days a week for fourteen-hour days that we need when it's busy here." While scholars and resort managers blamed gender role socialization that oriented women to home and family over work for women's lack of advancement,[10] research conducted toward the end of the twentieth century dispelled this notion, suggesting that women have diminished aspirations because their structural opportunities for advancement are fewer.[11]

Quite a few women we met complained of being sexually harassed.[12] Women reported being asked by their male managers to try on different outfits, received comments from their managers and co-workers about how they looked in these outfits, were asked about their weight and tone, were inappropriately touched by men, and were treated as sexual objects. Jane, a front desk clerk at the Hula Club Towers, reported being duped into going out to dinner with her manager for a professional staff meeting, only to find that there was no one there but them. Lisa, a secretary at the Lei Gardens, was flown by her assistant director to a hotel on another island for an alleged professional conference; but when she arrived, there was no conference, and the director wanted her to spend the night with him. Jill, a haole seeker who worked on the Kahana Surf's snorkel/cruise boat, described the general atmosphere of sexual harassment:

> I don't remember being sexually harassed so much in school, but I am constantly listening to degrading comments about women at my workplace. Some of them are very subtle, yet they are there. Men are always making jokes and sarcastic comments about women. I hear comments all the time about my woman manager who is a "bitch." However, they never refer to our male manager as a jerk. She always gets the bad rap because she is a woman telling men what to do. They go so far as to call her "it." I am the only woman who works on the boat, so the men are so used to

feeding off each other's jokes. Whenever they make comments I am always sure to tell them something back, although I choose to say it in a nice way because I don't take it personally. When our managers hire girls, they are always hiring pretty ones. One time I heard one say, "it's all about looks around here; men like to see pretty girls, and women like to see good-looking guys." The managers will approve the resort to hire girls, they will come out for the job, and within a few months they'll be gone. Whenever I ask why they didn't like a particular girl, it's always because she had an attitude or she was immature. Even the female manager of the boat seems to hire and fire lots of girls. Unfortunately, I believe they discriminate, harass, and even judge women according to their looks.

Lauren Hali, the assistant manager of beach and pool at the Lukane Sands, experienced a more direct form of sexual harassment from her director, Josh Bach. He told her about his previous experiences working on cruise ships, where the line employees had to submit to the sexual demands of management:

> For years he had been pressuring me. They had a tradition on the cruise ship where he worked that in the fall when they set the clocks back and you got to repeat an hour, that you could do whatever you wanted with that hour, and that you weren't accountable for it. Every time I asked him for a day off or something, he would tell me that I owed him another minute. Finally it got up to thirty minutes. Right before he left for his vacation he cornered me and told me he wanted five of those minutes now. He wanted me to take my clothes off and let him look at me. We might end up having sex or not, but he wanted me naked.

Lauren managed to escape when a line employee paged her. Subsequently, she hired a lawyer and reported Josh to the human relations director. When Josh returned from his vacation he was fired. But she felt that she paid a big price for standing up for herself:

> I went to a manager's meeting, a meeting of all managers held once a month and run by [the GM and deputy director]. It was right after I brought the sexual harassment case. Karen [the senior director of human resources] wasn't there yet, so [the GM] made a sexual joke, commodifying and sexually objectifying women. Then he said, "I can say that because Karen's not here." And then he looked right at me and said, "Unless Lauren's going to turn me in." And [the deputy director] just sat there. My friend Peter who works in sales says that they joke around and talk about women

all the time like that in his department. They shouldn't be talking like
that. It sets a bad tone for the entire hotel; it sets the attitudes for how
people can think and act. But now they look at me like I'm the narc, like
I'm the bad girl who wouldn't go along, like it's my fault. And I can feel that
it has shifted; I'm on the outside. Next time I go up before the panel it's
not going to be so friendly.

As Lauren expected, her career stalled, and she ended up, first, taking a
lower-ranked job at another resort, and then, leaving the resort industry altogether.

It was universally agreed by the female employees that all the Aliʻi resorts
were dominated by a sexist male culture at the top. At the Kahana Surf, the
powerful boys' club that ran the hotel and made all the important decisions
included the owner, his son who worked as the director of housekeeping, the
comptroller, the senior director of guest operations, the director of reservations, and the senior director of food and beverage. Hope described these
meetings at her hotel:

> There is a select group that starts off each day eating breakfast with him
> [the owner] nearly every day. It's a real clique. All they have to do is KA
> [kiss ass] to him. Even my own supervisor [a woman] sucks up to that
> group. It's a real boys' club, all top level salary-wise. None of them are lo-
> cal Hawaiian. Among management it's well known that when they come
> to hiring managers, they're more apt to hire a man. Pretty much all the
> women in management now are either at lower management or haole.
> There's only one or two that are in higher management. Upper manage-
> ment is so male-dominated, and it's impossible for a woman to break in.
> Even if they would hire one, she wouldn't be involved in making impor-
> tant decisions.

We talked to Barb Law one day when her husband Chuck was still working
at the Pono Beach Spa as the director of group sales and rooms division. She
said it was the same thing there, the guys at her hotel were close, they did
things together. They went on hunting trips together, like the Kahana Surf executives noted in chapter 5, where they camped, hunted, cooked, drank, and
sweated together. She referred to this as a form of male bonding and sardon-
ically noted that it translated back home into an exclusive preserve for the
formation of an old boy's network of power and privilege. This executive masculinity culture fostered an environment permitting management to act on

their greater comfort level, hiring and promoting male colleagues rather than women (Ibarra 1993).

Age

The age discrimination talked about in resorts was regarded as a more pervasive problem than in other types of organizations. Current and former Ali'i employees often said that appearance was a key factor affecting hiring and retention decisions, noting that the evaluation panels liked their people, especially women, "young and bouncy." This was exacerbated by the fact that the warm climate made these resorts oriented toward their beaches, pools, spas, and fitness centers, where wardrobe designers created scanty uniforms. Pool waitresses often complained about their attire, with their bare or blowing midriffs and micro-mini skirts. As they aged and were no longer youthfully tight, many felt less than comfortable revealing so much flesh. Guests could frequently be heard discussing the bodies of employees, both among themselves and to the workers directly.

Megan, a fitness trainer at the Pono Beach Spa, complained one day that a male guest told her that he would be more motivated to put effort into the program she was designing for him if she covered up less, so that he could have a better look at her "physique." She considered this an offensive and unprofessional remark. Palomi, the local Hula Club Towers concierge, noted that the modesty norms among locals were even stronger than those for mainland haoles, leading many to avoid working in departments with revealing uniforms.

One reason why these resorts employed such a youthful population was the presence of the young seekers and locals who came through and filled many of the line positions. These were usually time-outers between the ages of eighteen (the resorts' minimum employment threshold) and thirty. Ron, the Lei Gardens banquet bartender, talked about the placement of young people in resort jobs:

> I suppose it's more filled with young people, in that you have, not transients, but you have people coming to the island. Usually, if you have somebody older coming to the island, they're more set in what they're going to do, they know what they're gonna do. Where a younger person tends not to know what they're gonna do, and you don't need a lot of qualifications to be a beach and pool attendant. Whereas to jump into a bartender, you can't just get hired as a bartender unless you have a lot of experience, or if you're a bar porter, trainee for four or five years. It's a dif-

ficult job to get. So, beach and pool's easy, or houseman's easy, in that you can be trained quickly, and you can be hired without any experience. So those departments are pretty much young.

Ron also suggested that other types of resort employees were recruited and valued for their youth:

I would say the emphasis is for younger people, because you're catering to a little bit of a younger crowd. And I know that some hotel chains are progressive in that they're thinking, they're training people for a, not necessarily people they're gonna take care of today, but fifteen years from now. And that's part of hotel strategy. 'Cause I've had training classes in which I've been told that. So to that degree, they'd probably rather have younger people. A lot of it's physically demanding work, like, like I was saying, I work out every day, I'm in good shape. A lot of people my age wouldn't be able to do my job, or a wait help job, probably.

Physically demanding jobs tended to burn out workers at younger ages. Gary, the banquet captain at the Lei Gardens, talked about what drove people out of his department before they became too old:

It's not only our backs, which are always bad, and I've had two disk operations, but as we were walking, our feet would hurt in the morning. And all the hallways are concrete, and you're working on concrete, it's like working in a factory basically. And waiters, we're walking everywhere. And we go from grass to tile to concrete, we're not working on the same surface. Well, there's this new shoe, that is almost like a clog, that somebody got at one of these things, and all of a sudden their feet feels good, and all of a sudden everybody's wearing 'em, because our feet are hurting so much. So now all of sudden everybody's wearing these clog-type shoes, because our feet were hurting. So we go through cycles like this, and it seems like at each cycle someone just drops out because they can't take it anymore.

Departments where older people could find refuge were located in the less visible locations at the back of the house, such as housekeeping, hotel operator, room service, pantry (cutting vegetables), stewarding, and dishwashing, but still their numbers were small. In front-of-the-house departments, where the average age for employees was young, workers noted that an older person placed there might feel uncomfortable and excluded from the conversations and socializing. Kitchen staff and waiters/waitresses regularly went out for drinks after work with one another. Fitness staff, with a mean age from twenty-five to thirty-five, took advantage of half-price specials on drinks and sushi after 10 p.m. Older people did not fit in with these activities or the things people talked about while at work or afterward.

In addition to these informal forces discouraging older employees from feeling comfortable in their work environments, Palomi, the concierge, described hotel policies at the Hula Club Towers designed to drum out older workers:

> In my department people are required to cross-train. You cannot work all day just helping guests make restaurant reservations. And at the Towers, we stand behind a tall counter. Some of the others [resorts], they sit down and the guests sit down in chairs across from them. So even if you're just making reservations here, you have to stand on your feet every day. But in my department you have to do everything; you have to teach the lei-making classes, you have to teach the hula classes. We had a Japanese woman here who was in her late 50s and she wanted to just work with the Japanese guests, help them with their reservations. But they told her she would have to cross-train to stay. So she decided to retire. Carrying the heavy binders was hard for her, standing for eight hours, teaching the classes.

In sum, female Ali'i employees were more ghettoized, more harassed (individually and by the culture), and more likely to suffer in their promotions because they were loathe to move, resistant to working long hours through their childbearing and childrearing years, and subject to short job ladders with limited options for advancement. Ali'i employees of color (men) were less likely to have the educational credentials than their female counterparts and were also reluctant to move away from the Islands. Both groups suffered by being excluded from the old boys' club at the top of the management hierarchy and tended to sit for too long without promotions, as young, male haoles from the mainland were brought through by corporate management guiding their careers.

Large chain hotels were most likely to have formalized criteria for promotion, while the middle and smaller chains or independents often relied on hiring panels to screen people for various positions, a process that accommodated informal, ascriptive criteria and worked against both people of color and women. Management, who preferred to have agile, attractive employees servicing guests, favored the preponderance of younger employees in these re-

sorts. But factors such as the natural demographics of the applicant population, the physically demanding nature of the work, and the lack of comfort
older people felt in environments composed nearly entirely of younger workers naturally promoted a younger employee pool. Women, people of color,
and older workers usually saw their careers either stalled or terminated. If they
chose to accept a stagnant career trajectory, they remained in the same jobs
while younger white men passed them by.

Long-Term Resort Careers

As people moved through the age span, their likelihood of continuing to
work in a resort diminished. There were some, however, who made this their
career and stayed forever, or as long as they could. Even the longest-term resort employees rarely remained as long as individuals working in other fields,
as the hours and days were long, and the work was physically demanding.

Seekers

Seekers who kept their resort jobs for the long haul fell into several categories. *Ongoing seasonals* made transience a way of life, but they established a
regular home base, to which they returned annually. They left during the slow
season and came back for the high season. These migratory workers ebbed
and flowed, sometimes internationally, with the timing of the tourist industry.
Nick, a thirty-four-year-old seasonal transient who came for the Hawaiian
winters, discussed his attachment to both resort work and firefighting, making his stay at the Lei Gardens a regular seasonal venture:

> I've been doing firefighting for nearly fifteen years now. In the off season
> from that I've done a variety of jobs. For the first few off seasons I worked
> in a mountain resort. I did firefighting setup at first and learned to ski.
> Then I worked as a ski instructor for another few years. But then one fall
> I showed up the first day at the slopes and had to leave. I decided I
> couldn't face another winter. I had visited Honua three times before and
> knew a girl from home who was married and lived here, so I stayed with
> her until I found a place to live. Then I got a job here [at the Lei Gardens]
> in banquets and I've been doing it ever since. I'm way up the seniority
> ladder now, so I get a lot of work. I guess you could say that I'm pretty
> attached to both places. It's a good way of life.

Career seekers who made a life commitment to seeking, made another permanent adaptation, whether through high or low mobility. Some sought jobs that capitalized on their recreational interests, becoming kayak or windsurfing instructors at the beach, getting a degree in marine science to become "aquaculturists" in charge of the pools, fish tanks, and breeding ponds, or becoming dive masters to lead scuba groups. They took ribbing from other hotel employees who devalued such leisure-incorporated work as mere play ("cruise" jobs). Other careerists extended the transient adaptation permanently, moving around as they wished and finding jobs based on their repertoire of acquired skills. Janell, a thirty-five-year-old recreation attendant, decided after college that she could not pursue her business degree. Like Nick, she spent several years working in the ski industry and then shifted to Hawai'i when she could no longer stand the cold weather. Reflecting on her life, she noted: "There's no way I'll ever work any other kind of job or live any other kind of lifestyle. This is a career lifestyle for me."

Long-term seekers all eventually experienced the "existential crisis": grappling with abandoning the traditional career track and committing to the alternate lifestyle. Whether prompted from within, by parental prodding, or by the normative pressure of society, at some point they had to seriously consider their futures, as their options to return to the normative track began to fade.[13] Career seekers moved past this point by making a commitment to the alternative track. They resolved to remain free spirits rather than to spend the rest of their lives with their "noses to the grindstone."

A third group, *environmental seekers,* stayed for the long term without the intense interest in some form of serious leisure or outdoor recreation. They moved to Hawai'i because they found it beautiful, they craved the warm weather, they preferred the relaxed lifestyle, or they wanted to get away from the crowded mainland. Many of these paradise relocators adopted local lifestyles. Of these, some came over with the express intention of staying forever. Both Carol, the banquet server who split her time among three resorts, and Ron, the banquet bartender, decided before they moved to Honua that they wanted to make this place their home. After making the move, they looked around for work and adapted their occupational aspirations to what was available on the island.

Another relocator pattern involved coming over without a certain future. Bernie, a salesman at one of the shops at the Kahana Surf, moved to Honua when he was in his late thirties because his sister lived there. He thought he would try it out for a while to see how things went. He was fortunate to find a job in a high-end hotel arcade boutique where he could earn a living wage. Bernie enjoyed living on Honua and being able to take his vacations on adjoining islands. He liked his job at the Kahana Surf; and he had a regular cohort of return guests and celebrities who made it a point to stop in, shop with him, and take him out to dinner. His plan was to work at the store until he retired.

Relocator converts, who amended their initial intent of staying for a short time to moving to Honua permanently, were also apt to remain in resort work for the long term. They avoided having children or managed to figure out how to navigate the problematic local school situation. They did not get "island fever," the feeling that there was not enough to do on a tropical island, and managed to find an enjoyable lifestyle by making use of their work, home lives, available outdoor recreation, shopping, movies, and the shows and concerts that passed through Honua.

Some of these individuals had to make sure of their commitment by testing out the mainland one more time. John, a valet at the Kahana Surf, gave up his job after five years to move back to Wisconsin, his home state. After six months he was calling his buddies and his boss to see about the possibility of getting his old job back. After nine months, he was right back where he had left. Dennis, the bellman at the Lukane Sands, had moved to Honua with his wife, intending to settle there. She got a job as a teacher at the local public high school, but after five years she missed her family and wanted to move home. He did not want to go. They struggled with their conflict for a year. Finally, they reached a deal: she would move back without him and they would see how they liked it. If she missed him and/or Honua, she would move back. If he missed her or their families and the mainland, he would move to join her. She waited until the end of cheerleading camp in the summer, a commitment she had made to her school, and went back to Montana. She ended up liking it back there, and he preferred to stay where he was, so they made a "quick sale" on their condominium, drew up the division of their property to avoid spending much on lawyers, and got a divorce. The first couple of years, he used his vacation time to join his ex-wife and several of her family members when he went on vacation. After a few more years, though, he let that connection lapse and took his vacations the more usual relocator way: he went with another guy or two and they hopped around the country, visiting friends they had there and doing recreational things such as going to ball games. He eventually bought a new condo and became a member of the board. On his days off from the Sands, he golfed with his buddies in the bell department.

Some seekers, male or female, settled down and remained on Honua because they married a local. Brooke, an aerobics instructor at the Sands, had planned on living an international life. Expressing her aspirations one year, she said: "I like to travel. My 'American dream' is to travel 'till my feet fall off.'" But shortly after she said that, she fell in love with a local, an entertainer who performed nightly at the Lei Gardens' cocktail lounge, and married him. Although she never planned on having children, within five years she had three of them and a home mortgage. Her dreams of traveling the world were dampened. Referring to her husband, she said: "We're not going anywhere. Kamoka is a local boy. He's grounded." Three years after that, however, Brooke was divorced, the supervisor of the fitness classes at the Sands, and trying to piece together her life. Although she had never wanted to settle down, her three children and ex-in-laws tied her to Honua.

Seekers who settled into long-term resort careers often assumed active roles in the struggle for better wages and working conditions. Spurred by frustration when his friend Barry was fired over the ashtray incident, Dennis became one of the employees heading the drive to unionize his hotel. He met with the union representative and groups of workers in his department and others, talking about the benefits of the union. Since each department could decide on its own whether to accept unionization or not, he took his own department union, but continued to press others to follow. He found vocal support from relocated haoles in several other departments. Kevin, the local haole houseman at the Hula Club Towers, made this observation:

Q: So do the local people fight for their labor rights?
KEVIN: No. There are local people that will talk about it. They say, well, look at what they're doing, they can't do that. But they won't do anything about it. They don't want to stand out. But I think the haole worker that knows, you know, more so probably from the mainland, is more the one who knows, hey, contracts are, like, you know, I guess that's how it would be for anyone who really knows the law and goes hey, hey, hey, you can't do it. 'Cause they [the management] will try to get away with anything they can. But the haoles know they have rights. And they will stand up for them more. It's just a different background.

Some seekers held their resort jobs until retirement. But many departments that accommodated seekers wore them out eventually. Few remained in beach and pool or fitness well into their fifties. Most banquet workers began to find the work too exhausting by that age as well. Valets also found sprinting to the garage difficult as they got older. And bellmen grew tired of lugging heavy bags all over the hotels. At some point, most people who had adjusted to make their life on Honua permanent and their resort work a career, had to make a change. After Sam, the banquet server from the Pono Beach Spa, quit to become a fireman, he explained his decision:

> I saw what happened to Barbara's back [his wife herniated a disk lifting the heavy banquet trays], and I didn't want that to happen to me. I worked six years at the Pono Beach Spa, four years at the Kahana Surf. It's back-breaking work. I'll tell you, that's a hard way to make a living, although people do. You're on your feet eight hours, and you get maybe a half-hour break. It's hard on your feet, on your back, your knees. And I always wanted to be a fireman. I had looked into it before, but it's a tough enclave for a haole to get into. I finally decided to take the test and try out. And I passed the test. So I went for the training. On graduation day there were all these local guys with their whole families there, each one with twenty or so leis on their necks, picnics and food galore, and it was just me and Barbara. And my parents had come over for my graduation. But I like it a lot. The work is hard, but it's not as constant. It comes in spurts. You maybe get three calls a shift. In between you can rest or work out. People like and respect firemen. And I got great benefits.

Sam, like many other relocated seekers, blended into the local way of life.

Locals

Many locals remained within the resort industry for their working lives. For some, this was the job to which they aspired from the beginning. They had *specialized talents,* such as cooking or entertaining, which made resorts one of the best places to be employed. For example, Kamoka, Brooke's local ex-husband, made a good living singing and playing his guitar five nights a week at the Lei Gardens cocktail lounge. He supplemented this primary job with late-night gigs at a couple of restaurants and clubs, and he played his guitar and sang at weddings (by his estimate, three hundred a year). He supported his two ex-wives, his new wife, and his five children on his Lei Gardens' steady job.

Resort work may not have been the lifelong dream of other long-term local employees, but many found their *employment niche* there and either rose to their level of satisfaction or became satisfied with what they could attain. Nestor, the Kahana Surf houseman, for example, planned on remaining in his job for the duration. Hermio, the front desk worker at the Lukane Sands, also intended to keep his job forever. Joey, a local who worked his way from beach and pool into the spa, and finally into the information systems department at the Lukane Sands, planned on working there for the foreseeable future. These people viewed their jobs as permanent. They worked their way into positions that paid enough money to support them and looked no further. Like the housekeepers, they held "career jobs" within the Ali'i resorts. At the top of their earning curves, they were settled and stable. Taylor, a local bellman at the Lei Gardens in his late thirties, talked about his job and his lifestyle choices this way: "Once a bellman, always a bellman. This is one of the premium jobs in the hotel, because in this job you are capable of saving some money. Everybody's got a wife that works here except for two guys. This is a career-ending job. It's fun here, but we're not here because we love the work. A job is a job— it supports your lifestyle outside of the job."

Career jobholders regarded themselves as permanent fixtures of the hotel. In an industry with notoriously high turnover among employees, management, and ownership, they saw themselves as the foundation of stability. Hope further elaborated on this sense of permanence in distinguishing the locals' perspective from the managers':

> A lot of time the upper management come here and they don't adapt to the local ways. They're mainland haoles, and they come here for a couple of years, move up the career ladder, and move on. They don't take the time to learn the local culture, learn how to speak to the local people, learn how to motivate them and show them respect. These people are "short-timers," they're not here for the long haul. But the local people are. This is our island, and these are our jobs. When these management people are gone, when this owner is gone, we will still be here, making this island and this hotel what it is. It's funny how upper management can be oblivious to that.

Another alternative was to become a *mobile hotel careerist*, committing to resort work but not spending it all at the same hotel. Locals who worked their way up into the middle management ranks often sustained these careers over many years. Art Boggs, one of the general managers at the Lukane Sands, talked about the kinds of long-term management careers locals might have:

> ART: I would probably say that there are local mid-level managers that aren't looking to leave Hawai'i that are willing to relocate throughout

the Islands but won't leave the state—strong middle management, de-partment head levels, assistant managers, department managers. They are ambitious, they have left line positions to take sales and manage-ment, but they aren't going to become elite specialists in their indus-try, but they're looking to be strong managers and stay within the state.

Q: And are these people leaving their family behind in one location or are they taking them with them?

ART: No, they are taking them with them and they will jump from hotel to hotel so they'll do a twenty-year career between six hotels all in the same island. Nothing wrong with that, that's just your intermediate level. Say you get three years out of them at Hula Club Towers and three years out of them at the Sands and three years out of them at Lei Gardens, or then they might venture to another island.

Q: What kind of departments are these people in?

ART: Oh, anything. They could be in operations, it could be housekeep-ing, front of house, bell, valet, operations managers, front desk man-agers, restaurant outlet managers. That's a really popular one. Chefs, sous-chefs, a lot of those guys are your long-term ones. They will come to you committed and passionate and they will work hard, I'm here for you. But two years later they are going to go work somewhere else.

Long-term locals with jobs into which they had settled focused themselves on their families. Todd, a bellman at the Hula Club Towers in his forties, talked about the way his orientation toward his work had shifted over the course of his career: "When I was single it wasn't a top priority—I could still find another job, I was still young—I didn't care as much. Once I had my children it opened up a whole different meaning of why we are here. Local people care about their children a lot. They want to make a better life for them. You want to give them a good education that would provide them a really excellent job. It would be okay for them to become a bellman if that's how everything ended up. But I would rather not have them end up in a service job in the hotel industry."

As Bruce notes above, most local people did not put themselves into con-flict with management over labor issues. They grumbled to one another, but they did not press their rights. Todd tried to explain why this was the case by drawing on historical tradition: "Look at what happened to local people when the missionaries and colonialists came over. They were useless and help-less. They were passive in just accepting what these people did to them." He thought it was the "local way" to acquiesce. While this was mostly the case, there were some local employees who became involved in labor issues.

Lauren Hali, the beach and pool assistant manager, noted that Palo and Ku, two of the three longer-term beach and pool employees who provided the "customized" service for the Lukane Sands VIP guests, ended up leaving because of a labor dispute: "At that time beach and pool was one of only two non-union departments and the hotel was fighting it. They had the guillotine out chopping heads. Everyone could see that Palo and Ku were doomed. Palo quit and is now working at Leeward Nissan. Ku went on vacation and never came back. Marco got fired."

Whether they were fired or quit, most of the long-term locals eventually brought their employment to an end—usually, like the seekers, while they were no older than their fifties. Resort work was not something into which people grew old. When they reached their forties and fifties, many locals started looking around for what else they could do that would be easier. Don, a bellman at the Lukane Sands, noted that he had gotten his real estate license three years before. His plan was to make a gradual transition out of bell work. He began by first buying houses in new developments, living in them for a year or two, and then selling them. In this way, he, like many in the local area, capitalized on the rising cost of real estate: "That's my ticket too, is real estate. If I can 'burn and turn' a couple more houses I can get a job that doesn't pay as much money. And in the meantime, I'm trying to make some connections so I can get into selling houses for other people here that I know." Others pursued similar plans.

New Immigrants

New immigrant resort employees had simple needs from their jobs. They sought work that they could do, that would enable them to have a comfortable family life. They desired this for their children as well. They were not afraid of performing hard physical labor. They were not afraid of working long hours. They did not seek to retire early. In fact, their lifestyle outside their jobs was uncomplicated and undemanding. They spent time with family, church, and community; they watched television; some occasionally traveled back to their countries of origin.

As they aged and their responsibilities for raising and supporting children waned, new immigrants often pulled back from working for multiple employers, concentrating on one full-time job. They looked forward to their retirement years where they could spend time babysitting their grandchildren. Vida, the Pono Beach Spa housekeeper, planned to stay right where she was. Kam, the Lei Gardens cook, was expecting his children to return from college on the mainland and move into an extension he and his wife would build onto their house. Santo, the Pono Beach Spa steward, planned on caring for his parents and enjoying watching his children grow up and have their own children. Since her husband was already retired (and twenty-two years her senior), Agrifina, the Lukane Sands steward, planned on moving to near wherever her children were living (both in Las Vegas at the time of our interview) when she retired. As Mike, the Lukane Sands fitness manager notes above, they all planned to work as long as they could. Turnover rates in new immigrant departments were famously low.[14]

Not only were new immigrants lifetime workers, but they made few demands on management. As previous studies have shown, they rarely, if ever, complained when they were treated poorly, even illegally (Stepick and Grenier 1994). Kevin offered his explanation for the passivity of the new immigrants in dealing with management over labor issues:

> KEVIN: The new immigrants, they think they're so fortunate just to have a job. They don't want to speak up, say anything about anything.
> Q: Why? Why are they so quiet?
> KEVIN: Oh well, 'cause first of all, they just are. Their English is not good. They can't, you know, vocalize themselves well. But they're also, you know, they're eager; you know, they'll take any work. That's why they throw, that's why they take the Filipino worker and throw them in the damn, uh, stewarding jobs. Old people busting their asses for junk pay. You know they're getting paid crap to do that hard, hard work. But they, you know, who's working the hotel? Who's working? All the Filipinos. They'll take it. They'll take whatever they can get. You know. They're not proud. You know what I mean, they're not, you know, proud, proud people. They just want, you know, they're happy just getting by having that job so. Yeah. The Filipinos don't usually grumble.

Ty, the Lukane Sands bell captain, offered three reasons why he thought that the new immigrants who were getting cheated out of their benefits at the hotel did not complain. First, he noted, they did not know that what the resort was doing to them was illegal. Second, they did not know they could complain, or to whom to direct their complaints. Third, they were not the type of people who would go outside the hotel and complain. Stalwart and hardworking, new immigrants toiled in the resorts longer than any other group.

Management

Most people who embarked on management careers, who went to school for it or who entered management training programs with the hotel chains, lasted past the intermediate mark. Individuals on the fast track advanced rapidly. Most attained the highest position to which they would rise by the age of forty, if not younger. In fact, most general managers in hotels were no older than forty to forty-five (with some as young as thirty-five).

People with *stalled careers* at their highest level of attainment sometimes chose to stay the course and remain in their positions. Janice Thomas, the comptroller at the posh ski resort, and her husband had decided to settle at their jobs, in the same resort, for the rest of their careers in the industry. This was particularly likely for women, people of color, or those whose departments had short job ladders, where they had few directions where they could aspire for upward mobility.

But while many entered the hospitality career as young people, few remained in it all the way to the top. Like other service careers, the hospitality industry was characterized by early burnout (Cordes and Dougherty 1993). People left the business because they could no longer stand the hours, the boredom of doing the same thing over and over again, and the pressure of the demands and expectations that came from the guests, the ownership, and themselves. They thus spun out voluntarily. Art Boggs estimated that most upper-level managers only stayed in the field for fifteen to twenty years.

While few management professionals earned enough money to make outright early retirements, they more commonly *transitioned into related careers.* They found other, full-time "bridge jobs" (Feldman 1990) that could take them the rest of the way to retirement. People with hospitality management experience were eagerly recruited into other industries. Trade magazines were filled with articles touting the desirability of these employees, as they had valuable managerial skills and were used to working long hours for relatively little pay. Rooms executives were sought by hospitals, property management firms, university housing, and computer firms. People from food and beverage went into liquor and food service industries, worked for suppliers, and opened their own restaurants. People from human resources went into human resources in other industries. From sales they went into sales. Others went into the travel business, the convention business, travel and visitors bureaus, local and regional government, and other corporate management. In leaving the hospitality industry, they found other rewards. Hans Bjornstadt, a thirty-nine-year-old culinary executive at a large, downtown Chicago chain hotel, offered the observation that was repeated industrywide: "Let me tell you something about people that were in the business and left, people that were in hotels and they moved on to other things. There is a saying that they usually probably make twice as much and work half the time. That may not be exactly right, but they usually make some more and they work much less hours."

These kinds of assertions were often backed up with numerous specific examples. Larry Caplan, the former guest services/front desk/spa director at the Lukane Sands, talked about the "face point" required of managers at resorts, and how it drove people out of the business:

> LARRY: A lot of them get out of the management company corporate world of your name-brand hotel companies, meaning they get out of that bureaucratic process where face points are so popular, where you work ten hours a day, five to six days a week and that's the way it is. They get out of the Ritz, the Hyatt, the Marriott; they get out of the face-point phase.
>
> Q: What does face point mean?
>
> LARRY: Meaning that you have to do face time. You've got to work long hours just because that's the norm of the industry. You can't come in to work for eight hours, then go home, because we don't endorse that. You got to do eleven hours or we don't think you are working hard enough for us. We are only going to pay you for a department head level, only $45,000 a year, and you are going to work seventy hours a week or more. That's the way it is, take it or leave it. Well, that's tough when you can go work as a manager at a rental car company for forty grand a year and work forty-five hours a week. Or you can leave and go into the private world, I call it the private sector, where you go to a small hotel that is independently owned and operated and you might get an opportunity to work for them.

Rob Kumeho, the formerly wandering Ali'i chef and food and beverage executive, retired from resort work and took a job on the island where his wife had been raising their family. He became a purchasing agent for Costco Wholesale Foods at more money than he had been previously earning. Lorraine, our college secretary who had spent many years working for the Lukane Sands, began her work life at a hotel on another part of Honua. She moved over to the Lukane Sands three years later and worked there in purchasing for two years, in human resources for two years, and in purchasing for another five years. She and her husband moved to follow a job offer he got from a resort on Puerto Rico and stayed there for a year, then relocated to Los Angeles for a year.

Lorraine enjoyed Los Angeles until she and her husband had their first son. With no family support and the dangers of the city, they decided to move back to her family on Honua. She stayed at home to take care of her baby until she received a call from the new management of the Sands, inviting her back as a temp. Lorraine accepted the job offer and eventually landed a full-time position in human resources. She worked there for three years. But at that time she became concerned about the way the new management was running the hotel and decided to leave the hospitality industry. She explained her decision:

> My reason for leaving was seeing three people, in our office alone, laid off. One of them being a close friend and worked with the hotel for ten years. Even though I was in one of the key positions in the department, I didn't feel secure anymore. I felt that when it came down to number crunching, the bottom-line figures were only what mattered, not the employees. It was a tough decision to make because I did have a lot of benefits to lose. The pay was better, the medical benefits were good, free lunches, free dry cleaning, elaborate Christmas parties and numerous employee functions throughout the year. I really enjoyed the people I worked with. People in the hospitality industry, in my opinion, have great "aloha spirit." What more could I possibly have asked for? I applied for this civil service position while I was on maternity with my second son and on reduced hours after 9/11. I never expected to get the job [with the college], as I have applied for state jobs in the past. When I was offered this position, I had a lot of thinking to do. What made me come to my final decision to accept the position was that I now live two miles from work and didn't have to drive forty minutes each way to and from work to Lanikai. I also now have time to pick up my son from preschool on my lunch break, which is right across the street from [the college]. Also, I eventually want to return to school, which is practically free ($65 per course).

Lorraine's husband had been in the hospitality industry for many years as well. He was the assistant manager (manager on duty and manager of guest services) at the Kahana Surf. He left a year after she did for a sales manager position with the Bank of Hawai'i. Lorraine noted that he made the decision to leave because his hours had been insane. "He would work 11–13 hours a day. I worked days and he worked nights. We *never* saw each other. It was a very stressful job because he not only managed his department, but was the only manager on duty [rooms division] at night. He also took a big cut in pay, but he now has quality family time with us. And he also doesn't have to drive so far." Lorraine and her husband left their resort careers with at least fifteen years of management experience each. They burned out on the hours, the cost cuts, and the stress of their jobs.

Some resort managers planned their careers to afford them *softer senior years,* so that as they aged they advanced into shorter hours and more structured working time. Time demands became lighter for those who could move into general and regional management with the large chains. Bill Stone spoke about his plans for slowing down: "I feel now I have the energy, I have the life within me, pay my dues now, work hard, get to where I want to, and then enjoy my life. In the later years you'll learn to appreciate it even more, because you will have experienced the roughness, and what it took to get there, to actually be able to enjoy it. I will slow down; I will get to a point where I'll be able to appreciate the home life. . . . And then when I get to GM or whatever position it may be, I'll be able to take the weekends off, I'll have a more organized lifestyle."

Wes Morgan, a former executive director of food and beverage at the Hula Club Towers, was able to arrange such a lifestyle. He bounced around from one Hawaiian resort to another, looking for just the right job. He explained how he juggled his schedule: "I actually was easy to employ because I don't move my whole house, family, and kids with each location. My wife lives in [city on another island]. I commute every weekend back and forth. I work five days and take two days off and go home. Or sometimes I have to work longer, like six days, so I don't go home and then maybe she comes over for a day and a half, or maybe she doesn't, and we don't see each other for two weeks." Bill's philosophy involved deferring his leisure for his later life, concomitant with his entry into the higher ranks, while Wes's involved using his schedule to accommodate a transient family lifestyle.

Yet the *longest-term elite* of the resort management field, those top professionals who did not spin out into related industries and who wanted to remain working in the resort industry, faced difficult dilemmas. If they worked in large chains, they had regional and national management positions into which they could move. These were considered cushy and highly sought-after positions. But people released from independents and smaller chains had to fend for themselves. The ever-unpredictable nature of resort management jobs frequently left people stranded when hotels were sold, management companies were replaced, or individuals were simply terminated. Art Boggs lost his GM position at the Sands when the hotel sold. Chuck Law lost his GM position in the Hawaiian resort that recruited him away from the Pono Beach Spa when that hotel turned over. In fact, getting fired was so common in this field that it carried little shame. As Art Boggs noted, "It's not really a stigma in the management area to get bounced out of a job because the economic vicissitudes, and ownership changes, and management changes are so common."

Individuals were also often caught in the crossfire of complaints and bickering between owners and their management companies, both of whom accused each other of trying to enhance their profits and performance at the others' expense. When upper-echelon managers were released before they were ready to quit the industry, they went home and nursed their wounds, contacted their extensive networks of professional connections, and let people know they were available for new offers. Most found employment in another hotel within six months. When Chuck Law's Hawaiian hotel was sold, he picked up a GM position in Guam. A year later that property turned over as well, and he was out of work again. This time Nikko Hotels, for which he had previously worked, offered him a GM position in New Delhi.

Instead of finding another management position, some former managers went into *private consulting*. They sought work with people opening new properties, helping them design and open them. Sometimes this entailed working at the new property for six months to a year until they ironed out all the operating kinks. This was very common for former GMs, food and beverage directors, rooms executives, and executive spa directors, especially those with prestigious resorts, such as the Ali'i properties, on their resumes.

Consulting jobs paid good money. Larry Caplan set up his own spa consulting company after getting fired by the Lukane Sands, aided by the consulting experience he had obtained assisting other spas owned by the Sands' parent corporation. With two or three consulting jobs in the first year he was happy. But then one of these firms, a giant resort conglomerate, offered him a job as their corporate spa director overseeing the nine spas they planned to open over the following eighteen months. Although he had resisted leaving Honua (without being pried by a "crowbar"), they made him an offer too good to refuse. He explained his reasoning: "I held out as long as I could, and they wound up making an offer that was too lucrative to turn down. I would be foolish, be foolish to turn it down at this point. I'll do a year or two working for a strong company like this with another fabulous facility on my resume. . . . And then I can always go back to more consulting two years down the road if I want to, and I'll be just that much better at it because I'll wind up hopefully opening one or two facilities as well. So it's just that much more experience with a company that has financial stability and resources." Larry rented out his house on Honua and moved to the mainland.

Another option for former high-level resort managers who wanted to stay involved at the elite level was to start their *own management company*. Some got into this at the "boutique" or small hotel level, such as Ryan Jensen, a former vice president of business operations at the Lukane Sands. Jensen left the Sands for an elite Caribbean resort as the vice president of operations, and then became the GM at a resort on the west coast of Florida. As GM, he ran that for two years, and then he and two other partners formed their own management company, the "Sandy Beach" Hotel Corporation. When last we heard they owned three hotels up and down the east coast of Florida and managed six others. These were mostly little three- and four-diamond properties, and Ryan was the president. They also had two large golf country clubs that they managed on Florida's west coast.

Three other groups of Lukane Sands former executives established their own management companies as well, on a larger, international scale. One group set up a management company and opened resorts in Bali, Singapore, Shanghai, and other Eastern countries. The "elite of the elite," they recruited several executives from the Sands to join them. These people lasted with their own company for three years and then closed it, spinning back into high-level corporate management with exclusive chain hotels where they had previously worked. Art Boggs, who was recruited to join them noted: "They each got more lucrative offers to go and join big corporations, and it's hard not to get bought. These guys are already wealthy, but all of a sudden they realize that putting their own company together and forking all of the money out of their own pocket is not as easy as it sounds." These people exemplify the most elite postresort careers.

A second group of executives joined together and launched more international resorts. After a few years, they, too, went out of business. A third group of executives who worked during Larry Caplan's tenure tried to recruit him to a management company they were assembling. With Chuck Law in food and beverage, Art Boggs as the GM, Larry at spa, and several others joining them, they were trying to get something off the ground.

Eventually most managers reached the age where they wanted to stop working so hard. Tom Butterworth, a general manager at the Kahana Surf, talked about his retirement plans: "This industry dies out at around fifty. People either retire, burn out, or die. Some people go into their own business, they become entrepreneurs. Independent hotels have older management than the corporate hotels. This business's a young person's business. It's fast moving with fast attrition. My plan is to be independent by age fifty. Then I can run my own little business."

Other people *retired outright*. They saved their money, invested in retirement property or homes, cultivated their portfolios, and planned modest needs. Art Boggs spoke about his ultimate future plans: "I have no plans whatsoever for when I retire except to sit on my porch. I have a condo on [another island], and I will garden and read. Everything is paid for. And I will be out by fifty-five. My lifestyle's very simple. I don't need a boat. I can hike, bike, and read."

Resort Career Patterns

The demographics of resort work formed an age pyramid, with numerous youthful employees occupying the bottom rungs, a much smaller number of middle-aged (thirties) people filling the middle rungs, and a very small group of older workers (forties and beyond) occupying the apex. Even the longest die-hard workers left the hospitality industry at younger ages than was true of many other occupations.[15] Hawaiian resorts also evidenced a stratified pyramid demographically, with women and people of color filling the lower positions while the better-paying jobs with privilege and power went to white men. Those lasting the longest in the industry tended to be either new immigrants or mainland haoles. Barriers maintaining this demographic stratification were structural, cultural, and interactional, both subtle and highly overt. Depending on people's jobs, their work could be challenging and rewarding, or repetitive and boring. Ali'i employees tended to find their satisfaction most often in their location and in the fellowship of their co-workers.

11

UNDERSTANDING PARADISE LABOR

In this book we have offered an ethnographic portrayal of the Aliʻi resorts, five luxury Hawaiian hotels that have created the allure of paradise, and the people who work there. We have posited that four overarching categories of employees—new immigrants, locals, seekers, and managers—compose the work force in these resorts. While some of the phenomena that we describe are unique to Hawaiʻi, most of the patterns we observed can be extrapolated not only to resort workers in other locales but to workers in the global economy more generally. Here, we conclude by looking at some of the trans-situational elements of Hawaiian paradise work and how this serves to illustrate wider societal patterns in the global economy of the twenty-first century.

Resorts as Global, Postmodern Communities

Clifford (1997) referred to hotels as places of transit, not of residence. This depiction characterized the seekers and managers (as well as the guests, who only stay for short periods of time), as they passed through resorts relatively rapidly. Their individual values, aspirations, and motivations connected them, as workers and consumers, to the international capitalist enterprise, as they were part of the global flow of bodies, that "ethnoscape" (Appadurai 1996) of persons who constitute the shifting postindustrial world. With their movement, they took with them the material and conceptual ideas, artifacts, and customs that represented their "traveling cultures" (Clifford 1997), contributing to the "global flow of culture" (Appadurai 1996) that characterizes the new international community. They became central players in a local community that was defined by the international movement of capital, cultural forms, and tourist bodies—vehicles that transformed the local into a global panorama, a larger landscape where old typologies functioned to reproduce new cultural identities and social norms.

Workers who migrated to Hawai'i from abroad were unlikely to display the transmigration pattern described in the literature as predominant. Global immigrant workers were welcomed and assisted in finding housing and jobs by well-ensconced residential and occupational groups of current and former international migrants. They became highly valued, even crucial, workers in the hospitality and other local industries. While others have depicted globalized workers as transient, our new immigrants became heavily tied to and invested in their new country by opportunity, family, community, work, and fierce loyalty.

The feminization and subjugation of the international labor force so strongly noted in the literature was also not evident in Hawai'i. Two factors set the circumstances of our new immigrants apart from this trend. First, new immigrant women employed in the Ali'i resorts found their work relatively satisfying, neither demeaning nor repressed. As Glenn (1996) also noted in tracing the progression from servitude to service work of women employed in "reproductive" domestic labor, women of color found their subordination in hotels less direct and personal than in private households, mediated there by impersonal structures and the presence of work groups for sociability and support.[1] Sherman (2003) also noted that hotel workers enjoy their jobs because of their positive relationships with guests, their self-construction as professionals, and the distance they introduce from their work when they define themselves as nonprofessional.[2] Beyond the housekeeping area, new immigrant women also found comfortable and rewarding enclaves in laundry, wardrobe, and the kitchens. New immigrant women working in hotels, then, were liberated from the confines of the subjugated, secondary, and less remunerative household labor they would have found back home and given independence and economic resources through their resort employment.

Second, the Ali'i resorts welcomed and offered relatively fulfilling work to men as well. New immigrant men found secure and gratifying employment in the departments they dominated: landscaping, outdoor housekeeping, and stewarding. Their performance in these jobs doing heavy, difficult labor, often in outdoor settings, within primarily male groups, reinforced both their masculinity and their role as breadwinners.

Transient Communities and Postmodern Selves

The transience of our seekers and managers has fostered a changing conception of community as we move beyond the simple dichotomies of mechanical/organic and *Gemeinschaft/Gesellschaft* to the postmodern, global enclave. Community parameters are no longer geographically bounded but defined by shared consumption, interests, and lifestyle (Biggart 1994), subculturally and virtually forged.[3] People have gained a greater international heterogeneity and exposure. The resulting associations are neither folksy (*Gemeinschaft*) nor cosmopolitan (*Gesellschaft*), urban nor rural, but instead a postmodern bricolage or pastiche.

Transience, in fact, has become increasingly prevalent throughout society as we become more faddish and as styles change with increasing rapidity (Erickson 1995). Toffler (1970) forecast that ours would become a throwaway society characterized by transient and ephemeral commodities, services, images, and information. And Bell (1976) has suggested a movement toward conditions where the "temporary contract [will] become the hallmark of contemporary life." Erickson (1995) has pointed out that this "ethic of disposability" may lead beyond our perspective on society to a new view of the self as somehow transient or disposable.

Hawaiian resort workers displayed alternate careers and relationships from many in more conventional, traditional occupations. The question arises, then, as to what extent these postmodern people, these transients who have uncoupled themselves from the conventional lifestyles and social structures of society, reflect the postmodern self. On the one hand, in their transience they come together, displaying minimalist biography or identity, forging connections and communities based on flexible adaptation and survival skills, on open and creative social skills. They are fragmented through their loss of stability, evoked only situationally by the work, leisure, and relationships they encounter in their travels. Like others, they are driven to seek new and shifting disposable commodities and experiences by the media-driven mass culture. Much of their lives are emotionally flat, depthless, and decentered by the loss of their central base in recurrent and predictable place, people, structure, and routine. They form relationships that do not need to negotiate or touch a core base to function.

At the same time, changes in their surroundings, social structures, and relations have led these transient workers to adapt seriously. Relinquishing the anchors conventionally lodging others, they have made self-modifications. External structures have been replaced by internal ones. Materialist goals have been replaced by experientialist ones. Conventional forms of family, work, friendships, and communities have been replaced by modified modes. Stability, predictability, and the luxury of closure have been replaced by fluidity, adaptability, and the challenge of openness. To varying degrees they have created new social values and meanings to replace old ones, replacing dissolved social structures with new adaptations. In leaving behind the security of conventional life, they have stepped into a shifting global world, one where they were, even in the midst of makeshift or professional communities, fundamentally alone. They have looked inward for their source of strength, being resourceful, eschewing the consumerist lifestyle, forging their own paths.

This has not resulted for them, however, in the loss of core self. They have adapted by finding new ways of conceiving and lodging themselves. No longer tied to the tethers of traditional work, seekers, in particular, lodge their identity in their leisure.[4] Theories of the postmodern self focus on changes that have occurred to the more surface aspects of the self, and these are recognizable here. But these theories have not looked at the deeper aspects of the self, assuming that decentering has dissolved it. In fact, the selves of transient resort workers in the postmodern era have adapted and thrived, emerging with renewed self-orientation and a stronger driving center. They display a core, "existential" self that is still, despite Gergen's (1991) fears, the fundamental source of their driving agency. Rather than finding themselves fashioned by layers with no underlying core, they have become more mutable: they are anchored in change rather than stability and are impulse-process rather than institution-product oriented. While many theoretical depictions of the technological and cultural environment arising in the postindustrial world appear to be accurate, it seems that the postmodernists' most pessimistic view of the demise of the self has not been borne out; rather, the core, existential self has adapted to contemporary conditions and thrived.[5] For many, especially those who can afford it, this is a liberating experience.

Postmodern Temporality

Resorts also operate on a postmodern rhythm and time frame. Melbin (1987) proposed that we are in a period of transition from what might be considered the modern era of traditional temporality to the postmodern temporal era. In increasingly producing, servicing, and consuming under conditions of incessance, we have come to rely on this accelerated pace. Although people who worked in incessant organizations initially found themselves temporally displaced and culturally arrhythmic, Melbin predicted that this transitional group would be succeeded by a generation that takes incessance and its dislocation for granted. Those who might adapt most successfully would be what he called "recombinant" individuals: those with the skills to adapt to transience and socially fragmented environments, those whose mobility has enabled them to adapt to change by striking up acquaintances rapidly, those with interpersonal styles enabling greater flexibility, affability, and ability to maintain diverse alliances and relationships. In short, he described our transient workers.

Over a quarter-century has passed since Melbin (1978) first proposed this model, and it fits our population in part but not in whole. Workers at the Ali'i resorts adapted better to dislocation from the days of the week and seasons of the year than they did to having their hours of the day altered. This may be because their bodies, like others', were less adaptable to the social creation of reconstructed sleeping and waking hours than they were to the recast of their weekends and vacations (cf. Luce 1971). The Ali'i resorts' tropical location, with its seasonally consistent climate and its island resort atmosphere, may have more readily facilitated the year-round vacation environment and the socially constructed weekend. But being awake and available for social and recreational activities was critical there, due to the area's strong eco-natural ties to the sun and daylight, factors that attracted many seekers to this resort area in the first place. Urban dwellers, more detached from the eco-natural world, may adapt more easily to sleep and waking dislocations in an environment that hums around the clock than to weekly and seasonal arrhythmia, which may be exacerbated by the prominence of these rhythms in the urban society.

Our observations suggest that people resent these disturbances to their cultural entrainment. As Melbin (1987) predicted, they have opted for working over unemployment but have never accepted arrhythmia comfortably. This is somewhat surprising, given the fact that resort workers, with their occupational and geographic transience, their postmodern communities and friendships, and their nontraditional family arrangements probably fit the idealistic portrait of recombinant individuals more than most other populations. As a society, we are not where Melbin and those who initially theorized about the freedom that would be generated by technology have suggested. Our temporal rhythms, although socially constructed, have a power that may have been underestimated.

Paradise Tourist Labor

The Ali'i resorts were particular kinds of social systems, representing one facet of the largest international industry. As such, they occupied an organizational, occupational, and labor niche. We analyze the dimensions of their functioning that pertain to the tourism industry.

Tourism as Service Labor

In chapter 1 we note that the literature on service labor suggests that workers may find themselves overly demeaned, controlled, and exploited in their jobs. Unlike service workers in fast food and other similar establishments where the window of interaction with clients is brief and management may strictly regulate employees (cf. Talwar 2004), most Ali'i workers' engagements with guests were not routinized (see also O'Neill 2001).[6] Nor were they as closely scrutinized as casino or Disneyland workers, who had cameras and blind observation posts from which management could examine them at all times (Sallaz 2002; Van Maanen and Kunda 1989). Rather, these hospitality workers were given a fair amount of autonomy in which to carry out their jobs.[7] This empowerment approach was necessary, given the flexibility and spontaneity with which they had to act and the importance customers placed on their personal relationships with employees.[8] Management relied on its workers not only to ensure that guests had a good time during their stays but to bring customers back with their warmth, personal attention (the real and putative "aloha" spirit), and "recognition" (Sherman 2003); the more guests felt the continuity of being connected to the resort and its community of employees, the more like "home" it felt, and the more likely that they would return.[9]

As such, Ali'i employees had to perform deep rather than surface emotional labor (Hochschild 1983), infusing their selves into their jobs through a process of role identification (O'Neill 2001). While this may make service work more enjoyable, it has the potential to lead to greater levels of burnout (see Brotheridge and Grandey 2002). Ali'i employees burned out on their service to guests under a variety of circumstances. Timing was a critical variable, as work stress built up when customer demands accumulated past the point they could be satisfied, at the busiest times of the day and seasons of the year.[10] Low occupancy periods could also be dissatisfying to employees, especially for those in tip jobs, as boredom and dissatisfaction set in. As Hodson (1991) also noted, they preferred to deliver service in a "flow" state (Csikszentmihalyi 1975), in between boredom and anxiety.

Employees' skill levels also influenced their enjoyment of service delivery, as higher-qualified and credentialed workers such as massage therapists and trainers, who were hired by guests for their expertise, were more likely to be treated with deference and respect.[11] In addition, employees burned out and grew dissatisfied with providing service labor to guests more quickly at more elite Aliʻi resorts. They found the way they were treated by guests more demeaning at these hotels and the level of service expected considerably higher. Employees of hotels toward the less elite end of the spectrum claimed that guests treated them as equals and as people, were less arrogant and less demanding. While there is undoubtedly a self-selecting process at work here, with richer people accustomed to a higher level of service booking themselves into the most expensive of these luxury resorts, Sherman (2003) has suggested that the culture of each hotel socializes guests as to what kind of service they are "entitled" to expect.

Not surprisingly, new immigrants had the least desire to interact directly with guests and often sought jobs where they would not have to provide customer service labor. Locals grew disgruntled with tourist service labor the next most often, as they interpreted guests' obnoxious boorishness and demands as demeaning, symbolically reading it as the subjugation of their indigenous population by invading outsiders. They then sought refuge by transferring into nonservice departments. Seekers and managers had the easiest time placing guests' abrasive behavior within the context of the high expectations people brought with them to a Hawaiian vacation, and they understood that the guests' anticipation of being pampered was part of the image sold by these luxury resorts. But even they eventually grew tired of how the most demanding guests acted. Thus, while many workers had enjoyable experiences and relationships with guests,[12] and only a small percentage of guests were actually negative, this was occasionally enough to eventually sour some employees on interacting with tourists. Even so, as noted in chapters 9 and 10, servicing tourists was not considered especially difficult and was not one of the main reasons why people left resort work.

The *noninteractive dimensions* of tourist hospitality labor are underaddressed in the service work literature, but these had a profound effect on Aliʻi resort employees. Hawaiʻi is not a Third World country, where mega-resort development has been used by governments to induce dramatic socioeconomic change, such as Madsen Camacho (1996) described for the part of rural Mexico she studied. There, simple peasants were evicted from their neighborhoods and homes to make way for resort development. Displaced as well from the ways they had traditionally earned their living, they were forced to abandon small, independent businesses and work for large, foreign-owned, multinational hotel corporations.

Some measure of this subjugation of the indigenous population did occur in Hawaiʻi, as the state consciously planned and financially assisted resort

development so that it could reap the huge economic benefits that would accrue (Stern 1989). As a result, housing prices shot up, forcing locals to move
out of areas they had traditionally inhabited and to commute long distances
to work. Hierarchical inequalities were created where a sense of homogeneity
had predominated. Employees were forced to work in temporal arrhythmia,
thrown out of synch with their families, their friends, and their bodies. Divorce rates among locals rose sharply (Shamir 1981; Stern 1989). They had
to adapt to mainland haole standards of dress, language, grooming, and de-
meanor. As a result, locals were transformed into outsiders in their own communities. While individuals who burned out on servicing tourists could quit
their jobs and find employment elsewhere, these broader, more structural
costs of the tourist service economy affected the entire community.

Tourism as Contingent Labor

Demographically, the Ali'i resorts' seasonal contingency labor force con-
trasted with the broader national contingency pool.[13] While women pre-
dominate over men in national, year-round contingency jobs, the Ali'i resorts'
seasonal contingents broadly comprised both genders. This difference can
largely be attributed to the number of seekers who traveled to Hawai'i for work
and the higher predominance of men in this group. By age, young people, who
filled most mainland contingent jobs, were well represented in the Ali'i workforce. But seasonal contingency work also became a way of life for some people, who settled there into career jobs and attained middle age. As is common
in most hotels, few people of retirement age worked the Ali'i strip. Finally, as
one might expect in the ethnically diverse Hawaiian Islands, there were many
more people of color employed in Ali'i contingent jobs than the national
norm.[14]

Ali'i seasonal contingent workers had varied relations to the characteristics associated with this broader form of labor. In some ways they fit the portrait. While the national trend shows that involuntary contingent workers
outnumber those voluntarily engaged, the ratio was less severe in the Ali'i resorts. People hired into regular (integrated) departments that swelled during
busy times often hoped for more permanent work and were disappointed at
being laid off when occupancy shrank. Part-time seasonals, however, looked
forward to the opportunity to augment their salaries with this extra work,
which facilitated their survival in their full-time jobs. Full-time seasonals who
migrated during the off-season or stayed around to enjoy the leisure lifestyle
of the Islands were also pleased with this arrangement.

In other ways seekers diverged from the characteristics of traditional contingent workers. First, seekers represent a new type of postmodern seasonal migrant worker with very different characteristics from, and earning a significantly higher wage than, traditional migrant workers: when their work expands and constricts, they travel voluntarily, for recreation rather than necessity. Second, although contingent work has been noted in the literature as potentially offering less monotony (Osterman et al. 2001), Ali'i seasonal contingent workers, like the full-time employees, were primarily drawn from the secondary labor pool and found their jobs similarly rote, routine, and repetitive. Third, while research has shown that many traditional contingent workers become trapped in this employment category, seasonal contingent jobs sometimes served as points of origination, leading to full-time employment as turnover created openings in departments where full-time work was available.[15] No contingent retention positions existed in relatively low-skilled, high turnover, Ali'i resort work.[16]

While contingent jobs have generally been regarded as exploitive and disadvantageous, research of the late 1990s and beyond suggests that contingent workers vary greatly in their degree of satisfaction with their jobs. It is useful, then, to consider the effects of seasonal contingency work. Comparative research has been undertaken in several studies to better understand why some contingent workers feel exploited while others are enabled, why some contingent jobs are judged "good jobs" while others rank as "bad" (Tilly 1996). Tilly compared contingent clerical workers in retail operations with insurance industry salesmen and found that greater satisfaction was associated with skilled over unskilled labor, retention over origination jobs, and voluntary participation in the contingent workforce. Rogers (2000) compared contingent clerical workers with temporary lawyers, noting that greater skill, more autonomy, and enhanced professional status led the lawyers to feel better about their temp jobs than the clerical workers. Better jobs involved more flexibility, autonomy, skill, and voluntary participation.

Seasonal contingent workers at the Ali'i beach resorts varied in their job satisfaction, although by different variables from those previously reported; their happiness was tied to two factors, their seniority and their pay scale. As Rogers (2000) noted, people integrated with full-time workers tend to occupy the bottom rungs of the hierarchy. In our setting, part-time and casual seasonals, while performing the same work as full-time employees, had the lowest seniority and thus were called in for shifts at the last minute and received the least desirable assignments. In segregated departments composed nearly entirely of seasonal workers, however, they could ascend the seniority hierarchy and receive the same treatment as everyone else.

More importantly, seasonal contingents who earned more money were happier with their jobs. At the Ali'i beach resorts, seasonal contingents' pay scale was not tied to their skill (everyone was relatively unskilled), their age (young people earned the same wages and held the same jobs as middle-aged people), their experience (no pay increases accrued with greater seniority), or their gender (men and women were often mixed in departments and earned the same wages, and "male" departments tended to pay only slightly better than "female" departments). The most significant factor affecting the pay of seasonal contingent workers was their degree of service labor: their relative location in departments connected to the lucrative banquet sector of the resorts, and their placement in the better-paying front-of-the-house jobs providing direct guest (and tip) service. Both of these elements were affected by workers' ethnicity.

When workers earn more money at their seasonal contingent jobs, they are likely to be more pleased with them, to have the opportunity to work voluntarily, and to feel a greater status and respect associated with their labor. This explains why different groups among the Ali'i resorts' seasonal contingent workers could view their occupational arrangements as enabling, liberating, and rewarding versus exploitive, demeaning, and disempowering. The contingent labor market offers increasingly flexible working opportunities for those advantaged populations as the flip side of the coin to the exploitation of disadvantaged seasonal and unskilled labor in underemployed populations.

Ethnicity and Tourist Labor

Throughout this book we have noted the ghettoization and stratification of ethnic groups into different departments and jobs. Members of these groups gravitated toward and were assigned to their particular departments through a combination of their own preferences and the standardized, stereotypical hiring patterns in the resorts. This represents a system of institutionalized racism, where Ali'i management may not necessarily have adopted overtly racist practices but may have simply recruited and promoted into existing images. Human resources and management decisions that appeared to be based on overt, legitimate factors often led to unequal results. People used a series of legitimations to justify this inequality, based on the importance of haoles' language and service skills, locals' size and strength, and new immigrants' hard-work ethos and reliability. Such rationalizations are often based, Rogers (2000) found, on a customer service orientation that sweeps inequality under the rug in the name of pleasing the client.

It is clear that occupational hierarchies exist where dominant ethnic and racial groups monopolize the more attractive jobs, with each subsequent racial/ethnic group seizing the next most attractive job category on down the line (Lieberson 1980).[17] In much the same way that Reskin and Roos (1990) found job queues tied to gender queues, where higher-status women land the better jobs, the Ali'i resort job queues were tied to racialized/ethnic queues with corresponding job descriptions and pay scales.[18] Race and ethnicity thus join a host of other characteristics that queue workers for the better jobs including age, gender, social class, education, language skills, country of origin, and other forms of cultural capital.[19]

The Ali'i resorts offer us a laboratory to examine the occupational placement and patterns of three different ethnic/racial groups: haoles (whites), locals (brown), and new immigrants.[20] White people brought all the demographic advantages of class, education, and cultural capital to their employment. Those who sought management careers were quickly accelerated through the ranks. People whose interest lay in unskilled or semiskilled work received favorable positions with the highest pay. Moreover, whites captured many of the skilled positions in the resorts by coming in with specialized credentials in the spa, fitness, and recreation areas (although locals were represented there as well). White women were clearly handicapped, however, compared to white men.

Locals were disadvantaged by race/ethnicity, class, and education but benefited through their language skills and acculturation. In management, they moved easily into the middle ranks, with some reaching the executive levels. At the line positions, they mingled comfortably with whites in many departments (bell, beach and pool, guest services, spa, fitness) and occupied the middle rung of the stratified banquet arena. New immigrants were preferred over locals for jobs at the lowest levels, but locals generally disdained and avoided such dirty, demeaning work.

The notion, then, that indigenous, local populations were displaced by immigrant laborers was not really the case here.[21] Locals were exploited by management, however, being placed into highly visible token positions commodifying Hawaiian culture for the guests. As lei greeters and lei-making instructors, hula and lu'au dancers, and front desk clerks, for example, they fulfilled the objectified, commercialized notion of Hawaiians as "ideal natives": brown but not black (so they sidestepped the divisiveness of the black/white mainland conflict), graciously welcoming and not threatening to outsiders, alluring and sensual, different (the "other"), and primitive rather than modern (Desmond 1999). Where necessary, they further served as tokens, performing liaison work to local groups (Collins 1983, 1993; Jones 1986). Local women suffered the dual disadvantage of ghettoization into female positions and ethnic discrimination.

New immigrants, although the most severely demographically disadvantaged of the three groups, had high levels of job satisfaction. They voluntarily sought out and never looked beyond employment in linguistic, family, and ethnic occupational enclaves (Evans 1987; Grint 1998). As noted above, both genders fared well in resort employment, finding an abundance of jobs that offered them community, autonomy, and respectable wages.[22] Thus, although they occupied the lowest rung of the resort work strata, they had largely escaped dirtier, harder, and worse-paying work in agriculture; they worked in safe, clean environments;[23] and they were well underway toward attaining their American dream. They scrimped and saved to achieve material success, they attained citizenship and either brought their families to the United States or made their lives easier back home, and they watched their children enjoy the upward mobility they so fervently desired, moving into higher-strata resort work and a variety of other jobs held by locals.

Organizing Tourist Labor

Hawaiian resort hotels represent an important arena for the union movement, as they incorporate the conflicting trends of a strong state, democratic, and unionization background while employing populations that have traditionally been considered hard to organize. The Ali'i resorts presented a potpourri of union and nonunionization. Most hotels accorded the decision to unionize to each individual department, so that there were often mixtures of unionized and nonunionized departments in each resort. If enough departments and employees voted in favor of the union, however, the organization became a union hotel. For Ali'i workers, the presence of a union in their department or hotel usually resulted in a slight raise in pay, protection from management harassment, a guarantee that the management would adhere to state labor regulations, and a place to complain should they have a grievance. For Ali'i management, unions generally meant less navigability in their efforts to maintain a flexible workforce, to control costs, and to control workers. As a result, many of the Ali'i resorts, as they turned over management companies and changed ownership, engaged in a constant struggle against unionization, as noted in chapter 6.

Departments most likely to be unionized under the individual arrangement were always located in the back of the house, where highly stable new immigrants formed the preponderance of workers. The least likely department to be unionized was always beach and pool, with its labor force of transient, youthful seekers and locals. In Zamudio's (1996) study of hotel union organizing, she found that new immigrants were particularly difficult to recruit for unions, but that "natives" joined willingly. She attributed this to issues of ethnicity and citizenship. Yet the new immigrants in her Los Angeles hotel were Central and South Americans, many of whom planned to return to their countries of origin for retirement—that is, migrant immigrants.[24] Our new immigrants, however, made a firm commitment to remaining in America. Wells (2000) has documented more recent successes in organizing San Francisco hotel workers. She noted that San Francisco witnessed a huge influx of new immigrants over the last quarter of the twentieth century, fostering a local community highly receptive toward integrating new immigrants.

This suggests that the "trapped," or committed, factor may be more significant in determining workers' likelihood of participating in labor organization than race/ethnicity or citizenship. Ali'i workers most likely to be the active and vocal leaders of unionization movements were the ones "advantaged" by their cultural capital: some of the trapped locals, but most often the relocated seekers.[25] Committed, advantaged workers, then, particularly white men, stood at the forefront of the politics of union activism in the tourism industry.

The Political Economy of Tourism

The Ali'i resorts, as hospitality organizations, engaged in political and economic maneuvers to control costs and to manage employees. In contrast to other industries where this may not be possible, they used what Edwards (1979) has termed "loose modes of control" when times were busy, stretching and compressing their full-time staff and asking people to exceed their forty weekly hours. They used "tight [even coercive] modes of control" during slack periods, sending people home early and asking them to take less pay in underutilized areas, adopting "housecleaning" and other attrition strategies to weed out less desirable employees, leaving these positions unfilled, and stretching people to cover multiple jobs when business picked up again. But overwhelmingly, through their use of part-time, subcontracting, temporary, and casual positions, they were able to bring employees in and release them at will, assuming few obligations to this workforce. Like other organizations, those resort hotels manipulating their "flexible" labor force more adroitly to keep costs closely tied to occupancy were able to show greater profitability (see Krakover 2000b).

Theories of organizations' relations to their employees, the politics of their "human resources" (Kalleberg et al. 1996), are best understood, we argued earlier, by examining the broader context of labor relations in the local market economy. Each of the three forces we now consider—the organizations, the employees, and the local labor market—made a contribution to the political economy of this situation, and each was influenced by it in different ways.

From an *organizational* perspective, the resort hotels had several needs from their employee pool. First, they needed steady, long-term employees to form the backbone of their corporate identities, maintaining the institutional knowledge of policies and practices so necessary when the management was highly transient, and then providing the enduring relationships with returning guests who expected to be taken care of by their "family" at the hotels. Second, they needed a replenishing pool of youthful employees. Replacing older, "burned out" line employees with novices fresh out of the local high schools or new to the island boosted morale. Third, to fill the middle management ranks, the organizations needed to lure a small percentage of these individuals into making the hospitality industry a career. They were more successful in retaining locals for this purpose, as these people had fewer occupational alternatives. Fourth, the resorts also needed a flexible seasonal labor pool of workers to service the group functions. The larger the percentage of these who returned annually and needed no retraining, taking a leadership role, the smoother the hotels' banquets ran.

Finally, these organizations relied on a less seasonal pool of contingent workers, coming from the Hawaiian Islands and the mainland, to fill the employment gaps created when occupancy ran high, without draining their resources during slower periods. In seeking to hire the optimal proportion of workers from each of these categories, the Ali'i resorts, while they could have attained greater profitability by slashing their full-time workforce to the bare minimum and using a larger percentage of contingent workers, chose to keep a slightly greater percentage of full-time staff, expanding and shrinking their hours. Our research reveals that full-time employees can be made to work in a flexible manner that benefits their organizations, much like contingent workers.

From an *employee* perspective, different populations adapted to the seasonal fluctuation of work in various ways. Locals were a group with strong feelings toward their extended kinship networks and toward the land ('āina), their sense of place. They tended to have more casual work habits and to bring to their employment a low level of skills and education. While some were more dedicated and ambitious, most worked toward the goal of sustaining their lives outside work. When busy season came, they worked overtime to maximize their earnings, more fully utilizing the leisure opportunities available in this resort area during slow season by going to the beach, fishing, swimming, surfing, golfing, and hunting.

New immigrants were a group with dedicated work habits, who spent what little time they were not working involved with their extended and nuclear families, their church groups, and their ethnic communities. Not having grown up in America, they lacked the educational credentials to obtain more skilled work than resort employment. Most were extremely nervous about straying beyond their linguistic communities. They therefore found jobs within ethnic enclaves and stayed with them throughout their careers. Few new immigrants held contingent jobs; they preferred to work steadily for a lower paycheck than to make more money per hour in a seasonal job that could not be relied on year-round.

The wages of management workers were not affected by seasonality either, as managers were salaried. Their hours on property increased dramatically during the busy seasons, especially for those managing food and beverage departments. It was not uncommon to see these managers working without a day off for months, sleeping in their offices for weeks at a time, or going home for five hours of sleep and coming back to work again during group season. They saw little of their families unless their partner worked in the same resort. They took forced vacations during the slow seasons.

Seekers' seasonal work patterns varied with their departments. Like locals, they adapted their lifestyles to the patterns of the year. But having explicitly moved to Hawai'i for the beauty and recreation, seekers felt that their hard labor during the peak seasons was wasted if they were always too busy to enjoy their surroundings. Their choice to live in a resort area reflected their desire to incorporate leisure into their lives. Many voluntarily sought contingent employment to more fully dedicate themselves to their leisure, traveling the world during the off-season to scuba, surf, windsurf, and kiteboard. They considered their leisure time to be as valuable a resource as their money and deliberately eschewed careers that would have held them working steadily or in one place year-round. Their superior hourly pay compared to locals and new immigrants enabled them to work fewer hours and still maintain a reasonable lifestyle.[26]

Employees thus brought two different sets of offerings and needs to their working lives. Locals and new immigrants were unskilled or semiskilled, somewhat unambitious, and immobile, looking for steady jobs on which they could build settled lives and families. Seekers and management mainland haoles possessed significant cultural capital through their education, language skills, and cultural background. The former sought a lifestyle set in paradise with the time to enjoy it, while the latter enjoyed paradise on their way up and out of it. A symbiosis existed between the existing jobs and the people available to fill them.

Local labor markets are geographical areas within which labor is bought and sold. They encompass local social systems where capital and labor meet, representing the link between space and society (Schulman and Anderson 1993). Spatially, this string of hotels, like many resorts, was located in an isolated and geographically remote area, making commuter travel in and out difficult. Both employers and employees were constrained by the isolated geographic locale, making it a necessity for hotels to innovate with their scheduling. The brain drain resulting from the out-migration of bright young people left behind a largely trapped residual population (Manicas 1996). College education was neither highly valued in the local culture nor widely available, so most young people raised there went straight to work out of high school. Residents were restricted in their choice of available work to what the local economy offered. Limited jobs were available for those raised on the island beyond the tourist industry with the exception of retail sales, as agricultural production in Hawai'i has waned, leaving only government, social service, and a smattering of other occupations viable.[27]

Labor market studies have found that unemployment runs highest among those with lower educational attainment (high school versus college), particularly among men. Nearly all the increase in unemployment has fallen upon unskilled individuals, leading to a deterioration of job security, slowed earnings growth, and rising inequality (Addison 1997). When unemployment levels are high, people are prepared to accept the disadvantages of insecure work and low pay in return for the positive fact of having at least some paid employment. For less-skilled workers, it may be one of the few ways of earning money (Murphy 1996). Nevertheless, the beauty and wild spirit of the Islands drew outsiders, bringing a steady influx of mainland haoles seeking paradise and needing work.

In an area where the opportunities were few, costs were steep, and living conditions were highly desirable, the resort industry offered some of the best work available. Local inhabitants willingly adapted themselves to the seasonal employment fluctuations, although many worked long hours and multiple jobs. The situation of the poorly paid, less-skilled locals and new immigrants stood in contrast to the better pay of mainland haole management and banquet workers. As the structuralist theory of human resource organization suggests, the Ali'i resorts reproduced the inequality in the larger society through the internal system of stratification found in workers' earnings inequality and differential career mobility (Baron and Bielby 1980; Farkas and England 1988). Haoles were paid better and had greater opportunities to rise through the ranks; new immigrants were ghettoized into the lowest paid, dirtiest, and hardest jobs; and the locals fell somewhere in between, rising to middle management and being offered moderately paid seasonal work.

While it is clear that all three forces in the political economy of this tourist labor equation contributed symbiotically toward its ultimate functionality, at the same time there were exploitive dimensions. The organizations benefited as changes in the postwar labor market moved them into more powerful positions relative to their employees (Osterman 1999). Employees had differential outcomes, with those seeking greater leisure and the better-paid benefiting from this situation, accruing and enjoying the flexibility and freedom that their more meagerly paid fellow workers could not afford. The Euro-American system of preference perpetrated by the resort owners and their clientele reinforced the ethnic stratification of workers.

At the same time, less-advantaged workers, whom scholars might logically expect to be inclined toward organizing against their seasonal hiring and firing, embraced the temporal-flexibility model. Their occupational uncertainty, risk, and transience can be evaluated, as Smith (2001) has noted, in light of the organizational/industrial context, of the labor market, and of variations in their age, gender, class, race/ethnicity, and education.

The tourist labor market, while sustained, became disadvantaged over the long run as the availability of only unskilled and underpaid jobs reinforced the flight of smarter, more ambitious young people to the mainland and reproduced a subsistence labor market status quo. While the immediate, visible, and near-term adaptations benefited workers and the local labor force as well as the organizations, workers and their organizations were disadvantaged at the larger, less visible structural level, as the organization of human resources fostered a political economy of stratification that reinforced the reproduction of inequality and the impoverishment of the local market economy.

A P P E N D I X

THE PARTICIPANTS

Managers

Achmed, Kahlid	mainland hotel	rooms executive
wife Marion	mainland hotel	human relations manager
Bach, Josh	Lukane Sands	executive director spa
Bacon, Edward	Lukane Sands	rooms division/front office executive
Bjornstadt, Hans	mainland hotel	food and beverage executive
Boggs, Art	Lukane Sands	general manager
Butterworth, Tom	Kahana Surf	general manager
Caplan, Larry	Lukane Sands	guest services director/executive director spa
Clark, George	Lukane Sands	executive director of housekeeping/director internal operations
Direnzo, Elizabeth	Kahana Surf	restaurant manager
Douglas, Rick	Lukane Sands	executive director food and beverage
Garvey, Matt	Kahana Surf	senior director guest operations
Gregson, Bucky	mainland hotel	executive housekeeper
Holland, Terry	Hula Club Towers	DJ/nightclub manager/food and beverage
Jacobs, Denise	Kahana Surf	
Jensen, Ryan	Lukane Sands	vice president business operations
Keen, Richard	Hula Club Towers	executive director food and beverage

Kimble, David	Pono Beach Spa	sales executive
Kouchi, Dumar	international hotel	front desk night manager
Law, Chuck wife Barbara	Pono Beach Spa	deputy director
Levy, Steve	mainland hotel	rooms division executive/ deputy director
Masters, Ben	Lei Gardens	catering and banquet manager
McLeod, Daniel	Pono Beach Spa	beach and pool manager
McMurray, Vince	Pono Beach Spa	group sales executive
Michaels, Woody	Hula Club Towers	guest services director
Morgan, Wes	Hula Club Towers	executive director food and beverage
Peraud, Scott	mainland hotel	food and beverage executive
Rosen, Neil	Lei Gardens	restaurant manager
Stone, Bill	mainland resort	executive director food and beverage
Thomas, Janice	mainland resort	comptroller
partner Matt Marshall	mainland resort	executive
Thorpe, Frank	Kahana Surf	food and beverage executive
Williamson, Warren	Lukane Sands	director catering and conven- tion services

New Immigrants

Agrifina	Lukane Sands	housekeeper/steward
Alva	Hula Club Towers/ Lukane Sands	houseman
Claro	Lei Gardens	landscaper
Evelina	Lukane Sands	transportation department clerk
Favi	Kahana Surf	housekeeper
Kam	Lei Gardens	cook
Leonardo	Hula Club Towers	steward
Maximo	Hula Club Towers	steward
Miguela	Hula Club Towers	housekeeper
Nilda	Kahana Surf	housekeeper

| Duque Santo | Pono Beach Spa | stewarding manager |
| Vida | Pono Beach Spa | housekeeper |

Locals

Alex	Kahana Surf	beach and pool
Alika	Hula Club Towers	front desk
Annie	Hula Club Towers	concierge
Brandon	Pono Beach Spa	beach and pool
Bruce	Lei Gardens	bellman
Cory	Hula Club Towers	houseman
Dela Cruz, Thelma	Kahana Surf	accounting manager
Don	Lukane Sands	bellman
Eduardo	Lei Gardens	bellman
Enrique	Lei Gardens	houseman
Esmeralda	Lukane Sands	front desk
Felix	Pono Beach Spa	beach and pool/water features
Grego	Hula Club Towers	beach and pool
Hali, Lauren	Lukane Sands	beach and pool manager
Hermio	Lukane Sands	front desk
Hona	Hula Club Towers	houseman
Hope	Kahana Surf	human resources
Januaria	Hula Club Towers	front desk
Jeffrey	Pono Beach Spa	houseman/landscaper
Joseph	Hula Club Towers	houseman
Kaipo	Lukane Sands	room reservations
Kamoka	Lei Gardens	entertainer
Kaniho	Pono Beach Spa	fitness trainer
Kaona, Nestor	Kahana Surf	houseman supervisor
Karl	Lukane Sands	front desk
Ke'ahi, Tia	Lukane Sands	room reservations manager
Kevin	Hula Club Towers	houseman
wife Pua	Hula Club Towers	hair salon
Kiawe	Lukane Sands	houseman
Kiloa	Kahana Surf	beach and pool
Ko'ono	Lukane Sands	beach and pool

Koa	Pono Beach Spa	kitchen/beach and pool/water features
Ku	Lukane Sands	beach and pool
Kumeho, Rob	Ali'i resort	restaurant manager
Kyle	Lukane Sands	bell captain
Leroy	Hula Club Towers	beach and pool/assistant manager housekeeping
Lorraine	Lukane Sands	human resources
Nakamura, Chad	Pono Beach Spa	executive director food and beverage
Nohi	Pono Beach Spa	beach and pool
Palo	Lukane Sands	beach and pool
Palomi	Hula Club Towers	concierge
Pepito	Lukane Sands	fitness attendant
Pinedo, Mike	Lukane Sands	fitness manager
Romeo	Lei Gardens	houseman
Scott	Hula Club Towers	valet
Seth	Lukane Sands	fitness trainer
Tamora	Hula Club Towers	security
Taylor	Lei Gardens	bellman
Teresita	Lukane Sands	aerobics instructor
Tiare	Kahana Surf	beach and pool
Todd	Hula Club Towers	bellman
Ty	Lukane Sands	bell captain
Victor	Lei Gardens	landscaping
Wally	Lei Gardens	security
Willy	Lukane Sands	aerobics instructor

Seekers

Al	Hula Club Towers	beach and pool
Alan	Lukane Sands	front desk
Alexa	Lukane Sands	beach and pool
Andy	Lukane Sands	beach and pool/spa attendant
Barry	Lukane Sands	bellman
Bernie	Kahana Surf	retail sales
Bob	Kahana Surf	massage therapist
Brooke	Lukane Sands	aerobics instructor

Bud	Pono Beach Spa	fitness professional
Camille	Kahana Surf	scuba diver
Carlson, Jeff	Pono Beach Spa	retail shop owner
Carol	Lei Gardens/ Hula Club/Lukane	banquet/aerobics
Colin	Lei Gardens	bellman
Connor	Lei Gardens	banquet
Dana	Lukane Sands	banquet/beach and pool
Danielle	Pono Beach Spa	retail sales
David	Pono Beach Spa	banquet server
Deedy	Lukane Sands	pool waitress
Dennis	Lukane Sands	bellman
Don	Lukane Sands	massage therapist
Emily	Lukane Sands	beach and pool
Eric	Lukane Sands	kayak instructor
Ernie	Kahana Surf	beach and pool
Freddy	Pono Beach Spa	valet/bell
Gabriela	Kahana Surf	fitness trainer
Gary	Lei Gardens	banquet server
Hank	Hula Club Towers	fitness trainer
wife Susie	Hula Club Towers	pool waitress/restaurant cashier
Hila	Kahana Surf	waitress
Horowitz, David	Lukane Sands	retail shop owner
Iris	Lukane Sands	retail sales
Jake	Kahana Surf	beach and pool supervisor
James	Lukane Sands	chef
Jane	Hula Club Towers	front desk
Janell	Lukane Sands	beach and pool
Jennifer	Pono Beach Spa	hair salon
Jill	Kahana Surf	scuba diver
Joey	Lukane Sands	beach and pool/spa/info technology
John	Kahana Surf	valet
Kamala	Lukane Sands	banquet server
Kathy	Pono Beach/ Lukane Sands	aerobics instructor
Keiko	Hula Club Towers	pool waitress
Ken	Lukane Sands	beach and pool

Kim	Kahana Surf	banquet server
Kim	Lukane Sands	massage therapist
Kristy	Lukane/Pono Beach	beach and pool/waitress
Lance	Hula Club Towers	beach and pool
Lisa	Lei Gardens	secretary
Luke	Lei Gardens	beach and pool
Maia	mainland restaurant	waitress
Marc	Kahana Surf	chef
Marcos	Lukane Sands	banquet server
Matt	Lei Gardens	valet
Megan	Pono Beach Spa	fitness trainer
Milo	international hotel	doorman
Nick	Lei Gardens	beach and pool
Paul	Lei Gardens	beach and pool
Ray	Pono Beach Spa	scuba diver
Rick	Kahana Surf	beach and pool
Ron	Hula Club Towers	banquet server
Ryan	Lei Gardens	banquet bartender
Sam	Pono Beach Spa	banquet server
Sarah	Lei Gardens	pool waitress
Sosie	Pono Beach Spa	massage therapist
Tammy	Hula Club Towers	concierge
Ted	Lei Gardens	beach and pool
Tiffany	Kahana Surf	pool waitress
Tori	Lukane Sands	banquet server
Trevor	Lukane Sands	beach and pool

N O T E S

Chapter 1. Entering Paradise

1. Trask (1993) and Desmond (1999) have offered insightful analyses of the commodification of Hawaiian culture. They both look at the ways in which Hawaiian artifacts, cultural icons, and customs have been exploited to make the tourist experience seem more authentic.

2. Perhaps no other industry took a bigger hit than tourism in the wake of the September 11 terrorism attacks in New York and Washington. As of 2003, 6.6 million people in the tourist industry worldwide were out of work. One out of every twelve workers in the industry lost his or her job during 2001–2 ("Empty Beach Chairs" 2003, 1B). Surprisingly, though, the number of tourists around the world hit a record in 2002, despite the fears of terrorism. However, in contrast to past years, travelers stayed closer to home, made shorter visits, and spent less ("World Tourism Bags Record" 2003, 3B).

3. The rise in tourism was so dramatic that the numbers of tourists visiting the Hawaiian Islands rose from 171,000 in 1958 to 2,631,000 in 1973, a 20-percent increase every year. However, these gains leveled off in the 1990s, with the overall visitors to the Islands approximately the same in 1999 as in 1990 (see Blackford 2001).

4. Despite these impressive financial figures, tourism hit a huge slump in the Hawaiian Islands by the mid-1990s. For instance, in 1996, business failures climbed 47 percent, compared to 1 percent throughout the rest of the United States. During that same year, Hawai'i lost 4,000 residents due to out-migration and the hope of finding better opportunities elsewhere (Blackford 2001).

5. All names of people and places are pseudonyms.

6. By "trapped" we do not mean to suggest that they remain in Honua against their will or that they cannot leave. In fact, they do have the resources to travel and relocate, and many have moved from foreign countries to live in Honua. But the members of these two groups who live here have made a decision to make Honua their permanent home and will likely remain here for the rest of their lives. As a result, they are economically trapped in the local job pool and can seek work only within the confines of what is available on the island.

7. Madsen Camacho (1996) also posits that "cultural capital" is an important variable stratifying workers in the Mexican resort she studied.

8. See Hamburger 1983; Prus and Irini 1980; Rollinson 1990; and Stephens 1976.

9. See Chapman 1992 and Thompson 2002.

10. See Sherman 2003.

11. See Baum and Haveman 1997.

12. See Josephson 1956.

13. See Shamir 1981.

14. See Brown 1998 and Schwartz 2003.

15. See Stepick and Grenier 1994.

16. See Madsen Camacho 1996; Stern 1989; Wells 2000; and Zamudio 1996.

17. See Whyte 1949.

18. See Fine 1996 and Schroedl 1972.

19. See Butler and Skipper 1980; Cobble 1991; Hutter 1969; Mars and Nicod 1984; and Paules 1991.

20. See Butler and Snizek 1976.

21. See Marshall 1986.

22. See Leidner 1993; Newman 1999; and Talwar 2004.

23. The only full-length sociological treatment of the inner workings of a hotel we could find was ancient (see Haynes 1936).

24. See Bosk 1992; Cassell 1991; Millman 1976; and Zussman 1992.

25. See Eckert 1989; Eder 1995; and Wood 1986.

26. See Beynon 1972, 1975; Burawoy 1979; and Rinehart et al. 1997.

27. See Cock 1989; Constable 1997; Hondagneu-Sotelo 2001; and Rollins 1985.

28. See Devinatz 1999 and Kunda 1992.

29. See Burris 1983; Kanter 1977; and Smigel 1969.

30. See Jackall 1988 and V. Smith 1990.

31. See Chinoy 1955; Fink 1998; Gamst 1980; Hamper 1991; and Linhart 1981.

32. See Lois 2003; Manning 1977; Martin 1980; McCarl 1985; and Rubinstein 1973.

33. Sherman (2003) will help to ameliorate this dearth.

34. See Dirlik 1996; Hodson et al. 1998; and Kearney 1995.

35. Research has suggested that global labor migrants become caught in the interstices of nations because they are stunted in forming communities and becoming incorporated into the labor markets of their host countries (Glick-Schiller et al. 1995; Ong 1999; Parreñas 2001).

36. Scholarship on the rise of domestic work by international migrant women has become almost a cottage industry unto itself among feminist scholars. Numerous books, edited anthologies, and articles were published in the latter part of the twentieth century that documented the plight of women who were housed, employed, and often exploited by families, in the United States and elsewhere, that need inexpensive housecleaning, child care, and older adult care to maintain their standard of living and positions in the higher-strata labor force. While these domestic workers have been around for many decades, the influx of women into the middle-class labor force around the world has created an even greater need for domestic work. For examples of the scholarship on international migrant domestic workers, see Bakan and Stasiulis 1997; Chaney and Castro 1989; Chin 1998; Constable 1997; Garza 2001; Gregson and Lowe 1994; Heyzer et al. 1994; Hondagneu-Sotelo 1994, 2001; Kaplan 1987; Parreñas 2001; Romero 1992, 1994; and Wrigley 1995.

37. For a discussion of the rhythmic temporality of society, see Brissett and Snow 1993; Lauer 1981; Lyman and Scott 1989; Snow and Brissett 1986; and Zerubavel 1981.

38. For some excellent theoretical analyses of the relationship between self and society, see Gagnon 1992; Jameson 1984; Mead 1934; and Wood and Zurcher 1988.

39. For further discussion of the postmodern self, see Dowd 1991; Gergen 1991; and

Jameson 1984. Note, however, that some contemporary theorists challenge the postmodernists' image of self as centerless, fragmented, and situational. These authors reject the idea of bringing Goffman's concept of the multisituational self into an analysis of how the self operates in postmodern society (see Allen 1997 for further explanation and extrapolation).

40. Asian Americans—especially those from India—have begun to make significant inroads into the hospitality industry. As early as 1987, the *Wall Street Journal* reported that 28 percent of all motels in the United States were owned by Indians. Asians have become so visible in the hotel industry that they now have their own organization, the Asian Hotel Owners Association (AHOA) that boasts that 37 percent of all hotel properties in the United States are Asian-owned. See Fong 2002 for further discussion.

41. For an excellent and comprehensive overview of the changing labor market in the United States, see Osterman et al. 2001.

42. See Gronröos 1990; Kutscher 1987; Macdonald and Sirianni 1996; McCammon and Griffin 2000; and U.S. Department of Labor 2002.

43. See Blau and Ehrenberg 2000; Browne 2000; Cherry and Rodgers 2000; Moss and Tilly 2001; Reskin and Roos 1990; and Spain and Bianchi 1996.

44. See Bartik 2001; Freeman and Gottschalk 2000; and Holzer 1999.

45. See Appadurai 1996; Bean and Bell-Rose 1999; Blau and Kahn 2002; and Burawoy et al. 2000.

46. See Grint 1998; Macdonald and Sirianni 1996; McCammon and Griffin 2000; and Osterman 1999.

47. See Barker and Christensen 1998; Belous 1989; duRivage 1992; Hodson 2000; and Thompson 1995. For a review of the literature on contingency labor, see Kalleberg 2000.

48. See Belous 1989; Blossfeld and Hakim 1997; and O'Reilly and Fagan 1998.

49. See Belous 1989; Barker and Christensen 1998; and Rogers 2000.

50. See Barker and Christensen 1998; Buessing 1997; Cantor 1988; Gorz 1982, 1985; Klein et al. 1998; Meiksins and Whalley 2002; Murphy 1996; Olmsted and Smith 1989; and Rogers 2000. Rogers (2000) has suggested that higher levels of skill and professionalism yield greater degrees of autonomy for contingent workers.

51. See Golden and Appelbaum 1992; Horning et al. 1996; and Van Dyne and Ang 1998.

52. See Carré and Joshi 1997; Houseman 2001 Parker 1994; Smith 1998; and Witt and Witt 1989.

53. Lautsch (2002) has suggested that two different motivations impel management to hire contingent workers. When their objective is to cut costs, they are more likely to hire these workers into segregated departments. When maintaining a flexible labor force is their goal, they are more likely to hire them into integrated situations.

54. For an overarching review of this literature, see Belous 1989; duRivage 1992; and Tilly 1992, 1996.

55. For further empirical studies of the union prospects of youth and workers of color, see Laslett and Tyler 1989; Quadagno 1994; and Tannock 2001.

56. Discussions of the relationship between new immigrant status and unionization can also be seen in Piore 1979 and Waldinger and Der-Martirosian 2000.

57. In 2002, Hawai'i elected its first Republican governor, Linda Lingle, since it achieved statehood in 1959 and to date has never had a Republican senator in the U.S. Congress.

58. See, for example, Baron and Bielby 1980; Berg 1981; Farkas and England 1988; and Kalleberg and Berg 1987.

59. Even these older properties had to put in millions of dollars of renovation during the time of our study to keep pace with the highly competitive resort industry.

60. A relatively new style of resorts, fashioned in response to the success of Club Med, is "all-inclusive," meaning that with a single fee, practically everything that one does while within the confines of the property is complimentary. While none of the resorts we studied offered this option, they have become very popular in places such as the Caribbean and Mexico. All-inclusives represent the ultimate in destination vacations.

61. Throughout this book, we refer to people working in management positions by both their first and last names, as this is what appeared on the nametags that they wore daily. People in lower-end positions, however, only had their first names on their tags; in their cases, then, in line with the organizations' appellations, we use their first names exclusively. This is just one indication of the internal stratification that was so evident at the resorts.

Chapter 2. Researching Resorts

1. For some excellent background and history of the vacation in American society and elsewhere, see Aron 1999; Gini 2003; Lenček and Bosker 1998; Löfgren 1999; and Urbain 2003.

2. Markula (1997) has written about being a tourist from an ethnographic perspective. She chronicled her disappointing visit to Tahiti, where she expected an authentic culture, and how she, as a Westernized woman, related to the simulated culture of the resort world.

3. For an excellent discussion of the use of qualitative methods in leisure research, see Dupuis 1999. Here, she described the particular roles and roadblocks that researchers who study others' leisure might encounter.

4. For a discussion of the peculiar problems inherent in studying organizations from a qualitative perspective, see Van Maanen 1998, an edited volume gleaned from the past pages of the journal *Administrative Science Quarterly,* long a purveyor of organizational ethnographies. In addition, Hodson (2001) has created an archive at Ohio State University that lists all of the available studies of organizations conducted ethnographically.

5. Resort areas have been studied sociologically from the perspective of the tour guide (Schmidt 1979) and the tourist (MacCannell 1989; Markula 1997). Madsen Camacho (1996) used participant observation to study a resort hotel, Thompson (2002) got a job on a cruise ship to study the crew, Holyfield (1999) attended guide school for river rafters, and Jonas (1997) served as an apprentice and then became a river guide leader (what Arnould and Price [1993] call "experiential" service workers). For a fascinating article that contrasts the convergent and divergent experiences of these two river runners-turned-researchers, see Holyfield and Jonas 2003. Brown (1998) used a combination of personal history, in-depth interviews, and archival research to study the hotel where he was raised. Of course, there is a considerable literature on the planning, marketing, and developing of resorts, as well as other business and management factors. See King 1997 for a review of such works.

6. When we asked one bellman whom we did not know that well, for instance, what kinds of factors might affect the longevity of his career in resort work, he hesitated to answer,

worrying that if he made any critical remarks about the management it might affect his job. We also experienced repeated frustration getting the permission of new immigrant workers to use their photos for the book. Although they were willing to grant us oral permission, when we presented them with the model release form to sign, many balked in fear that they might lose their jobs, that it might cost them money, or from other unimaginable consequences.

7. Desmond (1999) discussed how Hawaiian hotels try to represent authentic Hawai'i for their customers through the clothing, décor, and sights within their establishments. Mac-Cannell (1992, 168) calls this "reconstructed ethnicity," by which he means "the maintenance and preservation of ethnic forms for the persuasion or entertainment not of specific others . . . but of a 'generalized other' within a white cultural frame."

8. This bears some similarity to the "phenomenological" interview approach that Pearson (1987) employed in conducting brief, on-the-spot interviews with Grateful "Deadheads" preceding, during, and after concerts.

9. Of course, there were other people who came to the resort annually or more often, but few stayed as long or were as visible as we.

10. Since we were doing research and teaching there, there were also certain tax benefits we received.

11. Kinship is a fluid and loose relationship in Hawaiian culture. The importance of kinship is central to all associations among Hawaiians, and thus fictive kin expressions, such as auntie and uncle, are liberally used with just about anyone who is in one's social network.

12. All quotes in this book reproduce as faithfully as possible the way the workers spoke to us. While other depictions of Hawaiians' speech often embody the particular rhythm, cadence, and colorful characteristics of the local dialect (see Ito 1999), resort workers do not speak that way to haoles. One of the hiring requirements at this strip of hotels was that prospective employees be able to speak standard American. Although we came to be known as regulars who taught on the island, resort workers spoke to us in "sanitized" English during both casual conversations and taped interviews.

13. Whether or not the term "haole" is derogatory has long been up for discussion among Hawaiians. While there are multiple answers to this question, most admit that there is at least a "hint of contempt" in the term (see Rohrer 1997).

14. Literally this term means "child of the land," but more commonly it refers to people who are "native born" (Ito 1999, 1). Colloquially and practically, though, it means anyone who has a Hawaiian driver's license.

15. See our chapter, "The Reluctant Respondent" (Adler and Adler 2002a), for a detailed discussion of types of people who are afraid to give interviews and strategies to use to circumvent some of these roadblocks.

16. Fortunately, we were aided by the phenomenon that Hawaiians call "talk story." This form of communication, which probably comes from the oral tradition of Hawaiian culture, involves a "relaxed, rambling, sometimes intense commentary or conversation" (Ito 1999, 12). Thus, once the respondents got past their initial nervousness and realized that all we wanted to do is "talk story," they often loosened up and felt more comfortable.

17. For further discussion of the problems of negotiating around the dictates of Institutional Review Boards, see Adler and Adler 2002b.

18. In 1987, we published a book, *Membership Roles in Field Research,* that argued that, in order to get the most accurate data and the nearest approximation of the "truth" in ethno-

graphic research, the best way is to maintain a type of closeness with the participants that heretofore had been considered methodologically unwise. The distance we had to travel in this project, though, made it impossible to establish the type of closeness that we have achieved elsewhere.

19. Thompson (2002) was able to conduct participant observation research with IRB approval by obtaining a job as a youth coordinator on a luxury cruise ship; and Sherman (2003) carried out ethnographic research in two hotels on the West Coast by working as a front desk agent, bellperson, room service server, telephone operator, and reservationist. However, Sallaz (2002) thought that announcing his research intentions would destroy his credibility and thus took a covert role in his study of Las Vegas casino dealers.

20. The position of ethnographers vis á vis their research subjects has been an ongoing debate, particularly during the postmodern turn of the 1990s. Denzin and Lincoln (2000), in their definitive *Handbook of Qualitative Research,* have defined the current "moment" in ethnography most critically as a time when ethnographers need to seriously consider who has the power and authority in a research project. Since we studied people who were both of higher social status and with greater financial means than ourselves, as well as many people whose stations in life were much less powerful than ours, these differences were items with which we had to grapple throughout the research.

21. There have been numerous accounts of the exploitation that native Hawaiian people have experienced at the hands of the white man. For a review of this history, see, for instance, Blackford 2001; Buck 1993; Halualani 2002; Kent 1993; and Trask 1993.

22. Kirby and Corzine (1981) first discussed the "contagion of stigma" that befalls researchers who study deviant groups. There, they explained that if one is involved in a study of a marginalized group it is assumed by others that the researcher is also a member of that group. Similarly, in our case, because we were involved in a setting that was considered to be a pleasant experience, many people assumed that our research was not important. Curiously, we felt, that if we were anthropologists studying an exotic culture such as Tahiti, for instance, no one would have said a negative word.

23. One of our deans acidly referred to our work as "the leisure of the theory class."

24. See Gallmeier (1991) for a discussion of the problems inherent in leaving the field. Maintaining relations with former research subjects is often a difficult part of an ethnographic project.

25. We did return there ten years later, however, for a follow-up study; see Adler 1993.

26. For some leading illustrations of and elaborations on the postmodern turn in ethnography, see Denzin and Lincoln 2000; Ellis and Flaherty 1992; and Richardson 1997.

Chapter 3. Trapped Laborers: New Immigrants and Locals

1. During the eight years we conducted our research (1995–2003), for example, the number of people employed at one of these resorts fluctuated between 900 and 1,600 workers.

2. Yamamura (1936) discussed the stratification of workers in Hawaiian hotels by ethnicity, and Zamudio (1996) noted it in the Los Angeles hotel she studied, but Madsen Camacho (1996) found that ethnicity was not a central organizing factor in her Mexican resort.

Rather, she found that class, and to a lesser degree, gender, were the variables most responsible for how hotel workers were stratified. Filipino laborers also make up the largest supplier of maritime labor, usually comprising a major percentage of the grunt workers on luxury cruise ships (see Chapman 1992).

3. For a fuller discussion of immigrant groups into Hawai'i, see Kent 1993; Lind 1996; Manicas 1996; and Wooden 1995.

4. In one of the seminal books on the different ethnic groups that have settled in Hawai'i, McDermott et al. (1980) profiled the following: the native Hawaiians, Caucasians, Chinese, Japanese, Portuguese, Okinawans, Koreans, Filipinos, Samoans, Vietnamese, and Laotians.

5. The hospitality industry has been referred to by some as the "new plantations" of Hawai'i (see Alegado 1991). Employment discrimination has stratified Filipinos into the lower segments of the labor force, particularly in the hotels (Okamura 1982). For a fuller discussion of the entry of new immigrant groups into the hotel industry, see Junasa 1996; Kent 1993; Okamura et al. 1991; and Okamura and Labrador 1996.

6. For a detailed discussion of the history and conditions of migrant Filipino workers in the late twentieth century, see Constable 1997; Espiritu 2003; and Parreñas 2001.

7. Both Bailey (1985) and Piore (1979) have reasoned that new immigrants are more likely than indigenous workers to take low-quality jobs, because these compare favorably to even worse conditions they have encountered in their countries of origin. Junasa (1996) further noted that immigrant children, accorded the lowly status of their poorly paid parents, were compelled by economic need to quit school early and to seek immediate employment, reinforcing their dependency on unskilled jobs. Talwar (2004) has added that managers of fast-food establishments are more likely to hire new immigrants, assuming that their work habits will be better than Americans'.

8. The global expanse of racialized and gendered occupations, with particular emphasis on paid domestic work, has been the subject of many studies. See Hondagneu-Sotelo 2001 and Parreñas 2001 for two excellent empirical examples and for reviews of others.

9. Zamudio (1996) stated that another reason to use immigrants in the lowest rung of the hotel industry was that they were more controllable than other groups. Keeping workers together allowed management to better watch and to channel immigrants' behavior. From the opposite standpoint, Hodson (2001) argued that the informal ties characteristic of these new immigrants create a foundation for workers to realize dignity at work. Having friendship cliques and ethnic homogeneity thus can help humanize an otherwise debased environment, as Talwar (2004) found in fast-food restaurants.

10. This is, in fact, an oversimplification, because immigrants from the Philippines brought many diverse dialects to Hawai'i and sometimes had difficulty communicating among themselves. Chief among these were the Ilocano, Visayan, and Tagalog dialects. For a discussion of the various Filipino dialects spoken in Hawai'i, see Ramos 1996.

11. Stepick and Grenier (1994) and Talwar (2004) have suggested that this "hard-working and uncomplaining" ethos is typical of new immigrant workers.

12. Kent (1993) noted that the Hawaiian hotel industry represented the lowest-paying form of work on the islands, comparable only to laundry work, which is also tourism-related. The average pay of local and new immigrant workers suffered considerably when the sugar and pineapple plantations were replaced with the tourism industry as the major employer in

Hawai'i, because the wages for comparable work were significantly poorer in the hotels than in the fields and factories. This is due not only to the lower hourly rate but also to the fact that many hotels employ a considerable number of their employees on a less than full-time basis, diminishing their benefits and keeping them involuntarily part-time. At the hotels we observed, the seasonal factor also worked against employees receiving full pay, as many people were hired in a "casual" status where they were not full-time, but given hours as needed, cut back during slow seasons and built up during "group" (banquet) season. Even full-time employees were hired with the understanding that their hours could be cut to less than full-time during slow seasons, although they, unlike casuals, received full benefits year-round.

13. According to Junasa (1996) and Tagaki and Ishisaka (1982), Filipino Americans stress cultural values, family solidarity, and familial cooperation over individualism, even among later generations.

14. Wu (1997, 130) noted that the 1994 census reported Filipino Americans' median family income as second highest of all Asian Pacific American groups. She remarked, however, that "this seeming affluence correlates not with higher wages, but with the fact that, on average, they have the largest number of household members."

15. Hondagneu-Sotelo (2001) also noted the importance of sending money home for new immigrant workers. She further claimed that one of the reasons that new immigrants were so willing to accept low-paying jobs was because, compared to their country of origin, they were still better off in the United States.

16. In contrast to earlier waves of Filipino immigration that were composed overwhelmingly of bachelor men, brought to Hawai'i to work on the sugar plantations, Filipino immigrants between 1966 and 1980 were composed mostly of women and young children, the relatives of citizens or resident alien Filipinos already in Hawai'i (Espiritu 1995; Junasa 1996).

17. For the Filipina domestic workers that Parreñas (2001) studied in Rome and Los Angeles, she found that there was a very strong sense of community. Hagan (1994), though, found that for Mayan women who migrated to Houston, there was a relatively low sense of community, mostly because they were concentrated in live-in domestic work and had few formal, public gathering places.

18. According to Ito (1999), "local" has a complex meaning. "In its simplest definition it refers to people born and raised in Hawai'i, but it is permeated by class distinctions, lifestyle preferences, speech patterns, and affective styles" (Ito 1999, 1). In contrast, Okamura (1980, 132) stated that nonlocals were "usually immigrants, people from the mainland, whites, landed gentry, tourists, developers, foreign investors, or big business representatives."

19. See Manicas 1996, 1998; Rohrer 1997; Trask 1993; and Whittaker 1986 for a fuller discussion of the state and politics of Hawaiian locals. Moreover, according to Rohrer (1997, 147) "the prevalent view among haoles is that pidgin is 'broken English'—that it is 'incorrect,' a sign of low intelligence." She suggested that children were punished for speaking pidgin in the schools of Hawai'i, although that was not our observation. What is being denied is the understanding that pidgin is a language in its own right, officially known as Hawai'i Creole English (HCE). Pidgin has its own rules, words, sentence structures, and vocabulary. Like Black English/Ebonics, HCE was born out of a need for a language of resistance, allowing communication among ethnically diverse slaves/workers, whether they are situated on southern cotton or Hawaiian sugar plantations.

20. For further discussion of local culture and its youth orientation, see Manicas 1998; McCubbin and McCubbin 1997; Okamura 1994; Weinstein et al. 1990, Whittaker 1986; and Yamamoto 1979.

21. Portes and Rumbaut (2001, 53) suggested that first- and second-generation parents and children often experienced role reversal: "This role reversal occurs when children's acculturation has moved so far ahead of their parents' that key family decisions become dependent on the children's knowledge. Because they speak the language and know the culture better, second-generation youths are often able to define the situation for themselves, prematurely freeing themselves from parental control."

22. See Portes and Rumbaut (2001) for a definitive study of second-generation immigrants and the varying criteria operating that can help predict the educational attainments of this group.

23. Some locals even complained that their parents "didn't really push us to success that much, maybe not enough."

24. Like many indigenous cultures, local people grew up eating the least expensive types of food available, while the better parts were sold to the richer people. These were then turned into culturally revered delicacies. Other examples of local food included poi, made from a tuber root starch that was ground, mixed with water, and either eaten plain, cooked, or fried; pork intestines; pigs' heads; and salmon and aku bellies. Ricky, a local boy, told us some of the secrets of his cooking: "Fillet the fish and leave the spine and bones—what little meat is left on it, cook it down and add lots of salt and pepper. Goat, you force-feed it with vinegar so the blood's cooking from the inside out, don't bleed it. Once you eat the goat, it's so 'ono' [good], you forget to go home. Broke da mouth."

25. Kent (1993, 168), quoting Hawai'i Business, declared that by 1981, "It has now become virtually impossible for most local residents to purchase a house."

26. See Macdonald and Sirriani 1996 for a discussion of burnout in service work.

27. Espiritu and Wolf (2001, 176) asserted that, among second-generation Filipinos, there was a great deal of rapid assimilation occurring. Their data suggest that there was a lack of cultural transmission occurring in Filipino-American families which they attributed to "the parents' long work hours and/or to the pressure that force (sic) immigrants to assimilate the mainstream culture."

28. While no study has thoroughly documented the exodus of Hawaiian locals from the islands, informal surveys suggest that the exodus is strongest among middle class and upwardly aspiring youth from private, college-preparatory academies (Miklius 1992). When a mixed population of public- and private-schooled youth was considered, one-third of high school graduates were found to have pursued careers outside of Hawai'i because of the limited state economy. Of those who stayed, half were living with their parents (The Honolulu Advertiser, June 10, 1996).

Chapter 4. Transient Laborers: Seekers and Management

1. Klapp (1969) felt that modern society was characterized by a lack of coherent identity, and used the term "seekers" to refer to people in search of identity. Our seekers incorporate some vestiges of the sixties mentality, or what Turner (1976) has called "impulse" selves.

Freud (cited in Guterl 2002) identified two sources of unconscious psychic energy, drives and libido. Aside from sexuality, the latter refers to the desire for stimulation and achievement. While Freud's theories are not as popular as they once were, by the end of the twentieth century neurologists began to find what they believed to be the roots of unconscious drives in the limbic system. They have expanded upon Freud's concept of unconscious drives to posit a modern suite of five drives: rage, panic, separation, distress, lust and "*seeking*" (our emphasis). The seeking drive has proven particularly fruitful for researchers, who have informally referred to it as "the urge to do stuff" (Guterl 2002).

2. See Irwin 1977 for similarities to the surfer and hippie ethos. These groups share some emphasis on spontaneity, lack of routinization, reduced complication, and freedom from responsibility.

3. Cohen (1972, 1973) has identified a closely related group, which he calls drifter-tourists. These individuals roam internationally, living with the indigenous population and taking odd jobs to keep themselves going. From predominantly affluent backgrounds, they escape adult, middle-class responsibility to seek spontaneous experiences and excitement.

4. Enloe (1989, 21) argued that women traveling alone were considered to be highly suspect. "A woman who travels . . . without the protection of an acceptable male escort is likely to be tarred with the brush of 'unrespectability.' She risks losing her honor."

5. In his analysis of "edgework" (voluntary risk-taking activity), Lyng (1990) also found that men were more likely than women to pursue extreme behaviors. Lyng suggested that male skill orientation might lead them to underestimate risk.

6. In traveling around the world and gathering data in different countries, we noted three different resort philosophies with regard to service labor and the employee-guest interaction. In some places, no matter what the makeup of the indigenous populations, resorts went out of their way to ensure that employees serving guests resembled them demographically. Like these Hawaiian organizations, most resorts that we visited in Africa, Europe, and the South Seas, whether or not their local population matched their guest composition, strove to hire individuals in point-of-service jobs who could most easily bridge the gap between guests and themselves. Management did this to encourage friendship and comfort between employees and guests. A second orientation (often found in Third World countries) involved employing higher-statused members of the indigenous population in contact positions, eschewing (for political, convenience, or other reasons) white, middle-class employees. This creates a demographic gap between employees and guests that may make their relations more distant linguistically, socially, and culturally. Relations may be polite and subservient, but they tend to be distant rather than intimate. A third orientation involves enhancing the intimacy between employees and guests beyond what we saw in the Ali'i resorts. Club Med organizations, for example, hire workers from the same class and educational background as guests, diminishing authority differences and stratification hierarchies by calling the guests *gentils members* (noble members) and the workers *gentils organizateurs* (noble organizers), banning tipping ("you cannot thank a friend with a tip"), and encouraging fraternization between the groups in such activities as dancing, water sports, lessons, and even sex (especially at the singles-oriented locations) (see Biggart 1994). Throughout the world, in providing service, members of other cultures see Americans as seeking a greater leveling between employees and customers, rejecting the more traditionally formal service relations of the British colonial empire and the European continent.

7. MacCannell (1989) has called tourism (a shallower mode of seeking) a form of pilgrimage, where people escape from the shallowness and alienation of modern life and rediscover the real. Zweig (1974) highlighted the adventurous dimension of such journeys, noting that they can restore values worn thin by domesticity.

8. Neumann (1992) observed that many tourists used their travels as metaphors for inner journeying.

9. Much like the adventure tourists studied by Neumann (1992) and the river-runner adventurers discussed by Jonas et al. (2003), seekers gained experiences that formed the basis for discovering, producing, and transforming their core identities. They then cast these, as Schiebe (1986) has noted, into the major, identity-supporting, life stories that they told.

10. For a discussion of the amount of commitment it takes to master extreme sports such as windsurfing, see Wheaton 2003. For a general sociological discussion of a variety of extreme sport devotees, see Rinehart and Sydnor 2003.

11. Fraternization among employees is common in all types of hospitality work, restaurants, bars, and hotels. Shamir (1981) found this was common among the hotel workers he studied.

12. Ironically, the seekers' philosophy has sunk deep enough into mainstream culture that in 2002 the Ford Motor Company kicked off the advertising campaign for a new SUV with the following slogan: "It's not what you do for a living, it's what you live to do." Thus, apparently, the instrumental goals and values of American society based on the Protestant ethic have been replaced, in part, with the notion that what you do with your leisure time can become more important than what you do during work.

13. Stories abounded about locals who had successfully risen through the management ranks in Hawaiian hotels, and the rare exemplars were well known. These exceptions to the general trend helped support the myth that the hospitality industry was structurally open to people of local origin with little educational background, fostering their aspiration and effort in this direction. This did not happen very often, however.

14. See Fine 1996 for similarities on the career entry patterns of chefs.

15. Wilensky's classic (1963) study noted the "long hour work" performed by managers and professionals. Kanter (1989), too, remarked on managers' commitment to long hours. Schor (1992) has observed that these professions have experienced a "shrinkage of leisure." A special issue of the journal *Work and Occupations,* published in 2001 and guest-edited by Cynthia Fuchs Epstein and Arne Kalleberg, contained several articles that challenged Schor's thesis that Americans were working more hours than ever before. Instead, the articles in the special issue suggested that the number of hours Americans work had not increased across the board, but just at the top and bottom strata of the work force (see Epstein and Kalleberg 2001).

16. Scholars have increasingly pointed to the congruity between work and leisure within certain types of occupations. Best and Stern (1977) suggested a more "cyclical life plan," where work, leisure, and education could be interspersed. Sayers (1987) called for more leisure aspects to be built into work. Heckscher and deGrazia (1959) had earlier concluded that American business executives' lives permit no clear-cut distinction between work and leisure.

17. Rafaeli and Pratt (1993), in discussing organizational attire, referred to this relative clothing autonomy as "stratified homogeneity." They posited that such wardrobe freedom

might lead to feelings of power and job satisfaction. Madsen Camacho (1996) also found that uniforms served to differentiate people, reflecting power relations within the hotel.

18. Fine (1996) also noted that opportunity to travel, to work where they wished, and to attain upward mobility attracted the chefs he studied.

19. It was not unusual for general managers to have a room in their hotels in which they primarily lived. In Shamir's (1981, 47) study of hotel managers, his respondents gave two reasons for living at the hotel: "(1) they claimed that good service and hospitality requires them to frequent hotel departments during all hours of the day and night, and (2) they emphasized the advantages of living-in in terms of information about and control of hotel operations."

20. This imbalance between work and family has become an increasing problem among Americans. Many workers have been looking for ways to accommodate the myriad demands of the job and household (Goldin 1997; Nippert-Eng 1996). Referred to as "the quiet revolution," a growing trend arose in the late twentieth century among people who voluntarily chose to work less than the standard forty-hour week. These people have sought to gain control over their time by reducing the number of hours they worked without sacrificing work or family. For a fascinating study of these workers, see Meiksins and Whalley 2002.

Chapter 5. Transient Lifestyles

1. Historically, transience has commonly been associated with lower socioeconomic groups and populations: drifters, tramps, and hobos (Allsop 1967; Anderson 1923, 1940; Harper 1982; Higbie 2003; Spradley 1970), hippies and dropouts (Cavan 1972; Snow and Anderson 1993), nomads (Aparna 1987; Khazanov 1984), indigent domestic workers (Anderson 2000; Parreñas 2001), and the homeless (Rosenthal 1994; Snow and Anderson 1993; Wagner 1993).

2. Some alight at their destinations just long enough to transact their work and return home (cf. Gryzb 1990 on railroaders; Hochschild 1983 on flight attendants; Ouellet 1994, on truckers; Prus 1989 on traveling salesmen). Others relocate in varying destinations, creating the concept of the mobile or transient dweller (cf. Hix 1998 on military personnel; Mitchell 1996 on migrant workers).

3. Many of these were students taking time off from college, either before they began, during their time there, or just after graduating. In the United Kingdom, for instance, the so-called "gap year" is so common that about 200,000 students a year take time off between high school and college (Paul 2002).

4. So common have the issues involved in this particular form of upper-middle-class families become that sociologists in the latter part of the twentieth century began to refer to them as corporate career families (Cuber and Harnoff 1965; Kanter 1977). "Many corporations tend to be all-inclusive, regulating every aspect of their employees' lives. Managers who are moved around the country from one corporate branch to another are expected to uproot their families, separate their children from their friends, and establish them in new schools as often as every few years. In this respect the corporation is rather like a career in the military" (Collins and Coltrane 1995, 202).

5. In looking at the British hotel industry, Adkins (1995, 84) noted that husbands al-

most always have the ability to control the labor of their wives. "Hotel and catering companies make use of these restricted employment opportunities for women, and of family relations, to derive their own benefits from these sets of relations."

6. This pattern is a distinct phenomenon among the upper middle class in America,
particularly those in the corporate career family (Collins and Coltrane 1995). Epstein (1971)
has suggested that the idea that one's career takes precedence over all other commitments
tends to reflect a male-centered view.

7. Trailing spouses, then, give up their work and search for another position in the location where the spouse has taken a job. Typically, it is wives trailing husbands, because men's
incomes are usually higher (Bielby and Bielby 1992). In a study of trailing spouses among the
clergy, Frame and Sheehan (1994, 202) found that wives: (a) lost contact with friends; (b) felt
a lack of support from husbands; (c) were anxious about the children's adjustment to new en-
virons; and (d) felt lonely and isolated. Thus, while about half of the major corporations have
established programs or have recruited outside firms to provide employment assistance for
trailing spouses, the social and psychological havoc that this causes for the family still per-
sists (Benokraitis 1996).

8. The absentee father syndrome has long been associated with families living in
poverty. While there has been a spate of research on the effects of the lack of a father on family life among the poor, recent controversial research indicates that there may be long-term
negative effects on children when a father is not present, regardless of social class (Popenoe
1996).

9. This represents a variation on the commuter marriage that began to proliferate in
the 1980s (Gerstel and Gross 1984).

10. Due to the high level of mobility found in both resort and military careers, several
comparisons can be made about the types of friendships people form in these organizations.
Little (1990) has described some of the reasons why military personnel easily form friendships, although he concentrated on some of the difficulties inherent in friendships among
highly mobile people. "The personnel policy of rotation—from one post to another, and from
home bases to overseas stations—precludes the establishment of a neighborhood. It produces
constant interruption of friendships and requires that they be established with other persons
at other places. The uncertainty of the duration of residence at one base limits the degree of
commitment to the friendship and fosters cynicism about the enduring value of such relationships" (Little 1990, 232).

11. This pattern is also similar to the one found in the military, where officers and en-
listed men rarely break ranks to form friendships. In the military, this limitation on friendships extends to spouses and children as well (Little 1990). In resorts, the divisions were not
as strict; but still—due to propinquity, social class, linguistic differences, schools, and extracurricular activities—most children of managers found themselves playing with children of
similarly statused parents.

12. In fact, the Lukane Sands owned a building for some years in a nearby town that
housed their workers. For the most part, this residence resembled the type of living that college students experienced in dorms. Living together also aided friendships within the resort.

13. Biggart (1994) has noted that Club Med moved their employees every six months
so that they did not become jaded or develop cliques with other employees.

14. Shortly after making this statement, Rick was hired away from the Lukane Sands

by its former deputy director, who had been recruited to rejoin a chain hotel for which he had previously worked.

15. In Shamir's (1981) study of British hotel workers, he found that it was common for groups of workers to leave one hotel and go to another hotel en masse. Usually, this was to follow a manager who had moved.

Chapter 6. Seasonal Laborers

1. For a discussion of the differences between "natural seasonality" and "commercial seasonality" in resorts, see BarOn 1975; Barry and Perry 1973; Boucher 1975; and Hartmann 1986.

2. Baum and Lundtorp (2001), Butler (1994), and Soesilo and Mings (1987) have all looked at the economic costs of seasonality in resorts.

3. Scholars have noted that resorts do not usually vary staff levels completely commensurate with guest fluctuation, so that they maintain slightly higher-than-needed employment during slow seasons and operate at slightly understaffed levels during busy seasons. They are usually quicker to fire than to hire employees, however, erring where necessary toward smaller labor pools (Krakover 1998, 2000b). Leidner (1993) and Fine (1996) have noted that all efficient organizations keep no more employees on duty at any given time than is absolutely necessary (see Krakover 1998, 2000a, 2000b; McMahon 1994).

4. Fringe benefits come in three forms: statutory benefits, which include social security, unemployment insurance, disability, workmen's compensation; compensatory benefits, which include paid vacation, holiday, and sick leave; and supplementary benefits, which include medical, dental, and life insurance, pensions, and profit sharing (Nollen et al. 1978).

5. Since the late 1980s, there have been a spate of authors who have discussed the conditions, needs, and rewards of contingency work, especially with regard to its pros and cons, including Barker and Christensen (1998), Belous (1989), duRivage (1992), Harrison (1994), Lautsch (2002), and Thompson (1995).

6. Beyond workers flexibly shuttling into and out of work, as we use the term here, the concept of a flexible labor force has been used to signify the flexible specialization of workers by Piore and Sabel (1984), referring to situations where employers move away from traditional, rigid, mass-production techniques toward different production processes and products in accord with changing market conditions. Characteristic of the new, postindustrialist economy, this situation requires workers to retool themselves at their own cost to changing market conditions and work demands.

7. For a fuller discussion of the benefits of flexible labor to employers, see Blank 1998; Kalleberg et al. 1997; Murphy 1996; Nollen et al. 1978; Olmsted and Smith 1989; and Osterman 1999.

8. Fortunately for these resorts, the attractions of Honua were such that the peaks and valleys in tourist visits were not as great as in other warm-weather climates, such as Florida and Arizona, or cold-weather venues, such as Colorado. While the winter months obviously drew the greatest numbers, considerable numbers of people still flocked to Hawai'i throughout the year.

9. During the economic boom of the 1990s, unemployment rates were so low and the

pay at resorts so meager that American teenagers were shunning these year-round jobs. Instead, a phalanx of foreign students, from Ireland, England, France, Spain, and Eastern Europe were imported to the summer resorts in 1999 to fill in the gaps. According to Dogar (1999, 38), "for seasonal employers these kids are a godsend—and one more byproduct of our new prosperity. . . . With teen unemployment at a 30-year low, American kids can afford to be choosy. Some take $200-on-a-good-night waitressing gigs. Those backed by parents with bulging stock portfolios may prefer unpaid but career-boosting internships. . . . Prosperity also means that people are vacationing more, resorts are thriving—and jobs like ride operator, beach attendant and even lifeguard are tough to fill. That's why there are 700 foreign kids spinning the Ferris wheels and frying funnel cakes at Cedar Point [an amusement park in Ohio], nearly a fourth of the summer work force."

10. Other hotels referred to this group of guests as "transients" or "families."

11. The exceptions to this are the international travelers, who come from countries where tipping is meager or absent, such as most of Europe, the South Seas, and Asia.

12. In contrast to waitresses in other types of venues (see Paules 1991), resort waitresses were more likely to have to declare their tips to the Internal Revenue Service because most guests charged their bills, including tips, to their hotel rooms, rather than tipping in cash. These tips then came to waitresses with their paychecks, and were both declared and subject to withholding. Thus, the numbers we describe here are before taxes. Stern (1989) estimated that those who work in "primary" tip positions (bartenders, bell, waitresses, door) received 45–57 percent of their total compensation in tips. Those in "secondary" tip positions (busboys, hostesses, housemen, housekeepers) received less than 20 percent of their compensation in tips.

13. Citing unpublished studies, Stern (1989) estimated that 25 percent of all workers employed in the Hawaiian visitor industry received tips.

14. Local students were another easy source for the Ali'i resorts to tap during the summer. While July was usually slow, August, before school began again, was a peak period and unemployed high school students were fair game. For excellent examinations of the benefits and detriments of work for high school students, see Entwisle et al. 2000 and Tannock 2001.

15. Because of the evenly temperate climate in Hawai'i, in contrast to locations featuring dramatic swings of temperature and rainfall, when the international economy was good, occupancy might not totally decline, even during these periods.

16. The only salaried employees whose income was not fixed were the sales force, particularly those in group sales who booked conferences and conventions attracting large numbers of individuals, and incentive trips for companies who brought their high-performing employees over as a reward. These people worked on a quota system, earning bonuses each quarter depending on their bookings.

17. For a useful volume that debates the pros and cons of part-time labor, see O'Reilly and Fagan 1998.

18. The worker shortage in some years has been so acute in the Rocky Mountain resort areas of Colorado that management has had to loosen up standards for employment. For instance, in 2000, low employment forced the Vail Resorts to drop a mandatory drug-testing program, lest they not get enough employees to fill their rosters ("Vail Resorts Drops" 2000). In 1998, the administrators of Copper Mountain Resort in Colorado dropped the grooming requirements for employees. To increase the potential for recruiting workers, men were al-

lowed to wear a ponytail, have facial hair, or sport an earring, all previously prohibited (Lipsher 1998).

19. This was not the case in all resorts, however, and depended heavily on the relation between the resort's internal labor market and the surrounding area's external labor market (Krakover 1998). In some types of locations, such as winter ski resorts, finding adequate numbers of seasonal employees could be a daunting and often impossible task (Aurand 2000; Lipsher 1998; Wolfson 2000). Resorts compete against each other and the major mountain lift operations to attract line and management employees. They hosted job fairs in the nearby metropolitan spots, placed advertisements around the country, recruited in the colleges, and sent solicitors overseas to establish seasonal internship and training programs. In spite of these efforts, many have reported that they operated on a short-staffed basis for most of the busy season.

20. According to a survey of hotel managers in the United Kingdom, moving staff from one department to another at peak times was not the most popular way to meet labor needs. Managers' first preference was to rearrange work rotations, and then to hire casuals and pay full-time employees overtime (McMahon 1994).

21. For a fuller discussion of the migratory patterns of farm workers, see Gardezi 1995; Martinez 1996; and Sosnick 1978.

22. Riley (1991) asserts that where the training period for workers is short, organizations can more easily release employees during slow periods and take on others when pressed by demand. Stepick and Grenier (1994, 186) state that, "the most widespread method for maintaining low labor costs in Miami's hotels and restaurants is through using part-time instead of full-time workers."

Chapter 7. Temporal Laborers

1. The logic behind this comes from the idea that technology makes people's lives less difficult. See Bosserman 1975; Cross 1990; Hammond 1933; and Owen 1969 for some discussion of this trend.

2. According to research by Robinson and Godbey (1999), even though Americans work longer hours than people in any other country, free time seemed to be increasing again by the end of the twentieth century.

3. See Melbin 1969; Roth 1963; and Zerubavel 1979.

4. See Fine 1996; Leidner 1993; and Paules 1991.

5. See Molstad 1986 and Robboy 1983.

6. See Charlton and Hertz 1989.

7. See Hood 1988.

8. Paul (2002) noted, in an article about the growing number of businesses offering their employees sabbaticals, that more Americans have realized the need to take time off from work and relationships. She cited a number of benefits, including de-stressing, re-energizing, and a renewed vigor and motivation to go back to work. This trend has become popular enough that Izzo and Withers (2001) predicted that the stigma associated with taking time off might even disappear.

9. For a fuller discussion of the differences and relations between objectively experi-

enced (clock) time and subjectively experienced (emotionally judged) time, see de Grazia 1962; Flaherty 1999; Hall 1983; Lauer 1981; Sorokin and Merton 1937; and Weigert 1981.

10. Melbin (1987) has discussed the historical development of around-the-clock shifts, noting that the traditional daytime hours marked the first and original shift, the "natural timetable." After that, during the "second schedule," organizations began extending their hours earlier into the morning and later into the evening, so that two shifts were required for staffing. The third movement—into continuous, or incessant operation—is the most recent development, and brought in the third working shift.

11. Melbin (1987) observed that predictability of work schedules was more important than their regularity. People could adapt to change if they knew far enough in advance what was coming. What they disliked more was having plans thrust on them with inadequate notice.

12. See Clarkberg and Moen (2001) for a discussion of the research on employee preferences for work hours.

13. People's increased vitality during the daytime and drowsiness at night may be tied to the body's production of the hormone melatonin, which rises during the dark hours and has a sedative effect (Åkersted et al. 1982; Lewy et al. 1980; Lieberman et al. 1984; Vaughan et al. 1979; Wurtman 1975).

14. Presser (1999, 2000) found that people who work at night might be subject to more physical symptoms caused by tension and stress, particularly relating to family life. Garey (1999), in contrast, in a study of night shift nurses, pointed out some of the advantages to working while others sleep. In particular, she looked at the advantages for "working mothers," who could appear like "stay-at-home moms" because they could participate in many of their children's activities. For an impressive review of extant knowledge on the physiological, psychological, and sociological adjustments that employees have to make to nonstandard work schedules, see Fenwick and Tausig 2001.

15. The sociological literature on night work is not extensive, but see Hood 1988; Melbin 1987; Molstad 1986; and Robboy 1983.

16. Research on sleep has shown that people who work nights and attempt to sleep days often feel disoriented and ill, have difficulty falling and staying asleep, sleep for fewer hours, and need to supplement this with naps (Czeisler et al. 1980; Luce 1971; Monroe 1967; Orem and Keeling 1980).

17. Zerubavel (1985) has noted that on vacations the days gradually lose their distinctiveness and begin to seem alike.

18. In hotel chains, this was measured by the length of affiliation with the company. In independents, which were often bought and sold by various individuals or conglomerates, length of service might (or might not) be vested during transfers (rolled over into the new contract), so that benefits and seniority were not lost.

19. For a discussion of the origins and construction of the weekend, see Rybczynski 1991.

20. Zerubavel (1979) noted that in hospitals, each weekday is regarded as a unit in its own right, whereas Saturday and Sunday are often considered together as one unsegmentable whole.

21. See Eisenberger 1989; Taylor 1967; Wright 1968; and Zerubavel 1979.

22. This is so acknowledged in Hawai'i that Fridays are known as "Aloha Fridays," when people can come in to work dressed casually, in more traditional Hawaiian garb.

23. One dimension scholars have noted is that time becomes compressed when experience is enjoyable and expanded when things become difficult or drudging (Flaherty 1999; Hall 1983; and Weigert 1981).

24. Melbin (1987) has suggested that people who work at night tend to be those at the bottom of the socioeconomic hierarchy: youths, women, and people of color who lack access to the highest-paying careers; people looking to break into an occupation who have to start in the night shift; blue-collar and service occupations, as opposed to white-collar and professional workers; minority groups and immigrants; people holding more than one job; and people dividing the daycare of children among themselves.

Chapter 8. Stratified Laborers

1. See Aguirre and Baker (2000) for a detailed discussion of occupational segregation in the United States.

2. While this type of semiskilled and unskilled work is often related to Marx's concept of alienation in the sociological literature (see Blauner 1967), the ethnic homogeneity of stewards in resorts counterbalanced many of the alienating factors for them. As far as we could tell, many of them truly enjoyed their work, liked the camaraderie of their fellow workers, and largely escaped some of the more heinous social psychological pitfalls usually associated with dirty work (see Fine 1996; Hughes 1971). Of course, Marxist scholars might quickly counter that these workers are simply suffering from false consciousness. Abu-Lughod (1990), with a nod to Foucault, suggested that power can not only work negatively on the powerless, but also positively, even producing forms of pleasure and thus not necessarily false consciousness. Applying this idea to the Filipina domestics in Hong Kong that she studied, Constable (1997, 210) stated that, even in the context of domination, these women "derive pleasure, or at least some satisfaction, from attempts to organize their work better and maximize their productivity, to get along better with employers, and to 'professionalize' their image, even at the cost of being ever more obedient and hardworking."

3. Thompson (2002) also found a relationship between occupation and race/ethnicity among the crew of the luxury cruise ship that he studied. Among the nearly six hundred crew members on his ship, there were more than forty countries represented. Interestingly, even though his ship traveled around the Caribbean islands, over 20 percent of the crew members were from the Philippines. In his case, for example, practically all of the people working in the security department were Filipino. In Chapman's (1992) study of seamen, he posited that management deliberately hired people from thirty-five to forty different nationalities to curtail the likelihood of crews protesting the working conditions on board. In their study of the Miami restaurant and hotel industry, Stepick and Grenier (1994) found that blacks are overrepresented in back-of-the-house jobs—menial, unskilled positions such as housekeeping and dishwashing that are out of the public's eye.

4. Chapman (1992) noted a similar type of ethnic funneling among the workers on the cruise ships he studied.

5. This is similar to the phenomenon known as "stacking" (Loy and McElvogue 1970) in intercollegiate and professional sports, whereby teams' management assumes that certain minority groups automatically should be funneled to specific positions. The result is that, as

in resorts, there is an over-representation of some groups at one position and an under-representation of those groups in other positions. The main argument is that minority groups are less likely to be chosen for positions of authority and centrality on the team.

6. Madsen Camacho (1996), in her study of the booming tourism and hotel industry in Oaxaca, Mexico, discussed what happens to workers when previously held agricultural land is transformed into luxury resorts. In her case, as with Agrifina's, workers were forced to give up the skills they already had working in the fields and turn to hotel service work, the only means of subsistence left to them.

7. This same type of differentiated pay structure by ethnicity was prevalent among the seafarers studied by Chapman (1992). He found that waiters, mostly young people enticed into the world of luxury cruising by glamour, generally made very good tips, while the workers in the kitchen, laundry, and sanitation received no tips at all.

Chapter 9. Careers in Paradise: Short-Term and Intermediate

1. The concept of "careers" has long held a fascination for sociologists (see Hall 2002 for a review). It can be looked at as used in the common vernacular: any kind of full-time employment that implies a continuing commitment to work (see Pavalko 1988). Sociologically, this can have two dimensions, taking a more subjective meaning (Stebbins 1970, 1971), involving the significance that individuals give to their work, or an objective meaning (Wilensky 1960), focusing on a series of stages that individuals pass through in their work lives. Some careers are "compressed," lasting for a shorter term, spiraling to rapid upward success and burning out shortly thereafter (Gallmeier 1987). Careers can also refer to illegitimate pursuits, referring to the span of people's involvement in a given activity, despite its shorter-term nature (Best and Luckenbill 1982).

2. A survey of major London hotels found that labor turnover ranged between 58 to 112 percent, well above such rates in other industries (Denvir and McMahon 1992).

3. Snow and Brissett (1986) have referred to this phenomenon as a "temporary withdrawal," where people rejuvenate or take stock (see also Weigert 1981).

4. These kinds of low-end service and retail jobs are referred to as "life cycle stopgap jobs" (see Jacobs 1993; Myles et al. 1993; Oppenheimer and Kalmijn 1995). For the most part, they are filled by youths and do not lead to career advancement or long-term employment. See Tannock 2001 for a discussion of the plight of these workers.

5. Drugs, sex, and alcohol were a big part of the after-work scene for resort workers. It was not uncommon for a big bonfire to be lit at a remote beach spot with dozens of workers, from all the resorts, congregating there. The high degree of deviance and the sexually charged atmosphere that exists in the hotel and restaurant industry have been amply documented (see Fine 1996; Giuffre and Williams.1994; Marshall 1986; Shamir 1981).

6. This sort of disinterest and lack of commitment to the workplace is common among young, stopgap workers. Gaskell and Lazerson (1981) have referred to this as "low job commitment" and Oppenheimer and Kalmijn (1995) have called it "marginal job attachment." Tucker (1993), in a study of young, temporary workers, stated that the easy option of leaving these jobs prematurely also contributed to workers' passivity.

7. Burnout has been a persistent problem plaguing corporations in the latter part of the

twentieth century (Maslach and Leiter 1997). Companies have tried to counterbalance this trend by offering stress management programs and employee assistance programs or simply by trying to recruit people who could handle stress. Hall (2002, 200) argued that, instead of these individually focused remedies, companies need to take a more organizational approach, including creating "challenging job assignments and workload (so that work is challenging but not overwhelming), the amount of control and autonomy that the employee has over his or her work, and the rewards that are provided for a job well done." Cordes and Dougherty (1993, 628) have posited that burnout is highest in the helping professions "because of the high level of arousal from direct, frequent, and rather intense interactions with clients." This parallels the high service demands from clients at luxury resorts.

    8. So popular was Las Vegas as a destination for Hawaiians that it was sometimes jokingly referred to as "the ninth Hawaiian island."

    9. Brianna and Steve brought their car with them, a sign of longer-term commitment. However, they never bothered to change the license plate from their home state, North Dakota, which looked rather odd in faraway Honua.

    10. It may be that our research failed to uncover cases where new immigrants left the resort industry, or the types of jobs they filled in it, after an intermediate period of time. But our observations suggest that once members of this group found work of this nature, they tended to stick with it over a longer tenure.

    11. This pattern is similar to the "ambivalent" middle managers studied by Tausky and Dubin (1965). These people were dissatisfied that they did not reach the upper levels of the corporation, but they then began to look for activities beyond the workplace for satisfaction. At that point, they stopped pursuing occupational success and career advancement and merely went through the traditional means of doing their jobs, following Merton's (1938) ritualistic mode of adaptation.

Chapter 10. Careers in Paradise: Long-Term

    1. See Baron et al. 1986; Cassirer and Reskin 2000; DiPrete and Soule 1988; Hartmann 1987; and Kanter 1977.

    2. See Maume 1999; Paulin and Mellnor 1996.

    3. See Baron and Bielby 1980; Reskin and Cassirer 1996; and Tomaskovic-Devey 1993.

    4. See Rosenbaum 1979. For a broader empirical study of the glass ceilings faced by Asian-Americans, specifically, and on the state of glass ceiling research, more generally, see Woo 2000.

    5. See the NAACP hotel report card, "Economic Reciprocity Lodging Industry Two-Year Comparison Report Card" (www.naacp.org/economic/lodging2002.shtml).

    6. Of course, this is not unusual in other industries as well. The professional sports world, for instance, is infamous for its over-representation of people of color in the playing ranks and their under-representation in coaching, managerial, administrative, and ownership positions (see Lapchick and Mathews 2000). Maume (1999) referred to this phenomenon as "racialized" jobs, in which minorities are placed in jobs that are chiefly liaisons to their ethnic communities. Almost all the existing data focus on African-Americans' attempts to make

inroads into managerial positions with virtually nothing available on other minority groups (but see Woo 2000 on Asian-Americans). For further discussion of the plight of African-American management personnel, see Collins 1997 and Jones 1986.

7. For quite some time now, the literature has shown that managers are becoming more resistant to relocation than they were in previous eras. Concerns about uprooting families, dual careers, and high costs are at the root of this changing attitude (see Veiga 1983).

8. Beller and Han (1984) have noted the predominance of women management in certain ghettoized areas, predicting that these enclaves will continue to become overwhelmingly female-dominated. Macdonald and Sirianni (1996) and Reskin and Phipps (1988) have particularly identified the service industry as stratified and segregated by gender.

9. See Colwill (1993) for a discussion of the way men's management careers are taken more seriously than women's.

10. See Acker 1990; Gilder 1995; and Zimmer 1988.

11. See Cassirer and Reskin 2000; Kanter 1977.

12. The highly charged sexual atmosphere endemic to restaurant work makes the atmosphere ripe for sexual harassment, although only a minority of women working in these milieus labels it as such (see Giuffre and Williams 1994). However, some have argued that as many as 70 percent of employed women have experienced behavior that can be legally termed sexual harassment (MacKinnon 1979; Powell 1986). For a review of the literature on sexual harassment see Williams et al. 1999.

13. In his study of temporary workers, Henson (1996) discussed the cultural stigma associated with being a "lifer." Newman (1988) has also noted the characterological flaws that our society places on those who remain "off track" for too long.

14. This is in direct contrast to the immigrant women in the microelectronics industry in California's Silicon Valley studied by Hossfeld (2002, 286): "Many immigrant women see their wage contribution to the family's economic survival not only as secondary but as *temporary,* even when they held their jobs for several years. They expect to quit their production jobs after they have saved enough money to go to school, stay home full time, or open a family business. In actuality, however, most of them barely earned enough to live on, let alone to save, and women who think they are signing on for a brief stint may end up staying in the industry for years" (emphasis in original).

15. With baby boomers hitting retirement age, the literature is rife with information about these later years of life. As an occupational group, managerial and administrative positions tend to have the largest number of older workers (Rones 1978). This may be the case because, in these jobs, wisdom, knowledge, skills, and authority are valued. However, for most resort executives, the hours were just too demanding to keep up with the pace.

Chapter 11. Understanding Paradise Labor

1. Glenn (2001) also pointed out that the invisible work done by people behind the scenes in nursing homes, restaurants, office buildings, and hotels, many of whom are women of color, served the latent function of giving these workers time and space segregation, which allowed them more autonomy and freedom, away from the prying eyes of supervisors, guests,

clients, or patients. However, as we note in chapter 7, the invisibility of their work also meant that it was probably less appreciated.

2. Housekeepers were especially able, Sherman (2003) noted, to use their access to intimate information about arrogant guests to criticize and make fun of them.

3. The advent of cyber-communities has served to mold these common interests based on lifestyle and interests even more than in previous eras, as people are no longer bounded by the confines of geographical location or physical proximity (see Shapiro 2001; Walker 2000).

4. As Wheaton (2000) has shown in her research on the windsurfing subculture, people's sense of identity has become increasingly fluid and fragmented. She illustrated how windsurfers lodged their identities within sport and leisure subcultures, a transformation in society that, perhaps, began in the 1960s but took full hold in the 1990s.

5. For a discussion of the nature of the existential self, see Douglas and Johnson 1977; Kotarba and Fontana 1984; and Kotarba and Johnson 2002.

6. Sherman (2003) has suggested that invisible workers in the back of the house are more easily routinized and monitored than front of the house employees.

7. Tolich (1993), in his study of supermarket clerks, posited that when emotion management is autonomous—regulated by the individual employee rather than by the employer—the result is likely to be a worker who finds the job more fulfilling and enjoyable. Stenross and Kleinman (1989) also found that autonomy of police officers produced happier workers when emotion management was more under their control.

8. For other discussions of the relationship between empowerment and flexibility, see Bowen and Lawler 1995; Fuller and Smith 1991; Macdonald and Sirianni 1996; and Sherman 2003.

9. The majority of all U.S. tourists to Hawai'i are repeat visitors (65 percent), as reported in the 1992 *Annual Research Report* of the Hawai'i Visitors Bureau Market Research Department (13), indicating that people liked what they saw the first time, that their experiences met or exceeded their expectations.

10. See also Sutton and Rafaeli 1988 on how cash register clerks dispensed with all pleasantries toward customers when the lines became too long, and Van Maanen and Kunda 1989 on how Disneyland employees harshly buckled customers into rides when they were squeezed for time.

11. Sherman (2003) has noted a variety of strategies employees used to cast themselves as powerful and professional rather than deferential or servile.

12. Sherman (2003) also found that hotel guests as a rule treated workers well.

13. For a critical analysis of the effects of globalization on contingent workers in the United States, see Parker 2002. His basic argument was that contingent work was not good for the global flow of workers more generally, as it denied workers job stability, benefits, or the possibility of union solidarity.

14. For further discussion of the existing broad-range demographic patterns of contingency workers, see Barker and Christensen 1998; Belous 1989; Bronstein 1991; Hudson 2001; Kalleberg 2000; Mangum et al. 1985; Osterman 1999; Rogers 2000; Sweeney and Nussbaum 1989; and Tilly 1996.

15. See Wacker and Bills 2000 for a study of the problems associated with contingent workers who try to make the transition to regular employment.

16. This is in distinct contrast to what little we know about the high-skilled side of contingent work. Contrary to the "employment relations" perspective, high-skilled contingent workers report getting better-paying jobs than their permanently employed counterparts. See Kunda et al. 2002 for further discussion of this particular segment of the contingent labor pool.

17. Glenn (1996), for example, found a hierarchy of job categories in the field of nursing, with individuals' occupational placement corresponding to the relative status of their ethnic group.

18. Cross-cutting the ghettoization of workers by ethnicity, of course, is the type of gender segregation that has long been the hallmark of hiring practices in the labor force (see Reskin 1993). Interestingly, Adkins (1995, 109–10), in her study of the British hotel industry, found that "what is most striking about the personnel specifications in relation to gender segregation is that those relating to occupations in which women were clustered (waitress, receptionist, and housekeeper) show remarkable continuity. According to the specifications, all these occupations 'require' workers to be 'attractive,' of 'average height and weight,' and to have a 'helpful and enthusiastic attitude' . . . In contrast, specifications for the occupations in which men were clustered (chef/cook, kitchen hand, barman, and porter) show no real continuity."

19. For a discussion of the confluence of gender, race, and ethnicity and their impact on occupational segregation, see Reskin and Cassirer 1996. For empirical data on the specific effects of ethnicity on labor market inequality, see Almquist 1997; Glass et al. 1988; Lieberson and Waters 1988; and Tienda and Lii 1987.

20. Others have also noted that service work is stratified by race (see Macdonald and Sirianni 1996; Talwar 2004), but most of this research focuses on African-Americans, particularly women (see Needleman and Nelson 1988; Woody 1989). Glenn (1996) is notable for considering the situation of African-American, Asian-American, Latina, and Native American women; and Sherman (2003) pointed out that the luxury hotels she studied were also divided along these lines.

21. Linton (2002) has looked at whether the presence of immigrants changed the nature of the internal labor market in the United States. She studied the relationship between immigration and labor-market demand and found that many immigrants fill occupational niches that would not exist in their absence.

22. Waldinger and Der-Martirosian (2000) have suggested that new immigrants are satisfied with low wages until they "assimilate" to norms of native-born workers.

23. Unlike the Silicon Valley new immigrants, who were employed in toxic settings surrounded by chemical pollution—see Pellow and Park 2003.

24. Similarly, Braham (1980), Leggett (1968), and Piore (1979) have found that migrant immigrant Middle Eastern workers have been difficult to organize.

25. Wells (2000) has also noted that white men stand out at the forefront of union organization. She has commented that white people were less likely than members of other racial or ethnic groups to be perceived as favoring their own group members.

26. Nollen et al. (1978) have noted the union claim that only the affluent can afford part-time work, because it does not pay a living wage. Contingent work is therefore less desirable, they argued, for the working than for the middle class.

27. Of the approximately 65,000 jobs in the local area, 90 percent were in the service

sector. Retail sales accounted for nearly 13,500 jobs, with hotels second, employing 11,600 people (although there were fewer hotels, so they were the larger employers). After that, most jobs could be found in government work, agricultural production, construction, and a variety of miscellaneous health, financial, business, social service, and "off-the-books" work ("Honua" County Annual Report 1996).

REFERENCES

Abu-Lughod, Lila. 1990. "The Romance of Resistance: Tracing Transformations of Power through Bedouin Women." *American Ethnologist* 17:41–55.

Acker, Joan. 1990. "Hierarchies, Jobs, and Bodies: A Theory of Gendered Organizations." *Gender and Society* 4:139–58.

Addison, John. 1997. "The U.S. Labor Market: Structure and Performance." In *Structural Change and Labor Market Flexibility,* ed. Horst Siebert. Kiel: Institut für Weltwirtschaft an der Universität Kiel, 187–222.

Adkins, Lisa. 1995. *Gendered Work.* Buckingham, Eng.: Open University Press.

Adler, Patricia A. 1993. *Wheeling and Dealing.* 2d. ed. New York: Columbia University Press.

——. 1985. *Wheeling and Dealing.* New York: Columbia University Press.

Adler, Patricia A., and Peter Adler. 2002a. "The Reluctant Respondent." In *Handbook of Interview Research,* ed. Jaber F. Gubrium and James A. Holstein. Thousand Oaks, Calif.: Sage, 515–36.

——. 2002b. "Do University Lawyers and the Police Define Our Research Values?" In *Walking the Tightrope: Ethical Issues for Qualitative Researchers,* ed. Will van den Hoonaard. Toronto: University of Toronto Press, 34–42.

——. 1998. *Peer Power: Preadolescent Culture and Identity.* New Brunswick: Rutgers University Press.

——. 1994. "Observational Techniques." In *Handbook of Qualitative Research,* ed. Norman K. Denzin and Yvonna S. Lincoln. Thousand Oaks, Calif.: Sage. 377–92.

——. 1991a. *Backboards and Blackboards: College Athletes and Role Engulfment.* New York: Columbia University Press.

——. 1991b. "Stability and Flexibility: Maintaining Relations within Organized and Unorganized Groups." In *Experiencing Fieldwork,* ed. William Shaffir and Robert Stebbins. Newbury Park, Calif.: Sage, 173–83.

——. 1987. *Membership Roles in Field Research.* Newbury Park, Calif.: Sage.

Aguirre, Adalberto, Jr., and David V. Baker. 2000. *Structured Inequality in the United States.* Upper Saddle River, N.J.: Prentice Hall.

Aikau, Hokulani. 2001. "Review of Staging Tourism." *Ethnography* 2:256–58.

Åkersted, T., M. Gillberg, and L. Wetterberg. 1982. "The Circadian Covariation of Fatigue and Urinary Melatonin." *Biological Psychiatry* 17:547–54.

Alegado, Dean T. 1991. "The Filipino Community in Hawai'i's Development and Change." *Social Process in Hawai'i* 33:12–38.

Allen, Kenneth. 1997. "The Postmodern Self: A Theoretical Consideration." *Quarterly Journal of Ideology* 20:3–22.

Allsop, Kenneth. 1967. *Hard Travellin': The Hobo and His History.* New York: New American Library.

Almquist, Elizabeth M. 1987. "Labor Market Inequality in Minority Groups." *Gender and Society* 1:400–14.

Andaya, Leonard Y. 1996. "From American-Filipino to Filipino-American." *Social Process in Hawai'i* 37:99–111.

Anderson, Bridget. 2000. *Doing the Dirty Work? The Global Politics of Domestic Labour.* London: Zed Books.

Anderson, Nels. 1940. *Men on the Move.* Chicago: University of Chicago Press.

———. 1923. *The Hobo: The Sociology of the Homeless Man.* Chicago: University of Chicago Press.

Aparna, Rao, ed. 1987. *The Other Nomads: Peripatetic Minorities in Cross-Cultural Perspective.* Cologne: Bohlau.

Apostolopoulos, Yiorgos, Stella Leivade, and Andrew Yiannakis, eds. 1996. *The Sociology of Tourism: Theoretical and Empirical Investigations.* London: Routledge.

Appadurai, Arjun. 1996. *Modernity at Large: Cultural Dimensions of Globalization.* Minneapolis: University of Minnesota Press.

Arnould, Eric J., and Linda L. Price. 1993. "River Magic: Extraordinary Experience and the Extended Service Encounter." *Journal of Consumer Research* 20:24–45.

Aron, Cindy S. 1999. *Working at Play: A History of Vacations in the United States.* New York: Oxford University Press.

Aurand, Anne. 2000. "Resorts Offer Workers Competitive Benefits." *The Daily Camera.* March 13, Business Plus, 15.

Bailey, Thomas. 1985. "A Case Study of Immigrants in the Restaurant Industry." *Industrial Relations* 24:205–21.

Bakan, Abigail, and Daiva Stasiulis, eds. 1997. *Not One of the Family: Foreign Domestic Workers in Canada.* Toronto: University of Toronto Press.

Barker, Kathleen, and Kathleen Christensen, eds. 1998. *Contingent Work: American Employment Relations in Transition.* Ithaca, N.Y.: Cornell University Press.

Baron, James N., and William T. Bielby. 1980. "Bringing the Firms Back In: Stratification, Segmentation, and the Organization of Work." *American Sociological Review* 45:737–65.

Baron, James N., Alison Davis-Blake, and William T. Bielby. 1986. "The Structure of Opportunity: How Promotion Ladders Vary within and among Organizations." *Administrative Science Quarterly* 31:248–73.

BarOn, R. V. 1975. "Seasonality in Tourism." *Economist Intelligence Unit,* London.

Barry, Roger G., and A. H. Perry. 1973. *Synoptic Climatology-Methods and Applications*. London: Methuen.

Bartik, Timothy J. 2001. *Jobs for the Poor*. New York: Russell Sage.

Baudrillard, Jean. 1983. *Simulations*. New York: Semiotext(e).

Baum, Joel, and Heather A. Haveman. 1997. "Love Thy Neighbor: Differentiation and Agglomeration in the Manhattan Hotel Industry, 1898–1990." *Administrative Science Quarterly* 42:304–38.

Baum, Tom, and Svend Lundtorp, eds. 2001. *Seasonality in Tourism*. Amsterdam: Pergamon.

"Beaches and Bucks." 2002. *Rocky Mountain News,* November 30:1C.

Bean, Frank D., and Stephanie Bell-Rose, eds. 1999. *Immigration and Opportunity*. New York: Russell Sage.

Becker, Howard S. 1960. "Notes on the Concept of Commitment." *American Journal of Sociology* 66:32–42.

Becker, Howard S., and Blanche Geer. 1960. "The Analysis of Qualitative Field Data." In *Human Organization Research,* ed. Richard Adams and Jack Preiss. Homewood, Ill.: Dorsey, 652–60.

Bell, Daniel. 1976. *The Cultural Contradictions of Capitalism*. New York: Basic Books.

Beller, Andrea H., and Kee-ok Kim Han. 1984. "Occupational Sex Segregation: Prospects for the 1980s." In *Sex Segregation in the Workplace,* ed. Barbara Reskin. Washington, D.C.: National Academy Press, 91–114.

Belous, Richard S. 1989. *The Contingent Economy*. Washington, D.C.: National Planning Association.

Benokraitis, Nicole. 1996. *Marriage and Family*. 2d ed. Upper Saddle River, N.J.: Prentice Hall.

Berg, Ivar, ed. 1981. *Sociological Perspectives on Labor Markets*. New York: Plenum.

Berger, Bennett M. 1967. "Hippie Morality—More Old than New." *Trans-action* 5:19–23.

Best, Fred, and Barry Stern. 1977. "Education, Work, and Leisure—Must They Come in That Order?" *Monthly Labor Review* July: 3–10.

Best, Joel, and David F. Luckenbill. 1982. *Organizing Deviance*. Englewood Cliffs, N.J.: Prentice Hall.

Beynon, Huw. 1975. *Working for Ford*. East Ardsley, Eng.: E. P. Publishing.

———. 1972. *Perceptions of Work: Variations within a Factory*. London: Cambridge University Press.

Bielby, William T., and Denise D. Bielby. 1992. "I Will Follow Him: Family Ties, Gender Role Beliefs, and Reluctance to Relocate for a Better Job." *American Journal of Sociology* 97:1241–67.

Biernacki, Patrick, and Dan Waldorf. 1981. "Snowball Sampling." *Sociological Research and Methods* 10:141–63.

Biggart, Nicole. 1994. "Labor and Leisure." In *The Handbook of Economic Sociology,* ed.

Neil J. Smelser and Richard Swedberg. Princeton, N.J.: Princeton University Press, 671–90.

Blackford, Mansel. 2001. *Fragile Paradise: The Impact of Tourism on Maui, 1959–2000.* Lawrence: University of Kansas Press.

Blank, Rebecca M. 1998. "Contingent Work in a Changing Labor Market." In *Generating Jobs: How to Increase Demand for Less-Skilled Workers,* ed. Richard Freeman and Peter Gottschalk. New York: Russell Sage, 258–94.

Blau, Francine, and Ronald G. Ehrenberg, eds. 2000. *Gender and Family Issues in the Workplace.* New York: Russell Sage.

Blau, Francine, and Lawrence M. Kahn. 2002. *At Home and Abroad.* New York: Russell Sage.

Blauner, Robert. 1967. *Alienation and Freedom: The Factory Worker and His Industry.* Chicago: University of Chicago Press.

Blossfeld, Hans-Peter, and Catherine Hakim, eds. 1997. *Between Equalization and Marginalization: Women Working Part-Time in Europe and the United States of America.* Oxford: Oxford University Press.

Bosk, Charles. 1992. *All God's Mistakes: Genetic Counseling in a Pediatric Hospital.* Chicago: University of Chicago Press.

Bosserman, Phillip. 1975. "Some Interpretations on the Dynamics of Time on Industrial Society." *Society and Leisure* 7:155–64.

Boucher, Keith. 1975. *Global Climate.* London: English Universities Press.

Bourdieu, Pierre. 1984. *Distinctions: A Social Critique of the Judgment of Taste.* London: Routledge and Kegan Paul.

Bowen, David E., and Edward E. Lawler III. 1995. "The Empowerment of Service Workers: What, Why, How, and When." *Sloan Management Review* 33:43–103.

Braham, Peter. 1980. *Class, Race, and Immigration.* London: Open University Press.

Bridges, William. 1994. *JobShift.* Reading, Mass.: Addison-Wesley.

Brissett, Dennis, and Robert P. Snow. 1993. "Boredom: Where the Fun Isn't." *Symbolic Interaction* 16:237–56.

Bronstein, A. S. 1991. "Temporary Work in Western Europe: Threat or Complement to Permanent Employment?" *International Labor Review* 130:293–310.

Brotheridge, Celeste M., and Alicia A. Grandey. 2002. "Emotional Labor and Burnout: Comparing Two Perspectives of 'People Work.'" *Journal of Vocational Behavior* 60:17–39.

Brown, Phil. 1998. *Catskill Culture.* Philadelphia: Temple University Press.

Browne, Irene, ed. 2000. *Latinas and African-American Women at Work.* New York: Russell Sage.

Buck, Elizabeth. 1993. *Paradise Remade: The Politics of Culture and History in Hawai'i.* Philadelphia: Temple University Press.

Buessing, A. 1997. "Working Time Scheduling and the Relations between Work, Family, and Leisure." In *Working Time: New Issues, New Norms, New Measures,* ed. G. Bosch, D. Muelders, and F. Michon. Brussels: Du Dulbea, 39–60.

Burawoy, Michael. 2003. "Revisits: An Outline of a Theory of Reflexive Ethnography." *American Sociological Review* 68:645–79.

——. 1979. *Manufacturing Consent*. Chicago: University of Chicago Press.

Burawoy, Michael, Joseph Blum, Sheba George, Zsuzsa Gille, Teresa Gowan, Lynne Haney, Maren Kalwaiter, Steven Lopez, Sean O'Riain, and Millie Thayer. 2000. *Global Ethnography: Forces, Connections, and Imaginations in a Postmodern World*. Berkeley: University of California Press.

Burgess, Robert G. 1991. "Sponsors, Gatekeepers, Members, and Friends: Access in Educational Settings." In *Experiencing Fieldwork*, ed. Shaffir and Stebbins, 43–52.

——. 1984. *In the Field: An Introduction to Field Research*. London: Allen and Unwin.

Burman, Patrick W. 1988. *Killing Time, Losing Ground: Experiences of Unemployment*. Toronto: Wall and Thompson.

Burris, Beverly H. 1983. *No Room at the Top: Underemployment and Alienation in the Corporation*. New York: Praeger.

Butler, R. W. 1994. "Seasonality in Tourism: Issues and Problems." In *Tourism: The State of the Art*, ed. A. V. Seaton, C. L. Jenkins, R. C. Wood, P. U. C. Dieke, M. M. Bennett, and R. Smith. Chichester, Eng.: Wiley, 332–39.

Butler, Suellen R., and James K. Skipper, Jr. 1980. "Waitressing, Vulnerability, and Job Autonomy: The Case of the Risky Tip." *Sociology of Work and Occupations* 7:487–502.

Butler, Suellen R., and William E. Snizek. 1976. "The Waitress-Diner Relationship: A Multimethod Approach to the Study of Subordinate Influence." *Sociology of Work and Occupations* 3:209–22.

Cantor, Sharon. 1988. "The Temporary Help Industry: Filling the Needs of Workers and Businesses." In *Flexible Workstyles: A Look at Contingent Labor*, ed. Ann McLaughlin and Shirley Dennis. Washington, D.C.: Conference Summary hosted by the U.S. Department of Labor and the Women's Bureau, 46–49.

Carré, Françoise J., Virginia L. duRivage, and Chris Tilly. 1995. "Piecing Together the Fragmented Workplace: Unions and Public Policy on Flexible Employment." In *Unions and Public Policy*, ed. Lawrence G. Flood. Westport, Conn.: Greenwood, 13–34.

Carré, Françoise J., and Pamela Joshi. 1997. "Building Stability for Transient Work Forces: Exploring the Possibilities of Intermediary Institutions Helping Workers Cope with Labor Market Instability." Radcliffe Public Policy Institute Working Paper Series, Working Paper No. 1. Cambridge, Mass.: Radcliffe Public Policy Institute.

Cassell, Joan. 1991. *Expected Miracles: Surgeons at Work*. Philadelphia: Temple University Press.

Cassirer, Naomi, and Barbara Reskin. 2000. "High Hopes: Organizational Position, Employment Experiences, and Women's and Men's Promotion Aspirations." *Work and Occupations* 27:438–63.

Cavan, Sherri. 1972. *Hippies of the Haight.* St. Louis: New Critics Press.

Chaney, Elsa, and Mary Garcia Castro, eds. 1989. *Muchachas No More: Household Workers in Latin America and the Caribbean.* Philadelphia: Temple University Press.

Chapman, Paul K. 1992. *Trouble on Board: The Plight of International Seafarers.* Ithaca, N.Y.: ILR Press.

Charlton, Joy, and Rosanna Hertz. 1989. "Guarding against Boredom: Security Specialists in the U.S. Air Force." *Journal of Contemporary Ethnography* 18:299–326.

Cherry, Robert, and William M. Rodgers, III, eds. 2000. *Prosperity for All?* New York: Russell Sage.

Chin, Christine. 1998. *In Service and Servitude: Foreign Female Domestic Workers and the Malaysian 'Modernity' Project.* New York: Columbia University Press.

Chinoy, Ely. 1955. *Automobile Workers and the American Dream.* Garden City, N.Y.: Doubleday.

Clarkberg, Marin, and Phyllis Moen. 2001. "Understanding the Time-Squeeze: Married Couples' Preferred and Actual Work-Hour Strategies." *American Behavioral Scientist* 44:1115–36.

Clifford, James. 1997. *Routes.* Cambridge, Mass.: Harvard University Press.

Cobble, Dorothy Sue. 1996. "The Prospects for Unionism in a Service Society." In *Working in the Service Society,* ed. Cameron L. Macdonald and Carmen Sirianni. Philadelphia: Temple University Press, 333–58.

———. 1991. *Dishing It Out: Waitresses and Their Unions in the Twentieth Century.* Urbana: University of Illinois Press.

Cock, Jacklyn. 1989. *Maids and Madams: Domestic Workers under Apartheid.* London: Women's Press.

Cohen, Eric. 1973. "Nomads from Affluence: Notes on the Phenomenon of Drifter-Tourism." *International Journal of Comparative Sociology* 14:89–103.

———. 1972. "Toward a Sociology of International Tourism." *Social Research* 39:164–82.

Cohen, Stan, and Laurie Taylor. 1976. *Escape Attempts.* London: Pelican.

Collins, Randall, and Scott Coltrane. 1995. *Sociology of Marriage and the Family.* 4th ed. Chicago: Nelson-Hall.

Collins, Sharon M. 1997. *Black Corporate Executives: The Making and Breaking of a Black Middle Class.* Philadelphia: Temple University Press.

———. 1993. "Blacks on the Bubble: The Vulnerability of Black Executives in White Corporations." *Sociological Quarterly* 34:29–47.

———. 1983. "The Making of the Black Middle Class." *Social Problems* 30:369–82.

Colwill, Nina L. 1993. "Women in Management: Power and Powerlessness." In *Women, Working and Coping,* ed. Bonita C. Long and Sharon E. Kahn. Montreal: McGill-Queen's University Press, 73–89.

Constable, Nicole. 1997. *Maid to Order in Hong Kong.* Ithaca, N.Y.: Cornell University Press.

Cooper, Chris, John Fletcher, David Gilbert, and Stephen Wanhill. 1993. *Tourism: Principles and Practice.* London: Pittman.

Cordes, Cynthia L., and Thomas W. Dougherty. 1993. "A Review and an Integration of Research on Job Burnout." *Academy of Management Review* 18:621–56.

Coser, Lewis. 1974. *Greedy Institutions.* New York: Free Press.

Crosette, Barbara. 1998. "Surprises in the Global Tourism Boom." *New York Times,* April 12.

Cross, Gary. 1990. *A Social History of Leisure since 1600.* State College, Penn.: Venture.

Csikszentmihalyi, Mihalyi. 1975. *Beyond Boredom and Anxiety.* San Francisco: Jossey-Bass.

Cuber, John F., and Peggy B. Harnoff. 1965. *The Significant Americans: A Study of Sexual Behavior among the Affluent.* Baltimore: Penguin.

Czeisler, Charles A., Elliot D. Weitzman, Martin C. Moore-Ede, Janet C. Zimmerman, and Richard S. Knauer. 1980. "Human Sleep: Its Duration and Organization Depend on Its Circadian Phase." *Science* 210:1264–67.

De Grazia, Sebastian. 1962. *Of Time, Work, and Leisure.* New York: Twentieth Century Fund.

Denvir, A., and F. McMahon. 1992. "Labour Turnover in London Hotels." *International Journal of Hospitality Management* 11:143–54.

Denzin, Norman. 1989. *Interpretive Interactionism.* Newbury Park, Calif.: Sage.

Denzin, Norman, and Yvonna Lincoln, eds. 2000. *Handbook of Qualitative Research.* 2d ed. Thousand Oaks, Calif.: Sage.

Desmond, Jane C. 1999. *Staging Tourism: Bodies on Display from Waikiki to Sea World.* Chicago: University of Chicago Press.

Devinatz, Victor G. 1999. *High Tech Betrayal: Working and Organizing on the Shop Floor.* East Lansing: Michigan State University Press.

DiPrete, Thomas A., and Whitman T. Soule. 1988. "Gender and Promotion." *American Sociological Review* 53:26–40.

Dirlik, Arif. 1996. "The Global in the Local." In *Global/Local,* ed. Rob Wilson and Wimal Dissanayake. Durham, N.C.: Duke University Press, 21–45.

Dogar, Rana. 1999. "The Boys (and Girls) of Summer." *Newsweek* August 30:38.

Douglas, Jack D. 1976. *Investigative Social Research: Individual and Team Field Research.* Beverly Hills, Calif.: Sage.

Douglas, Jack D., and John M. Johnson, eds. 1977. *Existential Sociology.* New York: Cambridge University Press.

Dowd, James J. 1991. "Social Psychology in a Postmodern Age: A Discipline without a Subject." *American Sociologist* 22:188–209.

Dubin, Robert. 1956. "Industrial Workers' Worlds: A Study in the 'Central Life Interests' of Industrial Workers." *Social Problems* 3:131–42.

Dupuis, Sherry L. 1999. "Naked Truths: Towards a Reflexive Methodology in Leisure Research." *Leisure Sciences* 21:43–64.

Durivage, Virginia L. 1992. *New Policies for the Part-Time and Contingent Workforce.* Armonk, N.Y.: M. E. Sharpe.

Durkheim. Emile. [1893] 1960. *The Division of Labor in Society.* New York: Free Press.

———. [1912] 1954. *The Elementary Forms of Religious Life.* New York: Free Press.

Eckert, Penelope. 1989. *Jocks and Burnouts.* New York: Teachers College Press.

Eco, Umberto. 1986. *Travels in Hyper Reality.* San Diego: Harcourt Brace Jovanovich.

"Economic Reciprocity Lodging Industry Two-Year Comparison Report Card." www.naacp.org/economic/lodging2002.shtml.

Eder, Donna. 1995. *School Talk: Gender and Adolescent Culture.* New Brunswick, N.J.: Rutgers University Press.

Edwards, Richard. 1979. *Contested Terrain: The Transformation of the Workplace in the Twentieth Century.* New York: Basic Books.

Eisenberger, Robert. 1989. *Blue Monday: The Loss of the Work Ethic in America.* New York: Paragon.

Ellis, Carolyn, and Michael Flaherty, eds. 1992. *Investigating Subjectivity: Research on Lived Experience.* Newbury Park, Calif.: Sage.

Emerson, Robert M., Rachel I. Fretz, and Linda L. Shaw. 1995. *Writing Ethnographic Fieldnotes.* Chicago: University of Chicago Press.

"Empty Beach Chairs." 2003. *Rocky Mountain News,* January 29:1B.

Enloe, Cynthia. 1989. *Beaches, Bananas, and Bases: Making Feminist Sense of International Politics.* Berkeley: University of California Press.

Entwisle, Doris R., Karl L. Alexander, and Linda Steffel Olson. 2000. "Early Work Histories of Urban Youth." *American Sociological Review* 65:279–97.

Epstein, Cynthia Fuchs. 1971. *Women's Place: Options and Limits in Professional Careers.* Berkeley: University of California Press.

Epstein, Cynthia Fuchs, and Arne L. Kalleberg. 2001. "Time and the Sociology of Work: Issues and Implications." *Work and Occupations* 28:5–16.

Epstein, Cynthia Fuchs, Carroll Seron, Bonnie Oglensky, and Robert Sauté. 1999. *The Part-Time Paradox.* New York: Routledge.

Erickson, Rebecca. 1995. "The Importance of Authenticity for Self and Society." *Symbolic Interaction* 18:121–44.

Espiritu, Yen Le. 2003. *Home Bound: Filipino American Lives Across Cultures, Communities, and Countries.* Berkeley: University of California Press.

———. 1995. *Filipino American Lives.* Philadelphia: Temple University Press.

Espiritu, Yen Le, and Diane L. Wolf. 2001. "The Paradox of Assimilation: Children of Filipino Immigrants in San Diego." In *Ethnicities,* ed. Rubén G. Rumbaut and Alejandro Portes. Berkeley: University of California Press, 157–86.

Evans, M. D. R. 1987. "Language Skill, Language Usage, and Opportunity: Immigrants in the Australian Labour Market." *Sociology* 21:253–74.

Ewen, Stuart. 1988. *All Consuming Images.* New York: Basic Books.

Farkas, George, and Paula England, eds. 1988. *Industries, Firms, and Jobs: Sociological and Economic Approaches.* New York: Plenum.

Feldman, Daniel C. 1990. "Reconceptualizing the Nature and Consequences of Part-time Work." *Academy of Management Review* 15:103–112.

Fenwick, Rudy, and Mark Tausig. 2001. "Scheduling Stress: Family and Health Outcomes of Shift Work and Schedule Control." *American Behavioral Scientist* 44:1179–98.

Fine, Gary Alan. 1996. *Kitchens: The Culture of Restaurant Work.* Berkeley: University of California Press.

Fink, Deborah. 1998. *Cutting into the Meatpacking Line: Workers and Change in the Rural Midwest.* Chapel Hill: University of North Carolina Press.

Flaherty, Michael G. 1999. *A Watched Pot: How We Experience Time.* New York: New York University Press.

Fong, Timothy P. 2002. *The Contemporary Asian American Experience: Beyond the Model Minority.* 2d ed. Upper Saddle River, N.J.: Prentice Hall.

Frame, M. W., and C. L. Sheehan. 1994. "Work and Well-Being in the Two-Person Career: Relocation Stress and Coping among Clergy Husbands and Wives." *Family Relations* 43:196–205.

Frankenberg, Ruth. 1993. *White Women, Race Matters: The Social Construction of Whiteness.* Minneapolis: University of Minnesota Press.

Freedman, Audrey. 1985. *The New Look in Wage Policy and Employee Relations.* New York: Conference Board.

Freeman, Richard B., and Peter Gottschalk, eds. 2000. *Generating Jobs: How to Increase Demand for Less-Skilled Workers.* New York: Russell Sage.

Fujimoto, Lila. 1998. "Resort Found Not Guilty in Age-Discrimination Case." *The "Honua" News,* Friday February 6:A3.

Fuller, Linda, and Vicki Smith. 1991. "Consumers' Reports: Management by Customers in a Changing Economy." *Work, Employment, and Society* 5:1–16.

Gagnon, John. 1992. "The Self, Its Voices, and Their Discord." In *Investigating Subjectivity,* ed. Carolyn Ellis and Michael G. Flaherty. Newbury Park, Calif.: Sage, 221–43.

Gallmeier, Charles P. 1991. "Leaving, Revisiting, and Staying in Touch: Neglected Issues in Field Research." In *Experiencing Fieldwork,* ed. Shaffir and Stebbins, 224–31.

———. 1987. "Dinosaurs and Prospects: Toward a Sociology of the Compressed Career." In *Sociological Inquiry: A Humanistic Perspective,* ed. Kooros Mahmoudi, Bradley W. Parlin, and Marty E. Zusman. 4th ed. Dubuque, Iowa: Kendall-Hunt, 95–103.

Gamst, Frederick C. 1980. *The Hoghead.* New York: Holt, Rinehart, and Winston.

Gardezi, Hassan N. 1995. *The Political Economy of International Labour Migration.* Montreal: Black Rose Books.

Garey, Anita Ilta. 1999. *Weaving Work and Motherhood.* Philadelphia: Temple University Press.

Garza, Cecilia. 2001. "Mexican American Domestic Workers." In *Sociological*

Odyssey, ed. Patricia A. Adler and Peter Adler. Belmont, Calif.: Wadsworth, 221–29.

Gaskell, Jane, and Marvin Lazerson. 1981. "Between School and Work: Perspectives on Working Class Youth." *Interchange* 11:80–96.

Geertz, Clifford. 1973. "Thick Description: Toward an Interpretive Theory of Culture." In Clifford Geertz, *The Interpretation of Cultures.* New York: Basic Books, 3–32.

Gergen, Kenneth J. 1991. *The Saturated Self.* New York: Basic Books.

Gerstel, Naomi, and Harriet Gross. 1984. *Commuter Marriage.* New York: Guilford Press.

Geschwender, James, Rita Carroll-Seguin, and Howard Brill. 1988. "The Portuguese and Haoles of Hawai'i: Implications for the Origin of Ethnicity." *American Sociological Review* 53:515–27.

Gilder, George. 1995. "The Glass Ceiling Is Not What Limits Women at Work." In *Male/Female Roles: Opposing Viewpoints,* ed. Jonathan Petrikin. San Diego: Greenhaven Press, 92–99.

Gini, Al. 2003. *The Importance of Being Lazy: In Praise of Play, Leisure, and Vacation.* New York: Routledge.

Giuffre, Patti A., and Christine L. Williams. 1994. "Boundary Lines: Labeling Sexual Harassment in Restaurants." *Gender and Society* 8:378–401.

Glass, Jennifer, Marta Tienda, and Shelly A. Smith. 1988. "The Impact of Changing Employment Opportunity on Gender and Ethnic Earning Inequality." *Social Science Research* 17:252–76.

Glenn, Evelyn Nakano. 2001. "Gender, Race, and the Organization of Reproductive Labor." In *The Critical Study of Work: Labor, Technology, and Global Production,* ed. Rick Baldoz, Charles Koeber, and Philip Kraft. Philadelphia: Temple University Press, 71–82.

———. 1996. "From Servitude to Service Work: Historical Continuities in the Racial Division of Paid Reproductive Labor." In *Working in the Service Economy,* ed. Macdonald and Sirianni, 115–56.

Glick-Schiller, Nina, Linda Basch, and Cristina Szanton-Blanc. 1995. "From Immigrant to Transmigrant: Theorizing Transnational Migration." *Anthropological Quarterly* 68:48–63.

Goffman, Erving. 1974. *Frame Analysis.* New York: Harper and Row.

———. 1959. *The Presentation of Self in Everyday Life.* New York: Anchor Books.

Golden, Lonnie, and Eileen Appelbaum. 1992. "What Was Driving the 1982–88 Boom in Temporary Employment? Preferences of Workers on Decisions or Power of Employers? *American Journal of Economics and Sociology* 51:473–93.

Goldin, Claudia. 1997. "Career and Family: College Women Look to the Past." In *Gender and Family Issues in the Workplace,* ed. Francine D. Blau and Ronald G. Ehrenberg. New York: Russell Sage, 20–64.

Gordon, David M., Richard Edwards, and Michael Reich. 1982. *Segmented Work, Di-*

vided Workers: The Historical Transformation of Labor in the U.S. Cambridge: Cambridge University Press.

Gorz, Andre. 1985. *Paths to Paradise: On the Liberation from Work.* Boston: Sound End Press.

———. 1982. *Farewell to the Working Class.* Boston: South End Press.

Graham, Laurie. 1995. *On the Line at Subaru-Isuzu.* Ithaca, N.Y.: ILR Press.

Gregson, Nicky, and Michelle Lowe. 1994. *Servicing the Middle Class: Class, Gender, and Waged Domestic Labour in Contemporary Britain.* New York: Routledge.

Grint, Keith. 1998. *The Sociology of Work.* 2d ed. Malden, Mass.: Blackwell.

Gronröos, Christian. 1990. *Service Management and Marketing: Managing the Moments of Truth in Service Competition.* Lexington, Mass.: Lexington.

Gryzb, Gerard J. 1990. "Deskilling, Decollectivization, and Diesels: Toward a New Focus in the Study of Changing Skills." *Journal of Contemporary Ethnography* 19:163–87.

Gunz, Hugh P., and R. Michael Jalland. 1996. "Managerial Careers and Business Strategies." *Academy of Management Review* 21:718–56.

Gusfield, Joseph R. 1967. "Moral Passage: The Symbolic Process in Public Designations of Deviance." *Social Problems* 15:175–88.

Gutek, Barbara A. 1992. "Women in Management: Change, Progress, or an Ephemeral Phenomenon?" In *The Ties That Bind,* ed. Louise A. Heslop. Ottawa: Canadian Consortium of Management Schools, 487–505.

Guterl, Fred. 2002. "What Freud Got Right." *Newsweek,* November 11:50–51.

Hagan, Jacqueline. 1994. *Deciding to be Legal: A Maya Community in Houston.* Philadelphia: Temple University Press.

Hall, Colin, and Ronald Lieber. 1996. *Taking Time Off.* New York: Noonday Press.

Hall, Douglas T. 2002. *Careers In and Out of Organizations.* Thousand Oaks, Calif.: Sage.

Hall, Edward T. 1983. *The Dance of Life.* New York: Anchor.

Halualani, Rona Tamiko. 2002. *In the Name of Hawaiians: Native Identities and Cultural Politics.* Minneapolis: University of Minnesota Press.

Hamburger, Robert. 1983. *All the Lonely People: Life in a Single Room Occupancy Hotel.* New Haven: Ticknor and Fields.

Hammond, J. 1933. *The Growth of Common Enjoyment.* London: Routledge.

Hamper, Ben. 1991. *Rivethead.* New York: Warner.

Harper, Douglas. 1982. *Good Company.* Chicago: University of Chicago Press.

Harper, Ida, and Richard L. Simpson, eds. 1983. *Research in the Sociology of Work: Peripheral Workers.* Greenwich, Conn.: JAI.

Harrison, Bennett. 1994. *Lean and Mean: The Changing Landscape of Corporate Power in the Age of Flexibility.* New York: Basic Books.

Hartmann, Heidi I. 1987. "Internal Labor Markets and Gender: A Case Study of Promotion." In *Gender in the Workplace,* ed. Clair Brown and Joseph A. Peckman. Washington, D.C.: Brookings Institution, 59–105.

Hartmann, R. 1986. "Tourism, Seasonality, and Social Change." *Leisure Studies* 5:25–33.

Hawai'i Tourism Authority. 2002. Annual Report to the Hawai'i State Legislature. Honolulu: Hawai'i Tourism Authority.

Hawai'i Visitors Bureau. 1992. *Market Research Department Annual Research Report.* Honolulu: Hawai'i Visitors Bureau.

Haynes, Norman S. 1936. *Hotel Life.* Chapel Hill: University of North Carolina Press.

Heckscher, August, and Sebastian deGrazia. 1959. "Executive Leisure." *Harvard Business Review* July:6–18.

Henson, Kevin D. 1996. *Just a Temp.* Philadelphia: Temple University Press.

Heyzer, Noellen, Geertje Lycklama á Nijeholt, and Nedra Weerakoon, eds. 1994. *The Trade in Domestic Workers: Causes, Mechanisms, and Consequences of International Labor Migration.* London: Zed Books.

Higbie, Frank Tobias. 2003. *Indispensable Outcasts: Hobo Workers and Community in the American Midwest, 1880–1930.* Urbana: University of Illinois Press.

Hill Collins, Patricia. 1987. "Learning from the Outsider Within: The Sociological Significance of Black Feminist Thought." *Social Problems* 33:14–32.

Hix, William. 1998. *Personnel Turbulence: The Personal Determinants of Permanent Change of Station Moves.* Santa Monica: RAND.

Hochschild, Arlie. 1997. *The Time Bind.* New York: Metropolitan Books.

———. 1983. *The Managed Heart: Commercialization of Human Feeling.* Berkeley: University of California Press.

Hodson, Randy. 2001. *Dignity at Work.* New York: Cambridge University Press.

———. 2000. "Introduction: The Expansion of Marginal Employment." *Research in the Sociology of Work* 9:xii–xix.

———. 1991. "The Active Worker: Compliance and Autonomy at the Workplace." *Journal of Contemporary Ethnography* 20:47–78.

Hodson, Randy, Richard L. Simpson, and Ida H. Simpson, eds. 1998. *The Globalization of Work.* Greenwich, Conn.: JAI.

Holyfield, Lori. 1999. "Manufacturing Adventure: The Buying and Selling of Emotions." *Journal of Contemporary Ethnography* 28:3–32.

Holyfield, Lori, and Lilian Jonas. 2003. "From River God to Research Grant: Identity, Emotions, and the Self." *Symbolic Interaction* 26: 285–306.

Holzer, Harry J. 1999. *What Employers Want.* New York: Russell Sage.

Hondagneu-Sotelo, Pierrette. 2001. *Doméstica: Immigrant Workers Cleaning and Caring in the Shadow of Affluence.* Berkeley: University of California Press.

———. 1994. *Gendered Transitions: Mexican Experiences of Migration.* Berkeley: University of California Press.

"Honua" County Annual Report. 1996. *"Island" Inc., The Annual:* 10–15.

Hood, Jane. 1988. "From Night to Day: Timing and the Management of Custodial Work." *Journal of Contemporary Ethnography* 17:96–116.

hooks, bell. 1984. *Feminist Theory: From Margin to Center.* Boston: South End Press.

Horning, Karl H., Anette Gerhard, and Matthias Michailow, eds. 1996. *Time Pioneers: Flexible Working Time and New Lifestyles.* London: Polity.

Hossfeld, Karen J. 2002. "'Their Logic Against Them': Contradictions in Sex, Race, and Class in Silicon Valley." In *Working in America: Continuity, Conflict, and Change,* ed. Amy S. Wharton. 2d ed. New York: McGraw-Hill, 281–91.

Houseman, Susan N. 2001. "Why Employers Use Flexible Staffing Arrangements: Evidence from an Established Survey." *Industrial and Labor Relations Review* 55:149–70.

Hudson, Ken. 2001. "The Disposable Worker." *Monthly Labor Review* 52(April):43–55.

Hughes, Everett C. 1971. *The Sociological Eye.* Boston: Little, Brown.

Hutter, Mark. 1969. "Summertime Servants: The Schlockhaus Waiter." In *The Participant Observer,* ed. Glenn Jacobs. New York: Braziller, 203–25.

Ibarra, Herminia. 1993. "Personal Networks of Women and Minorities in Management: A Conceptual Framework." *Academy of Management Review* 18:56–87.

Irwin, John. 1977. *Scenes.* Beverly Hills, Calif.: Sage.

Ito, Karen L. 1999. *Lady Friends: Hawaiian Ways and the Ties That Define.* Ithaca, N.Y.: Cornell University Press.

Izzo, John B., and Pam Withers. 2001. *Values Shift: The New Work Ethic and What It Means for Business.* Gloucester, Mass: FairWinds Press.

Jackall, Robert. 1988. *Moral Mazes.* New York: Oxford University Press.

Jacobs, Jerry. 1993. "Careers in the U.S. Service Economy." In *Changing Classes: Stratification and Mobility in Post-Industrial Societies,* ed. Gosta Esping-Anderson. London: Sage, 195–224.

Jameson, Fredric. 1984. "Postmodernism, or the Cultural Logic of Late Capitalism." *New Left Review* 146:30–72.

Jonas, Lilian M. 1997. "The Making of a River Guide: The Construction of Authority in a Leisure Subculture." Ph.D. dissertation, University of Denver, Denver, Colo.

Jonas, Lilian M., William P. Stewart, and Kevin W. Larkin. 2003. "Encountering Heidi: Audiences for a Wilderness Adventurer Identity." *Journal of Contemporary Ethnography* 32: 403–31.

Jones, Edward W., Jr. 1986. "Black Managers: The Dream Deferred." *Harvard Business Review* May–June:84–93.

Josephson, Matthew. 1956. *The History of the Hotel and Restaurant Employees and Bartenders International Union AFL-CIO.* New York: Random House.

Junasa, Bienvenido D. 1996. "Filipino Experience in Hawai'i." In *Ethnic Sources in Hawai'i,* ed. Bernhard L. Hormann and Andrew W. Lind. New York: McGraw-Hill, 79–87.

Kalleberg, Arne L. 2000. "Nonstandard Employment Relations: Part-Time, Temporary, and Contract Work." *Annual Review of Sociology* 26:341–65.

Kalleberg, Arne L., and Ivar Berg. 1987. *Work and Industry: Structures, Markets, and Processes.* New York: Plenum.

Kalleberg, Arne L., David Knoke, Peter V. Marsden, and Joe L. Spaeth. 1996. *Organizations in America*. Thousand Oaks, Calif.: Sage.

Kalleberg, Arne L., Edith Rasell, Ken Hudson, David Webster, Barbara F. Reskin, Naomi Cassirer, and Eileen Appelbaum. 1997. *Nonstandard Work, Substandard Jobs: Flexible Work Arrangements in the U.S.* Washington, D.C.: Economic Policy Institute.

Kalleberg, Arne, Barbara F. Reskin, and Ken Hudson. 2000. "Bad Jobs in America: Standard and Nonstandard Employment Relations and Job Quality in the United States." *American Sociological Review* 65:256–78.

Kanter, Rosalie Moss. 1989. *When Giants Learn to Dance*. New York: Simon and Schuster.

———. 1977. *Men and Women of the Corporation*. New York: Basic Books.

Kaplan, Elaine Bell. 1987. "'I Don't Do No Windows': Competition between the Domestic Worker and the Housewife." In *Competition: A Feminist Taboo?*, ed. Valerie Miner and Helene E. Longino. New York: Feminist Press, 92–105.

Kearney, Michael. 1995. "The Local and the Global: The Anthropology of Globalization and Transnationalism." *Annual Review of Anthropology* 24:547–65.

Kent, Noel J. 1993. *Hawai'i: Islands under the Influence*. Honolulu: University of Hawai'i Press.

Khazanov, Anatoli M. 1984. *Nomads and the Outside World*. Cambridge: Cambridge University Press.

King, Brian E. M. 1997. *Creating Island Resorts*. New York: Routledge.

Kirby, Richard, and Jay Corzine. 1981. "The Contagion of Stigma." *Qualitative Sociology* 4:3–20.

Kirschenman, Joleen, and Katherine M. Neckerman. 1991. "'We'd Love to Hire Them, But . . .': The Meaning of Race for Employers." In *The Urban Underclass*, ed. Christopher Jencks and Paul E. Peterson. Washington, D.C.: Brookings Institution, 203–32.

Klapp, Orrin. 1969. *Collective Search for Identity*. New York: Holt, Rinehart, and Winston.

Klein, M. H., H. S. Hyde, M. H. Essex, and R. Clark. 1998. "Maternity Leave, Role Quality, Work Involvement, and Mental Health One Year after Delivery." *Psychology of Women Quarterly* 22:239–66.

Kotarba, Joseph, and Andrea Fontana, eds. 1984. *The Existential Self in Society*. Chicago: University of Chicago Press.

Kotarba, Joseph, and John M. Johnson, eds. 2002. *Postmodern Existential Sociology*. Walnut Creek, Calif.: Alta Mira Press.

Krakover, Shaul. 2000a. "Seasonal Adjustment of Employment to Demand and Revenues in Tourist Hotels during Expansion and Stagnation." *International Journal of Hospitality and Tourism Administration* 1:27–49.

———. 2000b. "Partitioning Seasonal Employment in the Hospitality Industry." *Tourism Management* 21:461–71.

——. 1998. "Employment Adjustment Trends in Tourism Hotels in Israel." *Tourism Recreation Research* 23:23–32.

Kunda, Gideon. 1992. *Engineering Culture: Control and Commitment in a High-Tech Corporation.* Philadelphia: Temple University Press.

Kunda, Gideon, Stephen R. Barley, and James Evans. 2002. "Why Do Contractors Contract? The Experience of Highly Skilled Technical Professionals in a Contingent Labor Market." *Industrial and Labor Relations Review* 55:234–61.

Kutscher, Ronald E. 1987. "Projections 2000: Overview and Implications of the Projections to 2000." *Monthly Labor Review* (September):3–9.

Lapchick, Richard E., and Kevin J. Mathews. 2000. *Racial and Gender Report Card (for 1998).* Boston: Center for the Study of Sport in Society (Northeastern University).

Laslett, John, and Mary Tyler. 1989. *The ILGWU in Los Angeles 1907–1988.* Inglewood, Calif.: Ten Star Press.

Lauer, Robert H. 1981. *Temporal Man: The Meaning and Uses of Social Time.* New York: Praeger.

Lautsch, Brenda A. 2002. "Uncovering and Explaining Variance in the Features and Outcomes of Contingent Work." *Industrial and Labor Relations Review* 56:23–43.

Leggett, John. 1968. *Class, Race, and Labour.* New York: Cambridge University Press.

Leidner, Robin. 1999. "Emotional Labor in Service Work." *Annals of the Academy of Political Science and Sociology* 561:81–95.

——. 1993. *Fast Food, Fast Talk: Service Work and the Routinization of Everyday Life.* Berkeley: University of California Press.

Lenček, Lena, and Gideon Bosker. 1998. *The Beach: The History of Paradise on Earth.* New York: Viking.

Levenson, Alec R. 2000. "Long-Run Trends in Part-Time and Temporary Employment: Toward an Understanding." In *On the Job: Is Long-Term Employment a Thing of the Past?* ed. David Neumark. New York: Russell Sage, 335–97.

Lewy, Alfred J., Thomas A. Wehr, Frederick K. Goodwin, David A. Newsome, and S. P. Markey. 1980. "Light Suppresses Melatonin Secretion in Humans." *Science* 210:1267–69.

Lieberman, Harris R., Franz Waldhauser, Gail Garfield, Harry J. Lynch, and Richard J. Wurtman. 1984. "Effects of Melatonin on Human Mood and Performance." *Brain Research* 323:201–7.

Lieberson, Stanley. 1980. *A Piece of the Pie: Blacks and White Immigrants since 1880.* Berkeley: University of California Press.

Lieberson, Stanley, and Mary C. Waters. 1988. *From Many Strands: Ethnic and Racial Groups in Contemporary America.* New York: Russell Sage.

Lind, Andrew W. 1996. "Immigration to Hawai'i." In *Ethnic Sources in Hawai'i,* ed. Hormann and Lind, 3–12.

Linhart, Robert. 1981. *The Assembly Line.* Amherst: University of Massachusetts Press.

Linton, April. 2002. "Immigration and the Structure of Demand: Do Immigrants

Alter the Labor Market Composition of U.S. Cities?" *International Migration Review* 36:58–80.

Lipman, Elinor. 1999. *The Inn at Lake Devine.* New York: Vintage.

Lipsher, Steve. 1998. "State's Ski Areas Loosen up to Attract Workers." *The Denver Post,* November 2, 1A, 9A.

Little, Roger. 1990. "Friendships in the Military Community." In *Friendships in Context,* ed. Helena Z. Lopata and David R. Maines. Greenwich, Conn.: JAI, 221–36.

Lodge, David. 1991. *Paradise News.* New York: Penguin.

Löfgren, Orvar. 1999. *On Holiday: A History of Vacationing.* Berkeley: University of California Press.

Lois, Jennifer. 2003. *Heroic Efforts: The Emotional Culture of Search and Rescue Volunteers.* New York: New York University Press.

Loy, John W., and Joseph F. McElvogue. 1970. "Racial Segregation in American Sport." *International Review of Sport Sociology* 5:5–24.

Luce, Gay Gaer. 1971. *Body Time: Physiological and Social Stress.* New York: Pantheon.

Lurie, Alison. 1998. *The Last Resort.* New York: Henry Holt.

Lyman, Stanford M., and Marvin B. Scott. 1989. *A Sociology of the Absurd.* 2d ed. Dix Hills, N.Y.: General Hall.

Lyng, Stephen. 1990. "Edgework: A Social Psychological Analysis of Voluntary Risk Taking." *American Journal of Sociology* 95:851–86.

MacCannell, Dean. 1992. *Empty Meeting Grounds: The Tourist Papers.* New York: Routledge.

———. 1989. *The Tourist.* New York: Schocken.

Macdonald, Cameron L., and Carmen Sirianni. 1996. "The Service Society and the Changing Experience of Work." In *Working in the Service Society,* ed. Macdonald and Sirianni, 1–26.

MacKinnon, Catherine A. 1979. *Sexual Harassment of Working Women: A Case of Sex Discrimination.* New Haven: Yale University Press.

Madsen Camacho, Michelle E. 1996. "Dissenting Workers and Social Control: A Case Study of the Hotel Industry in Huatulco, Oaxaca." *Human Organization* 55:33–40.

Maines, J. 1993. "Long-Distance Romances." *American Demographics* (May):47.

Makimoto, Tsugio, and David Manners. 1997. *Digital Nomads.* Chichester, Eng.: Wiley.

Mangum, Garth, Donald Mayall, and Kristin Nelson. 1985. "The Temporary Help Industry: A Response to the Dual Internal Labor Market." *Industrial and Labor Relations Review* 38:599–611.

Manicas, Peter. 1998. "The Los Angelesation of Hawai'i." Paper presented at the annual meeting of the Hawai'i Sociological Association.

———. 1996. "Introduction." In *Ethnic Sources in Hawai'i,* ed. Hormann and Lind, v–xxviii.

Manning, Peter Kirby. 1991. "Strands in the Postmodern Rope." *Studies in Symbolic Interaction* 12:3–27.

———. 1977. *Police Work: The Social Organization of Policing.* Cambridge: MIT Press.

Mannon, James M. 1997. *Measuring Up.* Boulder, Colo.: Westview.

Markula, Pirkko. 1997. "As a Tourist in Tahiti: An Analysis of Personal Experience." *Journal of Contemporary Ethnography* 26:202–24.

Mars, Gerald, and Michael Nicod. 1984. *The World of Waiters.* London: Allen and Unwin.

Marshall, Gordon. 1986. "The Workplace of a Licensed Restaurant." *Theory, Culture, and Society* 3:33–47.

Martin, Susan Ehrlich. 1980. *Breaking and Entering: Policewomen on Patrol.* Berkeley: University of California Press.

Martinez, Samuel. 1996. *Peripheral Migrants: Haitians and Dominican Republic Sugar Plantations.* Knoxville: University of Tennessee Press.

Marx, Karl. [1845] 1972. "The German Ideology." In *The Marx-Engels Reader,* ed. Robert C. Tucker. New York: Norton, 110–64.

Maslach, Christina, and Michael P. Leiter. 1997. *The Truth about Burnout: How Organizations Cause Personal Stress and What to Do about It.* San Francisco: Jossey-Bass.

Maume, David J. 1999. "Glass Ceilings and Glass Escalators: Occupational Segregation and Race and Sex Differences in Managerial Promotions." *Work and Occupations* 26:483–509.

McCammon, Holly J., and Larry J. Griffin. 2000. "Workers and Their Customers and Clients: An Editorial Introduction." *Work and Occupations* 27:278–93.

McCarl, Robert. 1985. *The District of Columbia's Fire Fighters' Project: A Case Study in Occupational Folklife.* Washington, D.C.: Smithsonian Institution.

McCorkel, Jill, and Kristen Myers. 2003. "What Difference Does Difference Make? Position and Privilege in the Field." *Qualitative Sociology* 26:199–231.

McCormick, A. E., and Graham C. Kinloch. 1986. "Interracial Contact in the Customer-Clerk Situation." *Journal of Social Psychology* 126:551–53.

McCubbin, Hamilton I., and L. D. McCubbin. 1997. "Hawaiian American Families." In *Families in Cultural Context,* ed. Mary Kay DeGenova. Mountain View, Calif.: Mayfield, 239–66.

McDermott, John F., Jr., Wen Shing Tseng, and Thomas W. Maretzki, eds. 1980. *People and Cultures of Hawai'i.* Honolulu: University of Hawai'i Press.

McMahon, F. 1994. "Productivity in the Hotel Industry." In *Tourism: The State of the Art,* ed. Seaton et al., 616–25.

Mead, George Herbert. 1934. *Mind, Self, and Society.* Chicago: University of Chicago Press.

Meiksins, Peter, and Peter Whalley. 2002. *Putting Work in Its Place: A Quiet Revolution.* Ithaca, N.Y.: Cornell University Press.

Melbin, Murray. 1987. *Night as Frontier.* New York: Free Press.

——. 1978. "Night as Frontier." *American Sociological Review* 43:3–22.

——. 1969. "Behavioral Rhythms in Mental Hospitals." *American Journal of Sociology* 74:950–65.

Merton, Robert. 1938. "Social Structure and Anomie." *American Sociological Review* 3:672–82.

Miklius, Walter. 1992. "If Hawai'i Is Paradise, Why Do So Many People Leave?" In *The Price of Paradise,* ed. Randall W. Roth. Honolulu: Mutual. Vol. 1, 241–45.

Millman, Marcia. 1976. *The Unkindest Cut.* New York: Morrow.

Mitchell, Don. 1996. *The Lie of the Land: Migrant Workers and the California Landscape.* Minneapolis: University of Minnesota Press.

Mitchell, Richard G. 1983. *Mountain Experience: The Psychology and Sociology of Adventure.* Chicago: University of Chicago Press.

Molstad, Clark. 1986. "Choosing and Coping with Boring Work." *Urban Life* 15:215–36.

Monroe, L. J. 1967. "Psychological and Physiological Differences between Good and Poor Sleepers." *Journal of Abnormal Psychology* 72:255–64.

Morse, Dean. 1969. *The Peripheral Worker.* New York: Columbia University Press.

Moss, Phillip, and Chris Tilly. 2001. *Stories Employers Tell.* New York: Russell Sage.

——. 1996. "'Soft' Skills and Race: An Investigation of Black Men's Employment Problems." *Work and Occupations* 23:128–33.

Murphy, Edna. 1996. *Flexible Work.* London: Director Books.

Myles, John, Garnett Picot, and Ted Wannell. 1993. "Does Post-Industrialism Matter? The Canadian Experience." In *Changing Classes,* ed. Esping-Anderson, 171–94.

Needleman, Ruth, and Anne Nelson. 1988. "Policy Implications: The Worth of Women's Work." In *The Worth of Women's Work: A Qualitative Synthesis,* ed. Anne Statham, Eleanor M. Miller, and Hans O. Mauksch. Albany: State University of New York Press, 293–308.

Negrey, Cynthia. 1990. "Contingency Work and the Rhetoric of Autonomy." *Humanity and Society* 14:16–33.

Nelson, Joel I. 1994. "Work and Benefits: The Multiple Problems of Service Sector Employment." *Social Problems* 41:240–55.

Neumann, Mark. 1992. "The Trail through Experience: Finding Self in the Recollection of Travel." In *Investigating Subjectivity,* ed. Carolyn Ellis and Michael Flaherty. Newbury Park, Calif.: Sage, 176–201.

Newman, Katherine S. 1999. *No Shame in My Game: The Working Poor in the Inner City.* New York: Knopf.

——. 1988. *Falling from Grace.* New York: Free Press.

Nippert-Eng, Christena. 1996. *Home and Work: Negotiating Boundaries through Everyday Life.* Chicago: University of Chicago Press.

Nollen, Stanley D., Brenda Broz Eddy, and Virginia Hider Martin. 1978. *Permanent Part-Time Employment.* New York: Praeger.

O'Connell, Martin, and David E. Bloom. 1987. "Juggling Jobs and Babies: America's Child Care Challenge." *Population Trends and Public Policy* 12 (February).

Okamura, Jonathan Y. 1994. "Why There are No Asian Americans in Hawai'i: The Continuing Significance of Local Identity." *Social Process in Hawai'i* 35:161–78.

———. 1982. "Immigrant Filipino Ethnicity in Honolulu, Hawai'i." Ph.D. dissertation, University College, London.

———. 1980. "Aloha Kanaka Me Ke Aloha 'Āina: Local Culture and Society in Hawai'i." *Amerasia Journal* 7:119–37.

Okamura, Jonathan Y., A. Agbayani, and M. Kerkvliet. 1991. *The Filipino Experience in Hawai'i.* Honolulu: University of Hawai'i Press.

Okamura, Jonathan Y., and R. Labrador. 1996. *Pagdiriwang 1996: Legacy and Vision of Hawaiian Filipino Americans.* Honolulu: University of Hawai'i Press.

Olmsted, Barney, and Suzanne Smith. 1989. *Creating a Flexible Workplace.* New York: American Management Association.

O'Neill, Gillian. 2001. "'Find a Job You Love and You'll Never Have to Work Another Day': An Analysis of Emotion in the Work of Dive Instructors and Black Water 'Rafters.'" *Australian Journal of Communication* 28:47–62.

Ong, Aihwa. 1999. *Flexible Citizenship: The Culture Logic of Transnationality.* Durham, N.C.: Duke University Press.

Oppenheimer, Valerie, and Matthijs Kalmijn. 1995. "Life Job Cycles." *Research in Social Stratification and Mobility* 14:1–38.

O'Reilly, Jacqueline, and Colette Fagan, eds. 1998. *Part-Time Prospects.* New York: Routledge.

Orem, John, and Judith Keeling. 1980. *Physiology in Sleep.* New York: Academic Press.

Osterman, Paul. 1999. *Securing Prosperity.* Princeton, N.J.: Princeton University Press.

Osterman, Paul, Thomas A. Kochan, Richard M. Locke, and Michael J. Piore. 2001. *Working in America: A Blueprint for the New Labor Market.* Cambridge: MIT Press.

Ouellet, Lawrence. 1994. *Pedal to the Metal: The Work Lives of Truckers.* Philadelphia: Temple University Press.

Owen, John D. 1969. *The Price of Leisure.* Rotterdam: Rotterdam University Press.

Parker, Robert E. 2002. "The Global Economy and Changes in the Nature of Contingent Work." In *Labor and Capital in the Age of Globalization: The Labor Process and the Changing Nature of Work in the Global Economy,* ed. Berch Berberoglu. Lanham, Md.: Rowman and Littlefield, 107–23.

———. 1994. *Flesh Peddlers and Warm Bodies: The Temporary Help Industry and Its Workers.* New Brunswick, N.J.: Rutgers University Press.

Parker, Stanley. 1983. *Leisure and Work.* London: Allen and Unwin.

———. 1971. *The Future of Work and Leisure.* New York: Praeger.

Parreñas, Rhacel Salazar. 2001. *Servants of Globalization: Women, Migration, and Domestic Work.* Stanford, Calif.: Stanford University Press.

Paul, Pamela. 2002. "Time Out." *American Demographics* 24 (June):35–41.

Paules, Greta Foff. 1991. *Dishing It Out: Power and Resistance among Waitresses in a New Jersey Restaurant.* Philadelphia: Temple University Press.

Paulin, E. A., and J. M. Mellnor. 1996. "Gender, Race, and Promotions in a Private-Sector Firm." *Industrial Relations* 35:276–95.

Pavalko, Ronald M. 1988. *Sociology of Occupations and Professions.* 2d ed. Itasca, Ill.: Peacock.

Pearson, Anthony. 1987. "The Grateful Dead Phenomenon: An Ethnomethodological Approach." *Youth and Society* 18:4–18.

Pellow, David Naguib, and Lisa Sun-Hee Park. 2003. *The Silicon Valley of Dreams: Environmental Justice, Immigrant Workers, and the High-Tech Global Economy.* New York: NYU Press.

Piore, Michael J. 1979. *Birds of Passage: Migrant Labor and Industrial Societies.* New York: Cambridge University Press.

Piore, Michael J., and Charles F. Sabel. 1984. *The Second Industrial Divide: Possibilities for Prosperity.* New York: Basic Books.

Polivka, Anne E., and Thomas Nardone. 1989. "The Quality of Jobs: On the Definition of 'Contingent Work.'" *Monthly Labor Review* 112 (December):9–16.

Popenoe, David. 1996. *Life without Father.* Cambridge, Mass.: Harvard University Press.

Portes, Alejandro, ed. 1996. *The New Second Generation.* New York: Russell Sage.

Portes, Alejandro, and Rubén G. Rumbaut. 2001. *Legacies.* Berkeley: University of California Press.

———. 1996. *Immigrant America.* 2d ed. Berkeley: University of California Press.

Powell, Gary N. 1986. "Effects of Sex Role Identity and Sex on Definitions of Sexual Harassment." *Sex Roles* 14:9–19.

Presser, Harriet B. 2000. "Nonstandard Work Schedules and Marital Instability." *Journal of Marriage and the Family* 62:93–110.

———. 1999. "Toward a 24-Hour Economy." *Science* 284:1778–79.

Prus, Robert. 1989. *Pursuing Customers.* Newbury Park, Calif.: Sage.

Prus, Robert, and Styllianos Irini. 1980. *Hookers, Rounders, and Desk Clerks.* Toronto: Gage.

Quadagno, Jill. 1994. *The Color of Welfare: How Racism Undermined the War on Poverty.* New York: Oxford University Press.

Rafaeli, Anat, and Michael G. Pratt. 1993. "Tailored Meanings: On the Meaning and Impact of Organizational Dress." *Academy of Management Review* 18:32–55.

Ramos, Teresita V. 1996. "Philippine Languages in Hawai'i: Vehicles of Cultural Survival." *Social Process in Hawai'i* 37:161–70.

Reskin, Barbara F. 1993. "Sex Segregation in the Workplace." *Annual Review of Sociology* 19:241–70.

Reskin, Barbara F., and Naomi Cassirer. 1996. "Occupational Segregation by Gender, Race, and Ethnicity." *Sociological Focus* 29:231–43.

Reskin, Barbara F., and Polly A. Phipps. 1988. "Women in Male-Dominated Professional and Managerial Occupations." In *Women Working*, ed. Ann Helton Stromberg and Shirley Harkess. Mountain View, Calif.: Mayfield, 190–205.

Reskin, Barbara, and Patricia Roos. 1990. *Job Queues, Gender Queues*. Philadelphia: Temple University Press.

Richardson, Laurel. 1997. *Fields of Play*. New Brunswick, N.J.: Rutgers University Press.

Riley, M. 1991. "An Analysis of Hotel Labor Markets." In *Progress in Tourism, Recreation and Hospitality Management,* ed. Christopher P. Cooper. London: Bellhaven Press. Vol. 3, 232–46.

Rinehart, James W., Christopher Huxley, and David Robertson. 1997. *Just Another Car Factory? Lean Production and Its Discontents*. Ithaca, N.Y.: Cornell University Press.

Rinehart, Robert E., and Synthia Sydnor, eds. 2003. *To The Extreme: Alternative Sports, Inside and Out*. Albany: State University of New York Press.

Robboy, Howard. 1983. "At Night with the Night Worker." In *Social Interaction,* ed. Howard Robboy and Candace Clark. 2d ed. New York: St. Martin's Press, 506–19.

Robillard, Albert B. 1996. "'Typically Filipino.'" *Social Process in Hawai'i* 37:171–83.

Robinson, Jeffrey. 1997. *The Hotel*. New York: Arcade.

Robinson, John P., and Geoffrey Godbey. 1999. *Time for Life: The Surprising Ways Americans Use Their Time*. University Park: Pennsylvania State University Press.

Rogers, Jackie Krasas. 2000. *Temps: The Many Faces of the Changing Workplace*. Ithaca, N.Y.: Cornell University Press.

Rohrer, Judy. 1997. "Haole Girl: Identity and White Privilege in Hawai'i." *Social Process in Hawai'i* 38:140–61.

Rollins, Judith. 1985. *Between Women: Domestics and Their Employers*. Philadelphia: Temple University Press.

Rollinson, Paul A. 1990. "The Story of Edward: The Everyday Geography of Elderly Single Room Occupancy (SRO) Hotel Tenants." *Journal of Contemporary Ethnography* 19:188–206.

Romero, Mary. 1994. "Transcending and Reproducing Race, Class, and Gender Hierarchies in the Everyday Interactions between Chicana Private Household Workers and Employers." In *Ethnic Women: A Multiple Status Reality,* ed. Vasilikie Demos and Marcia Texler Segal. Dix Hills, N.Y.: General Hall, 135–44.

———. 1992. *Maid in the U.S.* New York: Routledge.

Rones, Phillip L. 1978. "Older Men—The Choice between Work and Retirement." *Monthly Labor Review* 101:3–10.

Rosenbaum, James E. 1979. "Tournament Mobility: Career Patterns in a Corporation." *Administrative Science Quarterly* 24:220–41.

Rosenthal, Rob. 1994. *Homeless in Paradise: A Map of the Terrain.* Philadelphia: Temple University Press.

Roth, Julius. 1963. *Timetables.* Indianapolis: Bobbs-Merrill.

Rubinstein, Jonathan. 1973. *City Police.* New York: Farrar, Straus, and Giroux.

Rybczynski, Witold. 1991. *Waiting for the Weekend.* New York: Viking.

Salaman, Graeme. 1971. "Two Occupational Communities: Examples of a Remarkable Convergence of Work and Non-Work." *Sociological Review* 19:389–407.

Sallaz, Jeffrey J. 2002. "The House Rules: Autonomy and Interests among Service Workers in the Contemporary Casino Industry." *Work and Occupations* 29:393–427.

Sayers, Sean. 1987. "The Need to Work." *Radical Philosophy* 46:17–26.

Schiebe, Karl E. 1986. "Self-Narratives and Adventure." In *Narrative Psychology,* ed. Theodore Sarbin. New York: Praeger, 129–51.

Schmidt, Catherine J. 1979. "The Guided Tour: Insulated Adventure." *Urban Life* 7:441–68.

Schor, Juliet B. 1992. *The Overworked American.* New York: Basic Books.

Schroedl, Alan. 1972. "The Dish Ran Away with the Spoon: Ethnography of Kitchen Culture." In *The Cultural Experience,* ed. James P. Spradley and David M. McCurdy. Chicago: Science Research Associates, 177–89.

Schulman, Michael D., and Cynthia Anderson. 1993. "Political Economy and Local Labor Markets: Toward a Theoretical Synthesis." In *Inequalities in Labor Market Areas,* ed. Joachim Singelmann and Forrest Deseran. Boulder, Colo.: Westview Press, 33–47.

Schwartz, David G. 2003. *Suburban Xanadu: The Casino Resort on the Las Vegas Strip and Beyond.* New York: Routledge.

Shamir, Boas. 1981. "The Workplace as a Community: The Case of British Hotels." *Industrial Relations Journal* 12:45–56.

Shapiro, Andrew. 2001. "The Net That Binds." In *Sociological Odyssey,* ed. Adler and Adler, 394–97.

Sherman, Rachel. 2003. "Class Acts: Producing and Consuming Luxury Service in Hotels." Ph.D. dissertation, University of California, Berkeley.

Simmel, Georg. 1950. *The Sociology of Georg Simmel.* Trans. and ed. by Kurt H. Wolff. New York: Free Press.

Smigel, Erwin O. 1969. *The Wall Street Lawyer: Professional Organizational Man?* New York: Free Press.

Smith, Dorothy. 1990. *The Conceptual Practices of Power.* Boston: Northeastern University Press.

Smith, Vicki. 2001. *Crossing the Great Divide: Worker Risk and Opportunity in the New Economy.* Ithaca, N.Y.: Cornell University Press.

———. 1998. "The Fractured World of the Temporary Worker: Power, Participation, and Fragmentation in the Contemporary Workplace." *Social Problems* 45:411–30.

———. 1990. *Managing in the Corporate Interest.* Berkeley: University of California Press.

Snow, David, and Leon Anderson. 1993. *Down on Their Luck.* Berkeley: University of California Press.

Snow, Robert P., and Dennis Brissett. 1986. "Pauses: Explorations in Social Rhythm." *Symbolic Interaction* 9:1–18.

Soesilo, J. Andy, and Robert C. Mings. 1987. "Assessing the Seasonality of Tourism." *Visions in Leisure and Business* 6:25–38.

Sorokin, Pitirim, and Robert Merton. 1937. "Social Time: A Methodological and Functional Analysis." *American Journal of Sociology* 42:615–29.

Sosnick, Stephen H. 1978. *Hired Hands.* Santa Barbara: McNally and Loftin, West.

Spain, Daphne, and Suzanne M. Bianchi. 1996. *Balancing Act.* New York: Russell Sage.

Spradley, James. 1970. *You Owe Yourself a Drunk.* Boston: Little, Brown.

Staines, Graham L. 1980. "Spillover versus Compensation: A Review of the Literature on the Relationship between Work and Nonwork." *Human Relations* 33:111–30.

Stebbins, Robert. 1979. *Amateurs.* Beverly Hills, Calif.: Sage.

———. 1971. "The Subjective Career as a Basis for Reducing Role Conflict." *Pacific Sociological Review* 14:383–402.

———. 1970. "Career: The Subjective Approach." *Sociological Quarterly* 11:32–49.

Stenross, Barbara, and Sherryl Kleinman. 1989. "The Highs and Lows of Emotional Labor: Detectives' Encounters with Criminals and Victims." *Journal of Contemporary Ethnography* 17:435–52.

Stephens, Joyce. 1976. *Loners, Losers, and Lovers.* Seattle: University of Washington Press.

Stepick, Alex, and Guillermo Grenier. 1994. "The View from the Back of the House: Restaurants and Hotels in Miami." In *Newcomers in the Workplace: Immigrants and the Restructuring of the U.S. Economy,* ed. Louise Lamphere, Alex Stepick, and Guillermo Grenier. Philadelphia: Temple University Press, 181–98.

Stern, Bernard W. 1989. *The Aloha Trade: Labor Relations in Hawai'i's Hotel Industry 1941–1987.* Honolulu: University of Hawai'i Press.

Sutton, Robert I., and Anat Rafaeli. 1988. "Untangling the Relationship Between Displayed Emotions and Organizational Sales: The Case of Convenience Stores." *Academy of Management Journal* 31:461–87.

Sweeney, John, and Karen Nussbaum. 1989. *Solutions for the New Work Force.* Cabin John, Md.: Seven Locks Press.

Tagaki, C., and T. Ishisaka. 1982. *Cultural Awareness in the Human Services.* Englewood Cliffs, N.J.: Prentice Hall.

Talwar, Jennifer Parker. 2004. *Fast Food, Fast Track: Immigrants, Big Business, and the American Dream.* Boulder, Colo: Westview Press.

Tannock, Stuart. 2001. *Youth at Work: The Unionized Fast-Food and Grocery Workplace.* Philadelphia: Temple University Press.

Tausky, Curt, and Robert Dubin. 1965. "Career Anchorage: Managerial Mobility Motivations." *American Sociological Review* 30:725–35.

Taylor, P. J. 1967. "Shift and Day Work: A Comparison of Sickness Absence, Lateness, and Other Absence Behavior at an Oil Refinery from 1962 to 1965." *British Journal of Industrial Medicine* 24:98.

Theroux, Paul. 2001. *Hotel Honolulu.* Boston: Houghton Mifflin.

Thompson, Allison. 1995. "The Contingent Workforce." *Occupational Outlook Quarterly* 39:45–48.

Thompson, Eric. 2002. "Engineered Corporate Culture on a Cruise Ship." *Sociological Focus* 35:331–44.

Tienda, Marta, and Ding-Trann Lii. 1987. "Minority Concentration and Earnings Inequality: Blacks, Hispanics, and Asians Compared." *American Journal of Sociology* 93:141–65.

Tilly, Chris. 1996. *Half a Job: Bad and Good Part-Time Jobs in a Changing Labor Market.* Philadelphia: Temple University Press.

——. 1992. "Short Hours, Short Shrift: The Causes and Consequences of Part-Time Employment." In *New Policies for the Part-Time and Contingent Workforce,* ed. Virginia duRivage. Armonk, N.Y.: M. E. Sharpe, 15–44.

Toffler, Alvin. 1970. *Future Shock.* New York: Random House.

Tolich, Martin B. 1993. "Alienating and Liberating Emotions at Work: Supermarket Clerks' Performance of Customer Service." *Journal of Contemporary Ethnography* 22:361–81.

Tomaskovic-Devey, Donald. 1993. *Gender and Racial Inequality at Work.* Ithaca, N.Y.: ILR Press.

Trask, Huanani-Kay. 1993. *From a Native Daughter: Colonialism and Sovereignty in Hawai'i.* Monroe, Maine: Common Courage Press.

Travel Industry Association of America. 2002. www.tia.org.

Trentham, Susan, and Laurie Larwood. 1998. "Gender Discrimination and the Workplace: An Examination of Rational Bias Theory." *Sex Roles* 38:1–28.

Tseëlon, Efrat. 1992. "Is the Postmodern Self Sincere? Goffman, Impression Management, and the Postmodern Self." *Theory, Culture, and Society* 9:115–28.

Tucker, James. 1993. "Everyday Forms of Employee Resistance." *Sociological Forum* 8:25–45.

Turner, Ralph H. 1976. "The Real Self: From Institution to Impulse." *American Journal of Sociology* 81:989–1016.

U.S. Department of Labor, Bureau of Labor Statistics. 2002. "Services: Business Demand Rivals Consumer Demand in Driving Job Growth." *Monthly Labor Review* 125 (April):3–16.

Urbain, Jean-Didier. 2003. *At the Beach.* Minneapolis: University of Minnesota Press.

Vail, Angus. 2001. "Researching from Afar: Distance, Ethnography, and Testing the Edge." *Journal of Contemporary Ethnography* 30:704–25.

"Vail Resorts Drops Employee Drug Testing." 2000. *The Daily Camera,* October 1:6B.

Van Dyne, Linn, and Soon Ang. 1998. "Organizational Citizenship Behavior of Contingent Workers in Singapore." *Academy of Management Journal* 41:692–703.

Van Maanen, John, ed. 1998. *Qualitative Studies of Organizations.* Thousand Oaks, Calif.: Sage.

——. 1988. *Tales of the Field.* Chicago: University of Chicago Press.

Van Maanen, John, and Gideon Kunda. 1989. "Real Feelings: Emotional Expression and Organizational Culture." *Research in Organizational Behavior* 11:43–103.

Vaughan, George M., Rodney Bell, and A. de la Peña. 1979. "Nocturnal Plasma Melatonin in Humans: Episodic Pattern and Influence of Light." *Neuroscience Letters* 14:81–84.

Veiga, John F. 1983. "Mobility Influences during Managerial Career Stages." *Academy of Management Journal* 26:64–85.

Wacker, Mary Ellen, and David B. Bills. 2000. "Barriers and Adaptations: Hiring Managers and Contingent Workers." *Research in the Sociology of Work* 9:231–52.

Wagner, David. 1993. *Checkerboard Square.* Boulder, Colo.: Westview.

Waldinger, Roger, and Claudia Der-Martirosian. 2000. "Immigrant Workers and American Labor: Challenge . . . or Disaster?" In *Organizing Immigrants: The Challenge for Unions in Contemporary California,* ed. Ruth Milkman. Ithaca, N.Y.: Cornell University Press, 49–80.

Walker, Katherine. 2000. "'It's Difficult to Hide': The Presentation of Self on Internet Home Pages." *Qualitative Sociology* 23:99–120.

Weigert, Andrew. 1981. *Sociology of Everyday Life.* New York: Longman.

Weinstein, Michael, Peter Manicas, and Joseph Leon. 1990. "On the Portuguese and Haoles of Hawai'i." *American Sociological Review* 55:305–8.

Wells, Miriam J. 2000. "Unionization and Immigrant Incorporation in San Francisco Hotels." *Social Problems* 47:241–65.

Wheaton, Belinda. 2003. "Windsurfing: A Subculture of Commitment." In *To the Extreme: Alternative Sports, Inside and Out,* ed. Robert E. Rinehart and Synthia Sydnor. Albany: State University of New York Press, 75–104.

——. 2000. "'Just Do It': Consumption, Commitment, and Identity in the Windsurfing Subculture." *Sociology of Sport Journal* 17:254–74.

Whittaker, Elvi. 1986. *The Mainland Haole: The White Experience in Hawaii.* New York: Columbia University Press.

Whyte, William Foote. 1949. "The Social Structure of the Restaurant." *American Journal of Sociology* 54:302–10.

Wilensky, Harold L. 1963. "The Uneven Distribution of Leisure: The Impact of Economic Growth on 'Free Time.'" In *Work and Leisure,* ed. Erwin Smigel. New Haven, Conn.: College and University Press, 107–45.

——. 1960. "Work, Careers, and Social Integration." *International Social Science Journal* 4:543–60.

Wiley, Juniper. 1987. "The Shock of Unrecognition as a Problem in Participant-Observation." *Qualitative Sociology* 10:78–83.

Williams, Christine L. 1989. *Gender Differences at Work: Men and Women in Nontraditional Occupations.* Berkeley: University of California Press.

Williams, Christine L., Patti A. Guiffre, and Kirsten Dellinger. 1999. "Sexuality in the Workplace: Organizational Control, Sexual Harassment, and the Pursuit of Pleasure." *Annual Review of Sociology* 25:73–93.

Witeck, John. 2001. "Public Policy in Hawai'i: Globalism's Neoliberal Embrace." *Social Process in Hawai'i* 40:36–68.

Witt, C. A., and S. F. Witt. 1989. "Why Productivity in the Hotel Sector is Low." *International Journal of Contemporary Hospitality Management* 1:28–33.

Wolfson, Hannah. 2000. "Resorts Have Trouble Finding Workers." *The Daily Camera,* September 10:F1, F4.

Woo, Deborah. 2000. *Glass Ceilings and Asian Americans: The New Face of Workplace Barriers.* Walnut Creek, Calif.: Alta Mira.

Wood, Michael R., and Louis A. Zurcher. 1988. *The Development of a Postmodern Self.* Westport, Conn.: Greenwood.

Wood, Peter. 1986. *Inside Schools.* London: Routledge and Kegan Paul.

Wooden, Wayne S. 1995. *Return to Paradise.* Lanham, Md.: University Press of America.

Woody, Bette. 1989. "Black Women in the Emerging Service Economy." *Sex Roles* 21:45–67.

"World Tourism Bags Record." 2003. *Rocky Mountain News,* January 29:3B.

Wright, Lawrence. 1968. *Clockwork Man.* London: Elek Books.

Wrigley, Julia, 1995. *Other People's Children: An Intimate Account of the Dilemmas Facing Middle-Class Parents and the Women They Hire to Raise Their Children.* New York: Basic Books.

Wu, Diana Ting Liu. 1997. *Asian Pacific Americans in the Workplace.* Walnut Creek, Calif.: Alta Mira.

Wurtman, Richard J. 1975. "The Effects of Light on the Human Body." *Scientific American* 233:69–77.

Yamamoto, Eric. 1979. "The Significance of Local." *Social Process in Hawai'i* 27:102–15.

Yamamura, Douglas. 1936. "Attitudes of Hotel Workers." *Social Process in Hawai'i* 2:15–19.

Zamudio, Margaret. 1996. "Organizing the New Otani Hotel in Los Angeles: The Role of Ethnicity, Race, and Citizenship in Class Formation." Ph.D. dissertation, University of California, Los Angeles.

Zerubavel, Eviatar. 1991. *The Fine Line.* New York: Free Press.

———. 1985. *The Seven Day Circle.* New York: Free Press.

———. 1981. *Hidden Rhythms.* Chicago: University of Chicago Press.

———. 1979. *Patterns of Time in Hospital Life.* Chicago: University of Chicago Press.

Zimmer, Lynn. 1988. "Tokenism and Women in the Workplace: The Limits of Gender-Neutral Theory." *Social Problems* 35:64–77.

Zurcher, Louis A. 1977. *The Mutable Self.* Beverly Hills, Calif.: Sage.

Zussman, Robert. 1992. *Intensive Care: Medical Ethics and the Medical Profession.* Chicago: University of Chicago Press.

Zweig, Paul. 1974. *The Adventurer: The Fate of Adventure in the Western World.* Princeton, N.J.: Princeton University Press.

I N D E X